D1566053

*Opera in Portugal in the Eighteenth Century*

This is the first detailed documentary history of opera in Portugal from the beginning of the eighteenth century to the inauguration of the still-existing Teatro de S. Carlos in 1793. The study shows how the introduction of opera into the country at the beginning of the century was connected with the recruitment of Italian singers and players during the reign of João V, even though the court's interest in opera was small and the activity of public opera houses was hampered by the Church and by the King himself.

It was during the following reign, that of José I, that court opera flourished, with the construction of three court theatres and the fostering of work by a number of excellent native Portuguese composers. The book thus traces the historical context of the opera business in eighteenth-century Portugal from the rejection of the 'secular art of opera' by a reactionary court to its adoption by a more enlightened elite, dedicated to the growth of bourgeois and private enterprise in opera towards the end of the century.

This study is valuable not only as a much-needed authoritative and thorough history of the Portuguese musical theatre in the eighteenth century, paralleling existing studies for all other major European operatic centres of the time, but also for the significant contribution it makes to the study of Italian opera with which it interconnects, and of musical theatre in general.

The work also includes a chronological listing of the operas, serenatas and oratorios performed during the whole period with a record of the extant copies of librettos and scores preserved in Portuguese libraries. These provide essential reference material for the specialist in pursuit of further research.

*The Royal Palace and the Terreiro do Paço in Lisbon before the 1755 earthquake.*

# OPERA IN PORTUGAL IN THE EIGHTEENTH CENTURY

*Manuel Carlos de Brito*

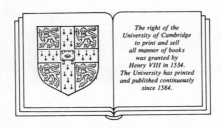

The right of the
University of Cambridge
to print and sell
all manner of books
was granted by
Henry VIII in 1534.
The University has printed
and published continuously
since 1584.

CAMBRIDGE UNIVERSITY PRESS

*Cambridge*

*New York   New Rochelle   Melbourne   Sydney*

Published by the Press Syndicate of the University of Cambridge
The Pitt Building, Trumpington Street, Cambridge CB2 1RP
32 East 57th Street, New York, NY 10022, USA
10 Stamford Road, Oakleigh, Melbourne 3166, Australia

First published 1989

Printed in Great Britain at the University Press, Cambridge

*British Library cataloguing in publication data*

Brito, Manuel Carlos de
Opera in Portugal in the eighteenth century.
1. Portugal. Opera 1700–1799
1. Title
782.1′09469

*Library of Congress cataloguing in publication data*

Brito, Manuel Carlos de.
Opera in Portugal in the eighteenth century / Manuel Carlos de Brito.
p.   cm.
Bibliography.
Includes index.
ISBN 0-521-35312-2
1. Opera – Portugal – 18th century. 1. Title.
ML1748.B75 1989
782.1′09469 – dc19   88-16925   CIP

ISBN 0 521 35312 2

# CONTENTS

## Contents

# ILLUSTRATIONS

# PREFACE

The first and so far the only general study of opera in Portugal in the eighteenth century was published by Teófilo Braga more than a century ago in one of the volumes of his *Historia do theatro portuguez*.[1]

Notwithstanding the contribution of several later studies towards the clarification of particular aspects of the subject,[2] until now no extensive and systematic research of all the relevant sources has been attempted.

The main purpose of the present study is thus to offer a detailed documentary history of opera in Portugal since the first recorded operatic manifestations at the beginning of the eighteenth century, and up to the inauguration of the still existing S. Carlos Theatre in 1793. Taking into account the state of research in this area, and the problems involved in the identification and subsequent treatment of a wide variety of relevant data, an early decision was made not to include any detailed study of the repertoire and its sources. On the other hand I defined as one of my primary aims the establishment of an accurate and, as far as possible, complete chronology of operatic performances during the period, which would also include serenatas, oratorios, and other types of theatrical music whose authors were known.

Another early decision was that of limiting my field of research almost exclusively to those materials which were available in the country. A search for related documents which may still exist abroad, particularly in Italy, would have been too slow and costly and its relevance by no means predictable. I was fortunate enough to obtain the manuscript of an unpublished work by Manuel Carvalhais, 'Subsidios para a historia da

---

[1] [Vol. 3] *A baixa comedia e a opera no seculo XVIII*.
[2] They are discussed in M. C. de Brito, 'Fontes para a história da ópera em Portugal no século XVIII (1708–1793)'.

opera e da coregraphia italianas em Portugal, no século XVIII'. Carvalhais, as is well known, amassed one of the largest libretto collections in the world, which he sold before he died to the Accademia (now Conservatorio) di Musica S. Cecilia in Rome. His manuscript work, however, is a detailed list of all the Italian operas, serenatas, oratorios and *balli* which were performed in Portugal during the period, including a transcription of the title page and other relevant information contained in each libretto, as well as a list of all the Italian works of the same title which were composed in the eighteenth century. Carvalhais' work, which was made available to me through the courtesy of his descendant Manuel Carvalhais Vasconcelos Pimentel (to whom I hereby extend my thanks), is the only one among previous lists I used which is reliable. Several of his listed librettos are unique copies, as far as Portuguese libraries are concerned, and only very few extant librettos were not apparently included in his collection. I made use of his list therefore as a check-list for the identification of libretto collections in Portuguese libraries, and for the establishment of my own chronology.

Considerable time was spent in the identification of relevant sources and documents in over a dozen main Portuguese libraries and archives, through extended perusal of available catalogues. To give two examples, opera librettos in the Biblioteca Nacional de Lisboa are listed (often inaccurately) in the main catalogue, mingled with every other species of printed books. Cataloguing of documents in the main national archives, the Arquivo Nacional da Torre do Tombo, is still very much in the state in which it was left by nineteenth-century librarians.

In these circumstances, the possibility that significant new sources may still come to light in the future cannot be ruled out altogether. This is, however, less likely as regards the first half of the century, in view of the widespread destruction caused by the 1755 earthquake. In my own research I was able to identify only a limited number of completely new sources. These include a few librettos and a certain number of documents in the Faculdade de Letras de Coimbra, the Biblioteca da Ajuda, the Biblioteca Nacional de Lisboa, the Arquivo Nacional da Torre do Tombo and the Teatro Nacional de S. Carlos. Among these I should mention the *Certidão de medição da obra do Officio de Pedreiro pertencente a Caza da Opera* (1759), the *Apolices dos accionistas* of the Sociedade para a Subsistencia dos Theatros Publicos de Lisboa (1771) and the *Reflexoens sobre O restabelecimento do Theatro Do Porto* by Ricardo Raimundo Nogueira (1778). On the other hand, collections of documents which had been used previously by other historians were for the first time submitted to a systematic scrutiny. This was the case for instance with the *Escripturas do Theatro da Rua dos Condes*, the *Contas do Principio do Theatro da Caza da Opera do Bairro Alto*, and in particular with the accounts of the Arquivo Histórico do Ministério das Finanças. It should be noted in passing that most earlier studies of the subject were carried out by general or literary historians, or even by mere amateurs, who lacked the background and training which would have been needed for a correct interpretation of the source materials.[3]

I was less fortunate in my search for references to the operatic scene in contemporary literature, especially in travel books and published memoirs and diaries. As regards periodical literature, those few periodicals which were published in eighteenth-century Portugal only rarely include references to theatrical events, and theatrical criticism as such is almost non-existent.

In spite of the above-mentioned limitations, I hope that the present study, while offering a sample case of the European spread of eighteenth-century Italian opera, will also constitute a useful basis and a stimulus for future research in this area and in particular for the study of the works of Portuguese eighteenth-century opera composers which still lie forgotten in the Biblioteca da Ajuda or the Palácio Ducal de Vila Viçosa. A steady, albeit slow revival of these works began in the 1940s: 1985 saw the first modern production of *Lo spirito di contradizione* by Jerónimo Francisco de Lima, and 1987 that of *Testoride argonauta* by João de Sousa Carvalho.

This study was originally presented as a thesis for the PhD degree of the University of London in 1985. I should like to thank my supervisor, Professor Reinhard Strohm, for his invaluable advice and criticism, which he first dispensed in London, and later from across the Atlantic, after his appointment as Professor of Music History at Yale University. I should also like to thank my examiners, Professors Brian Trowell, Michael Robinson and Jack Sage, for various suggestions and corrections which I incorporated in my final version, and Professor Marita McClymonds, who was kind enough to read my typescript, share her knowledge of the field with me and offer invaluable advice. Various other people have helped me at different stages of my work: my good friend and colleague David Cranmer read large parts of my manuscript, corrected my English, and offered valuable advice on several matters, while passing on to me any information related to my subject which he gathered during his own research on the S. Carlos Theatre; my friend Bernard Brauchli looked up for me L. E. Lindgren's thesis on the Bononcinis in the Music Library of Harvard University; Maria da Conceição Carvalho Geada, of the Biblioteca da Ajuda, brought to my attention the letters of Sebastião José de Carvalho e Melo on the castrato Gizziello and the *Osservazioni Correlative alla Reale, e Patriarcal Cappella di Lisbona*, and helped me in various ways while I worked in that library: Maria José da Silva Leal, of the Arquivo Nacional da Torre do Tombo, brought to my attention a number of rare librettos and documents in that archive; Emília Mariano, of the Biblioteca Geral da Universidade de Coimbra, procured information for me on a number of rare librettos;

---

[3] Earlier literature on the subject is discussed in M. C. de Brito, 'Fontes para a história da ópera em Portugal no século XVIII (1708–1793)'.

Maria Fernanda Cidrais, of the Music Department, Gulbenkian Foundation, kindly allowed me to consult the Foundation's libretto collection, which is not yet available to the public; the staff of the Biblioteca Nacional de Lisboa, the Biblioteca da Ajuda, and the Arquivo Histórico do Ministério das Finanças generally tried in various ways to make up for the technical deficiencies of those institutions. I should also like to express my gratitude to Professor Macario Santiago Kastner and Professor Pierluigi Petrobelli for their steady friendship and support during my research. I should finally like to thank Margaret Jull Costa and Penny Souster, of Cambridge University Press, for all the care and attention to detail they bestowed on the revision of my typescript. I shudder to think of all the small mistakes which would have gone unheeded without their help.

A final note about Italian names. First names of Italian musicians working in Portugal were usually 'portuguesified' (and conversely, first names of Portuguese composers were italianised in the librettos). To the best of my ability I have tried to restore the original Italian names.

*Carcavelos, March 1988*

# ABBREVIATIONS

*Libraries and archives (RISM siglas where available)*

| | |
|---|---|
| *B-Bc* | Brussels, Conservatoire Royal de Musique |
| *BR-Rn* | Rio de Janeiro, Biblioteca Nacional |
| *C-Lu* | London, University of Western Ontario, Lawson Memorial Library |
| *D-B* | Berlin, Staatsbibliothek Preussischer Kulturbesitz |
| *D-SWl* | Schwerin, Wissenschaftliche Allgemeinbibliothek (former Mecklenburgische Landesbibliothek) |
| *F-Pn* | Paris, Bibliothèque Nationale |
| *GB-Lbm* | London, British Library |
| *I-Bc* | Bologna, Civico Museo Bibliografico Musicale |
| *I-Vnm* | Venice, Biblioteca Nazionale Marciana |
| *P-Cug* | Coimbra, Biblioteca Geral da Universidade |
| *P-Cul* | Coimbra, Faculdade de Letras (Sala Dr Jorge de Faria) |
| *P-Em* | Elvas, Biblioteca Municipal |
| *P-EVp* | Évora, Biblioteca Pública e Arquivo Distrital |
| *P-La* | Lisbon, Biblioteca da Ajuda |
| *P-Lac* | Lisbon, Academia das Ciências |
| *P-Lan* | Lisbon, Arquivo Nacional da Torre do Tombo |
| *P-Lcg* | Lisbon, Fundação Calouste Gulbenkian (Serviço de Música) |
| *P-Ln* | Lisbon, Biblioteca Nacional |
| *P-Lt* | Lisbon, Teatro Nacional de S. Carlos |
| *P-Mp* | Mafra, Palácio Nacional |
| *P-Pa* | Oporto, Ateneu Comercial |
| *P-Pm* | Oporto, Biblioteca Pública Municipal |

## Abbreviations

| | |
|---|---|
| *P-VV* | Vila Viçosa, Palácio Ducal |
| IPPC | Lisbon, Instituto Português do Património Cultural (Departmento de Musicologia) |
| AHMF | Lisbon, Arquivo Histórico do Ministério das Finanças (Arquivo da Casa Real) |
| AHTC | Lisbon, Arquivo Histórico do Tribunal de Contas |
| TNM | Lisbon, Teatro Nacional D. Maria II |

## Others

| | |
|---|---|
| b.c. | basso continuo |
| f., ff. | folio, folios |
| l | libretto |
| m | music |
| mod. edn | modern edition |
| sc | extant score |
| ov. | overture |
| p. sc. | piano score |
| pts | extant parts |
| t | text |
| rpt | repeat |
| rec. | recording |
| CX. | CAIXA |
| *Hebd. Lisb.* | *Hebdomadario Lisbonense* |
| *MGG* | *Die Musik in Geschichte und Gegenwart* |

# NOTE ON CURRENCY

The monetary unit in eighteenth-century Portugal was the *real*, plural *réis* (rs).

$$1\$000 = 1,000 \text{ rs}$$
$$1{:}000\$000 = 1,000,000 \text{ rs (`um conto de réis')}$$

One *cruzado velho* was the equivalent to $400 rs and one *cruzado novo* the equivalent to $480 rs. Here amounts in *cruzados* have been conservatively estimated on the basis of the *cruzado velho*. The *moeda* was worth 4$800 rs.

According to Twiss (*Travels through Portugal and Spain in 1772 and 1773*, p. 2), one *cruzado novo* in 1772 was the equivalent to 2s 8½d.

# I

# Opera during the reign of João V (1708–50)

## The general background: Spanish theatrical music at court

On 27 October 1708 Marie Anne of Austria, daughter of the Emperor Leopold I, arrived in Lisbon to marry King João V.[1] She was twenty-five and the King only nineteen, having been on the throne for less than two years. The influence of the new Queen seems to have immediately brought new customs into court life. A contemporary diarist, in an entry for 30 November, tells us that

> there are parties [*saraos*] at court on Sunday evenings, with music by the ladies. The King and Queen attend them, together with all the nobility, who after the Queen's arrival continue to attend at court willingly and with enjoyment, as is the custom in the foreign courts, and in the same way the Queen observes the custom of always having her meals with the King, and accordingly at a state table, the which had not been done since the death of King João IV [in 1656].[2]

In a manuscript collection of notices on Portuguese composers written *c.* 1737[3] we are informed that in that same year a certain Frei Pedro da Conceição composed music consisting of solos, duets and four-part choruses for the comedy *Eligir al inimigo*, which was performed at court before the Queen by the singers of the Royal Chapel. According to Mazza[4] this was done to celebrate the Queen's arrival. The fact should be noted that the composer was a friar, and not a layman, and also that he was Portuguese. It is not known in fact whether the new Queen had brought any musicians with her from Vienna, but if she did it is very unlikely that there were any composers among them. In any case this new interest in court music apparently prompted the King to take into his service the sons of a certain Caim for their ability to sing and play, which seems to have aroused the envy of other young nobles.[5]

I

In his ironical description of a tragicomedy staged by the Jesuits at their College of Santo Antão in 1709, our diarist reports that on the first day only the King, the Queen and their children attended, on the second the three estates, clergy, nobility and the people, and on the third ladies and non-ladies ('Senhoras e não-Senhoras'). He adds that the production, 'for all that is known, and can be done among us', was like any ordinary opera of France or Italy.[6]

The term opera is defined thus in the first large Portuguese dictionary, published at the beginning of the eighteenth century:[7]

From the Italians and the French this word was communicated to the other nations of Europe, and nowadays it is used at this Court, when one talks about the celebrated Comedies, invented by the Venetians, which are recited in music, and performed with delicious symphonies, remarkable machines, and admirable sets [*apparencias*]. In the month of March of the year 1672 the first opera, entitled *Pomona*, was performed in Paris.

Still in 1709[8] the terms *aria* and *recitativo* appear for the first time in the libretto of the *villancicos* for the feast of St Vincent at Lisbon cathedral. Bluteau only registers *aria*, which he derives from the French *air*, and *ariêta*, which he takes to be an Italian word, meaning the same as *tonilho*, *cantiginha* (*sic*; short song), in the two-volume supplement to his dictionary, published in 1727–8. In the seventh volume he defines *recitativo*, *canto recitativo*, as a kind of singing invented by the Italians, midway between the natural voice, or ordinary pronunciation, and counterpoint, used in the theatrical works called operas.

Italian operatic influence is roughly contemporary in the Portuguese and the Spanish *villancicos*, and in the Portuguese case it was very probably mediated through Spain. The fortunes of the religious villancico in Lisbon would in any case soon come to an end: Christmas *villancicos* were sung for the last time in the Royal Chapel in 1715, in which year the rites of the Papal Chapel were introduced, and in Lisbon parish churches in 1723.[9]

Spanish musical influence is still present, however, in the various comedies with music or in the *zarzuelas* which were performed in Lisbon until at least 1739. The publication in November of that year of a *Discurso apologetico em defensa do Theatro Hespanhol*, written by the Marquis of Valença, seems to sound the death knell for Spanish theatre in Portugal.[10]

Nevertheless, there is no reason to assume that the slow penetration of Italian opera into the country at the beginning of the eighteenth century was due to the existence of a very strong local theatrical tradition, either of Spanish or of national origin. In 1710 there was apparently only one theatre in Lisbon, the Pátio das Arcas or das Comédias, which had burnt down in 1697 or 1698 and had been rebuilt with capacity for some 500 spectators.[11] A Portuguese company performed there, directed by a certain Ferrer. Another Portuguese company directed by José Ferreira worked there in

1715–16. Various Spanish companies also appeared in the same theatre on and off until 1727.[12] Their repertoire seems to have consisted mainly of Spanish comedies. Cotarelo y Mori[13] mentions the names of a few Spanish actress-singers active in Lisbon, such as the famous Petronilla Gibaja, *La Portuguesa*, who left in 1721, Juana and Rita de Orozco, who stayed a full twelve years until 1736, Juana de Inestrosa, who went there in that same year, and Rosa Rodríguez, *La Gallega*. Of the two Orozco sisters he says that Juana was a better actress than singer. Rita had a better voice, such a fine, high soprano that she might have been mistaken for the playing of a violin, something she sometimes imitated to perfection.

In view of the almost total darkness still surrounding the history of the Spanish (and the Portuguese) theatre in Lisbon in this period, two facts that Cotarelo y Mori establishes with reference to Madrid should be noted here. One concerns the existence of companies with all-women casts. The other is the influence exerted by Italian opera on those companies.[14]

The introduction of Italian opera in Madrid is connected with the arrival in 1703 of a company known as *de los Trufaldines*, which was protected by the new King Philip V, a grandson of Louis XIV, and which was active until 1714.[15] As their name indicates, their repertory was essentially in the *comedia dell'arte* tradition, but they also produced several operas. At the same time the seventeenth-century tradition of the courtly *zarzuela* and of the popular comedy with music was still very much alive. The Spanish companies tried to compete with the Italians, and in doing so their comedies and *zarzuelas* became more operatic, both in the amount and in the style of their music, to which a number of Italian composers, such as Antonio Duni or Francesco Coradini, began also to contribute.

Both the *zarzuela* and the comedy usually alternate spoken dialogue with music in varying proportions, and it is very difficult, if not impossible, to distinguish what is a comedy, or what a *zarzuela*, from contemporary references alone, when, as is often the case in Portugal, neither the text nor the music is extant. For Spain, Cotarelo y Mori notes the following names: *comedia, comedia de música, comedia de teatro y música, zarzuela, fiesta, melodrama harmónico al estilo de Italia, melodrama harmónico, drama para representarse en música, drama para música, melodrama escénico, drama harmónico*. *Drama para música* and *melodrama* are obviously of Italian origin.

In Portugal the first such work recorded during the reign of João V is a *Fabula de Acis y Galatea fiesta armonica com Violines, Flautas, e Ubues, a la celebridad de los felizes anos del Augustissimo Señor D. Juan V* [...], *que en su aplauso le dedica la Reyna nuestra Señora D. Marianna da Austria*, which was performed at court on 22 October 1711.[16] The printed libretto does not mention the names of either the composer or the librettist.[17] There are only three roles, Galatea, Acis and Polifemo, and it is sung throughout, including 'a quatro', 'arias', 'recitados', 'coplas', 'a duo', etc. The singers were probably members of the Royal Chapel, as would have been the instrumental band of violins, basses, oboes and flutes.

The first known list of court players in the eighteenth century, published by Walther,[18] refers to 1728, and there is almost no evidence of orchestral music, or even of music with obbligato instrumental parts connected with the Royal Chapel at the end of the seventeenth century and the beginning of the eighteenth. An exception to this are two Christmas *villancicos* with parts for *rabeca* and for *violines* by António Marques Lésbio, master of the Royal Chapel from 1698 until his death in 1709.[19] Oboes in any case would have been a novelty.[20] It is not known whether the players were the French Latur and the Bohemian Veith mentioned by Walther, but they were almost certainly foreigners.

In 1712 and 1713 two other *zarzuelas* were performed at court, the first on 24 June, nameday of João V, and the second on his birthday on 22 October. They were the *Fabula de Alfeo y Aretusa fiesta armonica con toda la variedad de instrumentos musicos con que la Reyna Nuestra Señora D. Marianna de Austria celebro el Real Nombre Del Rey Nuestro Señor* . . . and *La Comedia – El poder de la Armonia fiesta de zarzuela*. . . . The librettos of both were written by Luis Calisto da Costa e Faria.[21] The composer of the second was Don Jayme de la Te y Sagau.[22] According to a manuscript note on Costa e Faria written before 1745, the second *zarzuela* was performed by one of the Princesses and seven court ladies.[23]

Thus during her first years in Portugal the daughter of the Emperor-composer Leopold I of Austria put on Spanish *zarzuelas* to pay homage to her husband and King. She was certainly familiar with the repertoire, which was also performed at the court of Vienna.[24] However, as the historian Oliveira Marques puts it,[25]

the profound cultural revolution which was under way in Portugal [in the eighteenth century] meant also the replacement of Spanish influence by French, English, Italian and German influences . . . Until the end of the seventeenth century Spain was considered among the leading nations in Europe. . . ; after that her role was in constant decline, and Spain itself needed to search for stimulus and standards of development outside her own borders. It is not surprising that Portugal . . . should have looked elsewhere and should tend to despise whatever came from her neighbour . . . From the eighteenth century onwards Portugal realised that her place among the civilised nations and her individuality as a European nation depended on her reacting against Spain. Portugal started to hate and despise Spain as an obstacle between her and the rest of Europe, something which stood in the way and prevented her from communicating easily with France and the remaining [European] countries.

The war of the Spanish Succession, in which Portugal had sided against Spain, ended in 1713. For the remainder of João V's reign the country was at peace, except for a brief naval intervention on the side of the Pope and Venice against the Turks in 1716 and 1717. Meanwhile the gold from the recently discovered mines in Brazil began to flow in in ever greater quantities: 514 kg in 1699, 2,000 kg in 1701, over 4,460 in 1703, 14,500 kg in 1712. This flow began to decline only after the middle of the century, until it practically came to a halt at the beginning of the nineteenth century.[26] João V could look forward to a future of political stability and financial prosperity that neither his father nor his grandfather had ever known.

The way he made use of this wealth is still a matter of dispute among historians. A very small part of it was actually used in productive investments, but responsibility for this should not be exclusively laid with the King, absolute monarch though he may have been:

> The lack of an elite was patent in every area: in culture, in art, in politics, in the economy. The lack of active managers prevented any productive investments during the golden decades. The river Tagus was only a port of call for this money which flowed towards areas where the economy was more developed and where the goods that the Portuguese consumed, but did not know how to produce themselves came from. Of these areas England was the most richly rewarded.[27]

In the fields of art and culture João V's main undertakings were the creation in 1720 of the Royal Academy of History, whose members were to publish a number of important historiographical works, and the gigantic Monastery of Mafra, which took the best part of his reign to erect (1717–50) and occupied 45,000 forced labourers, as well as 7,000 soldiers who kept them at work. Most of its statues were made in Italy; 'the religious vestments, the church furnishings, the candlesticks, the sets of bells were ordered from Rome, Venice, Milan, France, Holland, Genoa and Liège'. Even the pinewood for the scaffolding and for the workers' shacks came from Northern Europe.[28] The King also sent a number of Portuguese sculptors and painters to study in Italy, and hired several Italian and other foreign artists.

The reform of musical institutions itself was largely connected with the reform of the religious cult. In the words of his contemporary, Frederick the Great of Prussia, João V had a 'strange passion for church ceremonies. He had obtained the Pope's permission to establish a Patriarchy, and to say Mass himself, excluding consecration. Priestly functions were his amusements, convents his buildings, monks his armies, and nuns his mistresses.'[29]

The irony of the Protestant King does not show the whole picture: the 'strange passion' of João V was shared by the greater number of his subjects. Lisbon at the beginning of the eighteenth century was the capital of a country where the Church still dominated public life.[30] No wonder then that the King, out of a personal and in a way sincere devotion that may appear bizarre to modern eyes, and for reasons of prestige, tried to invest as much as he could in the religious establishment in general and in his own Royal Chapel in particular, which he tried to convert into a cathedral immediately after he ascended the throne.[31] On 1 March 1710 it was elevated to the status of Collegiate Church in a Bull issued by Pope Clement XI, and in another Bull dated 7 November 1716 it was elevated to Metropolitan and Patriarchal See, under the title of Our Lady of the Assumption.[32] Lisbon became divided into two dioceses: that of Lisboa Oriental, corresponding to the old Metropolitan See, and that of Lisboa Ocidental, corresponding to the new Patriarchy.[33]

A large number of crown rents was attributed to the new Patriarchy. The richness and pomp of its furnishings and its religious services are generally underlined in contemporary descriptions:

The seat of the Lisbon Patriarchy is in the chapel of the King's palace. As regards its architecture and paintings they are very ordinary: but the temple is vast. Besides the main altar, there are twelve other altars, with magnificent decorations. There is a large two-storey tribune, with lattices, where the King and Queen usually attend Mass. On Sundays and feast days the Patriarch always officiates, accompanied by eighteen mitred canons. The choir, composed of some thirty or forty beneficiaries, is accompanied by music in the Roman style, without any instruments; and there are a number of excellent voices among the many heard there.[34]

In his desire to follow the liturgy of the Papal Chapel, João V ordered copies to be made of all the choirbooks used in the Vatican. He also had copies made of the Ambrosian ceremonial in Milan, with its music, as well as those of the Greek and Armenian Churches, the Syriac Mass, and the liturgical books of the Maronites, the Nestorians and the Syrian Orthodox Church, translated by the librarian of the Vatican, G. S. Assemani. All these books were lost in the 1755 earthquake.[35]

In 1713 a music school was created adjoining the Patriarchal See, the Seminário da Patriarcal. It was to remain the main music school during the eighteenth century, being replaced by the Lisbon Conservatory only in 1835. In 1729 the King created another music school at the Monastery of Santa Catarina de Ribamar for the teaching of the *canto capucho* (a *falsobordone* harmonisation of plainsong), and hired the Venetian composer Giovanni Giorgi (João Jorge) to direct it, helped by two Italian singers from the Patriarcal. Vieira[36] is certainly right in saying that the only object of study in these schools was church music, with the result that the study of secular music would have had to remain a marginal activity.

With funds from the Patriarcal the King sent a number of scholars to Rome to study music. The first to go was António Teixeira (1707–after 1770) in 1716 or 1717. Having taken holy orders, he returned on 11 June 1728 and was appointed chaplain singer of the Patriarcal and examiner in plainsong of all the ordinands in the Patriarchy.[37] We also know of three others: Joaquim do Vale Mexelim, João Rodrigues Esteves, and Francisco António de Almeida. Another, Romão Mazza (1719–47), was sent by Queen Marie Anne to study at one of the Naples conservatories.[38] Francisco António de Almeida had two oratorios performed while he was in Rome: the first was *Il pentimento di Davidde*, with libretto by Andrea

Trabucco, in 1722, and the second was *Giuditta*, in 1726. A caricature of him drawn by Pier Leone Ghezzi in 1724 bears the following legend:[39]

Signor Francesco, a Portuguese, who has come to Rome to study, and who is already a very fine composer of concertos and church music, amazingly so given his youth and he sings superbly. Having come to my musical academy, I, Cavalier Ghezzi, have recorded his memory, this 9th day of July, 1724.

By April 1728 he was already back in Lisbon, where a serenata with music by him, *Il trionfo della Virtù*, was performed at the Palace of the Cardinal da Mota, and where he was employed as organist of the Patriarcal.

## Italian court music: serenatas and operas

From 1716 onwards the *Gazeta de Lisboa*, created the previous year, begins to mention the performance of serenatas at court on the King's, the Queen's, and the Prince's birthdays and namedays, or more occasionally on those of their foreign relatives, the Austrian Emperor and Empress, the King and Queen of Spain, etc. Meanwhile in Rome Domenico Scarlatti had been employed as *maestro di cappella* by the Portuguese ambassador extraordinary, the Marquis of Fontes. In 1714 he composed an *Applauso Genetliaco alla Reale Altezza del Signor Infante di Portogallo* which was performed in the palace of the ambassador.[40] The following year he became chapelmaster of Saint Peter's Cappella Giulia. In 1717 three singers left the Papal Chapel to enter the service of the King of Portugal and in 1719 another did the same.[41] On 24 September 1719 a serenata was performed in the King's apartment 'sung by the new and excellent musicians which His Majesty . . . had brought from Rome, in the Presence of Their Majesties and Royal Highnesses'.[42]

Scarlatti himself left Rome in August or September of that year, and even if he did not immediately take over his new post as master of the Portuguese Royal Chapel and went instead to Palermo in Sicily, as the recent findings of Roberto Pagano seem to indicate,[43] from 1720 onwards serenatas by him were performed at the Lisbon court. Extant Lisbon librettos of this period only rarely mention the names of the librettist or the composer of the music, and it is likely that, until his departure for Spain in the retinue of his pupil Princess Maria Bárbara in January 1729, he may have written more of these works than are actually attributed to him.[44] The same is probably the case with Francisco António de Almeida, António Teixeira, or the Barón d'Astorga, who resided in Lisbon in this period.

On the other hand, the libretto or the title of many serenatas which the *Gazeta de Lisboa* registers is not known, and in several cases they may have been repeats of works already performed. Thus in 1735 the Princess Mariana Vitória wrote to her mother in Madrid saying that the Queen had asked which serenata she wished for her birthday.[45] Also the term serenata may not always have meant any particular work, but simply an evening of vocal and instrumental music. This must have been especially true of serenatas performed at the houses of the aristocracy.

Serenatas were usually performed either in the King's or the Queen's chambers, according to which of the royal spouses was offering this entertainment to the other. In some cases they were part of a court gala, and sung in the presence of the court and the foreign dignitaries, but more often they seem to have been performed in private (*em particular*). The singers, whose names never appear, belonged to the Royal Chapel. Walther[46] mentions the names of 'Floriani, Discantist, ein Castrat und Römer' and 'Mossi, Tenorist, ein Römer' as belonging to the Chapel in 1728, and says that most of the remaining thirty or forty singers were also Italian.[47] He gives the following list of the most notable players in the Chapel:

> Scarlatti, chapelmaster, a Roman
> Joseph Antoni, vice-chapelmaster, a Portuguese[48]
> Pietro Giorgio Avondano, first violinist, a Genoese
> Antonio Paghetti, first violinist, a Roman
> Alessandro Paghetti, second violinist, a Roman
> Johann Peter, second violinist, a Portuguese, but of German parents
> Thomas, third violinist, a Florentine
> Latur, fourth violinist, and second oboist, a Frenchman
> Veith, fourth violinist, and first oboist, a Bohemian
> Ventur, viola player, a Catalan
> Antoni, viola player, a Catalan
> Ludewig, bassoonist, a Bohemian
> Juan, cellist, a Catalan
> Laurenti, cellist, a Florentine
> Paolo, contra-violinist [i.e. double-bass], a Roman
> Antonio Joseph, organist, a Portuguese[48]

Even if there had been no other players, this orchestra would have been sufficient to accompany a small work with few singers, such as a serenata. Horns and trumpets, when needed, would probably have been supplied by the King's military band, or *Charamela Real*.

In accordance with the genre, the librettos of these serenatas do not contain any indications of stage sets, and only in the case of Scarlatti's *Festeggio armonico*, sung for the wedding of Prince Ferdinand of Spain and Princess Maria Bárbara on 11 January 1728 does the *Gazeta de Lisboa* refer to 'hūa especie de theatro, que para este fim se fabricou' ('a kind of theatre which was built for this purpose'). This must have been the same which was used the following month for the *intermezzi* of *Il D. Chisciotte della Mancia*, the first Italian operatic work known to have been performed at court, and may have consisted simply of a stage erected in one of the rooms of the palace.

It is interesting to note that the term opera first appears in connection with works performed outside the court, such as the 'Opera ou Comedia em musica' *Atis & Cybelle* performed at the house of the Secretary of State, Diogo de Mendonça Corte Real, on 3 August 1717, or the *Acis & Galatea* performed on 25 August that same year in the gardens of the French ambassador, the Abbé de Mornay. The titles of these works suggest that they were serenatas, and in the first instance it may well have been a case of a word being misapplied on account of its prestige. (The same probably happened with the word serenata and its broader use to mean any kind of musical entertainment during the first half of the century, especially outside Lisbon.) But in the second case the *Gazeta* specifies that it was performed 'com todas as decorações e perspectivas pertencentes a sua representação', leaving us in no doubt that it was actually staged with sets. Again for the 'Comedia' *Acis & Galatea* performed at the palace of the Count of S. Vicente on 23 January 1718 the *Gazeta* states that it was performed in a 'theatro com perspectivas'.

From the beginning one has the feeling that the interest in opera was much more quickly aroused among the aristocracy than at the royal court itself, and later developments confirm this. It is not known, however, whether the singers and players in these early performances outside the court were members of the Royal Chapel, or whether they belonged to any of the Spanish companies mentioned above.

The continuing tradition of the Spanish musical theatre was certainly helped by the *zarzuelas* and *comedias de música* produced at the palaces of the Spanish ambassadors Marquis of Capicilatro and Marquis de los Balbases, the second of whom had a theatre (i.e. a stage) built for the purpose but which was demolished before his departure in 1728.[49] But even here Italian influence was beginning to show itself, as may be seen by the *Gazeta* calling one of these works, *Las Amazonas de España*, performed in January, 'Melodrama, ou Comedia harmonica, pelo estylo Italiano'.[50]

A sure sign of the lack of interest in opera on the part of the court is the small number of Italian operas – as opposed to serenatas – performed there during the whole reign, as well as the fact that none of them was an *opera seria* (the true *instrumentum regni* of eighteenth-century music). They were *La pazienza di Socrate* in 1733 and 1734, *La finta pazza* in 1735, *La risa di Democrito* in 1736, *La Spinalba* in 1739, and *Madama Ciana* in 1740.[51] To these we may add the intermezzi of *D. Chisciotte* of 1728 (possibly with music by Domenico Scarlatti), which were repeated in 1730, 1731, and 1734, and the three-act *Pastorale a tre voci* of 1734, whose libretto indicates that it was *da rappresentarsi*.

Information on these court performances is very scarce. In contrast to the numerous announcements of serenatas, the semi-official *Gazeta de Lisboa* makes only two short references to operatic performances during the whole reign.[52] The reason for this is probably that, while serenatas were usually connected with royal birthdays or an important event such as a royal wedding,[53] operatic productions were simply seen as a private courtly entertainment during Carnival. This impression is confirmed by two partially related manuscript diaries or newsletters, the Évora diaries and the *Diário do Conde de Ericeira*,[54] as well as the letters written by Princess Mariana Vitória, the betrothed of the heir to the throne Prince José, to her mother the Queen of Spain.[55]

In two entries for 21 February 1730 and 5 February 1731[56] the Évora diaries mention the Italian comedy of D. Quixote and the burlesque operas that were performed at the court by the Italian singers, reporting that they were only attended by ladies. On 20 January 1733 the diary of the Count of Ericeira[57] says that a large theatre was being set up in the royal palace for three operas (probably meaning three performances of the same opera) written by Alexandre de Gusmão,[58] with music by Francisco António (de Almeida). It was thought that the three excellent singers, the Paghetti sisters[59] would sing in the palace on the same days (of Carnival). The entry in the Évora diaries for 3 February[60] adds that a rehearsal held on the birthday of the Infanta D. Francisca had been attended by many ladies, several of whom wore new dresses (!). The theatre, which had wings, had already been completed. On 10 February the diary of the Count of Ericeira states that those ladies who had been attending rehearsals in the palace had arranged to hear the Paghetti singers in some of their homes, as it was not certain they would sing in the palace, or whether the King would attend those performances.

On 17 February the same diarist reports that the King was going to spend Carnival in Mafra, and that he had not seen the opera, even though he had a box prepared. The costumes were very rich and the singers had kept them, as they wanted to perform the opera for the nobles. Those of the nobles who had asked the Queen's permission to do so had been allowed to hide in the wings to watch it. Only the Queen's own servants had seen it in public, but even the Captain of the Guard, D. Manuel de Sousa, was not allowed to stay among them, and he had gone away, refusing to hide in order to watch. The last performance was on Shrove Tuesday, but the King, who had returned from Mafra on Monday, had not attended it, and neither had his brother, the Infante D. António.[61]

The King's absence is probably the reason why only ladies were allowed to attend those private performances. The changes in court life mentioned at the beginning of this chapter do not seem to have lasted very long, and court etiquette continued to impose the strict separation between the sexes described by a foreign visitor *c.* 1723–6:[62]

The way visits are made in Portugal is rather odd: the gentlemen are in one room, and the ladies in another, and as both enjoy dancing very much, the ladies dance with each other in their room, and the men do the same in theirs. If one is lucky enough to be admitted to the ladies' room, one will find them sitting on a straw mat on the floor, and the men standing talking to them on the border of the mat, some fifteen feet away.

An entry in the Évora diaries for 27 December 1735 mentions that a new opera (*La risa di Democrito*) and two of the old ones would be performed at court during the following Carnival. Another entry for 7 February 1736 states that opinions were divided on which of the two was the better, the court opera or that of the Paghetti sisters (Schiassi's *Alessandro nell'Indie* at the Academia da Trindade). Only two foreign ministers, the gentlemen of the chamber, the *veadores*,[63] the Duke of Lafões and the Count of Ericeira were allowed to see it in public. Other nobles, whose names were included in a list, were allowed to watch it from the wings, but not from the orchestra.[64]

In 1739 the same diary reports that on Sunday, 25 January, the comedy of the mad old man (*La Spinalba*) had been performed at court, and that it had lasted four hours. It had been attended by only a few servants and the Count of Ericeira in public, and three or four nobles in private (i.e. from the wings), as the other nobles had gone to the opera in the public theatre.[65]

Further data on the court's musical life are found in the letters of Princess Mariana Vitória, who was eleven years old when she arrived in Portugal in 1729. Between the ages of four and seven she had lived at the French court as the betrothed of the future Louis XV, and for this reason her letters are written in a kind of phonetic French, mingled with a few Spanish and Portuguese words. Besides serenatas and operas, she mentions other musical entertainments, such as an excursion on the river, accompanied by violins, trumpets, kettledrums, and a singer, on 1 May 1729,[66] or the fact that the Queen played the harpsichord, while she herself sang the cantatas of the Baron d'Astorga.[67] From 1736 onwards, however, the young Princess starts to complain of the lack of entertainment available at court. Her own remaining pleasures were her singing and music lessons, but even these were sometimes interrupted for months on end, due to royal mourning:

yesterday it was a month since the death of the Infante D. Carlos. I am only waiting for tomorrow to have my music lesson, for I can't stand the importunity of these mournings any longer.[68]

I do what I can to relieve my melancholy, since you are so kind to want it thus, even though this is very difficult in a country where there is no entertainment. My only one is singing, as I love music passionately. Lately we have gone out a lot, but only to churches ... [69]

I am very happy to know that you take pleasure in listening to Farinelli and that you have found him so good. Everybody says that there is no one who can sing like him, and one can see from his arias (for I have sung some of them and have also heard others) the great agility that he possesses, and the Queen told me yesterday that the Princess [Maria Bárbara] had written to her that he could not go very high any more, but I do not know how that can be as I had heard that he could go as high as the top end of the harpsichord. I would take great pleasure in listening to him but one must have patience since God wants it thus.[70]

I feel the lack of freedom more and more every day and I do not know how I could live if I did not have such a liking for music. I wait every day to see when they will take a dislike to it too and deprive me of this entertainment, because then I would be quite desperate.[71]

we are very sad as the mourning still goes on with the same severity, which everyone finds rather ridiculous, and thus we do not have any music on gala days; I have only my lesson in my room but there are no serenatas . . .[72]

we are in the midst of great mourning now for the death of the Queen's sister, there seems no end to it at this court.[73]

On Sunday we heard Reginelle whom I found admirable. The King also heard him from one door.[74]

everything is in the most miserable state. The King thinks of nothing else but the Patriarcal and the Queen does nothing; . . . so that you may see how far the importunity of this court goes, I have some ladies here who organised small private balls; the Queen sent them orders for them not to hold them any more. Thus until now the importunity was only towards me, but now it is towards everybody. These ladies are desperate, but there is nothing for it but to be patient;[75]

here we now have sermons every day and we do not have any entertainments.[76]

The growing austerity of court life described by Princess Mariana Vitória was also a result of the King's illness. In April 1740 João V suffered the first of a series of strokes, the second of which, on 10 May 1742, resulted in his becoming hemiplegic. At the same time he became obsessed with a religious fervour which made him forbid most entertainments not only at the court but, as will be seen below, in the public theatres as well.

## Opera in the public theatres

A foreign visitor, the Swiss César de Saussure, writing in 1730,[77] says that he had no idea what kind of entertainment the Portuguese had, apart from the guitar. They did not have any comedy, or opera, or any concerts, except those in the churches. The English, French and Dutch merchants of Lisbon had organised a nice concert once a week composed of some twenty instruments and eight or ten voices, two or three of which had been embellished by 'a cruel operation'. Most of these singers were Italian (he does not specify whether they were members of the Royal Chapel or not). The subscribers to these concerts did not pay anything and occasional visitors only paid a small sum. During the winter the concerts alternated with balls, which cost twice as much. Chocolate, tea, wines, sweets and such things were served. Both the concerts and the balls were attended by a large and brilliant company of English, French, Dutch and other foreign persons of both sexes, but by very few Portuguese gentlemen and even fewer Portuguese ladies, except for two or three whose husbands had been ambassadors in France, England, and other countries, and had thus humanised themselves a little. Adjoining the concert or ballroom there were two rooms where the buffet was served and where the gentlemen often played hard at cards.[78]

Saussure stayed in Lisbon less than a month, not long enough to be fully aware of the rapidly changing habits of the Portuguese aristocracy. In fact the diaries or newsletters quoted above indicate that serenatas, balls and card games were becoming increasingly frequent around this time.[79] In late 1729, according to them, the dances held by the English and French ladies went on until morning and there were card games several days a week even in the houses of certain canons of the Patriarcal, and at the house of the Marquis of Abrantes as well. In November of that year the dances held by the English ladies were suspended by order of the judge João Marques Bacalhau. They were resumed again in January of the following year, although the scrupulous did not attend them.[80] It is apparent that while these social changes were being enthusiastically adopted by a large part of the aristocracy, they were also meeting with strong opposition in certain sectors of the Church and of the civil authorities.[81]

Increasing references to private performances of serenatas and comedies with music are also a sign of a need for theatrical entertainment which did not find its outlet in the public theatres. In 1729 a Spanish company to which Rosa Rodriguez, *La Gallega*, belonged was giving private performances in Lisbon, but it was disbanded before the year was out.[82] In 1727 the King had ordered that the Hospital Real de Todos os Santos, which was administered by the Santa Casa da Misericórdia, and which owned the Pátio das Arcas or das Comédias, should cease to have any dealings with the actors, and in consequence all theatrical performances had ceased. Two years later, on 30 November 1729, the purveyor of the Misericórdia, the Count of Ericeira, in view of the fact that the Hospital was in risk of having to close, due to its diminishing rents, determined to ask the King's permission to appoint someone who would organise the theatrical companies, or rent the Pátio to anyone who would reopen it. He asked the opinion of several theologians, wishing to know whether the *comedias* in themselves were sinful or indifferent, while recalling that the Spanish comedies were not of the kind which had been condemned by the Fathers of the Church. On his part he promised to fulfil the following conditions:[83]

1  The men's boxes would have a different access from those of the women, and not even the husbands would be allowed to see the plays together with their wives.
2  The actresses would not dress in male apparel, nor would there be any indecent objects among the props.
3  The *comedias*, *bailes* and *entremezes* would be examined beforehand, so that no indecent word or action would be allowed on the stage.
4  A court injunction would be sought to the effect that no one would be able to take any player away from the theatre during his period of contract.

He also recalled that in such a serious court as that of Lisbon there had always been comedies, even in the royal palace and in the monasteries, and that the holiest Popes and the more moderate Kings had always allowed them in their states for public entertainment, and in order to prevent worse evils.

Appended to the application are the opinions of two Jesuit theologians, one of them in favour, as long as those conditions were observed, the other against, adding that the way actresses performed excited *ad venerem*, even when their subject was holy, and that the Spanish actresses who used to come to Portugal were generally of ill repute and would certainly try to earn money in their usual way. He ended by saying that 'Non sunt facienda mala, ut veniant bona' (Good deeds may not come from bad deeds) and that the Hospital should therefore look for other means to solve its financial problems.

The Évora diaries indicate that in February 1730 the Count of Ericeira presented this petition to the King, signed by thirty of the best theologians, and that the King had it examined. In January a comedy, *Endimión y Diana*, 'quasi toda de musica', was performed by amateurs in the Lisbon borough of Santos. It was attended by all the ladies of the aristocracy and some of the court ladies, 'but all the Princess' eagerness was not enough to make the Queen see it.'[84]

A year later, on 15 January 1731, the diaries announced that an Italian opera company, which included a painter, carpenters, costumes and a singer, had arrived in Lisbon. They would be happy to perform in the Pátio das Comédias, but they were waiting for the King's permission. On 27 February the diaries stated that those who wished to introduce the opera had hired the female singers for 20,000 *cruzados* (8:000$000 rs) and that they had a plan for a theatre to be built in the Pátio das Comédias. The Patriarch did not raise any difficulties, but they were still waiting for the King's licence.[85]

These projects seem to have failed, however. Whether as a consequence of the King's opposition, or for some other reason, there is no evidence of public opera performances in Lisbon during the next five years. They continued to be replaced by serenatas, in the probable sense of concerts of vocal and instrumental music, some performed by amateurs, especially ladies of the aristocracy, others performed on a more regular basis by professional singers. In October 1731 serenatas were being held twice a week at the houses of a certain Jorge and of D. Maurício.[86] The following year a Venetian singer married to an archlute player performed at the houses of D. Maurício and of Lázaro Leitão, a canon of the Patriarcal. Opinions were divided on which music was best: that of the serenatas or the one which was sung at the Patriarcal or at the Church of S. Roque.[87]

In January 1733 the Paghetti sisters, daughters of a violinist of the Royal Chapel, Alessandro Maria Paghetti, were giving performances twice a week and had moved to better houses at the Boavista. One of their performances had been attended by forty ladies and in a month they had earned over 3,000 *cruzados* (1:200$000 rs). While their *Casa das Músicas*, as well as the balls and the *presépios*, were well attended, the Pátio das Comédias itself was in danger of falling down.[88]

In April they began giving their serenatas every Wednesday in the houses belonging to Rodrigo de Sousa, near the Convent of the Trindade.[89] Commenting on their performance, the diarist says that, while they did not have great voices and they did not make their words very clear, they were admired for their style and variety. In December two other female singers and a cello player were being expected for their serenatas. Meanwhile it was said that Canon Lázaro Leitão was preparing a theatre in his own house, and at his own expense, where, during the winter, he intended putting on operas with the Italian singers, to which he would invite many nobles.[90]

However, the first public production of an Italian opera which is recorded is that of *Farnace* in December 1735, in the 'sala dell'Academia alla Piazza della Trinità', in the words of the libretto. The company director was Alessandro Maria Paghetti and the composer was Gaetano Maria Schiassi, from Bologna, who had arrived in Lisbon in November, as he himself states in a letter to Padre Martini, dated 3 December ('Io stò travagliando per l'opera che anderà per la sera di S. Stefano'). In the following sentence Schiassi mentions that Giovanni Bononcini, Handel's rival at the Royal Academy, was in Lisbon at the time.[91] A setting of the aria 'Mio sposo t'arresta/Io vuolo nella morte', from the end of Act III of *Farnace*, preserved in the Bibliothèque Nationale in Paris, is attributed to 'Domenico Bonuncini, attempato d'85 anni, in Lisbona 1737'.[92] It is not known whether Domenico was a relative of Giovanni Bononcini, but according to Cotarelo y Mori[93] he was a member of the first Trufaldines company, which had been active in Madrid between 1703 and 1714. He had been known in Italy since 1698, when he performed the role of Brighella in a *commedia dell'arte* company from Rimini. His wife, Giusta or Giustina Francesca Paghetti, belonged to a family of actors famous since the mid-seventeenth century, but it is not known whether she was a relative of Alessandro Paghetti, or if she was the same Francesca Paghetti who also sang in Lisbon in 1738 and 1739.

The only composers whose names appear in the librettos of operas performed at the Academia de Trindade are Leonardo Leo (*Siface* of 1737 and 1739) and Gaetano Maria Schiassi. The latter became a member of the Royal Chapel and composer to the Infante D. Manuel, a brother of King João V.[94] The author of the theatrical sets was Roberto Clerici, a disciple of Ferdinando Bibiena and painter to the Duke of Parma. There is no reason to believe that, as has often been stated, there was any connection between this company and the one that had visited Lisbon in 1731.[95]

In December 1735 the Évora diaries stated that the Italian company had made a profit of 230 *moedas* (1:104$000) in six operas (probably in the sense of six performances). This was not enough, however, as their expenses amounted to 25,000 *cruzados* (10:000$000). In January 1736 there were two private performances of *Farnace* attended only by ladies, who paid 50 *moedas* (240$000) between them for each performance. For the first of these there were twenty-one ladies, who brought with them their daughters and servants up to ten persons each, and for the second forty-six ladies. The Cardinal da Cunha, the Bishop of Leiria and the Dean of the Patriarcal also watched the opera from a public box, but the Nuncio did not want to go to the theatre as he was not allowed to have curtains to his box.[96]

*Farnace* was followed by Schiassi's *Alessandro nell'Indie*, which was considered better. It had 'two kinds of intermezzi' and was performed three times a week. In March the King's second son, the Infante D. Carlos, died. This was soon followed by the death of his aunt, the Infanta D. Francisca. All theatrical performances were suspended until November at least, when *O labirinto de Creta* by António José da Silva was performed at the Teatro do Bairro Alto.[97]

In November an Italian company 'of both sexes' arrived in Lisbon and began performing comedies in their own language in the palace of D. António Henriques, which they rented for 2,000 *cruzados* (800$000). In February 1737 the ladies attended the opera twice a week. For one performance forty-two ladies paid 4$430 for each ticket, which gave them the right to bring two other people with them. The total cost of the performance was 40 *moedas* (192$000). In January Elena Paghetti had had a stroke for the second time, and she was away from the theatre until November.[98]

Meanwhile the Misericórdia had made a representation to the King in which it recalled its century-old privilege on all theatrical performances in Lisbon, and which seems to have been favourably received.[99] On 17 October 1737, it rented out the Pátio das Comédias for 600$000 a year to João Vilanova, Luis Trinité and António Forestier, who had recently presented the Italian comedy company, with the right to perform comedies, tragedies, *entremezes*, *bailes*, etc., in Spanish, Portuguese, French or Italian. They could not however perform any operas, and if they did they would have to pay a fine of 400$000 each time, half to the Hospital de Todos os Santos, and half to the opera managers.

A few months earlier Paghetti had applied to the Misericórdia to be released from the tax he was paying to the Hospital, complaining about the competition he was suffering from the managers of the Italian comedy company and claiming that he had spent 1:000$000 on the theatre, plus 35,000 *cruzados* (14:000$000) on overheads, and that his singers had not yet been paid. If he could not be released from paying his tax, at least he asked to be allowed to establish himself where he wished or, if he had to remain in the same place, that his tax be calculated on a different basis. He also asked to have the exclusive rights to operatic performances. On the other hand the French impresarios should not be allowed to employ musicians in their comedies or even in the *entremezes*. The same should apply to the *presépios*, which should reduce the size and quality of their figures, or puppets.

On 17 July 1737, the Hospital granted a ten-year privilege on the operas to the Academia da Trindade, in return for a yearly payment of 700$000, which was lowered to 600$000 on 28 July. As for the French impresarios the Hospital declared that it could not prevent them from presenting their comedies in the same way in which they were done everywhere else. As to the *presépios*, it would try to forbid them exceeding their traditional rights.[100] The Évora diary of 30 July indicates that the nobility took sides concerning all these dealings.[101]

In September new singers for the opera had been hired in Italy. In November Elena Paghetti fainted during a rehearsal of Schiassi's *Anagilda*. She was replaced by her sister Anna but there was a significant drop in the number of opera-goers. Sixty ladies were invited to one performance but only sixteen went, paying 35 *moedas* (168$000). The dancers were admired for their high kicks, which had never been seen before.[102]

In January 1738 *Sesostri, Re d'Egitto* brought a full house. In only one night there was a profit of 60 *moedas* (288$000). Elena Paghetti was singing again and two new singers, Giacoma Ferrari and Francesco Grisi, had seemed excellent to the public. In February however the Patriarch forbade Giacoma Ferrari to continue to dance in male costume.

Meanwhile a few businessmen asked the Count of Ericeira for part of a riding arena and the corner of a street, with a total area of 270 ×110 spans (59 ×24 metres), to build an opera house. The Count fixed the rent at 2,000 *cruzados* (800$000) a year. In June the Hospital transferred Paghetti's privilege, which had not yet been paid, to António Gomes Figueiró.[103] Beside the 600$000 he paid to the Hospital, Figueiró also paid 840$000 a year, not to the Count, but to his original tenant, Agostinho da Silva.[104]

In July the new theatre was being built in the *horta* (vegetable garden) of the Count of Ericeira, with a courtyard for the carriages and a private box with a separate entrance for the Count. Figueiró was trying to hire the Paghetti sisters and Gaetano Valetta. In Italy he also tried to hire the famous Anna Peruzzi, offering her 8,000 *cruzados* (3:200$000) for three winters, but the singer apparently wanted 10,000 (4:000$000). In August the husband of Angela Paghetti stole her jewels and left a knife stuck in her house.[105]

In November the 'Teatro novo alla Rua dos Condes' opened its doors with *La clemenza di Tito*, performed by the same company which had appeared at the Academia da Trindade.[106] The Marchioness of Valença took five boxes with venetian blinds and a separate entrance and other ladies took five other boxes without blinds but also with a separate entrance. After their first visit(s) to the theatre the blinds were made to close more tightly. Meanwhile the Marquis of Abrantes and other nobles entertained themselves with the introduction of Italian opera texts that were being printed.[107] The new opera was attracting a large audience and on certain nights there was a profit of over 300$000. On 28 December

Felice Cecacci, Giacoma Ferrari and Gaetano Valetta sang a two-act serenata at a party given by the Marquis of Cascais.

In November 1739 there were two new singers in the company, Giuseppe Schiavoni and Petronilla Trabò Brasili,[108] who seemed very good. Agostinho da Silva started a law-suit against Figueiró but lost. In January 1740 the singers Francesca Polli (the *Brescianina*) and Maria Caterina Negri and two dancers arrived from Italy, but the Marquis of Abrantes, who was not pleased with the opera company, intended to start his own company in the houses of the Presépio of the Mouraria district of Lisbon. His productions would be free and he and his wife would invite whomsoever they pleased to attend them. The male roles would be sung by Felice Cecacci, Francesco Grisi and Gaetano Valetta, and the female roles by Elena and Anna Paghetti.

The Misericórdia however raised objections to these plans, even though the Marquis proposed to give only seven performances on days when there would be no opera at the Rua dos Condes. As the royal privilege stated that there could not be any public or private opera performances without the Misericórdia's permission, the jurists were of the opinion that Figueiró would be able to sue the Marquis for damages.

When the Marquis saw that the King was asking for a written application, and that the Misericórdia insisted on keeping its privilege on the operas, he decided to give up his plans, even though he had incurred considerable expenses for the theatre and the costumes. He also paid over 40 *cruzados* (16$000) to the singers for their work in learning the opera. It was said that the Marquis and other nobles wanted to take over as impresarios of the Rua dos Condes from Figueiró.[109]

In February the new *prima donna*, Francesca Polli, was preferred by many to Angela Paghetti. Some admirers had offered her valuable gold rings and necklaces. Due to Angela's illness the performances were suspended for three days, but she was already back on the stage at the end of the month. She and her sisters meanwhile had rented some houses belonging to the Count of Soure for 300$000. They had them painted and furnished with embroidered velvet and damask cloths. It was said that they would invite the nobles for card games, music, and refreshments.[110]

From 1740 onwards, the librettos from the Rua dos Condes show in fact that there had been considerable changes in the company's cast. Angela was the only member of the Paghetti family who remained in the company.[111] Two interesting additions were Annibale Pio Fabri and Maria Caterina Negri, who had previously sung in Handel's company in London. Fabri sang in Madrid, in the Teatro de los Caños del Peral, between 1738 and 1740.[112] In Lisbon he also apparently worked as a set-painter.[113] In 1751 he was hired for the Royal Chapel at 60 *scudi romani* a month.[114]

Besides the already mentioned Leonardo Leo and Schiassi, the only other composer whose name is identified in the Rua dos Condes librettos is

Table 1 *Singers in the Public Theatres, 1735–42*

| Singers | Academia da Trindade | | | | Teatro novo da Rua Dos Condes | | | |
|---|---|---|---|---|---|---|---|---|
| | 1735 | 1736 | 1737 | 1738 | 1739 | 1740 | 1741 | 1742 |
| Bambini, Laura, from Pesaro | | | | | | | * | * |
| Brasili, Petronilla Trabò, from Rome | | | | | * | * | | |
| Cecacci, Anna | | | | | * | | | |
| Cecacci, Felice, from Pistoia (tenor)[a] | * | * | * | * | * | | | |
| Fabri, Annibale Pio from Bologna (tenor) | | | | | | * | * | * |
| Ferrari, Giacoma, from Naples | | | | * | * | | | |
| Franchi, Giovanna, from Rome | | | | | * | * | * | * |
| Galetti, Domenico Giuseppe, from Cortogna | * | * | * | | | | | |
| Grisi, Francesco, from Brescia | | | | * | * | | | |
| Lamparelli, Agata, from Rome | | | | | | * | * | |
| Mugnaini, Isabella | | | | * | * | | | |
| Negri, Maria Caterina, from Bologna (*primo uomo*)[a] | | | | | | * | | |
| Paghetti, Angela Adriana, from Bologna | * | * | * | * | * | * | * | * |
| Paghetti, Anna, from Bologna | * | | * | * | | | | |
| Paghetti, Elena, from Bologna | * | * | * | * | | | | |
| Paghetti, Francesca, from Bologna | | | | * | * | | | |
| Passerini, Carlo | | | * | | | | | |
| Polli, Francesca, from Brescia (*prima donna*)[a] | | | | | | * | * | * |
| Santini, Antonio, from Pisa | | | | | * | * | | |
| Schiavoni, Giuseppe, from Siracusa | | | | | * | * | * | |
| Valetta (Valetti), Gaetano, from Milan | * | * | * | * | * | * | * | * |
| Veroni, Alessandro, from Urbino | * | * | * | | | | | |
| Zanardi, Teresa, from Bologna | | * | * | * | | | | |

[a] According to J. Monfort, 'Quelques notes sur l'histoire du théâtre portugais (1729–1750)', p. 592.

Rinaldo di Capua. On 18 March 1740, he left Italy for Lisbon with an annual contract of 1,000 *scudi*. In 1742 he was already back in Rome. His operas *Catone in Utica* of 1740 and *Didone abbandonata* and *Ipermestra* of 1741 were apparently written for the Rua dos Condes.[115] The painter of the sets was now the Roman Salvatore Colonelli.

The librettos of the Rua dos Condes, like those of the Academia da Trindade, are generally bilingual. Several of them claim to have been printed in Bologna ('nella Stamperia di Giuseppe de Longi'). According to Carvalhais, however,[116] the frequent mistakes present in the Italian texts show that they were actually printed in Lisbon. He notes that in one case (*Demetrio* of 1739) the printing types are the same as those used by António Isidoro da Fonseca, the printer of the librettos for the Academia da Trindade.

A royal provision of 15 September 1737 extended the Hospital's privilege on theatrical performances to another kind of opera that had recently been introduced in Lisbon, and which was performed by artificial figures (i.e. puppets) with music, in imitation of the other comedies and operas.[117] The first known of these puppet operas is the *Vida do grande D. Quixote de la Mancha e do gordo Sancho Pança*, which according to the Count of Ericeira's diary was being attended by the people and part of the nobility in June 1733.[118] Its author, António José da Silva, was a Jewish lawyer who was born in 1705. In 1712 he came to Lisbon with his parents, who were under arrest, and whose property had been confiscated by the Inquisition. In 1726 he was arrested and tortured by the Inquisition, along with his mother and two brothers. Between 1733 and 1738 eight of his puppet operas were performed in the Teatro or Casa dos Bonecos (Puppet House) of the Bairro Alto. On 5 October 1737 he was again arrested and on 18 December 1739 he was burned at the stake. His operas were published anonymously throughout the eighteenth century, but he is identified as their author by his contemporary Barbosa Machado in his *Bibliotheca Lusitana*.

With the exception of the *Vida do grande D. Quixote de la Mancha* ... and of *Guerras do alecrim e manjerona*, which is a kind of middle-class comedy, his operas are all based on mythological subjects, which are treated in a baroque mixture of serious and comic styles. The serious characters talk in a pedantic manner, full of metaphors, while their servants mock this style and occasionally criticise their betters quite boldly. In *As variedades de Proteu* Maresia exclaims, when she sees the princess her mistress bleeding: 'In the end royal blood is red like any other blood.'[119]

António José da Silva is generally considered to be the most original dramatic author in eighteenth-century Portugal, but his work has not yet been the object of any major literary study.[120] No relation has been established yet between his literary activity, which was not even mentioned in his trial, and his persecution by the Inquisition.

Musically his operas are somewhat akin to the French *opéra-comique* or to the German *Singspiel*. They sometimes start with a *sinfonia*, and include recitatives, arias, vocal minuets, duets, trios and other choruses, as well as choirs, alternating with spoken dialogues, with an average of twenty-one musical numbers in each opera. The original music for two of these operas is preserved in the library of the Ducal Palace at Vila Viçosa. The music of the *Guerras do alecrim e manjerona* is attributed to António Teixeira, and that for *As variedades de Proteu* is anonymous. The Évora diaries also name António Teixeira as the composer of *Os encantos de Medeia*, and it is likely that he composed the music to António José da Silva's other operas as well.[121] The music that survives (and which has been revived more than once in modern times) shows him to have been perfectly at ease in the Italian operatic style. Nothing is known about the actor-singers who performed these operas at the Bairro Alto Theatre.

The popularity of António José da Silva's operas is certainly connected with the fact that they were acted and sung in Portuguese. An entry in one of the Évora diaries for 12 November 1737 says that the Pátio das Comédias was beginning to put on operas in Portuguese, because the public was turning away in boredom from those performed in Italian.[122] This probably refers to the performances of the Italian comedy company which had appeared in the Pátio das Comédias the previous year. It is possible that they presented spoken versions of Italian librettos with occasional music, and this certainly became the fashion on the Portuguese stage during the whole of the eighteenth century. Of António José da Silva's two immediate successors, Alexandre António de Lima and José Joaquim de Sousa Rocha e Saldanha, the first is mainly responsible for translations of Italian opera librettos, while the second published an original collection of *Óperas segundo o gosto e costume português* in 1761.[123] Those 'Portuguese' operas known to have been performed at the Bairro Alto and Mouraria Theatres during the first half of the eighteenth century have been included in my Chronology.[124] With the exception of António Teixeira's scores, no music has survived for this kind of repertoire.

The texts of António José da Silva's operas were frequently reprinted throughout the eighteenth century. His *Guerras do alecrim e manjerona* in particular seems to have been performed often both by professionals and amateurs, not only in Lisbon and in the provinces but in Brazil as well.[125] It has often been stated that they were originally intended for a middle- and lower middle-class public which did not have access to the Italian operas presented at the Academia da Trindade or the Rua dos Condes. It is true that the Italian opera librettos of this period are usually dedicated 'alla Nobiltà di Portogallo', but this does not necessarily mean that the middle class did not have access to performances of them. Conversely, the above-quoted reference shows that at least part of the nobility did also attend the Bairro Alto Theatre (and the popular *presépios* as well).[126] The title of a sonnet published by João Cardoso da Costa in 1736 mentions a performance by ladies of *Os encantos de Medeia*.[127] In the light of the slender evidence available, and of the few extant studies of the repertoire itself, a proper sociological characterisation of the theatrical public in Lisbon in the first half of the eighteenth century does not yet seem possible.[128]

Nothing is known about the way in which the puppet theatre was introduced in Lisbon at this time, or whether all the operas produced at the Bairro Alto were performed by puppets, but it seems that they were the cause of certain difficulties with the censors. The Évora diaries for July 1738 mention some artificial figures that the ignorant could not believe were 'natural', and whose curious movements had been examined by the Inquisition.[129]

The last Italian opera to have been performed at the Rua dos Condes during the reign of João V was *Bajazet* in January 1742 and the last theatrical performances in Lisbon during the first half of the eighteenth century that are mentioned in the Évora diaries are those of António José da Silva's *As variedades de Proteu* in April 1742.[130] On 28 January of the following year the privilege on theatrical performances of the Hospital de Todos os Santos was revoked by royal decree, being replaced by an annual contribution of 1:300$000, paid out of the Mint's profits.[131] This suggests that at that time all theatrical performances in Lisbon had ceased, very probably as a consequence of the King's illness.[132]

A contemporary author[133] indicates that Queen Marie Anne of Austria also contributed towards the extinction of the lay theatres, adding that as an example of a safer occupation she used to make frequent visits to the churches.

This prohibition seems to have remained in force in Lisbon until the King's death in 1750. In the absence of any theatrical performances in the capital, the Évora diaries mention those few performances that were put on in the provinces. On 26 February 1746 they announced that all public and private balls in Lisbon had been suspended and that at that time there was no entertainment in the city.[134]

In a letter written to Padre Martini on 1 May 1747,[135] the composer Schiassi informs him that

All entertainments have been forbidden here due to the illness of the King, who, since the first day that he had a stroke, has forbidden all theatrical performances and balls, and wants to force people into becoming saints. Church feasts and oratorios have not been forbidden and from this I also take some advantage.

As pointed out above (p. 9), during the first half of the century the term serenata seems to have been broadly used outside Lisbon in connection with performances of vocal and instrumental music. Thus the *Gazeta* of 7 August 1721 mentions the performance of a serenata during a visit of the Patriarch of Lisbon to the monastery and town of Alcobaça. In December 1727, during the festivities at Ponte de Lima for the birth of the first son of the Viscount of Vila Nova de Cerveira, a comedy by Luís Calisto da Costa e Faria was accompanied by a serenata. On 7 February 1728 a serenata was also performed in Oporto during the festivities for the wedding of the Portuguese and Spanish Princes.[136]

The same ambiguity exists in relation to the use of the term 'opera'. Thus the 'kind of opera with sets of several choirs', performed at Covilhã in July 1735,[137] was probably just a comedy with music.

An interesting case is that of the oratorio for five voices 'with recitatives and arias, in the manner of the operas', performed in Oporto on 13 September 1747, on the occasion of the King's (temporary) recovery.[138] The text was in Portuguese and it alluded to that recovery. Neither its author nor the composer of the music are mentioned by the *Gazeta*. This was the last event in a four-day celebration for which the Bishop had had a wooden hall erected in the courtyard of his palace. It measured 115 × 50 spans (25 × 11 metres) and was lined on the inside with silk and gold. It had six windows on either side, and enough chairs and benches for 1,200 spectators (!). At the top of the hall the portraits of the King and Queen had been placed on a throne under a canopy, and the portraits of their ancestors had been hung from the walls. The performance lasted three hours and was followed by refreshments.

# 2

# Court opera during the reign of José I (1750–77)

### Court opera before the 1755 earthquake

Princess Mariana Vitória, referring to her husband in one of her letters to her mother written in 1743, says: 'I think that if his Father happens to die, which God forbid, the face of things will change, for he himself does not love the Patriarcal so much.'[1] João V died on 31 July 1750 and as early as March of the following year José I was already involved in negotiations to hire some of the best Italian opera singers then available. A series of letters written by the then Foreign Secretary and later all-powerful Prime Minister and Marquis of Pombal, Sebastião José de Carvalho e Melo, to the ambassador in Rome, António Freire de Andrade Encerrabodes, deals with the contract of Gioacchino Conti (Gizziello), and shows that the King was sparing no expense to secure his services.[2] Negotiations dragged on for a whole year until March 1752, and involved a lot of wheeling and dealing (including the use of a Portuguese special agent and a proposed bribe to a certain Abbate who kept company with the singer) as well as secrecy.[3] Whereas in the first letter the Foreign Secretary specifies that Gizziello was to serve both in the Patriarcal and the Royal Chamber, this condition was later changed to include only the latter.[4]

In one of the letters Sebastião José agrees with the ambassador that the singer's own conditions were exorbitant, but that they had not appeared so to the King's magnanimity, who had ordered that they be accepted. They included house, board and carriage, the freedom to leave after a year's service, and an unspecified sum of money.[5] Gizziello, who was at the time at the Milan Opera, was to start his journey after Carnival and travel by land. Regarding his route, the Foreign Secretary draws a detailed itinerary which would prevent him from passing through any other courts where he

*Fig. 1 'Reggia con vedutta di Cartagine'. Set for* Didone abbandonata *by David Perez, Act 1, Scene 1 (Teatro de Salvaterra, Carnival 1753). Drawing by Giovanni Carlo Sicini Bibiena.*

might be held up. He was to have his own carriage from the moment he arrived in Rome, as by then he would be in the service of the King of Portugal.

The letters also deal with the contracts of other lesser singers, among them the tenor Anton Raaff (whom Sebastião José calls *Racca*), who was to be found in Bologna. He was to be offered up to 300$000 rs a year, not being considered to be worth more.[6]

Meanwhile all the other elements needed for the organisation of an operatic establishment were being gathered in Lisbon. The architect Giovanni Carlo Sicini Bibiena, the son of the famous Ferdinando Bibiena, arrived in early 1752. In May or June the singer Francesco Feracci was sent to Rome to fetch the whole company which had been hired by Giovanni Bibiena, as well as the composer David Perez.[7] According to Volkmar Machado,[8] Bibiena sent his assistant Giovanni Berardi ahead of him with drawings of the opera sets and plans for the Theatres of Salvaterra, Ajuda and the short-lived Ópera do Tejo. Besides Berardi he brought with him other assistants, like the painter Giacomo Azzolini and the architect and theatrical machinist Petronio Mazzoni, who were to be active in the royal theatres throughout the second half of the century.[9]

*Fig. 2 Plan of a theatre identified as the Casa da Ópera.*

Gizziello was already in Lisbon on 6 June 1752 when a serenata for the King's birthday was sung at the Paço da Ribeira.[10] On 12 September a new theatre was inaugurated in the palace. This was in the Torreão da Casa da Índia, in the room formerly used for the reception of foreign ambassadors, and came to be known as the Teatro do Forte.[11] Perez's *Il Siroe* was sung by Giuseppe Gallieni, Gizziello, Raaff, Niccolà Conti, Giovanni Simone Ciucci and Domenico Luciani, the last three being described in the libretto as 'Virtuosi della Cappella Reale'. The *balli* were by Andrea Alberti, *Il Tedeschino*, who was to remain one of the court theatre's choreographers until his death in 1780. They were danced by himself and by Giovanni Battista Grazioli, *Il Schizza*, Vincenzo Magnani, Andrea Marchi, *Il Morino*, Gasparo Pieri, Michele Ricciolini, Giuseppe Salomoni and Filippo Vicedomini. The sets were designed by Giovanni Bibiena, the costumes by Antonio Bassi, and the *abbattimenti* or combats by Alessandro Pizzi.

During Carnival of 1753 *Didone abbandonata* by Perez and the intermezzo *La fantesca* by Hasse were performed at the new theatre of Salvaterra, alternating with a Portuguese comedy.[12] Between spring and autumn *L'Olimpiade* and *L'eroe cinese* by Perez were also produced at the Teatro do Forte in the Paço da Ribeira. As well as the above-mentioned singers their cast included Giovanni Manzoli. In 1754 *L'Adriano in Siria* by Perez alternated with an Italian comedy, or comedies, at Salvaterra, and *L'Ipermestra* and *L'Artaserse* by the same composer were performed at the Teatro do Forte. The names of Tommaso Guarducci, Giuseppe Morelli, and Pietro Serbolloni, 'Virtuosi della Cappella Reale', appear among the cast.

By then the erection of a new court theatre in Lisbon must have been well under way.[13] It was situated not far from the palace, approximately where the Arsenal da Marinha now stands, west of the Praça do Comércio. The basement plan and a sectional drawing of a court opera by Bibiena preserved at the Academia Nacional de Belas Artes have been identified as belonging to this theatre, which is frequently known today as the Ópera do Tejo, because of its proximity to the river Tagus, but is simply called Casa da Ópera in contemporary documents.[14] The Chevalier des Courtils, an officer in the French fleet that visited Lisbon in 1755, described it thus:[15]

The King maintains an Italian opera house that costs him two million a year. The spectacle he offers to his court twice or three times every week is truly majestic and full of pomp. To this purpose he had a beautiful and magnificent theatre built. It is octagonal with four tiers of boxes.[16] That of the King is at the end, and is decorated with imitation marble columns,[17] covered with gilded bronze mouldings. Two other boxes in the same style are placed at the right and left on the sides of the stage. Those on the first and third tiers have gilded balustrades; those on the second and third tiers are fully open in front and magnificently gilded with a shining gold glittering like diamonds. Richness, delicacy and good taste vie with each other. The theatre is superb. It is one hundred and eighty feet long and sixty feet wide.[18] The stalls occupy the whole length of the room. One is comfortably seated; there is no amphitheatre, as in France. Beautiful though this beautiful and kingly place is, its magnificence conceals defects. The room is not large enough in relation to the stage. The columns with pilasters that support the boxes and are crowned with figures of giants, are too big for the size of the room. There are only three boxes in each tier; there should have been more.[19] I find it too small for a stately theatre and too big for a private theatre. In relation to the stage it should have been three times as large as it is. Notwithstanding these defects, one cannot deny that one is struck when entering this room, by the gold and magnificence which shines and glitters from all sides.

There were two performances there during our stay in Lisbon. The King invited us to attend both times.[20] He had recommended to his main courtiers that they give us the honour of the house and offer us the good places. The Portuguese, who are naturally polite and affable, fulfilled this order wonderfully. The *Clémence de Titus* by the celebrated 'maître Astasi' [*sic*], the Corneille of the Italian theatre, was performed. The decorations and the spectacle are superb. The immense stage, sumptuously decorated, charmed our eyes. Most of us found our ears equally charmed by the Italian music. There were others whom it did not please. Male and female roles are both played by castrati. The recitative seemed very boring to me. The Italian music may not be to the taste of those French not used to it. Not that I think their taste should prevail over that of the rest of Europe, which prefers Italian music, merely that I did not care for it much.

A slightly different view of the theatre is expressed by Francisco Coelho de Figueiredo, who was speaking from hearsay:[21]

The curious found two defects in the big theatre built by Bibiena in 1753: that the room was too large, and did not have the grace of the room at Salvaterra, which, being smaller, was well proportioned, and in which one had a good view of the stage from every part of the theatre, something which was impossible in the larger theatre. The second was that the spectators were unwittingly distracted from the stage by the richness of the house and all the gilded decorations.

A list of the people who were allowed to attend the royal theatres has been preserved.[22] It includes both Portuguese and foreign noblemen (as well as those with the status of noblemen or 'fôro de fidalgo'), dignitaries of the Church, higher-ranking judges, military officers and cadets, commanding officers of the militia and their deputies ('Capitaens mores, e Sargentos mores das ordenanças e auxiliares'), the King's and the Queen's servants, ministers and Government officials, and Portuguese and foreign businessmen. All these were seated in the stalls. Box no. 11 had places for those people who had no place in the stalls, box no. 12 twenty-seven places for the noblemen's female servants, and box no. 22 ten places for a number of officials, including two priests ('Padre Gaspar e Padre Francisco do Tojal'), the surgeon José Carvalho, and the court blood-letter. According to Matos Sequeira,[23] six boxes were reserved for the Patriarch, the 'Meninos de Palhavã' (three illegitimate sons of João V), the Lord Chief Butler ('Mordomo-mór'), officers of the King's Household and chamber servants ('camaristas'). Eight boxes on the second storey were reserved for foreign envoys, officers of the Queen's House, and ladies of the first rank. Eight boxes on the third storey were for the most important members of the court, and were distributed by the Lord Chief Butler. In the stalls ten or twelve benches were also reserved for the court.

The inauguration of the Ópera do Tejo was on the Queen's birthday, 31 March.[24] Referring to it Burney says:[25]

the new theatre ... surpassed, in magnitude and decorations, all that modern times can boast. On this occasion Perez new set the opera of *Alessandro nell'Indie*,[26] in which opera a troop of horses appeared on the stage, with a Macedonian phalanx. One of the King's riding-masters rode Bucephalus, to a march which Perez composed in the *Manege*, to the *grand pas* of a beautiful horse,[27] the whole far exceeding all that Farinelli had attempted ... at Madrid, for the fitting out of which he had unlimited powers. Besides these splendid decorations, his Portuguese Majesty had assembled together the greatest singers then existing.

These singers were Caffarelli, Gallieni, Luciani, Morelli, Raaff and Carlo Reina. The libretto includes nine engravings of the sets by Berardi, Le Bouteux and Dourneau. The libretto of *La clemenza di Tito*, with music by Mazzoni[28] the first performance of which was on 6 June, and which included the singer Giacomo Veroli among its cast, also includes eight engravings. According to Volkmar Machado, during summer and autumn *L'Olimpiade* and *L'Artaserse* by Perez were also performed.[29]

The Chevalier des Courtils gives some hints concerning the role that opera was supposed to play in court life:[30]

There is no court in Portugal as there is in France. One never sees the King nor the Queen eat. Nobody attends the King's *lever* and *coucher*. The Queen does not have her *toilette* in public. There are never any games or *appartements*. Their Majesties live

*Fig. 3 'Padiglione d'Alessandro'. Set for* Alessandro nell'Indie *by David Perez, Act 1, Scene 11 (Casa da Ópera, March 1755). Drawing by Giovanni Carlo Sicini Bibiena.*

in their court as private citizens. One only sees them at the opera and by audience when one wishes to talk to them. The King has the excellent custom, which cannot be too highly praised in a monarch, of holding two public audiences every week, one for the people, the other for the nobility, so that his subjects are able to talk directly to their master.

Elsewhere he says that the monks from Mafra had threatened the King with the Pope's authority when he insisted on having opera performed in the monastery.[31]

Scarcely seven months after its inauguration the Ópera do Tejo crumbled in the 1 November Lisbon earthquake, one of the biggest ever recorded. It has been estimated that as many as 10,000 lost their lives, out of a total population of 150,000. Two thirds of the houses became uninhabitable, and out of forty parish churches only five remained standing.[32] The earthquake and the fires that ensued destroyed also a large part of the city's and the court's archives, as well as the royal library, thus creating particular difficulties for the historian. A few documents from this period are preserved in the AHMF, Caixas 1, 2, and 315. A number of them are receipts of payments relating to the construction, decoration and stage productions of the Casa da Ópera [do Tejo], and some are dated from the eve of the earthquake, while later payments concern the clearing away of the debris.

Four receipts are for another theatre, the Casa da Comédia da Quinta de

Casa da Ópera                    Sale de l'Opera

*Fig. 4  Ruins of the Casa da Ópera.*

Cima da Ajuda or Casa da Comédia de Belém, and one of them refers to
comedies performed there, which suggests that this theatre may have been
originally intended for spoken drama. Another payment in Caixa 2 is for
2:976$000 rs to Francesco Feracci to pay the Companhia cómica to return
to Italy, which also shows the court's interest in Italian drama. I have not
found any details concerning the construction of the Casa da Comédia or
Teatro da Ajuda.

Feracci also received 470$000 rs to dismiss the last dancers. The King's
operatic establishment had no doubt been totally disrupted by the earthquake.[33] Many singers fled from Lisbon in terror. The British ambassador
in Madrid, writing to his colleague in Lisbon on 20 November, says:[34]
'Your musitians [*sic*] come tumbling in naked upon us everyday'. This was
certainly the case with the composer Antonio Mazzoni, Gizziello, and
probably also with Carlo Reina and Pietro Serbolloni (if he is the same as
the Pietro Servellini who received remuneration from the Madrid court in
1756).[35] Others had left for Madrid even before the earthquake, like Raaff

and Manzoli, who sang in Galuppi's *Demofoonte* for the birthday of Ferdinand VI on 23 September.[36] Both Manzoli and Veroli had sung in Madrid prior to coming to Portugal, and returned there afterwards.[37]

Burney says of Gizziello that

> he was impressed with such a religious turn by that tremendous calamity, that he retreated to a monastery where he ended his days. It was soon after this event that Guadagni shut himself up in the same convent, not so much for spiritual consolation as musical counsel.[38]

Burney says, quoting Pacchierotti, that Guadagni was in Lisbon in 1754–55 as second serious man, or *secondo uomo serio* under Gizziello, and as late as 1790, being old and poor, he asked for a subsidy from the Portuguese court, claiming that he had only abandoned the royal service for the fear that the earthquake had caused in him. He was sent 96$000 rs.[39] Anton Raaff himself had a chapel built in his native place of Holzen bei Bonn, in gratitude for having escaped the earthquake.[40] The *Berliner musikalische Zeitung* of 1805[41] says that he received from the King of Portugal a tobacco case with a piece of solid gold inside weighing 1½ pounds 2 ounces, and a solitaire ring estimated to be worth 8,000 gulden.

## *The reorganisation of the operatic establishment. Purchase of scores, librettos, and theatrical costumes*

The above-mentioned facts are a possible indication that José I had not intended to keep all the first-rate singers that he had gathered for the inauguration of the Ópera do Tejo permanently in his service. Equally, however, it is not possible to guess what his plans for the future might have been. As it was, the earthquake brought operatic activity to a complete standstill. It was only in 1763 that it was again resumed on a somewhat more modest scale,[42] at least as far as singers were concerned.[43]

It must have been sometime before 1764 that a Director of the Royal Theatres was appointed in the person of Pedro José da Silva Botelho, a member of the Overseas Council, Knight of the Ordem de Cristo, Porter of the Royal Chamber, and Robekeeper to José I, who after his death in July 1773 was replaced by João António Pinto da Silva, an official in the Navy Department, Knight of the Ordem de Cristo, Robekeeper, and after 1776 also Keeper of the Royal Jewels and of the King's Privy Purse, who in turn occupied that post until his death in 1801. All their transactions with Italy were carried out through the intermediary of the Portuguese consuls in Genoa and general agents to the Portuguese crown in that country, the Piaggios, of whom three succeeding generations occupied that post: Niccolà (up to 1772), Giovanni and Lorenzo.

Beside being charged with hiring singers, dancers and players, the Piaggios supplied the Lisbon court theatres with scores, librettos, theatrical costumes and ornaments, instruments, strings, and music paper, and even wick for the candles.[44] Many other commodities for the court were acquired in Italy through the Piaggios, such as tea, chocolate, wine, etc. Silva Botelho also managed to squeeze in his own personal orders for Parmesan, Stracchino and Lodi cheese, tuna fish in olive oil, anchovies, wine from Florence and even rice.[45] Caixa 260 in the AHMF preserves a few bills for librettos and scores sent to D. Luca Giovine, Knight of the Ordem de Cristo and Capelão Fidalgo da Casa Real, in 1775 and 1776.[46] A letter from Piaggio dated 3 March 1765 in the same box, also mentions the dispatching of *argomenti* and music for the *balli*, including those from the Milan Opera, and those by Manetti for two Rome operas. No music for the *balli* has been preserved; however, the Ajuda library alone possesses over 700 manuscript scores of operas, serenatas and oratorios from the second half of the century, nearly three times as many as those that were actually performed in Lisbon during the period (including those performed in the public theatres up to 1793).

A few general comments should be made concerning this collection. First of all the great majority of the scores of the operas and serenatas which were actually performed at court are copies made in Lisbon. These are all carefully written copies in the same style of hand throughout, which contrast sharply with the hasty and disorderly appearance of the scores of Italian origin.[47] A typical complaint regarding Italian copyists is in fact voiced by Pinto da Silva in a letter to Piaggio of 7 April 1772, in which he asks for copies of Jommelli's operas.[48] There he insisted that these should be made by the best hand available, as the scores which came from Italy were usually badly and hastily written. Some copyists frequently left out the second violin, or the oboes, or the flutes, while others, to increase the number of pages, wrote only two or three bars on each page, which besides being dishonest forced the performers to keep turning the pages.

In certain cases complete sets of parts have been preserved, along with separate arias from the operas, occasionally with the names of the players and the singers who used them. Several scores, by way of contrast, are richly bound in red leather with gold decorations, and they do not seem to have been used in performance. This is the case with the Lisbon copies of Perez's operas, in contrast with the original (possibly autograph) scores, which show signs of great use.[49]

Besides the operas and serenatas which were actually performed in Lisbon, the Ajuda library holds over five hundred scores of operas by nearly one hundred different composers, mainly from the second half of the century, which were not performed, at least during our period. Some of them bear the name of Olimpia Perez, the sister of David Perez, from whom they were probably acquired. A number of non-Italian composers are included, such as J. C. Bach, Gassmann, Gluck, Holzbauer, Mysliveček, Naumann, Pleyel and Wagenseil. The three Milan operas by Mozart are also to be found. Concerning the score of *Mitridate* (*P-La* 45-III–22/24), a letter from Leopold Mozart, written from Venice on 1 March 1771, says that the Milan copyist was making five complete copies of the opera, one for the 'impresa', two for Vienna, one for the Duchess of Parma, and one for the Lisbon court.[50] The library of the Paço Ducal at Vila Viçosa, one of the royal residences, also preserves several scores from our period, some of which were performed in the court theatres.

Two letters from Pinto da Silva in 1774 and 1775 mention the receipt of books of Italian theatrical news ('Livro das Noticias dos Theatros de Italia', possibly volumes of Cacciò's *Indice de' spettacoli teatrali di tutto l'anno*).[51] The Lisbon court was thus kept fairly well informed on the current Italian operatic scene and was supplied with a wide and regular assortment of operas from which to choose.

Many letters and a few accounts preserved in the AHMF and also in the Ajuda library deal with the costumes and ornaments for the operas *Alessandro nell'Indie*, *Demofoonte*, *Enea nel Lazio*, *Ezio*, *Pelope*, *Solimano*, *Fetonte*, *La Nitteti*, *L'Olimpiade* and *Il trionfo di Clelia*.[52] In a letter to Piaggio dated 1 March 1768[53] Silva Botelho complains that in Lisbon ornaments were bad and very expensive and gives a detailed list of ornaments for which he asks Piaggio's correspondent in Milan, Antonio Zucchi, to send him samples and a price list.[54] In the same letter he writes that the great amounts of smoke from the theatre lights which obscured the theatre were caused by the bad quality cotton used for the wicks, which came from Maranhão (Brazil), as the candle maker was not allowed to import cotton from abroad. The King had therefore ordered twenty *arrobas* (300 kg) of cotton from the Levant to be bought by Piaggio in Genoa.

Detailed orders for the costumes of *Alessandro nell'Indie*, *Demofoonte* and *L'Olimpiade* by Jommelli, along with contracts for the same signed by the Milan theatrical tailor Francesco Motta, are preserved in AHMF, Caixa XX/Z/77 (14). Theatrical costumes ordered from so far away did not always arrive in time for the productions, and in certain cases did give rise to complaints. This was the case with *L'Olimpiade*: those for the nymphs and the shepherds were considered too light and poorly ornamented, and those for the men too long.[55]

The answers of the Milan tailors Motta and Mazza (i.e. eredi Mainini) to these accusations make interesting reading.[56] They argued that in opera theatres and in *drammi seri* costumes *all' eroica* were used and that for these only two types existed: either short, in the Roman style, or long in the Persian or Turkish style. *L'Olimpiade* had been staged in Milan, Turin, Venice, Rome, and all the major theatres in Italy with long dresses, even though these were worn with trousers, and they had never been criticised. And if the dresses were really too long, they could always be accommodated to the height of the singers. As to the nymphs and the shepherds, they argued that in an opera it was the singers who really mattered, and these should be distinguished from the extras. These last, whether they were shepherds, nymphs, priests, pages, noblemen, soldiers, guards or sailors, need only be modestly well dressed, according to their own characters. The tailors had also asked the opinion of Lieutenant Gamerra, who was the Poet of the Regio Teatro Ducale in Milan, and he said that the singers were always against wearing long dresses, preferring to wear short trousers in the French style. They added that they suspected the whole question to have originated with Carlo Reina, a singer in the court of Lisbon who before leaving Milan had sworn that the orders for the costumes would come to his father Antonio Reina. Zucchi adds that Motta and Mazza had been theatrical tailors for around forty years, and that they had worked for many theatres in Italy. He himself had read *L'Olimpiade* and had noticed that it took place in Greece, and that both the Greeks and the Persians wore long dresses, as one may read in the works of Metastasio.

Another complaint voiced by Pinto da Silva shortly after taking over the direction of the royal theatres concerns the prices, which he considered to be excessive.[57] He also insisted that the quality and variety of the colours was more important than the actual quality of the silks, which, even if they were slightly damaged by mould, would not be noticed from a distance in the theatre. Still this slight damage should make them come down to a more convenient price.

Occasionally orders were placed with other suppliers outside Italy. This was the case with a certain M. Dupont, who supplied the jewels for the opera *Solimano* by Perez, and was also asked to obtain a collection of coloured drawings of the dresses and masks of the Paris Opera, among them those designed by Bouquet.[58]

## Hiring of singers, dancers, and players

Singers were now usually hired to serve both in the court theatres and the Royal Chapel,[59] but this may not always have been the case. A rare example, dating from 1764, of two alternative drafts for a contract to be offered to the tenor Tibaldi, who was at the time at the court of Vienna, is preserved in AHMF, Caixa 260. They deserve to be quoted here in full. According to the first contract he would receive a monthly salary of 60$000 rs, plus 30$000 a month for his food allowance, 100$000 allowance on his arrival and one silk cloak and cassock. His voyage by sea or land from Genoa would be paid for. He would serve for twelve years, and if he wished to leave at the end of this period he would be pensioned with a quarter of his salary. If he wished to serve a further twelve years, he would be pensioned at the end with 30$000 a month. If he decided to remain in Portugal after twenty-four years he would keep his full salary and food allowance, even if he were too old, or too sick, to serve any longer. He was expected to sing in the Royal Chapel, in the Patriarcal, in the Royal Chamber, and in the Royal Theatre.

In the second alternative draft his yearly salary would be 1:000$000, plus 360$000 for his food allowance, and he would also receive a chaise with two mares, and two servants. The voyage by sea or land would also be paid for. His contract would be for only six years, after which he might, if he wished, be pensioned with 200$000 a year. If he wished, with the King's agreement, to remain in service a few more years, his pension would remain the same. In this second alternative he would be obliged to sing in the Royal Theatre and in the Royal Chamber, and also on any occasion when the King might wish to hear him in the Chapel, even in secular dress, but then only in solos with orchestra, and not in the choir ('em alguma muzica de Capella concertada, e naõ pᵃ os cheyos, e ripienos da mesma muzica'). In addition, he would have to sing wherever the King might be staying, whether at the court or outside it. He would be paid in Portuguese currency, both while in Portugal and after he retired abroad. His name never appears again in Lisbon, which means that he was not actually hired.

Different conditions for retirement pensions offered to the singers in the Portuguese royal service are mentioned in a letter from the court poet Gaetano Martinelli to Niccolò Jommelli of 18 March 1771.[60] In it he says that these pensions had originally been established by João V for those singers who had served for twenty-four years, and amounted to half of the salary they received from the Patriarcal. Later the demanded period of service had been reduced to twelve years. This, however, was only reserved for singers with greater merit and 'virtù'. After having served for twelve years Carlo Reina would get 30$000 a month, but Jozzi, who had served six years, only received 10$000.

The following list of Chapel singers dating from 1761 is preserved in AHMF, Caixa 315 (names in italics are those that appear in the opera librettos):[61]

> *Jozzi*
> *Conti*
> Michelotti
> *Vasquez*
> *Marchetti*
> Ristorini
> Poma
> Gallini
> Scharinei
> D. Ambrosio
> Mossi
> Federici
> Seri
> Marchetti
> *Ciucci*

Ceccoli
Tedeschi
*Principii*
Pocher
Palmazzi
Lombardi
Assisi
Baldi
*Giorgetti*
Sanpieri
De Porcheris
Pera
*Maruzzi*
Ducci
Franceschini
Barzi
Barnabei
Profili
Jassi
Grassi
Constantini
Appoloni
Baregi
Fratta
Pocarazza
Vallucci
Bertocchini
Pennacchiari
Durrelli
Bertozzi
D. Orazio

Correspondence between the Directors of the Royal Theatres and the Piaggios mentions the arrival of four singers, including Giuseppe Marocchini 'to act in comic female roles [parte jocoza]' in 1765, of the basses Bernardo Cocuccioni and Taddeo Puzzi ('de Nação húngaro') and the double-bass player Michele Giordani in 1767, of the singer Filippo Cappellani in 1770, of the singers Cosimo Banchi, Giuliano Giusti, Filippo Viotti, and the contralto Ansano Ferracuti in 1772,[62] the bass Anton(io) Scheifler or Scheiffer and seven dancers in 1774, the tenor Antonio Tomiatti and the soprano Luigi Bianchini also in 1774, and the tenor Michele Mazziotti and the bass Luca Manna in 1776.[63]

Contracts were usually signed in Genoa, but in some cases the artists arrived in Lisbon without having been previously hired. Thus François Sauveterre, who decided to accompany his favourite pupil, Pietro Colonna, was recommended by Piaggio as a choreographer, in a letter to Silva Botelho of 4 June 1767.[64] He was taken on at 400$000 a year to replace

Andrea Alberti, *Il Tedeschino*, 'whose imagination was becoming exhausted', and to act also as dancing-master to the Prince.[65]

Sauveterre had preceded Noverre in Stuttgart, where he had been responsible for the *balli* in Jommelli's *La Nitteti* and *Endimione* of 1759 and *Alessandro nell'Indie* of 1760.[66] Sasportes[67] gives some titles of Sauveterre's *balli* for the Lisbon court and remarks that he attempted to give them a certain degree of independence within the framework of operatic performance, and give them a certain dramatic and mimetic content, probably under the influence of the *ballets d'action*. In fact a list of *balli* drawn up by Carvalhais[68] on the basis of the librettos shows that Sauveterre's *balli* usually had their own independent titles. Still, as Sasportes adds, the fact that only male dancers were employed in the court theatres (and after 1775 in the public theatres as well) may have driven the best dancers away from Lisbon: they would have refused to dance ridiculous *travesti* roles. It also prevented development in the important area of female dancing – in which such names as Anna Camargo, Madeleine Guimard, Marie Sallé, Barbara Campanini, and Mlles Heinel and Allard were already well-known.

Livro xx/z/38 in the AHMF includes a record of contracts with court dancers from which the following alphabetical list has been drawn:

| *Name* | *Period of Service* | *Yearly salary* |
|---|---|---|
| Luigi Bardotti | June 1772–8 | 504$000 |
| Luigi Bellucci | June 1772–8 | 504$000 |
| Ridolfo Butti | December 1774–80 | 480$000[a] |
| Gherardo Cavazza | 26 May 1775–June 1779 | 480$000[a] |
| Pietro Colonna | August 1767; from 1775 also dancing-master to the Prince | 432$000 |
| Teofilo Corazzi | October 1764–December 1774 | 480$000[b] |
| Francesco Curioni | December 1774–December 1778 | 480$000[a] |
| Giambattista Flambò (Jean Baptiste Flambeau) | January 1770– | |
| Francesco Fontanella | December 1774–December 1778 | 480$000[a] |
| Luigi Gori | December 1774–December 1778 | 480$000[a] |
| Benedetto Lombardi | October 1764–December 1774 | 480$000[b] |
| Niccolà Midosi | June 1769– | 200$000 |
| Paolo Orlandi | January 1770–†6 November 1780 | 400$000 |
| Pietro Picchelli | December 1774–December 1778 | 480$000[a] |
| Francesco Picchi | December 1774–December 1778 | 480$000 |
| Antonio Porri | April 1767–January 1770 | 400$000 |
| François Sauveterre | November 1767–†18 January 1775 | 400$000 |
| Antonio Villa | May 1774–December 1778 | 480$000[a] |
| Carlo Vitalba | April 1767–December 1774 | 346$000 |
| Francesco Zucchelli | July 1767; after 1791 also wardrobe master | 432$000 |
| Tommaso Zucchelli | October 1764–December 1774 | 480$000[b] |

[a] plus 30$000 for accommodation
[b] plus 20$000 for accommodation

Some of these dancers appeared in the public theatres before being hired for the court theatres, and in the next reign they were to perform alternately in both places.[69]

After Sauveterre's death in 1775 Andrea Alberti once again became choreographer of the court theatres until his death in 1780, when he was replaced by Pietro Colonna. In the eighteenth century composers of the music for the *balli* were usually anonymous, but we know that in December 1773 António de Freitas de Silva was hired at 260$450 to play viola and cello and also to compose the music of the *balli* for the royal theatres.[70] In 1769 Pedro António Avondano is also mentioned as composer of the dances for the operas.[71]

With the partial disbandment of the Duke of Württemberg's operatic establishment in 1768–9, efforts were made to hire some of the dismissed artists. Writing to Niccolò Jommelli on 28 March 1769,[72] Silva Botelho asked for details concerning the capacities of the tenor Arcangelo Cortoni ('s'è buono, o ordinario, si sà ben la musica, o solamente a buon orrechio') and also of the two virtuosi Francesco Guerrieri and Giuseppe Robinelli. He also wished to know what kind of positions and salaries the members of the orchestra had, and whether there was any good dancer of *mezzo carattere*. One player who was hired was the Catalan oboist Juan Baptista Plà, who had belonged to the Duke's orchestra between 1755 and 1768.[73] Curiously enough, both he and his brother José had been in Lisbon in 1751, but had not wanted to accept the 320$000 salary which was offered them.[74] Plà was now offered 352$000.[75]

Scherpereel[76] has made a detailed study of the players in the Royal Chamber and concluded that their average salary was 260$450. As regards singers, their salaries were paid partly by the Patriarcal, partly by the King's Privy Purse, but I have not been able to find these payments, either in the Lisbon Cathedral Archive, or at the AHMF. From 1778 onwards a record of food allowances paid to singers and other personnel exists at the Arquivo Histórico do Tribunal de Contas.[77] It includes eight singers, who received 120$000 a year each. Of these only two are connected with the court theatres: Giovanni Marchetti and Giuseppe Romanini. Another opera singer, Luigi Torriani, appears in AHMF, Livro xx/z/38 as receiving a 120$000 salary.

Other contracts and payments listed in Livros xx/z/38 and xx/G/61 are for the composer and organist João Cordeiro da Silva, who received 240$000; the architects Giacomo Azzolini and Inácio de Oliveira [Bernardes], who received 600$000 and 280$000 respectively from September and November 1766 onwards; the poets Gaetano Martinelli (528$400 from March 1769 onwards) and Marianno Bergonzoni Martelli (230$400 from 1763 onwards); the copyist António Bernardo[78] (230$400 from 1767 onwards); the clerk Matias António de Azevedo (307$200 from 1773 onwards); the prompter Giovanni Ambrosini (172$800 from 1763, raised to 288$000 in

1771); the wardrobe master Francesco Piolti (172$800 from 1763 onwards); the tailor Paolino Solenghi (216$000 from 1763 onwards); the foreman and storekeeper Manuel José de Vasconcelos (216$000 from 1770 onwards); and the porter and watchman João Pereira ($400 a day, i.e. 146$000 a year, if he were paid every day, from 1764 onwards). The players Andrea Marra, Antonio Rodil and Jerónimo Groneman, and the chaplain singer of the Ajuda Chapel Bernardo Joaquim Álvares, also received a supplement to their salary out of the opera funds (the first two 115$200, the third 230$400, and the last one 38$400). The daughters of the wardrobe master Francesco Piolti and of the player João Francisco Avondano also received 38$400 and 76$800 respectively out of the opera funds.

Mention has been made of the pension scheme offered to court singers, but this scheme extended itself also to other artists and even to their relatives. A list of yearly pensions paid by Piaggio in Italy in 1770[79] includes the names of the singers Giuseppe Jozzi, Simone Ciucci and Francesco Bertocchini, and the widow of the player Vitto Manarelli, the son of the trumpet player Filippo Marcelli, and a brother of Bibiena. The dancer Antonio Porri, who had broken his legs while dancing in the presence of the King, received 100$000, after having served for three years.

## Relations with Niccolò Jommelli and Carlo Goldoni

According to Mattei,[80] Jommelli's relations with the court of Lisbon date back to the end of 1753, when the latter court was vying with those of Mannheim and Stuttgart to hire him as a composer. Mattei adds that Jommelli decided to go to Stuttgart 'per la delicatezza del gusto del Duca di Wurtemberg'. Contacts with the Portuguese court probably started earlier than that as a libretto of a *Componimento drammatico rappresentato in musica* for the birthday of José I, with music by Jommelli, was published at Ronciglione in 1751.[81]

The way in which Jommelli's relations with the Portuguese court were resumed after he left the Duke of Württemberg's service in 1769 has been studied in detail by Marita McClymonds.[82] Here they will be only briefly examined, on the basis of documents preserved in the AHMF and also in the Archive of the Teatro de S. Carlos.

The first letter from Silva Botelho to Jommelli preserved in the AHMF dates from 27 June 1768[83] but his first opera to have been performed in Lisbon was *Enea nel Lazio*, during Carnival of 1767, while Jommelli was still in the Duke's service. In this letter the Director of the Royal Theatres praises the Lisbon orchestra ('L'Orchesta di S.M.F. è di tal maniera unita e discreta nel chiaro e oscuro de'suoi andamenti, che tutti i signori Forestieri che quì la sentono le danno mille lodi.'), and says that Jozzi, who had sung both in *Enea nel Lazio* and in *Pelope*, had been very happy with the way they had been produced by a certain young Portuguese composer and harpsichordist called Giovanni Cordeiro [João Cordeiro da Silva],[84] who was passionately fond of Jommelli's music, always attempting when writing to imitate as much as he could its exquisite style. Cordeiro de Silva was a very welcome support, since it was impossible to get help from Jommelli himself.

Silva Botelho proceeds to discuss the difficulty of the fire in *Fetonte*, and begs Jommelli to ask the theatrical machinist at Ludwigsburg (the Duke's residence near Stuttgart) how he achieved it and with what materials. He is also surprised by the great number of extras who appeared in the opera,[85] and wants to know the exact dimensions of the Ludwigsburg stage. He explains that before the earthquake the King had a large theatre near his Lisbon palace, but that at present he uses a smaller one near his residence at the Ajuda. Finally he mentions that Jozzi,[86] who had an 'ottimo portamento di voce' and a 'gran scienza nella Musica', and had been hired for six years, would be leaving at the beginning of the following year, and that lately a first soprano called Carlo Reina had been hired, who had a good voice, large range, a good figure and good acting. He was finishing his contract at the Theatre in Padua, before coming to Portugal. Silva Botelho does not mention the fact that Reina had already sung in Lisbon before the earthquake.

In another letter of 19 October[87] he informs Jommelli that, following his recommendation, Gaetano Martinelli (who was one of the poets at the court of Württemberg, and had written several librettos for Jommelli) had been hired for the court of Lisbon at a yearly salary of 300 zecchini, the same as he had been receiving at Ludwigsburg, and with the same duties.

Martinelli arrived in Lisbon on 20 May 1769, in time to put the final touches to the production of *Fetonte*. He was to remain the court's librettist all his life,[88] and was also responsible for all the court's stage productions. An earlier director had been the singer Giovanni Leonardi, briefly replaced between 1768 and 1769 by another court poet, Marianno Bergonzoni Martelli.[89] The latter is associated with the texts of only two librettos, those of *La vera felicità* of 1761 and *Il ritorno di Ulisse in Itaca* of 1774, both with music by Perez. He must have died before 1777, as in January of that year his heirs received 115$000.[90] Martinelli himself, naturally, was also concerned with revisions to librettos of Metastasio or other authors for production in Lisbon.

On 28 March 1769, on learning of Jommelli's departure from Stuttgart to Naples, Silva Botelho offered him a 300 zecchini annual pension, with the only stipulation that he should write two operas each year, one serious and the other comic, either for the King's or the Queen's birthday, and some a cappella masses, psalms, sequences or motets, for the Royal Chapel. The contract became effective on 1 April[91] and on 10 July this pension was raised to 400 zecchini, on condition that he compose only for the Lisbon court, or, if he did write for other places, that this would not be offered as an excuse for not fulfilling his obligations towards Lisbon.[92] McClymonds[93] comments that this amounted to about a third of the 6,000 gulden he was receiving from Karl Eugen of Württemberg.

In the same letter Silva Botelho informs him that the operatic pro-ductions for the following year had all been chosen already, and that they included Jommelli's *Il Re pastore* and *Il matrimonio per concorso* for Salvaterra in January, *La schiava liberata* for the Queen's birthday on 31 March, and *La Nitteti* for the King's birthday on 6 June. Meanwhile Martinelli had been ordered to write an *opera seria* in the modern taste, into which trios, quartets and quintets could be introduced, but with no *balli* other than those that could be performed between the acts, while Jommelli himself was requested to write a number of works for the Royal Chapel, whose choir had over sixteen or eighteen singers (in another letter of 26 August he says that there were twenty-six).

Jommelli's collaboration with the court of Lisbon was relatively brief, as the composer died on 26 August 1774, and was marred by his illness and by his failure to deliver his promised work on time, while writing other operas for Naples and elsewhere.[94] In the end only three of his last operas were actually written for Lisbon: *Le avventure di Cleomede* and a new version of *Ezio* of 1772, and *Il trionfo di Clelia* of 1774, his last dramatic work.

Silva Botelho was repeatedly forced to voice his strong complaints regarding Jommelli's failure to fulfil his obligations, as in the following letter of 5 March 1771, concerning the revised version of *Ezio*:[95]

Who would have thought, dear Signor Jommelli, that instead of receiving the rest of the opera of *Ezio*, I would find myself with only the recitatives for Acts II and III of the same opera, which he now sends me without any of the respective arias? Who would have expected such a failure, due to the deplorable illnesses that he mentions, when one sees three operas written in Italy for other theatres? Who would have imagined that Signor Jommelli would have preferred the venal Theatre in Rome to the Royal Theatre of His Most Faithful Majesty, who provides him with an annual pension of four hundred zecchini, which were added later although he had been satisfied with three hundred? To whom will it not be more than strange to hear the same Signor Jommelli say in his letter that he was seduced by the profits he could make with the Roman Opera, forgetting his private contract of 20 August 1769 . . .

In his letter he goes on to ask for pardon before writing the Roman opera, which he wrote soon afterwards. To ask for pardon and then proceed to commit the sin is a new form of repentance. Neither my friendship nor my protection and good will, to which he recommends himself, can help him; for friendship requires true reci-procity; and protection and good heart require sincerity and genuine excuses.

I fear greatly that the opera for the birthday of His Most Faithful Majesty, our august sovereign, will have the same fortune as *Ezio*; for Signor Jommelli does not take into account the time taken by the post, the time needed for the singers to study the parts, the many rehearsals that are needed, and that are usually made to reach that accurate perfection with which his operas are per-formed here.

In fact, particular care seems to have gone into the production of Jommelli's operas at Lisbon. In several letters to the Director of the Royal Theatres the composer gave recommendations concerning the performance of his works. Thus on 25 September 1770,[96] he insisted that his works should be taken at precisely the tempo indicated, so as to express the right sentiment he had given them, and that this could only be achieved through rehearsals, it could not be guessed 'a prima vista': a slightly quicker or a slightly slower tempo might make all the difference. He did not press the subject further, as he knew that he was in good, indeed excellent hands.[97] In another letter of 28 December 1773 he said of the first aria in the second act of *Il trionfo di Clelia* ('Dei di Roma') that it was written in E, 'tuono scabroso', and difficult to play in, but that he hoped it would not prove too difficult, as he had kept to the natural notes. It would be particularly difficult for the transverse flutes, but he knew that in the King's orchestra there were excellent players of this instrument.[98]

Replying to the first of these letters on 30 October 1770,[99] Silva Botelho assured the composer that his music was studied, enjoyed and given that faithful and exact expression which he had written of and indicated. He himself demanded frequent rehearsals, and Cordeiro da Silva's diligence was untiring. During one performance the King had told him that he would have been very happy if Jommelli could have been present to hear how well his music was performed.

The sovereigns certainly took an active interest in the choice of the texts and in the music of the operas. Referring to a new libretto being written by Martinelli for Jommelli (probably *Le avventure di Cleomede*) Silva Botelho says that the King had read the first act and had enjoyed and approved it, and elsewhere he informs Jommelli that he could not send him an aria and a duet from *Demofoonte* because the score was in the hands of the Queen, who guarded his music so jealously that he did not dare ask her for it.[100]

In her study, McClymonds remarks that 'it is small wonder that Jommelli's later style received greater approbation in places like Stuttgart and the Portuguese court, where silence and attention were demanded for the audience, than it did in Naples, where opera was more a background for a social evening'. She describes this style in the following terms:[101]

Besides his pioneering work with the orchestra Jommelli's Stuttgart years were also distinguished for the incorporation of French spectacular elements such as chorus, ensembles, ballets, programmatic instrumental pieces, and spectacular stage effects, all banished from Italian operatic dramaturgy by a reform early in the century that was pioneered by Zeno and achieved by Metastasio. Jommelli further contributed to the breakdown of the rigid precepts of Metastasian dramaturgy with its succession of recitatives and exit arias in four ways: one, by cutting the moralizing from Metastasian texts and thus tightening the action; two by replacing the finale scenes and arias of the first two acts with ensembles; three by interspersing short arias not requiring an exit . . . and four by combining chorus, recitative, ensemble, solo and programmatic instrumental commentary in large, dramatic scene complexes.

McClymonds considers *Fetonte*, Jommelli's final opera for Stuttgart, his crowning achievement in the synthesis of French and Italian operatic styles, reflecting the taste for French spectacular elements, and adds that since no French opera had ever been done in the Portuguese royal court, there were neither the personnel nor the equipment required for French spectacle.

The problems that the Portuguese court theatre encountered with such a spectacular production serve to illustrate the extraordinary resources available to Jommelli at Ludwigsburg, resources comparable to those at the Opéra in Paris. Lisbon's now limited resources more surely represented conditions in the average Italian city, where such productions as *Fetonte* were unknown.

Mention has been made of certain difficulties related particularly to the stage production of *Fetonte*, but Jommelli's scores were also adapted to local conditions through the transposition or adaptation of certain arias by Cordeiro de Silva, or the commission of new arias from Jommelli himself. A detailed example of such a commission connected with the production of *La Nitetti*, is transcribed below:[102]

On 6 June 1770, which is the birthday of His Most Faithful Majesty, our common and beloved sovereign, the opera *La Nitteti* will be performed. New musical compositions are outlined below, hence my writing on this occasion. The role of Sammete will be performed by Signor Carlo Reina, for whom all four arias and the duet need to be rewritten. That is to say the arias

| | |
|---|---|
| 'Sono in mai: non vego sponde' ⎫<br>'Se d'amor, se di contento' ⎬ | from Act I |
| 'Mi sento il cor trafiggere' ⎭ | from Act II |
| 'Decisa è la mia sorte' | from Act III |

This actor sings very expressively and dramatically. His voice has a good range, as you can see from the examples included herewith.

As the above-named second aria 'Se d'amor, se di contento' is only separated from the first by one aria, this one should be short, so that if the second part is inserted beside the first it will form a *cavatina* virtually avoiding the necessity to start again da capo.

The four above-named arias should be like the one in *Vologeso*, with the [da capo] sign in the middle of the aria, so that they are not overlong.

In Act I, Scene X, which precedes the duet, in such place as you should find opportune, the recitative should be accompanied by the orchestra so that the singer can go straight into the duet; this duet (as well as the other pieces of music) should be of the same calibre as Maestro Jommelli's music.

The first soprano in the said duet will be sung by Battistini [Giambattista Vasquez], and should not be too *sfogato*,[103] as the same singer only goes up to *Amirè* and *Bemi* [a" and b"] without sustaining them; Reina will be the second soprano, and for him you may be guided by the above-mentioned example. The role of Beroe will be performed by Signor Battistini Vasquez, for whom a new composition is required for the aria which goes

'Per costume o mio bel Nume'

This fellow has sung all the arias in *Vologeso* with a great ability and to great applause, and they were found to suit his style and manner of singing very well. The said singer performs well. He has a small voice, but it is good, graceful, and expressive. Finally he is a musician, so that you may write for him and feel sure of a good performance.

You should be guided for this aria as for the four above-named for Reinino, that is with the sign in the middle of the aria.

The music of the march indicated in the libretto in Act I, Scene VI, does not appear in the score; only the bass part without the instruments was found, therefore music for it is needed and should not be too short.

Even in the case of operas originally written for the court of Lisbon, such as Jommelli's new version of *Ezio* of 1772, João Cordeiro da Silva had to make certain revisions to suit the music to local conditions. McClymonds, who has studied these revisions in detail, concludes that in most cases the orchestral music was relatively unrevised, as the orchestra must have been as fine as Silva Botelho claimed.[104] As to the singers she is of the opinion that 'Jommelli was clearly accustomed to writing for singers who had greater flexibility, stamina and a better command of the extremes of their ranges than did the singers in the Portuguese court.' She adds that Cordeiro da Silva's task was in fact an impossible one. Far better if he had been allowed to write anew rather than forced to fit beautifully tailored music to singers for whom it was ill-suited.[105] Still, as the above example and others that could be quoted also show, some alterations were required for dramatic reasons, or simply for reasons of local taste, in accordance with current eighteenth-century practice. Another reason might be the high pitch adopted by the court orchestra.[106]

Silva Botelho attempted to collect Jommelli's complete works both before and after the composer's death. In a letter of 7 April 1772 he lists twenty-seven operas that already existed in Lisbon and asks the composer for copies of half a dozen other operas, which he could choose himself. Concerning Jommelli's new operas for Naples and Rome, he asked Piaggio to obtain copies of them without the composer's knowledge.[107] After the composer's death his brother and sisters sent a list of all his remaining manuscripts, from which Pinto da Silva ordered those which did not yet exist in Lisbon.[108]

Cordeiro da Silva was not the only composer who was involved in revising and adapting operas for the court productions. In a letter to Sousa Carvalho of 12 June 1774[109] Pinto da Silva asked him to compose any arias or recitatives he might deem necessary for *Li napoletani in America* (by Sousa Carvalho's former teacher Piccinni), omitting from the original score anything that he might find insipid. For this purpose he was sending him Martinelli's revised version of the libretto along with the original Naples version. Unfortunately the score of *Li napoletani* is not extant, but occasional evidence for the elimination of arias and whole scenes appears in other scores, such as that of Piccinni's *L'incognita perseguitata*, performed at the Ajuda Theatre in 1766 (*P-La* 46–1–13/15), where twenty-four pages corresponding to the first three scenes of Act III were sewn together.

As regards commissions for new works from any other composers abroad besides Jommelli, Silva Botelho assured him in his letter of 16 October 1770[110] that neither Sacchini, nor Piccinni nor any other composer had been commissioned to write for Lisbon. Concerning librettists a puzzling case is that of Carlo Goldoni, who says in his memoirs[111] that around 1763 he had received 1,000 écus for a small work that he had written for the court of Portugal, and which had met with success (this may have been one of the comedies named on p. 46 below). In a letter of December of that same year he also mentions that he had been commissioned to write an *opera buffa* for Lisbon.[112] Sousa Viterbo[113] has published a number of letters from the Portuguese ambassador in Paris, and of Goldoni himself, which prove that Goldoni in fact wrote two hitherto unidentified operas for Lisbon in 1765. Costa Miranda[114] has suggested that these two operas may have been simply revisions by Goldoni himself of his own librettos for operas such as *L'Arcadia in Brenta* or *Il mondo della luna*, but these were both performed before Goldoni delivered his librettos (July 1765). One other possibility is *Notte critica*, first performed at the Teatro S. Cassiano in Venice in 1766 with music by Antonio Boroni, and which had its premiere at Salvaterra in Carnival 1767, with music by Niccolò Piccinni.

## Calendars of performances and details of operatic productions

The way in which the court's theatrical season was organised may be gathered from a number of calendars which have been preserved, concerning performances of operas and spoken drama during the years 1769 to 1772.[115] Below is the calendar for Salvaterra in 1770, in which *Il Re pastore* and *Il matrimonio per concorso* by Jommelli were sung, alternating with a tragedy and a comedy:

| | |
|---|---|
| 18 January | Seria 1 |
| 19 | Seria 2 |
| 20 | Burletta 1 |
| 21 | Burletta 2 |
| 22 | Seria 3 |
| 23 | Burletta 3 |
| 24 | Seria 4 |
| 25 | Burletta 4 |
| 26 | No performance |

| 27 | Seria 5 |
|---|---|
| 28 | Burletta 5 |
| 29 | Seria 6 |
| 30 | Burletta 6 |
| 31 | Tragedia 1 |
| 1 February | Opera seria 7 |
| 2 | Tragedia 2 |
| 3 | Burletta 7 |
| 4 | Seria 8 |
| 5 | Comedia D. [i.e. dancers] 1 |
| 6 | Burletta 8 |
| 7 | Comedia D. [i.e. dancers] 2 |
| 8 | Seria 9 |
| 9 | No performance |
| 10 | Comedia Muzicos 1 |
| 11 | Burletta 9 |
| 12 | Comedia Muzicos 2 |
| 13 | Tragedia |
| 14 | Seria 10 |
| 15 | Comedia D. [i.e. dancers] 3 |
| 16 | No performance |
| 17 | Burletta 10 |
| 18 | Opera seria 11 |
| 19 | Comedia Muzicos 3 |
| 20 | Burletta 11 |
| 21 | Seria 12 |
| 22 | Burletta 12 |
| 23 | No performance |
| 24 | Seria 13 |
| 25 | Burletta 13 |
| 26 | Comedia D. [i.e. dancers] 4 |
| 27 | Comedia Muzicos 4 |

Spoken drama was thus interspersed among the operatic performances and performed by the dancers and the singers themselves. The following Goldonian titles were performed by the dancers up to 1771: *O amor paterno* (1764), *O servitore di due padroni*, *O amante militar* and *A bottega del caffè*. Despite the half-Portuguese spelling used in the document in Caixa 5 which mentions them they were certainly performed in Italian. A manuscript copy of '*L'irrisoluto*, commedia tradotta dal francese Da rappresentarsi nel Real Teatro di Salvaterra Nel Carnavale del'Anno 1773' is also preserved in the Ajuda library (*P-La* 50–1–46).

Other non-operatic performances included groups of acrobats ('equili-bristas', 'bolantins'), such as those who appeared in the Ajuda Theatre on 9 June 1771 and 15 August 1772. The first of these performances was accompanied by an exceptionally large orchestra of forty-three players and the second by twenty-five players.

The Salvaterra seasons, centred around Carnival, seem to have been particularly crowded in terms of performances and productions. Rehearsals usually took place at the Ajuda from October onwards. Performances at the Ajuda were more scattered throughout the rest of the year. Thus for instance *L'amore industrioso* by Sousa Carvalho was performed ten times in 1769: on the Queen's birthday on 31 March, 13 May, 2 July, 5, 15, 24 and 25 August, and 21, 26 and 28 December. From 6 June onwards it alternated with Jommelli's *Fetonte*, which had twelve performances. In 1771 Jommelli's *La clemenza di Tito* had eight rehearsals in May and June and was performed nine times. The composer's *Il cacciatore deluso* (which had been earlier produced at Salvaterra during Carnival) had three rehearsals in July and was repeated eight times. The calendar of these two operas was as follows:

| | |
|---|---|
| 6, 12, 13 June, 5 July | *La clemenza di Tito* |
| 25 July | *Il cacciatore deluso* |
| 26 July | *La clemenza di Tito* |
| 10, 15 August | *Il cacciatore deluso* |
| 21 August | *La clemenza di Tito* |
| 24 August | *Il cacciatore deluso* |
| 1 September | *La clemenza di Tito* |
| 28 October, 7, 10 November | *Il cacciatore deluso* |
| 17 November, 17, 18 December | *La clemenza di Tito* |
| 21 December | *Il cacciatore deluso* |

Jommelli's *Semiramide* had three rehearsals in March and seems to have been performed only once, on the Queen's birthday.

The Ajuda Theatre's calendar for 1772 was as follows:

| | |
|---|---|
| 20 April | *Ezio* |
| 6, 9, 13 June | *Le avventure di Cleomede* |
| 5 July | *Ezio* |
| 12, 19 July | *Le avventure di Cleomede* |
| 25, 26 July | *Ezio* |
| 10 August | *Le avventure di Cleomede* |
| 21 August | *Ezio* |
| 24 August | *Le avventure di Cleomede* |
| 7 September | *Ezio* |
| 13 September | *Le avventure di Cleomede* |
| 29 September, 4 October | *La scaltra letterata* |
| 12 October | *Ezio* |
| 25 October | *La scaltra letterata* |
| 4 November, 17 December | *Ezio* |
| 18 December | *Le avventure di Cleomede* |

Jommelli's *Le avventure di Cleomede* had fourteen rehearsals in May and June and one in August and the composer's *Ezio* eight rehearsals in March and April and one in July. Piccinni's *La scaltra letterata* was rehearsed twice in September. These data give us some idea of the relative importance which was attributed to these different operas.

As we shall see in chapter 4 (pp. 90, 103–4) during these years the sovereigns also paid frequent visits to the Theatres of the Bairro Alto and Rua dos Condes. At the summer palace of Queluz, near Lisbon, a few small one-act dramatic works (*farsette* and *componimenti drammatici*) were also performed along with a number of serenatas. Available evidence points to five such dramatic works and eight serenatas between the years 1761 and 1774.

The Queluz palace belonged to José I's brother, the future Pedro III. Its construction began in 1747 and was completed in 1786. Over the years several parts of the palace were used for musical performances, starting with the Sala de Música, which was completed in 1759, and where a stage for opera, or Casa da Ópera, was sometimes set, and chamber music was also performed during the reign of Maria I and her husband and uncle Pedro III.[116]

The Casa da Ópera was also set in the Sala do Trono, in the small garden at the back of the Sala dos Espelhos, or in this last room, which is also known as Sala dos Embaixadores, das Talhas or das Serenatas. The palace's present director, Simonetta Luz Afonso, has identified and published a plan of the theatre set in the garden, which exists in the Biblioteca Nacional.[117] It shows that the Casa da Ópera must have been fairly small: the house measured seventy-seven spans (*c.* 17 metres) in depth. It had a large royal box and two side boxes, one of which was for the Patriarch, and nine rows in the stalls.

Caldeira Pires[118] gives a slightly different description of the Casa da Ópera, for which he transcribes a few accounts, but it should be noted that the above plan is only a sketch and that the dismountable theatre may have been modified over the years. According to him it had twelve doors, four decorated boxes and one royal box, and three chandeliers. Its walls and roof were covered by greased cloth and lined on the inside with damask.

A few serenatas and oratorios were also performed at the Ajuda palace, namely on 19 and 21 March, namedays of José I and the Princess D. Maria Francisca Benedita, but librettos do not seem always to have been printed for them, as was the case with the serenata of 19 March 1770, which was repeated on 31 March.[119]

Further details on the way operas were produced at Salvaterra and at the Ajuda may be gleaned from documents in AHMF, Caixas 5 and 257. In 1768 and 1769 seventy-six men were employed on the sets in both theatres: 4 riggers, 46 journeymen, 2 apprentices and 24 workmen. The number of extras who appeared in the operas varied. For *Il Vologeso* at Salvaterra in 1769, there were sixty-three, distributed as follows: 13 royal guards, 4 ministers, 4 gentlemen, 20 guardians, 13 Roman guards, 4 pages and 5 animals (!).[120] Most of the extras were soldiers, led by an ensign and a sergeant. In *Il Vologeso* there were 53. In *L'amore industrioso* by Sousa Carvalho there were 66 soldiers and 9 civilians, and in *Fetonte* 106 soldiers and 17 civilians. Finally in Jommelli's *Il Re pastore* of 1770 there were 79 extras: 13 grandees of Alexander, 6 noblemen from Sidone, 2 royal shepherds, 6 Greek captains, 13 guards of Aminta, 19 people, 8 shepherdesses and 12 shepherds.

*Fetonte* had seven singers, a choir of eight members (Principii, Ceccoli, Francisco dos Reis, Cavalli, Puzzi, Pecorario, Franchi and Giorgetti) and sixteen dancers (as against nine in *L'amore industrioso*). The orchestra had 14 violins, 2 violas, 3 cellos, 4 double-basses, 2 flutes, 2 oboes, 2 bassoons and 2 trumpets ('clarins') plus João de Sousa Carvalho on the harpsichord (who may thus have conducted the opera in place of Cordeiro da Silva), making thirty-two players in all. In his study of the Royal Chamber, Scherpereel gives the total number of its members in 1782 as being fifty-one, and publishes a list of the number of players in seventeen other European orchestras in the same period, which suggests that the Lisbon orchestra was the largest, but it is unlikely that they ever all played together at the same time. Serenatas and oratorios must usually have required fewer players than the operas: there were only nineteen players for instance for the oratorio performed at the Ajuda palace on 19 March 1772. For the audition of new singers even fewer players were employed: there were seventeen players for the audition of the tenor Afferri on 22 August 1771 and nine for that of the tenor Policarpo José da Silva on 2 August of the same year.[121]

Documents in AHMF, Caixa 5, show that rehearsals were partly held at the house of the Director of the Royal Theatres, Pinto da Silva, at the Bom Sucesso, near the Ajuda. Thus on 9 April 1771 a rehearsal was held there to choose the *burlette* for the Salvaterra season of the following year. For the rehearsals and performances the singers and players were fetched from their homes in Lisbon by carriages which were requisitioned by the *corregedor* of the Bairro Alto district. In 1774 the owner of the livery stable which supplied the carriages spent a day in prison because one of his carriages had failed to take two players to a performance at the Ajuda Theatre. In his note to the *corregedor*, Pinto da Silva complained that the carriages often left late, and that others which started on time were so bad that they also arrived late at the theatre.[122] In another letter of 1768,[123] Silva Botelho informs the *corregedor* that some singers, dancers and players were arriving late at the theatre because they stopped on the way to pay private visits, and tells him that if they insisted on doing so their drivers should leave them and proceed to the theatre, where they would report where they had left them.

Fairly strict discipline seems to have been in force in the royal theatres. In 1774 two players, Jerónimo Nonnini and Francisco Xavier de Figueiredo, were arrested on account of some quarrel. On their release they were made to sign a declaration, according to which they would not fight again. Nonnini was again put in prison for ten days in 1776. In 1775 another player, Filippo Marcelli, spent seven days in prison for unspecified reasons and in 1776 the dancer Bellucci was jailed for two days, during which he was taken under armed guard to dance in the theatre. He was to be told that he would be set free only after he returned from the theatre on the second day. In 1777 the dancer Gherardo Cavazza was also jailed for a week.[124]

The singers and other participants received special payments for their performance in the operas. For the *Olimpiade* and *Il trionfo di Clelia* of 1774 the singers received between 33$600 and 9$600 each. For the Ajuda operas of 1775 they received between 144$000 and 96$000 each. The nine members of the choir in *Li napoletani in America* received 24$000. In 1773 João de Sousa Carvalho received 240$000 for his opera *Eumene*.[125]

Very interesting details on court opera between 1772 and 1776 have been recorded by an English visitor, Sir Nathaniel William Wraxall:[126]

Two passions or pursuits, hunting and music, principally occupied his [José I's] time, absorbed his thoughts, and divided his affections: nor was it easy to decide which of them possessed the strongest ascendant over him. In the former diversion he passed the far greater part of the day: to the latter amusement his evenings were principally or wholly dedicated, either in public, when at the Opera; or in private, with his family. No royal house in Europe was then so musical as that of Portugal. Joseph himself performed with considerable execution on the violin; and the three Princesses, his daughters, all were proficients in a greater, or in a lesser degree, on different instruments. If he was prevented by the weather from going out to chace, the King had recourse for occupation to his manege. On Sundays he seldom or never missed attending the Italian Opera in Lisbon; but he likewise maintained another Opera at Belem [i.e. Ajuda], his residence near the capital. I have been present at this latter performance, to which only foreign ministers, officers, persons belonging to the Court, and foreigners of condition, were admitted; all of them gratuitously. The house itself was of very contracted dimensions; the pit not being calculated to contain more than about one hundred and thirty individuals. Boxes indeed, in the proper acceptation of the term, there were none; the King, Queen, and Royal Family being seated in a gallery fronting the stage, elevated considerably above the body of the house. One small box was constructed on each side; that on the right hand had been appropriated to the Patriarch, or head of the Portuguese church, whom I have seen present at the performance. The other usually remained vacant, being reserved for any stranger of high rank who might visit Portugal.

The circumstance which distinguished this entertainment from any other of the same kind which I ever witnessed; and which may appear so extraordinary as hardly to obtain credit; consisted in the total exclusion of women, not only from the pit, but from the stage; either as spectators, or as actresses. No female could obtain admission. The reason commonly assigned by the Court, for proscribing the whole sex from any participation in an amusement of which, in all other European countries, they constitute the principal ornament and soul; was, that there were no proper places for ladies. But it might have been answered, that nothing could be easier than to construct side-boxes for their reception. Even this reason could not explain their exclusion from the stage, on which none except Italian *Castrati* were ever admitted to sing, or to perform any part. *Battistini*, who filled with great distinction the first female characters, was selected and engaged, not only for his superior vocal excellence, but for his feminine appearance, and admirable resemblance to a woman, when he was dressed in female attire. So complete indeed was the deception, that I think it never would have occurred to any uninformed person, to doubt for an instant, of his being what he personated. Even the *Ballets* were all performed by men or boys, habited in the Costume of nymphs, shepherdesses, and goddesses. This exclusion of all females, except the Queen and Princesses, rendered the spectacle, though otherwise magnificent in machinery and decorations, as well as scientific in point of musical execution; comparatively insipid, dull, and destitute of interest or animation. Incredible as it may seem, the passion of jealousy constituted the cause of so singular a prohibition. The Queen of Portugal, though at this time she was considerably advanced towards her sixtieth year, yet watched every motion of her husband, with all the vigilant anxiety of a young woman. Nor was her vigilance by any means confined to the Opera. She displayed the same apprehensions, and took similar precautions, against any rival or intruder in the King's affections, whenever he went out to the chace.

According to another English visitor, Richard Twiss, who attended a performance of Jommelli's *Ezio* in November 1772,[127] the theatre had only ten rows of benches in the stalls. It cannot therefore have been much larger than the Queluz Theatre. Twiss says that total silence was observed during the whole performance, which lasted from seven to ten in the evening, and during the intervals the audience turned so as to face the royal family. He found that 'the dancing between the acts ... by men with great black beards[128] and broad shoulders, dressed in female apparel, was a disgusting sight.'

It will be noted that before the earthquake the audience of the Ópera do Tejo had included ladies and female servants.[129] As regards foreigners, an article in the French *Journal de Littérature, des Sciences et des Arts* of 1781[130] says that any foreign traveller or merchant had access to the theatre, as long as he went there in advance and declared his name.

## The repertoire. Total expenditure on the opera

A few remarks may be made concerning the repertoire of the court theatres during the whole reign. In the first period, 1752–5, only *opere serie* with music by Perez, and two with music by Antonio Mazzoni, were performed (the only known exception is the intermezzo *La fantesca* by Hasse). When performances were again resumed in 1763, the Lisbon court theatres seem also to have been invaded by the current vogue for *opera buffa* which in the meantime had spread throughout Europe.

The continuing interest in *opera seria* was now associated with an enthusiasm for Jommelli's works, of which twenty operas and four smaller dramatic works were performed between 1767 and 1780. Of Perez's works only three *opere serie* were still performed at court: *Demetrio* in 1765, *Solimano* in 1768 and *Creusa in Delfo* in 1774, besides several other smaller works. Five other of his operas were performed at the Bairro Alto, the Rua dos Condes and the Oporto Theatres. As an opera composer the now ageing Perez seems to have gone relatively out of fashion, as happened with Jommelli on his return to Naples. It may be interesting to recall here the parallel which Burney draws between the two composers:[131] 'Jommelli ... was chiefly admired for the ingenious and learned texture of the instrumental parts; and Perez for the elegance and grace of his melodies and expression of the words.'

Among *opera buffa* composers Piccinni was clearly the favourite. As regards Portuguese composers, the part that their works played in the total repertoire is relatively small (details on these composers appear in chapter 3, pp. 78–9).

Until 1773 we find only scattered bills and expense notes relating to the royal theatres. If more complete accounts ever existed they are now difficult to trace. A rare account in AHMF, Caixa 257, is of a new theatrical fund for 1768–9 ('Fundo Novo do Teatro athe 16 de Setembro de 1769') amounting to 9:141$830.[132] In fact attempts towards some form of systematic account-ing seem to have started only with Pinto da Silva's administration. Livro xx/z/39 registers the total expenditure on the theatres for the years 1773 to 1777, which was as follows:

| | |
|---|---|
| 1773 | 5 5:6 1 1$1 1 1 |
| 1774 | 46:776$ 587 |
| 1775 | 4 3:27 5$929 |
| 1776 | 42:299$890 |
| 1777 | 1 1:8 38$00 5 |

The much smaller expenditure in 1777 is due to the fact that José I died on 24 February. Of this amount 1:868$765 refers to the Salvaterra operas which were not put on the stage. The steady decline in expenses in the remaining years is explained by the diminishing balances which were carried over from the preceding year, as may be seen in the following detailed list of expenses:

*1773*

| | |
|---|---|
| Carried over from 1772 | 8:64 5$70 3 |
| Salvaterra operas | 19:498$474 |
| *Armida*, for the Queen's birthday | 6:204$9 3 5 |
| *Eumene*, for the King's birthday | 6:294$4 16 |
| Salaries paid from the opera funds | 2:2 36$800 |
| Salaries of the dancers | 5:84 3$200 |
| Payments, Ajuda Theatre | 1: 574$400 |
| Extraordinary payments | 827$200 |
| Small expenses | 67 5$44 5 |
| [Carriage] rentals | 506$800 |
| New warehouse | 1: 380$000 |
| Wax for the Ajuda Theatre | 1:924$00 8 |
| | |
| TOTAL | 5 5:6 1 1$38 1 |

## 1774

| | |
|---|---|
| Carried over from 1773 | 2: 162$933 |
| Salvaterra operas | 22:649$976 |
| *Olimpiade*, for the Queen's birthday | 3: 160$926 |
| *Clelia*, for the King's birthday | 3:727$519 |
| Salaries paid from the opera funds | 1:658$400 |
| Salaries of the dancers and others | 6:684$000 |
| New stable, Ajuda Theatre | 1:288$750 |
| Payments, Ajuda Theatre | 1:588$800 |
| Extraordinary payments | 502$400 |
| Small expenses | 825$955 |
| [Carriage] rentals | 609$600 |
| Wax for the Ajuda Theatre | 1:917$328 |
| **TOTAL** | **46:776$587** |

## 1775

| | |
|---|---|
| Carried over from 1774 | 512$374 |
| Salvaterra operas | 21:595$233 |
| *I napoletani in America*, for the Queen's birthday | 2:996$653 |
| *Demofoonte*, for the King's birthday | 4:004$700 |
| Salaries paid from the opera funds | 1:512$000 |
| Salaries of the dancers and others | 7:382$008 |
| Payments, Ajuda Theatre | 1:590$400 |
| Extraordinary payments | 569$600 |
| Small expenses | 577$155 |
| [Carriage] rentals | 942$000 |
| Wax for the Ajuda Theatre | 1:593$806 |
| **TOTAL** | **43:275$929** |

## 1776

| | |
|---|---|
| Carried over from 1775 | 480$975 |
| Salvaterra operas | 24:469$191 |
| *Alessandro nell'Indie*, for the King's birthday | 4:238$087 |
| Reprise of *La contadina superba*, which was not put on stage | 96$635 |
| Salaries paid from the opera funds | 1:032$000 |
| Salaries of the dancers and others | 8:284$800 |
| Payments, Ajuda Theatre | 1:152$200 |
| Extraordinary payments | 409$600 |
| Small expenses | 630$852 |
| Expenses with the kitchen at Salvaterra | 328$950 |
| Expense with the King's small [sedan?] chair at Salvaterra | 33$080 |
| Wax for the Ajuda Theatre | 291$920 |
| Extraordinary [carriage] rentals | 851$600 |
| **TOTAL** | **42:299$890** |

Table 2 Career of court singers, 1752–93, according to the librettos

Bands across the year columns: 1756–1760 labelled "NO DOCUMENTED PERFORMANCES"; 1761–1763 labelled "NO NAMES IN THE LIBRETTOS".

| Singer | Voice | 1752 | 1753 | 1754 | 1755 | 1756 | 1757 | 1758 | 1759 | 1760 | 1761 | 1762 | 1763 | 1764 | 1765 | 1766 | 1767 | 1768 | 1769 | 1770 | 1771 | 1772 | 1773 | 1774 | 1775 | 1776 | 1777 | 1778 | 1779 | 1780 | 1781 | 1782 | 1783 | 1784 | 1785 | 1786 | 1787 | 1788 | 1789 | 1790 | 1791 | 1792 | 1793 |
|---|---|---|---|---|---|---|---|---|---|---|---|---|---|---|---|---|---|---|---|---|---|---|---|---|---|---|---|---|---|---|---|---|---|---|---|---|---|---|---|---|---|---|---|
| Aloisi, Venanzio | A | | | | | | | | | | | | | | | | | | | | | | | | | | | | | | | * | | | | | | | | | | | |
| Angelelli, Francesco | S | * | * | * | * | | | | | | | | | | | | | | | | | | | | | | | | | | | | | | | | | | | | | | |
| Bartolini, Antonio | B | * | * | * | | | | | | | | | | | | | | | | | | | | | | | | | | | | | | | | | | | | | * | * | |
| Botticelli, Salvatore | T | | | | * | | | | | | | | | | | | | | | | | | | | | | | | | | | | | | | | | * | * | * | * | * | * |
| Cappellani, Filippo | | | | | | | | | | | | | | | | | | | | | | | | | | | | | | | | | | | | | | | * | * | * | * | * |
| Capranica, Giuseppe | | | | | | | | | | | | | | | | | | | | | | | | | | | | | | | | | | | | | | | | | | * | * |
| Cavalli, Francesco | T/B | | | | | | | | | | | | | | | | | | | | | * | * | | | | | | | | | | | | | | | | | | | | |
| Ciucci, Giovanni S. | | * | * | * | * | | | | | | | | | | | | | | | | | | | | | | | | | | | | | | | | | | | | | | |
| Conti, G. (Gizziello) | S | * | * | * | * | | | | | | | | | | | | | | | | | | | | | | | | | | | | | | | | | | | | | | |
| Conti, Niccolà | | | | | | | | | | | | | | | | | | | | | | | | | | | | | | | | | | | | | | | | * | | | |
| Contucci, Carlo | | | | | | | | | | | | | | | | * | | | | | | | | | | * | | | | | | | | | | | | | | | | | |
| Contucci, Giovanni | | | | | | | | | | | | | | | | | | | | | | | | | | | | | | | | | | | | | | * | * | | | | |
| Ferracuti, Ansano | A | | | | | | | | | | | | | | | | | | | | | | | * | | | | | | | | | | | | | | | | | | | |
| Forlivesi, Giuseppe | T | | | | | | | | | | | | | | | | | | | | | | | | * | | | | | | | | | | | | | | | | | | |
| Franchi, Loreto | T | | | | | | | | | | | | | | | | | | | | | | * | | | | | | | | | | | | | | | | | | | | |
| Gallieni, Giuseppe | | | | | | | | | | | | | | | * | * | * | * | * | * | * | * | * | * | * | * | * | * | * | * | * | * | * | * | * | * | * | * | * | * | * | * | * |
| Gelati, Giovanni | S | | | | | | | | | | | | | | * | * | * | * | * | * | * | * | * | * | * | * | * | * | * | * | * | * | * | * | * | * | * | * | * | * | * | * | * |
| Giorgetti, Lorenzo | | | | | | | | | | | | | | | | | | * | * | | | | | | | | | | | | | | | | | | | | | | | | |
| Giusti, Giuliano | | | | | | | | | | | | | | | | | | * | * | | | | | | | | | | | | | | | | | | | | | | | | |
| Guadagni, Gaetano | S | | | * | * | | | | | | | | | | | | | | | | | | | | | | | | | | | | | | | | | | | | | | |
| Guarducci, Tommaso | | | | | | | | | | | | | | * | | | | | | | | | | | | | | | | | | | | | | | | | | | | | |
| Jozzi, Giuseppe | S | * | * | * | * | | | | | | | | | | | | | | | | | | | | | | | | | | | | | | | | | | | | | | |
| Leonardi, Giovanni | B | | | | | | | | | | | | | | * | * | * | * | * | | | | | | | | | | | | | | | | | | | | | | | | |
| Leonardi, Vincenzo | T | | | | | | | | | | | | | * | * | * | * | * | * | * | * | * | * | * | * | * | * | * | * | * | * | * | * | * | * | | | | | | | | |
| Luciani, Domenico | | | | | | | | | | | | | | | | | | | | | | | | | | | | | | | | | | | | * | | | | | | | |
| Maiorano, G. (Caffarelli) | | * | * | * | * | | | | | | | | | | | | | | | | | | | | | | | | | | | | | | | | | | | | | | |

54

| Name | Voice | | NO DOCUMENTED PERFORMANCES | NO NAMES IN THE LIBRETTOS |
|---|---|---|---|---|
| Marchetti, Giovanni | S | | * | |
| Marini, Vincenzo | A | | | |
| Marrocchini, Giuseppe | A | | * | |
| Martini, Giuseppe | S | | | |
| Martini, Leonardo | | | * | |
| Maruzzi, Lorenzo | T | | | |
| Morelli, Giuseppe | S | | | |
| Oliveira, Joaquim de | T | | | |
| Orti, Giuseppe | S | | | |
| Perilla, Francesco | B | | * | |
| Principii, Ottavio | B | | | |
| Puzzi, Antonio | B | | | |
| Puzzi, Taddeo | B | | | |
| Raaff, Anton | T | | * | |
| Reina, Carlo | S | | * | |
| Ripa, Giovanni | S | | * | |
| Rocchi, Agostino | B | | | |
| Romanini, Giuseppe | S | | | |
| Schettini, Innocenzo | T/B | | | |
| Serbolloni, Pietro | | | * | |
| Silva, Policarpo José da | T | | | |
| Tomiatti, Antonio | T | | | |
| Torriani, Luigi | T | | | |
| Totti, Giuseppe | S | | | |
| Vaccai, Francesco | | | * | |
| Vasquez, Giambattista | S | | | |
| Venturi, Fedele | S | | | |
| Veroli, Giacomo | | | * | |
| Violani, Valeriano | S | | | |

S = soprano; A = contralto; T = tenor; B = Bass. Voice types according to the librettos, and also to *Osservazioni Correlative alla Reale, e Patriarcal Cappella di Lisbona* (1788) in *P-La*.

55

Historians have repeatedly talked about José I's extravagance over the opera, but it is difficult to assess the relative importance of these expenses in the absence of precise information on the total court expenditure. However some measure of their magnitude may be given by the generous yearly salaries received by the Secretaries of State: they received 9:600$000 each.[133]

Table 2 shows that a large number of singers were simultaneously employed as soloists during the same period to perform operas, serenatas and oratorios.

# 3

# Court opera and music in the reign of Maria I (1777–92)

*Changes in court music after the death of José I. Serenatas and chamber music*

With the death of José I and the fall of his Prime Minister, the Marquis of Pombal, in what came to be known as the 'viradeira', or overthrow, the court seems to have embarked on a course of relatively strict economy. In a letter of 24 July 1777[1] the Austrian envoy, Lebzeltern, says that the Queen had ordered that the court's servants, who had not received their salaries for fourteen years, should immediately be paid. To effect this a great number of horses, mules and carriages had been sold. Bullfights had been suppressed and there was also talk of doing away with hunting and the opera, which would produce a total yearly saving of 2,000,000 cruzados (800:000$000, probably a grossly exaggerated figure). In fact for the first three years of the new reign there were no operatic productions, with the exception of the one-act *componimento drammatico Il ritorno di Ulisse in Itaca* by Perez, which was repeated at the new Queluz Theatre on 17 December 1778. Also during the sixteen years between 1777 and 1792 there were a total of only twenty-eight operatic productions (including small works), as against sixty-four productions for the sixteen-year period between 1761 and 1776.

In September 1776 Pinto da Silva was put in charge of the King's Privy Purse ('encarregado das Despezas do Particular') and all expenditures which had previously been administered through the *Repartição da Ópera* were now incorporated into this account. A fairly detailed and accurate accounting system was introduced. All expenses were now entered in a journal, and monthly summaries of them entered in another book. Documents relating to these expenses and books containing detailed accounts of operatic productions were filed in boxes.[2] Through these accounts it is possible to establish a much more complete picture of musical activity and theatrical entertainment at court in this period than at any other during the eighteenth century, even though it is still impossible to evaluate its total expenditure, as most of the singers and players continued to be paid by other separate departments.

As regards dancers the accounts show that in May 1778 Luigi Bellucci and Luigi Bardotti, who had terminated their contracts, received 249$600 each as payment and to cover travelling expenses for their return to Italy. In December (seven?) other dancers received 1:747$200 for the same reason, and in April 1779 Gherardo Cavazza also received 249$600.[3] Some of these dancers, however, seem to have stayed on in Lisbon, as their names appear both in the court's and in the public theatres' librettos up to 1792.[4] But the idea of keeping a permanent *corps de ballet* was obviously abandoned. Of the original list of dancers only three names are exclusively connected with the court theatre performances after 1780: those of Pietro Colonna, Giambattista Flambò (= Jean Baptiste Flambeau) and Niccolà Midosi. As for new dancers, only one name appears exclusively in the court theatres in 1780, one in 1785, and three in 1789–91.

In the case of singers, players, and the rest of the operatic establishment, there is no evidence of any significant alterations, except in the way in which they were now employed. Serenatas, which had been rare during the previous reign, were now the main form of courtly musical entertainment. They were much cheaper to put on, requiring no scenery, costumes, dancers, or extras, and only few rehearsals. Probably for reasons of prestige, they are often identified in the librettos as *drammi per musica*, although they are usually called *serenatas* in the account books. During Lent oratorios were also performed, particularly on 19 and 21 March, namedays of the heir to the throne, Prince José, and of his aunt and wife Princess Maria Francisca Benedita.

The average cost of the forty-seven serenatas and oratorios performed during the period was 327$947. The most expensive was *Artemisia, Regina di Caria* (Ajuda, 1787), which cost 396$885, and the cheapest was *L'omaggio de' Pastori* (Ajuda, 1779), which cost 213$300.[5] Repeats were even cheaper: their average cost was 178$042.

Typical expenses for a serenata (*Palmira di Tebe*, Queluz, 1781) are given below:[6]

| | |
|---|---:|
| Payment to the composer, Luciano Xavier dos Santos | 96$000 |
| Payment to the librettist, Gaetano Martinelli | 48$000 |
| Payment to five singers,[7] at 24$000 each | 120$000 |
| To João Caetano dos Santos, for copying the music | 30$640 |
| Carriage rentals for the first and second rehearsals | 26$400 |
| idem, for the performance | 16$000 |
| Refreshments for the performers in the two rehearsals | 4$740 |
| Printing of the librettos | 9$870 |
| Binding of same | 34$095 |
| | |
| TOTAL | 385$745 |

When the music director was different from the composer, or when his own serenata was repeated, he received only 24$000, the same as the singers.

For serenatas and oratorios there were usually only two rehearsals. In many cases these were held at the house of Pinto da Silva in the Bom Sucesso, near the Ajuda. The bills for the refreshments usually include coffee, biscuits, venison scraps, and also bitter lemons, sugar, eggs, syrup and sugar cane brandy, with which some kind of punch must have been prepared particularly for the benefit of the singers. The orders issued to the singers and players include a list of their names and often indicate the addresses where each of them should be picked up by the carriages. They show that the orchestra for these performances comprised between twenty-three and thirty-two players, with an average number of twenty-eight players. According to the orders both the rehearsals and the performances were held at four o'clock or sometimes at five. The journal of the French ambassador, the Marquis of Bombelles, shows however, that the serenatas of 1787 at the Ajuda were performed between 7.30 or 8.00 and 10.30 or 11.00 in the evening.[8] It is therefore also possible that actual performances may have been preceded by a 'dress rehearsal' in the afternoon. At Queluz there was sometimes a display of fireworks in the gardens after the performance.[9]

Bombelles also gives very interesting details concerning these perform-ances, as he describes his protests against the improper way in which the members of the diplomatic corps were placed during them. He went so far as to draw a diagram showing the way in which the performers, the royal family and the various guests were placed in the room.[10] According to it, only the royal family and the musicians (i.e. the singers) seem (while at rest) to have had seats, or stools. Male guests were apparently standing, while the court ladies sat crouching on the floor behind the royal family (in truly Arabic fashion). Bombelles could not accept that the foreign ambassadors should stand behind the orchestra and the singers, mixed up with other outside guests. To this the Foreign Secretary Martinho de Melo e Castro replied that they should not regard the singers in front of them other than as pieces of furniture, and that in any case these were only private performances, something with which the French ambassador could not agree, as the Queen appeared in state and followed by all her retinue, and after the concert all the musicians (the singers?) went and kissed her hand and those of the royal family.[11]

The performances that aroused Bombelles' protest were those of *Alcione* and *Telemaco*, which seem to have been held in different rooms in the Ajuda palace. But that of *Artemisia, Regina di Caria* on 17 December was certainly held in the Sala da Serenata, and this time the Queen and her family sat on a dais under a canopy, separated from the audience by a balustrade, and the ambassadors were placed in one of the two existing boxes on the left-hand side of the dais, of which the other was reserved for the Queen's uncles, the 'Meninos de Palhavã'. On the right-hand side there were two glass doors which opened into two adjoining rooms, where the court ladies sat. This Sala da Serenata, or Casa de Música, had been rebuilt in 1783, in a room formerly used for the Council of State.[12] After the serenata Bombelles repaired to a ball in the English long-room in Lisbon (the English club, or Assembleia Inglesa) where he stayed until two in the morning.[13]

According to the bills preserved in the AHMF, Caixas 9 to 39, the number of librettos which were printed for the serenatas varied widely between a maximum of 423 and a minimum of 296, of which between seven and ten, intended for the royal family, were bound in silk. This suggests that the exact number of guests attending these performances was known in advance.

Besides serenatas proper, the documents in the AHMF also register the performance of music in the chamber on the following dates:

| | | |
|---|---|---|
| *1778* | Ajuda palace | 19, 20, 21 March |
| | | 13 May |
| | | 13 (to audition the singer Giovanni Gelati), 24, 29 June |
| | Queluz palace | 26 July |
| | | 3, 5, 10, 11 August |
| | Ajuda palace | 15, 18 December |
| *1779* | Ajuda palace | 19, 21 March |
| | | 13 May |
| | | 24 June |
| | | 26 July |
| | | 4 November |
| | | 15 December |
| *1780* | Ajuda palace | 2 January |
| | | 13 May |
| | | (?) September |
| | | 4 November |
| | | 15 December |
| *1781* | Queluz palace | 26 July (with a foreigner who played the musical glasses) |
| | | 4 November |
| | | 15 December |
| *1782* | Ajuda palace | 13 May |
| | Queluz palace | 26 July |
| | Ajuda palace | 4 November |
| *1783* | Ajuda palace | 19 March |
| | House of Pinto da Silva | 17 May (some music by Gluck was rehearsed) |
| | Ajuda palace | 6, 24 June |
| | Queluz palace | 26 July |
| | Ajuda palace | 7 October |
| | | 4 November |
| | | 15 December |

| | | |
|---|---|---|
| *1784* | Ajuda palace | 13 May |
| | | 24 June |
| | Queluz palace | 28 (?) September (with Franz Gottlieb Reispacher, who played on the musical glasses and the kettledrums) |
| | | 4 November |
| | | 15 December |
| *1785*[14] | Queluz palace | 26 July |
| | | St Laurence's day (10? August) |
| | | 7 October |
| | | 4 November |
| | | 15 December |
| *1786* | Ajuda palace | 25 April |
| | | 11, 13 May |
| *1787* | Lisbon palace | 26 July |
| | Sintra palace | 7 October |
| | Ajuda palace | 4 November |
| | | 15 December |
| *1788* | Ajuda palace | 25 April |
| | | 29 June |
| *1789* | Ajuda palace | 8 May |
| | | 26 July |
| | | 7 October (with the violinist Antonio Ronzi, who received 96$000) |
| | | (?) December (with a harpsichord and a harp player, probably the Maréchals,[15] who received 192$000) |
| *1790* | Ajuda palace | 24 May (with a Spanish violinist and his wife, who played the psaltery, and with the Maréchals, who played the pianoforte and the harp; they all received 384$000) |
| | | 7 October |
| *1791* | Ajuda palace | 30 July |
| *1792* | Lisbon palace | 16–24 February |

It will be noticed that many of these dates are those of royal birthdays or namedays, which were thus celebrated in a less solemn fashion than when serenatas or operas were performed (cf. Chronology, pp. 122–3).

These chamber music recitals were typically performed by several of the opera singers, who sang arias accompanied by the full orchestra. The following music was copied, for instance, to be sung at Queluz on 4 November 1785:[16] two arias and one trio; the aria 'Per quel paterno amplesso', by order of Pinto da Silva; four arias from the opera *Antigono* by an unnamed composer, by order of Cordeiro da Silva ('E frà tante tempeste' and 'A torto spergiuro', from Act I, and 'Misero e sarà ver' and 'Ah non t'inganni', from Act II).

Occasionally one of the players was ordered to bring along instrumental music ('Cordeiro will bring a symphony', 'Lenzi and Blayek will bring a symphony', 'Felner will bring a concerto'). This suggests that these pieces belonged to the players, and may account for the fact that so little orchestral music from the period has been preserved in the Ajuda library.[17]

Several lists also exist of the music which was copied to be performed in the chamber at Salvaterra. Thus in 1779 arias, duets, trios and quartets from *Armida, Bellerofonte, Calliroe, Catone, Merope, Quinto Fabio* and *Ricimero* were copied, along with single arias by Bertoni, Guglielmi, Radicchi and Sarti. In 1781, as well as many single arias, the overtures and several arias from *Adriano in Siria, Armida, Creso in Media* by Schuster, *Demetrio* by Bianchi, *Il gran Cid, Montezuma, Nitteti* by Anfossi, and *Solimano* by Alessandri. In 1784 the overture, three arias and one duet from *Piramo e lisbe* [*Tisbe*] (probably by Bianchi), the overture and two arias from Act I of *La Nitteti* by Rispoli, and an aria and scene from Act II of *La Nitteti* by Giuseppe Curci.[18] The largest list of Court copyists available relates to copying of music for Salvaterra in 1783.[19] It includes the names of José Maria de Almeida, Bernardo Joaquim Álvares, João Caetano, João Bernardo Henriques, José Cláudio Henriques, Eugénio Gonçalo Nogueira, José António Paulo and António dos Santos.

In 1780 trios (identified as op. 1 and 3) and quartets (identified as op. 2, 5, 6, 7, 9 and 10) by Haydn, and trios (*idem*, op. 2, 7 and 9), quartets (op. 1, 6, 10 and 11), quintets (op. 12 and 13) and serenades by Boccherini were acquired for royal use,[20] and these may also have been used in the chamber.

Being a deeply religious person, the Queen sent her singers and players to take part in a large number of religious festivities in various churches in Lisbon and its outskirts. As might be expected, these religious feasts and their music were frequently very operatic in style. William Beckford, the author of *Vathek*, for instance, describes thus the performance of Vespers for St Cecilia's day at the Church of Mártires in 1787:[21]

It was dark when we arrived. Having driven at a rapid rate, we seemed suddenly transported not to a church, but to a splendid theatre, glittering with lights and spangled friezes. Every altar on a blaze with tapers, every tribune festooned with curtains of the gaudiest Indian damask. A hundred singers and musicians executing the liveliest and most brilliant symphonies. Much fanning, giggling and flirting going on in the spacious nave, which was comfortably carpeted for the accommodation of a numerous group of ladies. A recess in front of the great entrance, in which the high altar is placed, looked so like a stage and was decorated in so operatic a manner that I expected every moment the triumphant entrance of a hero or the descent of some pagan divinity, surrounded by cupids and turtle doves.

Speaking of High Mass at the Mártires on 22 November, Beckford says that he was but little pleased with the music as 'it had nothing solemn or pathetic, but was made up of odds and ends of overtures and the beginnings and cadences of opera arias'. But he has this to say of the music that was performed in the same church on 26 November:[22]

I went to the church of the Martyres to hear the matins of Perez and the dead mass of Jommelli performed by all the principal musicians of the royal chapel for the repose of the souls of their deceased predecessors. Such august, such affecting music I never heard, and perhaps may never hear again; for the flame of devout enthusiasm burns dim in almost every part of Europe, and threatens total extinction in a very few years: as yet it glows at Lisbon, and produced this day the most striking musical effect. After the requiem the high mass of Jommelli in commemoration of the deceased was performed; that famous composition which begins with a movement indicative of the tolling of bells,

'Swinging slow with sullen roar'

These deep majestic sounds mingled with others like the cries for mercy of unhappy beings, around whom the shadows of death and the pains of hell were gathering, shook every nerve in my frame.

Beckford was a well-informed amateur musician, who had had the privilege of receiving some lessons from Mozart when they were both children, and so his musical opinions carry a certain weight, even though they sometimes seem slightly exaggerated. He considered the Queen of Portugal's Chapel to be the first in Europe. According to him no other establishment of the kind, the papal not excepted, could boast such an assemblage of admirable musicians. The Queen was always surrounded 'by a bevy of delicate warblers, as plump as quails, and as gurgling and melodious as nightingales. The violins and violoncellos at her Majesty's beck are all of the first order, and in oboe and flute players her musical menagerie is unrivalled.'[23]

Seeing that he proceeds to describe how six of these musicians were put at his disposal by the Marquis of Marialva while he was staying at the Ramalhão, in Sintra (in the vicinity of Lisbon), it may be that he is also trying to impress his readers. The musicians played music by Haydn and Jommelli, while Beckford himself sang arias by Sacchini, Gian Francesco di Majo, Sousa Carvalho, and Jerónimo Francisco de Lima (accompanied by the composer). Elsewhere he refers to a *lingua franca*, half-Italian and half-Portuguese, which was very prevalent at the Ajuda palace, where Italian singers were in much greater demand and fashion than persons of deeper tone and intellect.[24] It is unfortunate for us that during his stay in Lisbon he did not attend any operas either in the public theatres or in the court theatres.

Besides regular serenatas, chamber music recitals, and religious feasts, the documents also mention several other courtly entertainments, many of which have remained hitherto unknown, and which were frequently accompanied by music:[25]

| *1779* | | |
|---|---|---|
| 8 July | Queluz palace | A man with trained horses, who received 96$000 |
| *1780* | | |
| June | Belém farm (near the Ajuda palace) | Pierre Delaval presented a self-propelled car ('Carrinho que anda per si') and received 57$600 |
| 17 September 14 November } | Ajuda Theatre | Shadow puppets ('Bonecos de sombras') Company of acrobats ('Bolantins') which received 192$000 |
| *1782* | | |
| 9 March | Ajuda Theatre | Company of acrobats directed by José Cortez, which received 192$000 |
| July 28 and 4 August August } | Queluz Theatre | Puppet company ('Compagnia di Fantoccini') directed by Giuseppe Castagna, which received 384$000 Pierre Delaval, who presented a figure which spoke, suspended by strings, and received 96$000 |
| *1783* | | |
| Carnival | Salvaterra Theatre | Company of acrobats |
| *1788* | | |
| 14 August | Ajuda Theatre | Company of acrobats, directed by Paulino José da Silva and Tomás Crespo, which received 310$520 |
| *1789* | | |
| 26 and 28 May | Ajuda palace | Puppet opera or comedy ('Opera ou Comédia de Bonecos') |
| *1791* | | |
| March | Ajuda palace | The Italian poet Angelo Talassi improvised in front of the Queen and received 480$000[26] |
| May | Queluz palace | Men with ponies who received 288$000 |
| | Ajuda palace | Men who performed with machines [?] and received 480$000 |
| August | | 'Homem das Poloticas [?] Pinetti, que trabalhou no Teatro da Ajuda e Queluz'; he received 960$000 and 122$690 |

For the shadow puppets of 1780 there were seventeen players. Rodil was ordered to bring a concerto and Lenzi to bring a symphony. For the puppet company of 1782 there were seven players and for the puppet opera of 1789 twelve.

## Correspondence with Italy. Hiring of new singers and purchase of scores

In October 1777 Giambattista Vasquez received 1:000$000 before retiring to Italy. In 1778 five other singers did the same: Giovanni Marchetti,

Pasquale Marchetti, Pasquale Franceschetti, Niccolò Appolini and Massimo Barnabei.[27] Each of them received 96$000. In 1782 Domenico Barzi retired to Italy and Giuliano Giusti died.[28] In 1783 Lorenzo Giorgetti retired, as did Giuseppe Romanini in 1788, Giovanni Ripa in 1791, and Antonio Fratta, Cosimo Banchi and Salvatore Carobene in 1792.[29] At the same time the court continued to hire new singers. Livros xx/G/20–7 register the auditions of the following singers, accompanied either by a small orchestra, or sometimes by a harpsichord or pianoforte: Giovanni Gelati on 13 June 1778; Vincenzo Muccioli in July 1779; Giuseppe Totti in March 1780; the alto Francesco Fariselli in August 1781 (he left in May 1787; the alto Venanzio Aloisi in June 1782; Biagio Mariani on 6 January 1783; Vincenzo Marini and Antonio Bartolini in April 1783; the alto Carlo Contucci in June 1788 (at the spa of Caldas da Rainha, where the Queen was staying); the bass Salvatore Botticelli on 23 December 1790; Valeriano Violani, Giuseppe Capranica and Francesco Angelelli in July 1791; the tenor Giuseppe Forlivesi and the soprano Antonio Balelli on 16 October 1791.[30]

Despite this steady inflow of new singers to replace those who died or retired, there was increasing difficulty in hiring good castrati, as is shown by the stream of correspondence on the subject exchanged between Pinto da Silva on the one hand, and Piaggio, the retired singers Giuseppe Jozzi, Giovanni Marchetti and Giambattista Vasquez, and several Portuguese diplomats on the other.[31]

Referring to the audition of Biagio Mariani in a letter to Piaggio dated 20 January 1783, Pinto da Silva says that he had sung three arias in the presence of the royal family and in all of them he had shown his defects, managing to sing even an *andante* out of tune. The altos who had arrived earlier (probably Fariselli and Aloisi) were almost of the same calibre. In another letter of 7 April he refers to Vincenzo Marini, who had a very beautiful voice and very good style, and had therefore been chosen by the Queen to sing in the Royal Chapel, whereas Antonio Bartolini, who was very ordinary, would go to the Patriarcal.

Writing from Rome on 18 July 1782, the Portuguese ambassador D. Diogo de Noronha says that music was in a state of decadence. He had heard many different operas in more than ten theatres all over Italy and there was nothing new as regards the music, and no singer of distinction, except for Marchesini (Luigi Marchesi), who was in the service of the King of Turin, and would be coming to sing in Rome during Carnival. In a letter of 7 April 1783, Pinto da Silva agrees with him regarding the bad state of music and singing, and with an amusing touch of chauvinism declares that at present there was no other composer like 'our own João de Sousa Carvalho', and that both he and his disciple António Leal (Moreira) had recently composed excellent serenatas.

On 5 July 1784 Pinto da Silva asked D. Diogo de Noronha to search in the Roman theatres for a male *prima donna* to replace Battistini (Giambattista

Vasquez), to which he replied on 30 September that owing to the current dearth of good singers, those who had any merit only wanted to sing as *primi uomini*. Regarding the contract of a tenor whom he had auditioned (D. Luigi Giglioni) he relates on 2 September that he was a subdeacon, which would not allow him to sing in His Majesty's theatres, despite the fact that D. Diogo's advisers, the singers Jozzi and Battistini, had produced certificates from good theologians to prove that this was not an impediment. He was finally hired for the Patriarcal at 50$000 a month only on the strong recommendation of Jozzi, as there were enough good tenors in Lisbon, some of whom were Portuguese.[32]

In 1786 D. Diogo was still trying to find a good male soprano and had persisted in inviting Andreini (Andrea Martini, *Il Senesino*) who had earlier sung in the Teatro Valle and had recently been hired for one of the Naples theatres, but he could not be persuaded to come to Lisbon. Leaving Rome shortly afterwards, D. Diogo de Noronha left the embassy secretary and chargé d'affaires *ad interim* José Pereira Santiago with the additional duty of looking out for new singers (and new music).

In February 1788 the latter was searching for a *prima donna*, a *servetta*, and a bass. He had visited all the Roman theatres, where first parts were now taken up by singers who in earlier days would not have made decent second parts, as a result of the scarcity of good sopranos, those still alive being now too old. According to him one of the difficulties in hiring singers for the Portuguese royal service, even in earlier days, was the condition that they should serve for twenty-four years, which frightened all but the very young and inexperienced singers. Because of the scarcity, good singers would not accept engagements for so long a period and in such a remote place, and the others were not fit for the job.

Pereira Santiago also wrote to Naples, and he was informed that there were hardly any decent singers in the Naples conservatories. Having asked the secretary to the ambassador in Naples, José de Sá Pereira, to look for a *servetta* in the Conservatories of the Loreto and the Pietà dei Turchini, the latter reported back on 10 September 1790 that the only 'livestock' ('rês') he had been shown was not totally ignorant, had a good figure, and a good voice, but he was not a perfect soprano, not being able to sing firmly above f'' ('effaut'). Even though he was still at the Conservatory, he was reluctant to sing *servetta*, and Sá Pereira had to try and persuade him that in the Portuguese court theatres this was not considered such a despicable role as it was in Italy.

Among other names that Pereira Santiago mentions are those of Domenico Caporalini, who would make a good *servetta*, of the tenor Domenico Mombelli, and of the basses Morelli and Francesco Bernucci. Caporalini, who was then in his late teens, was initially prevented by his parents from coming to Lisbon. When he finally accepted in 1790, it was apparently too late. Speaking of Andrea Martini in two letters of September

1790, the singer Giovanni Marchetti says that he had been told that either the *primo uomo* Crescentini, or Rubinelli, was better than him.[33]Mombelli would be willing to come to Lisbon but only for five or six years. These first-rate singers would not come except for a few years and with very good pay.

In other letters written in 1791, Pereira Santiago mentions having travelled to Lucca, Pisa, Livorno and Florence in the preceding Carnival to hear singers both in the theatres and in the churches, and says that owing to the scarcity of good singers, any that appeared were immediately requested to go to London, Moscow or Vienna, with stupendous salaries. Speaking of Giuseppe Capranica, the tenor Giuseppe Forlivesi, and the soprano Valeriano Violani, he says that the latter would only come for eight years, under the same conditions enjoyed by Carlo Reina (the *primo uomo* at Lisbon). These conditions were, according to a letter from Piaggio, dated 2 May 1791, a twelve-year contract at 100$000 a month (60$000 paid by the Patriarcal and 40$000 from the Queen's Privy Purse or *Real Bolsinho*), 20 gold *moedas* for house rent, and a payment of 30 gold *moedas* each time he were to appear as *primo uomo*. He would leave to Her Majesty's good will the decision to give him a carriage. Elsewhere Piaggio tells us that in turn Forlivesi was willing to come for twelve years at 80$000 a month, 50$000 paid by the Patriarcal and 30$000 from the Queen's Privy Purse, while Crescentini asked for 1,500 zecchini a year, and was only willing to do four or five operas a year, as *primo uomo*.

D. João de Almeida (Melo e Castro), who had meanwhile become ambassador to Rome, also tried to help choose singers for the royal service, but he too complained in a letter of 13 April 1789 that the singers who could be found either in the theatres during Carnival, or in the Papal Chapel itself, were so bad that he would pay not to be forced to listen to them. In another letter he says that the situation was such that he had had to send for Crescentini, who was then a member of the Neapolitan Royal Chapel, to sing the poem [*sic*] in honour of the Pope at the embassy.

Melo e Castro left in 1790, without being able to hire any new singers. He was replaced by D. Alexandre de Sousa Holstein, who suggested that in future some other method should be devised to choose the singers, so that inferior singers would not be hired. The details quoted above clearly show however that the problems facing the Portuguese Queen's musical establishment were probably insoluble, given the sort of conditions it set. Good castrati were becoming rarer, at a time when there were more women singers available, and those that existed would not accept long-term contracts for such a distant place as Lisbon.

In the correspondence quoted above more relevant information on the Italian operatic scene and singers is available than can possibly be given here. Before leaving the subject, however, two interesting facts should be mentioned: first-rate singers like Crescentini or Domenico Mombelli, who would not agree to serve in the court theatres, were soon to play a leading role in the first and probably most brilliant period of the Lisbon's S. Carlos Theatre; Caporalini also appeared at the S. Carlos from its inauguration onwards as *prima buffa assoluta*; on the other hand singers like Angelelli, Capranica, or Forlivesi, who would have little opportunity to sing in the court theatres before they closed, were to appear afterwards in public concerts in Lisbon.[34]

Portuguese diplomats in Italy were also requested to look for and acquire new music for the court. In a letter to D. Diogo de Noronha of 17 June 1782[35] Pinto da Silva refers to the sacred music which was sung in Rome by the priests of the Congregation (of the Oratory?) and elsewhere, and asks him to send through Piaggio in Genoa those oratorios of which he had the best information, as they were in great need of them for Lent, and particularly for St Joseph's and St Benedict's day (19 and 21 March), and some good serenatas, which were also in considerable demand in Lisbon. Replying on 18 July, D. Diogo de Noronha said that he needed the help of Battistini and Jozzi, who were not in Rome at the time, to choose the music. Most arias that he had ordered himself were all pretty well known, but in one of the Venice Conservatories or Asylums he had heard an oratorio by Anfossi which did not seem too bad. Elsewhere he says that the best composers there at present are Sarti for the *opera seria* and Cimarosa for the *opera buffa*.

On 8 August he sent a list of nineteen oratorios, of which the following, marked with an asterisk in the original, were probably ordered:

| | |
|---|---|
| *Giuseppe riconosciuto* | by Anfossi |
| *Salomone Re d'Israeli* | by Casali |
| *S. Elena al Calvario* | by Anfossi |
| *Pastorale a 4 voci* (?) | by Casali |
| *L'Ester* | by Sacchini |
| *L'Abigaille* | by Pigna |
| *Il trionfo di Mardoccheo* | by Borghi |
| *Gianetta* | by Pigna |

Of these only *S. Elena al Calvario*, *Ester* and *Il trionfo di Mardoccheo* were finally sent, as the others had not seemed suitable to Battistini. As for serenatas (in fact three are operas) he sent the following that had been chosen by the Queen and procured in Naples by José Pereira Santiago:

| | |
|---|---|
| *L'isola disabitata* | by Schuster |
| *Alceste* | by Gluck |
| *Paride ed Elena* | by Gluck |
| *Matrimonio inaspettato* | by Paisiello |

It is interesting to note that *Paride ed Elena* had been originally dedicated by Gluck to his friend D. João de Bragança, Duke of Lafões, an uncle of the Queen, while he lived in exile in Vienna.

Pinto da Silva himself, in a letter of 16 September 1782, offered to send D. Diogo de Noronha any of the serenatas composed by João de Sousa Carvalho, or one which had been written by a young boy from the Seminário da Patriarcal (António Leal Moreira) for the birthday of Prince José. In another letter of 19 May 1783 he tells him that the music that he had sent (probably the oratorios) had been examined by their Royal Highnesses with their usual curiosity and that they had agreed that at present in Italy good taste in composition was lost, and there were no composers as good as those in Portugal.

In 1784 the Portuguese ambassador was again asked by the Queen's confessor, the Archbishop of Tessalonica, to procure a few *opere buffe* for Lisbon. He wrote to Naples and Florence asking for librettos of operas performed there, because those that were being performed in Rome were very bad. He finally decided to send a *burletta* by Paisiello of the preceding year, which was one of the best that he had heard in Rome. Again in 1786 he sent a collection of librettos of *burlette*, one of them with music by Paisiello, and another with music by Fabrizi. He also sent the music of the *burletta* sung that year at the Capranica, the best there had been during the season, especially the quartet, which was greatly admired, being written by a young man who was at most twenty-four years old. All the operas produced in the other theatres were very inferior.

In 1789 the ambassador in Turin, D. Rodrigo de Sousa Coutinho, also sent several librettos and additionally scores of *burlette* and *opere serie*, including the one which had been performed at the wedding of the Duke of Aosta.

Occasionally the Queen also sent operas and serenatas as gifts to foreign courts. The serenatas *Seleuco*, *Everardo II*, *Re di Lituania*, *Penelope* and *Adrasto* (2 copies), by Sousa Carvalho, were copied between 1781 and 1784 to be sent to the Madrid court.[36] In a letter to her cousin, the Princess Maria Josefa of Bourbon, of 12 May 1783 Maria I writes that she was very happy to know that the serenata she had sent her had pleased, and that João de Sousa [Carvalho] certainly composed in an agreeable manner and according to the rules of music.[37] In 1784 and 1786 the operas *Solimano* (by Perez?), *Li fratelli Pappamosca* by Guglielmi and *La finta giardiniera* by Anfossi were copied to be sent to the court of Russia.[38]

## Calendars and details of operatic performances

Until 1785 there were only three operatic productions at the court, of which the first was the above-mentioned repeat of the *componimento drammatico Il ritorno di Ulisse in Itaca* in 1778, to inaugurate the new Queluz Theatre, which was built by Inácio de Oliveira Bernardes on a site now occupied by the small palace originally intended for Prince José and his wife and later inhabited by Queen Maria I when she became a widow. It was all in wood and had several boxes. It was demolished in 1784.[39]

The next production at Queluz was the two-act *dramma per musica Testoride Argonauta*, with music by Sousa Carvalho, which had eight rehearsals and was performed twice, on 5 and 25 July 1782.[40] The list of thirty-two players included the composer, who received 144$000, and his colleague Jerónimo Francisco de Lima, who probably shared the harpsi-chord continuo part with him. The singers Carlo Reina and Giuseppe Romanini received 96$000 each and the other singers 72$000. Each of the seven dancers received 48$000. Of these, only three, Pietro Colonna, Niccolà Midosi and Francesco Zucchelli, appear in the libretto as being in the service of the Queen. The others were Giorgio Binetti, Ridolfo Butti, Giambattista Flambò and Pedro António Pereira. There were also seven-teen extras, sixteen of whom were soldiers. The sets returned to the Ajuda Theatre in January.[41]

The book relating to the Salvaterra productions of 1784[42] indicates that besides the *burletta Dal finto il vero*, with music by Paisiello, two Goldoni comedies, *L'antiquario* (i.e. *La famiglia dell' antiquario*) and *99 disgrazie di Pulcinella*, were performed. The first four rehearsals of the *burletta*, and one of the comedy (*L'antiquario?*) were held at the house of Pinto da Silva between 7 and 21 January, at three o'clock. On 21 January the carpenters and the boat with the sets arrived at Salvaterra, on the 22nd the wardrobe master Francesco Piolti, the tailor Paolino Solenghi, and the boat with the costumes, on the 24th Pinto da Silva and the remaining theatrical per-sonnel.[43]

The calendar for the season was the following:

*January*

| 25, 26, 27 | Rehearsal of the *burletta* |
| 28 | Rehearsal of *L'antiquario* |
| 29, 30 | Rehearsal of the *burletta* |
| 31 | Dress rehearsal of the *burletta* |

*February*

| 1 | Music in the chamber |
| 2 | First performance of the *burletta* |
| 3 | Second performance of the *burletta* |
| 4 | Rehearsal of *L'antiquario* in the morning; music in the chamber in the evening |
| 5 | First performance of *L'antiquario* |
| 6 | Rehearsal of the cut in the *burletta* in the morning; music in the chamber in the evening |
| 7 | Third performance of the *burletta* |
| 8 | Fourth performance of the *burletta* |
| 9 | First and second rehearsal of *99 disgrazie di Pulcinella* |
| 10 | Rehearsal of the cut in *L'antiquario* and second per-formance |
| 11 | Rehearsal of *99 disgrazie* and fifth performance of the *burletta* |

| 12 | Rehearsal of *99 disgrazie* and third performance of *L'anti-quario* |
| 13 | Dress rehearsal of *99 disgrazie* and music in the chamber |
| 14 | First performance of *99 disgrazie* |
| 15 | Sixth performance of the *burletta* |
| 16 | Second performance of *99 disgrazie* |
| 17 | Seventh performance of the *burletta* |
| 18 | Fourth performance of *L'antiquario* |
| 19 | Third performance of *99 disgrazie* |
| 20 | Music in the chamber |
| 21 | Eighth performance of the *burletta* |
| 22 | Fourth performance of *99 disgrazie* |
| 23 | Fifth performance of *99 disgrazie* |
| 24 | Ninth performance of the *burletta* |
| 25 | Ash Wednesday |
| 26 | Pinto da Silva and the musicians returned to the Ajuda |

Between 30 January and 3 February the singers Ansano Ferracuti and Antonio Puzzi came to Salvaterra to sing at Candlemas, and between 20 and 26 February two other singers came for the Forty Hours and Ash Wednesday. João Cordeiro da Silva, the singers Reina, Torriani, Ripa and Marini and twelve players, plus the court's harpsichord tuner Matias Bostem, the wardrobe master Piolti and the copyist António Bernardo, stayed on for the chamber until 3 March. The players were 4 violinists, 1 viola, 2 cellos (or more probably 1 cello and 1 double-bass), 2 flautists or oboes, 1 bassoon and 2 horns. The repertoire performed in the chamber that year has already been mentioned (see p. 62 above).

For the opera itself there were twenty-five players, who received 24$000 each. Cordeiro da Silva and the singers Reina, Leonardi and Marrocchini received 144$000 each, Martinelli and the singers Torriani, Romanini, Cappellani, Manna and Bartolini 96$000, and the singer Marini 24$000. The singers and Martinelli also received 24$000 each for the comedies. The singers, players and other regular personnel received food allowances in money as well. Other payments were for 13 extras, 4 copyists, 6 tailors, painters, 64 carpenters, 4 night guards, a glazier, an Italian hairdresser (Pietro Antonio Chiesa), a shoemaker, and different materials for the sets and costumes. Of the 787 librettos printed of the *burletta*, 7 were bound in silk.

A curious note concerns the clothes that were usually given to each singer or actor who appeared on the stage. It shows that besides the singers and the dancers, other members of the personnel occasionally also took part in the comedies:

When in the year 1764 the Comedy *Amor Paterno* was performed each actor received two shirts, two pairs of socks, and two pairs of shoes.
The singers used to receive the same when they sang in the opera; and again the

same for each *burletta*. But if they performed one or two comedies at the same time, they did not receive any extra clothes, but only five *moedas* each.

When Nonnini [one of the violinists in the orchestra] [the prompter] Ambrosini and others, who were not singers ['músicos'] performed the comedies, each of them received only one pair of socks and one pair of shoes, besides five *moedas*.

As now Ripa and Marini are taking part in the comedies, it must be decided what clothes they shall receive, as they are not singing the *burletta*.

In 1785 the double wedding of the Portuguese Prince João and Princess Mariana Vitória to the Spanish Princess Carlota Joaquina and Prince Gabriel was the occasion for several musical events which were given special reports and conventional praise in the *Gazeta de Lisboa*. The first of these was the serenata *L'imenei di Delfo*, with music by Leal Moreira, performed in the Sala da Música, or da Serenata, at the Ajuda on 28 March, with the foreign ambassadors in attendance. On 13 April the Spanish ambassador, the Count of Fernan Nuñez gave a reception in his palace in the Rossio square[44] for 100 ladies and 388 gentlemen that began with refreshments. Each lady received a bouquet of artificial flowers, made in Madrid, and all the guests received a copy of the libretto of the serenata *Le nozze d'Ercole ed'Ebe*, with music by Jerónimo Francisco de Lima. After the performance supper was served, followed by a ball which lasted from one o'clock till seven in the morning.

The court returned on 8 June from the palace of Vila Viçosa, where it had gone for the exchange of the Portuguese and Spanish Princesses, and on the following evening the *favola pastorale Nettuno ed Egle* had its premiere at the Ajuda Theatre. As already mentioned, no documents have been preserved concerning this production, except for a note in AHMF, Caixa 258, which says that thirty-three soldiers were employed as extras. It was performed four times, and again repeated on 16 and 17 December. The *Gazeta* refers to the 'exquisite and admirable taste' of the music of Sousa Carvalho and praises the Porter of the Chamber (Pinto da Silva) for the quality of the production. For the December performances a new *Licenza* was composed.[45]

On 15 June the Spanish ambassador gave another reception in his palace which again started with refreshments, followed by the serenata *Il ritorno di Astrea in Terra*, the music of which, composed by the Spanish violinist of the Royal Chamber, D. José Palomino, is compared by the *Gazeta* to that of Jommelli. After the serenata supper was served to the 370 guests.

From 1785 onwards mentions of court serenatas became more frequent in the *Gazeta*. Operatic productions themselves became more regular again, although it is not possible to say if this was due to the influence of the Spanish Princess, who was only eleven years old when she arrived in Portugal. Four operas were produced in 1785, including the three Salvaterra productions early in the year. In 1786 there were again three operas at Salvaterra, but King Pedro III, the husband of Queen Maria I, having died on 25 May, the court did not go to Salvaterra the following year, and there were no operas. In 1788 there were again two operas during Carnival, but Prince José died in September and again the court did not go to Salvaterra in 1789. There were however two operas at the Ajuda, one in May and one in December. In 1790 there were four operas, plus one performance by the company from the Rua dos Condes Theatre at the Ajuda. In the last two years of court opera, 1791 and 1792, there were five and four productions respectively.

In 1785 nine rehearsals for the Salvaterra operas of the following year were held at the house of Pinto da Silva at Queluz (where the court was staying) between 17 October and 1 January, followed by four more rehearsals at the Ajuda Theatre.[46] The Salvaterra calendar itself shows how performances and rehearsals were alternated (*m* = morning; *e* = evening):

| *January* | | *Pappamosca* | *Giardiniera* | *Don Facilone* |
|---|---|---|---|---|
| Wednesday | 25 | 1st rehearsal    *e* | | 1st rehearsal    *m* |
| Thursday | 26 | 2nd rehearsal    *m* | 1st rehearsal    *e* | |
| Friday | 27 | 3rd rehearsal    *e* | | |
| Saturday | 28 | | 2nd rehearsal    *m* | 2nd rehearsal    *e* |
| Sunday | 29 | | 3rd rehearsal    *e* | |
| Monday | 30 | Dress rehearsal | | |
| Tuesday | 31 | | | Dress rehearsal |
| *February* | | | | |
| Wednesday | 1 | 1st performance | | |
| Thursday | 2 | 2nd performance | | |
| Friday | 3 | [Music in the] chamber | Dress rehearsal | |
| Saturday | 4 | | | 1st performance |
| Sunday | 5 | | | 2nd performance |
| Monday | 6 | | 1st performance | |
| Tuesday | 7 | | 2nd performance | |
| Wednesday | 8 | 3rd performance | | |
| Thursday | 9 | | 3rd performance | |
| Friday | 10 | | [Music in the] *chamber* | |
| Saturday | 11 | 4th performance | | |
| Sunday | 12 | | | 3rd performance |
| Monday | 13 | 5th performance | | |
| Tuesday | 14 | | 4th performance | |
| Wednesday | 15 | | | 4th performance |
| Thursday | 16 | 6th performance | | |
| Friday | 17 | | [Music in the] *chamber* | |
| Saturday | 18 | | 5th performance | |
| Sunday | 19 | | | 5th performance |
| Monday | 20 | | 6th performance | |
| Tuesday | 21 | 7th performance | | |
| Wednesday | 22 | | 7th performance | |

| | | | |
|---|---|---|---|
| Thursday | 23 | 8th performance | |
| Friday | 24 | | [Rest] |
| Saturday | 25 | | 8th performance |
| Sunday | 26 | 9th performance | |
| Monday | 27 | | 9th performance |
| Tuesday | 28 | 10th performance | |

As in 1784, three singers came to Salvaterra between 29 January and 3 February, and again between 24 February and 1 March, to sing at Candlemas, the Forty Hours and on Ash Wednesday. At the end of the Carnival season some fifteen singers and fourteen players stayed on at Salvaterra until 10 March.

Among other personnel employed in the operas there were thirty-nine extras, twenty-two of whom were soldiers (including a drummer in *Li fratelli Pappamosca*). Eight of the civilian extras were Martinelli's godsons (!). Each of the extras received 200 rs a day. The sets were moved by 131 carpenters.

For *La finta giardiniera* 815 librettos were printed, for *Gl'intrichi di Don Facilone* 814 and for *Li fratelli Pappamosca* 816. In each case seven librettos were bound in silk and cost 120 rs each, while the others cost 45 rs. For the music of *La finta giardiniera* fourteen books were bound at 200 rs each, for *Li fratelli Pappamosca* thirteen and for *Gl'intrichi di Don Facilone* seven.

The following notes concern the production of *La finta giardiniera* (according to the names of the singers they quote) and are very probably in Martinelli's hand. They provide us with a rare example of the kind of planning involved in preparing a court production:

Plan of the Opera

Recitatives of the original Burletta, as may be seen in the red libretto

| Lines | in Act I | 411 | |
| | in Act II | 472 | |
| | in Act III | 204 | |
| | | ------- | |
| | Totals | 1087 | |

Recitatives in the composed Opera

| Lines | in Act I | 328 | |
| | in Act II | 363 | |
| | in Act III | 87 | |
| | | ------- | |
| | | 778 | 778 |
| Therefore the opera has been reduced in lines | | | 309 |

In the reduced opera it is inevitable that there should be an aria before the duet; for when the scene opens the two actors, Reina, and Gelati, should be asleep. The aria which in the manuscript libretto has been given to Leonardi takes three minutes; so that if His Majesty should decide that the aria in Act III should be sung by Ripa, or Romanino (which are both similarly short [who both have equally short arias?]) it could be newly accommodated without any harm.

Plans of the Arias, etc.

| Act I | Act II | Act III |
|---|---|---|
| 1 Introduction | 1 aria by Romanino | 1 aria by Leonardi |
| 1 aria by Ripa | 1 aria by Cappellani | 1 duet |
| 1 aria by Leonardi | 1 aria by Reina | 2 |
| 1 aria by Gelati | 1 aria by Gelati | |
| 1 aria by Reina | 2 cavatine by Gelati | |
| 1 cavatina by Bartolini | 1 Finale | |
| 1 cavatina by Cappellani | 7 | |
| 1 aria by Gelati | | |
| 1 cavatina by Gelati | | |
| 1 Finale | | |
| 10 | | |

| | | | | |
|---|---|---|---|---|
| Act I | 10 | pieces | | 21 |
| Act II | 9 | pieces | sinfonia | 1 |
| Act III | 2 | pieces | chorus | 2 |
| | 21 | | | 24 |

The next book in Caixa 258 concerns the opera *La vera costanza*, which was repeated at the Ajuda Theatre in 1789. It shows that the singers received the usual payments (Reina and Gelati 144$000 and the others 96$000). The composer, Jerónimo Francisco de Lima, received 48$000, and so did Cordeiro da Silva when he replaced him, while Martinelli received 96$000. The dancer Antonio Marrafi,[47] author of the *ballo Aminta e Silvia* which was performed with the opera, received 110$000, and the other dancers 96$000. The court violinist Pietro Rumi received 24$000 for the dance music. Twenty extras in the opera received 200 rs a day and eight extras in the *ballo* 480 rs. 395 librettos were printed, 8 of which were bound in silk. The tailor's accounts, signed by Paolini Solenghi, still preserve samples of blue and pink silk, fixed with pins, with the amounts needed ('Six ells of blue silk as sample for Gelati; twelve ells of pink silk for Todi [Totti]; twelve ells of light blue silk').

A list of the porters gives a vague idea of the number of entrances that existed in the theatre: one for the Queen, several court entrances, one for the musicians and the servants, one for the guests and the riding-masters, one for the theatre personnel, one on the farm side, and stable doors.

Documents in Caixa 259 are for *Axur, Re di Ormus, Le trame deluse*, and *L'amore ingegnoso* of 1790/91. For *Axur* 800 librettos were printed, eight of which were bound in silk. A list of the extras and a note on the costumes, in Martinelli's hand (?), is transcribed below:

Set
Ajuda Theatre 17 December 1790

Extras
Eight Priests

Four soldiers, and Four Slaves     These should be played by the choristers
   No 4 Female Slaves: as above.     Boys

---

Four Grandees
Eight Soldiers with Altamor
Eight Guards and noblemen with Axur
Twelve Soldiers with same
Ten people
Eight comprising Incendiaries, Players, and Servants

Note
for the wardrobe of the Extras

---

This opera is in oriental, or rather, Persian character. The different actions in the drama require many extras; and many other extras must take part as choristers and mix among them. One can anticipate that few, or even none of the costumes that the opera requires are to be found in the wardrobe. With all that, many old costumes that are kept in the said wardrobe (which are rotting away because they have not been used in the opera for so long) may be torn up; and new costumes can be made for the different characters needed.

Beside the 8 singers, 8 dancers, and 16 choristers, 76 extras were employed: 48 soldiers, 22 civilians, including 4 boys, and 6 extras for the *balli*. A letter requisitioning the soldiers mentions the name of Sergeant Aleixo Duarte, who had many years' experience of operas and was already able to understand Martinelli. One of the civilian extras was a servant of Cordeiro da Silva, and another a servant of Martinelli.

For *Le trame deluse* there were 24 civilian extras and 14 extras in the *balli*, who received their usual salaries. It is also interesting to note the salary of several theatre workers: 3 riggers received 400 rs a day, 75 workmen 300 rs, 4 journeymen 240 rs, 85 journeymen 200 rs, and one foreman ('apontador') 500 rs. Ten porters received 400 rs a day each, and 4 stable servants 200 rs.

On 30 October 1790 the Italian company of the Rua dos Condes Theatre performed a *burletta* at the Ajuda Theatre, accompanied by 30 players of the Royal Chamber, with António Leal Moreira (the musical director of the Rua dos Condes) at the harpsichord. There were four singers who, with the impresario and Leal Moreira, received 398$400. The *burletta* may have been either *Il marchese di Tulipano* or *I filosofi immaginari* by Paisiello, both of which have only four singing parts.

On the basis of individual entries in Livros xx/G/20 to 27, it is possible to establish with a certain degree of accuracy the sum total of expenses for operatic productions between 1780 and 1792:

| Year | No of productions | Total expense |
|------|-------------------|---------------|
| 1780 | 1 | 2:388$015 |
| 1784 | 1 | 7:815$422 |
| 1785 | 4 | 16:653$857 |
| 1786 | 3 | 10:427$392 |
| 1788 | 2 | 9:329$525 |
| 1789 | 2 | 5:034$198 |
| 1790 | 4 | 32:547$784 |
| 1791 | 5 | 31:674$586 |
| 1792 | 4 | 11:844$494 |

A contemporary manuscript note in Carvalhais' copy of the libretto of *Riccardo Cor di Leone*,[48] produced at Salvaterra in Carnival 1792, says that during one of the performances Queen Maria I had one of her stronger fits of madness, and that the operas in the royal theatres came thus to an end.[49]

It is interesting to note that still in June of that year eighty-five prints of Spanish characters and eighty-one prints of Asian characters were bought for the use of the royal theatres. But with the opening of the S. Carlos Theatre in June 1793, court opera was finally over. None of the Royal theatres has survived to our own day. As mentioned above (p. 69), the theatre at Queluz was demolished in 1784. That of Salvaterra was auctioned along with the palace in 1862–3. The theatre, with the ruins of the palace, was acquired for 3,260$810 and demolished, its stone being used to pave the road between Salvaterra and Coruche.[50] The Ajuda Theatre still existed in 1868, when the junior officers of the Queen's 2nd Lancers performed some comedies there, but later it was also demolished.[51]

## The repertoire. Data on Portuguese court composers

During the reign of Maria I the court theatres' repertoire was mainly centred on the *opere buffe* or *burlette* of Pietro Alessandro Guglielmi, Paisiello, Cimarosa, etc. Exceptions are *Attalo, Re di Bitinia*, by Robuschi, and the Italian version of that famous example of French pre-romantic opera, *Riccardo Cor di Leone* by Grétry. The Portuguese composers' contribution to the theatrical repertoire is small: four works only (as against five in the previous reign). These are the *dramma per musica Testoride argonauta* of 1780 and the *favola pastorale Nettuno ed Egle* of 1785, by Sousa Carvalho, the *dramma giocoso La vera costanza* of 1785, by Jerónimo Francisco de Lima, and the *dramma serio-comico Lindane e Dalmiro* of 1789, by João Cordeiro da Silva.[52]

On the other hand, more than three dozen serenatas and oratorios by Portuguese composers were performed during the period, as against a dozen by foreign composers. This much larger participation by local talent is probably explained by the fact that the Italian David Perez, who died in October 1778, was replaced by the Portuguese João de Sousa Carvalho as music teacher to the Princes and unofficial court music director. However, a plausible explanation still remains to be found for their much more modest contribution to the operatic repertoire itself.

A few biographical data should be given here concerning these composers, most of whom had already been active during the previous reign. Only one of them, Pedro António Avondano (1714–82), did not apparently have any work performed at court during the reign of Maria I. He was a member of the Royal Chamber, where he played the violin. His father, Pietro Giorgio Avondano, had belonged to the orchestra in the reign of João V, and four other members of his family appeared in it during the second half of the century.[53] Pedro António seems to have been the most active member of the family. After the 1755 earthquake he reorganised the Irmandade de Santa Cecília. From at least 1766 onwards he was also the founder of a club in his own house, the Assembleia das Nações Estrangeiras, where the British colony in particular gathered twice a week to play cards and dance, and where concerts were also held. For these balls he also composed minuets which were printed in London at the expense of the said colony.[54] Besides the opera and the two oratorios he wrote for Lisbon (*Il voto di Jefte* of 1771 and *Adamo ed Eva* of 1772), he also wrote the opera *Berenice*, performed at Macerata (Italy) in 1742. He was a Knight of the Ordem de Cristo, a dignity which he bought for 480$000.[55]

Luciano Xavier dos Santos (1734–1808) studied with Giovanni Giorgi at the monastery of Santa Catarina de Ribamar and later became first organist and master of the Royal Chapel of the Bemposta.[56]

João Cordeiro da Silva has already been mentioned several times in connection with the court opera productions. The dates of his birth and death are not known but his signature appears in the register of the Irmandade de Santa Cecília for 1756. He may have studied in Naples and in 1763 he appears as organist and composer of His Most Faithful Majesty in the Royal Chapel of the Ajuda, in a letter of commendation which accompanies the *Nova instrucção musical* by Francisco Inácio Solano. In the librettos he is simply designated as 'Virtuoso della Cappella Reale'.

João de Sousa Carvalho (1745–98), generally considered to be the greatest Portuguese composer of the second half of the eighteenth century, was born at Estremoz. He attended the Colégio dos Santos Reis Magos at Vila Viçosa,[57] and between 1761 and 1767 he studied at the Conservatorio di S. Onofrio a Capuana in Naples, where he had Giovanni Paisiello among his colleagues. His opera *La Nitteti* was performed at the Teatro delle Dame in Rome during Carnival of 1766.[58] On his return to Portugal he was made counterpoint teacher and later first chapelmaster at the Seminário da Patriarcal, where he had among his pupils António Leal Moreira and Marcos Portugal. From 1778 onwards, as mentioned above, he replaced David Perez as music teacher to the Princes, at a monthly salary of 40$000, with use of a carriage. Having made a wealthy marriage, he later retired to the Alentejo, where he died.

Jerónimo Francisco de Lima (1741–1822) was a pupil of the Seminário da Patriarcal and also attended the Conservatorio di S. Onofrio a Capuana between 1761 and 1767. On his return he was appointed teacher at the Seminário da Patriarcal and in 1798 he succeeded João de Sousa Carvalho as chapelmaster there.

Braz Francisco de Lima (?–1813) was also a pupil of the Seminário, and he also studied in Naples with his brother Jerónimo Francisco. In 1785, according to the libretto of *Il trionfo di Davidde*, he taught at the Seminário da Patriarcal, but he may later have abandoned music as a profession. Writing in 1788, Beckford[59] refers to him as 'Signor Biaggio, an odd mysterious character, no indifferent composer, as I am told, but who for what reason I have not discovered, thought proper to be introduced to me as a merchant totally ignorant of music.'

José Joaquim dos Santos (*c.* 1747–1801) also studied at the Seminário da Patriarcal, where he later became a teacher.

António Leal Moreira (1758–1819) studied in the Seminário da Patriarcal, where he also became a teacher and in 1783 chapelmaster. In 1790 he became music director at the Rua dos Condes Theatre, and between 1793 and 1799 he was music director at the S. Carlos Theatre, where he was replaced by Francesco Federici (and not, as is commonly stated, by Marcos Portugal, who only took over the direction in 1800).[60]

António da Silva Gomes e Oliveira signed the register of the Irmandade de Santa Cecília in 1774 and may have died after 1817. He is called 'Virtuoso di musica Portoghese, sotto la scuola, e direzzione del celebre Sig. Maestro Davidde Perez' in the libretto for *Gioas, Re di Giudà* of 1778, but in that of *Calliroe* of 1782 he appears as organist of the Royal Chapel of the Ajuda.[61]

# 4

# Commercial opera 1760–93

### The general theatrical scene and its repertoire

A fact which has confused earlier historians of the opera in Portugal is the
growing vogue in the second half of the eighteenth century for translations
and adaptations of Metastasian dramas and Goldonian comedies. Most of
these plays and other theatrical literature of the period were published as
cheap booklets and sold in the streets by blind men and other vendors, who
hung them from a string fixed to a wall or to a door, and have thus acquired
the collective name of 'teatro de cordel' (string theatre). They are often
classified as operas ('ópera nova', 'ópera drama', 'ópera joco-séria') on the
title-page, and follow the trend begun by António José da Silva in the
second quarter of the century by including 'arias' and other indications of
incidental music interspersed throughout the text. Thus for example the
'ópera' *Ciro reconhecido*, which was performed at the Rua dos Condes
Theatre in 1762,[1] includes eight arias and one duet (which are not identified
as such) in Act I, nine arias in Act II, and seven arias and a final chorus in
Act III. At the end there is a recitative and aria, 'which Ciro sings in place of
the duet'. The *Opera que se intitula: Memorias de peralvilho e disgraças
graciosas*[2] includes five arias and one recitative in Act I, and six arias, two
duets and a 'Coro Final' in Act II.

Several of the plays which were published in the repertoire of the 'teatro
de cordel' bear an indication of having been performed in one of the Lisbon
theatres, and there is evidence to the effect that many, if not all, of those
arias were in fact sung. Thus for instance the Bairro Alto accounts[3] show
that arias and duets were copied for the following plays, among others: *Inês
de Castro*, *O sábio ... (?)*, and *Alexandre na Índia*.

The article on the Portuguese theatre published in the *Journal de littérature, des sciences et des arts* of 1781[4] says that between the acts airs were sung, or more rarely some player showed his talents. There were also *balli*, which were very mediocre, but when they were popular they remained on the stage for two months at least. The second play usually had music. One aria, poorly sung, was applauded in such a way by the supporters of the singer, that sometimes it had to be repeated three or four times, to the great displeasure of the rest of the audience. While a few of the actors had some merit, none was extraordinary, with the exception of Cecília Rosa de Aguiar. This last let herself be carried away by sentiment to the point of falling ill after performing *Inês de Castro*, and needing a few days' rest. She also sang in a very agreeable manner. The performance of the other actors was uneven and lacking in feeling. The only plays they were able to perform with success were Portuguese or Italian. *O pai de família* had been booed; Molière made the public fall asleep; only *O avarento* (*The Miser*) and *Tartufo*[5] found favour. Italian plays were so much in fashion that the translations, particularly those from Goldoni, took on a special colour, and were considered by the audience to be originals.

It is worth dwelling a little longer on the Portuguese theatrical scene of this period, in order to appreciate the role that opera played within it. In general the opinion of foreign visitors agrees with that of the *Journal de littérature*. The French general Dumouriez, writing in 1766,[6] said that the Portuguese theatre was even worse than the Spanish, and that only the burlesque genre was cultivated with success.[7] The actors were bad, but well dressed. On the other hand the *balli* and the music were excellent, and provided good *intermèdes* in the two Lisbon theatres, where very good Italian operas were also performed. The *Travels of the Duke of Chatelet*, probably written in the early years of Maria I's reign,[8] says that the Portuguese theatre was beneath criticism. It lacked both plays and actors. These last, however, sang and danced very gracefully. Short Portuguese plays, known by the name of *intermèdes* [*entremezes*], were very good. The music in them was indeed very good and in excellent taste, but the acting was wretched.[9]

Even if we discount a certain amount of prejudice which is common to many negative criticisms of the country voiced by foreign visitors in the eighteenth century, the picture they paint is probably true enough. It is confirmed by the unsuccessful efforts of Portuguese dramatists and intellectuals to reform the theatre. This was one of the avowed aims of the Arcádia Lusitana, which was created in 1756 by the lawyers António Diniz da Cruz e Silva, Teotónio Gomes de Carvalho and Manuel Esteves Negrão.[10] One of its members, Pedro António Correia Garção, wrote the comedy *Teatro novo*, which was performed at the Bairro Alto Theatre on 22 January 1766[11] and which includes a classical debate on the respective importance of the text, the sets, and the music of the drama. The play itself was booed, due to the poverty of the action. Another member of the

Arcádia, Manuel de Figueiredo, who wrote thirteen volumes of original plays and adaptations, only one of which was performed, says in his preface to the translation of Addison's *Cato*[12] that Portuguese theatre-goers did not care about the quality of the play, as long as there was an *entremez*, two arias, and four dancers jumping about the stage.

The enthusiasm for Italian opera gave rise to the figure of the *peralta*, the poor but 'estrangeirado' *fidalgo*, who disdains to speak his own language, making use only of French and Italian. He is satirised in many plays of the period, among them the *Incisão anatomica ao corpo da Peraltice* of 1771:[13]

| | |
|---|---|
| *Claudio* | Did you go to the Bairro Alto? |
| *Júlio* | I would not waste my time on such things! |
| | I do not go to these *bairros* [boroughs], |
| | my friend, I cannot stand it |
| | when there are not two lines of Italian.[14] |
| *Matilda* | That's a good one! |
| (aside) | After all he understands it as well as I do Greek. |
| *Júlio* | Bairro Alto! Not on your life. |
| *Cláudio* | Don't be an ass: |
| | today our stage |
| | can hold its own |
| | with the best in Europe. |
| *Júlio* | I said: |
| | si non habemo de quello |
| | de parola italiana |
| | non me piaxe, y con aquesto |
| | um pouco de areliquino |
| | oh Dio, charo dilecto![15] |

It should be noted in this respect that already in 1754 and 1755 the children of the singers and actors hired by José I performed several comedies in Italian at the Bairro Alto Theatre.[16] Two of them were certainly *Il cavaliere e la dama* and *La vedova scaltra*, whose bilingual libretto indicates that they were performed there in 1755.[17]

The widespread use of the term opera in connection with spoken drama (with or without music?) also bears witness to the prestige and popularity of the genre, while making it sometimes difficult to know what kind of spectacle is meant. Thus the *Gazeta de Lisboa* of 12 November 1785, referring to the festivities in the provinces to celebrate the double marriage of the Portuguese and Spanish Princes, says that in Alter do Chão during the last three days of September full performances of three different operas were presented, for which the costumes had been brought from the court (i.e. Lisbon). In August at Vila Real two operas were performed by amateurs in a theatre which was built in the square (*Gazeta* of 17 December 1785). In Brazil, at Maranhão, the opera *Demofoonte* by Metastasio was also performed by amateurs the following year.[18] On the island of Madeira Metastasio's *Artaserse* was performed on 17 and 21 November 1759.[19]

Another fact which we have already noted is the continuing tradition of the puppet opera (or theatre) in the second half of the century.[20] A letter written by the dramatist Alexandre António de Lima to the future Director of the Royal Theatres, Pedro José da Silva Botelho, on 23 January 1755 is entitled 'Familiar, informative, and mainly critical letter, on the bad digestion of the harmony of the Puppet Opera which in those days was being performed in the Entertainment House of the Bairro Alto'.[21] It is a satirical review, criticising the texts of the arias and the bad quality of the translation. It refers to the song of Achilles and the actor Pedro António. The 'opera' was Metastasio's *Achiles em Sciro*, whose 1755 translation states that it was performed at the 'Casa do Theatro Publico do Bairro Alto'.[22]

The authors of the music for this type of repertory are generally unknown, but Sousa Bastos[23] has transcribed a few receipts of payments to composers, among other theatrical receipts to which he had access and which are not now extant. Thus in November 1771 António José de Sousa received 6$400 for an *entremez* entitled *O licenciado*, with all the music and the score pertaining to it (it is not clear whether he was the author of the text, the composer of the music, or both). In November 1772 Frei Manuel de Santo Elias received 19$200 for composing three arias with recitatives, one quartet, one duet and a finale for the tragicomedy *D. Afonso de Albuquerque*.[24] Nor have any musical sources for the repertory survived, with the possible exception of Marcos Portugal's scores for *Licença pastoril* and *Pequeno drama*, both performed at the Salitre Theatre in 1787.[25]

The subject of theatrical music, and of the dramatic repertoire performed at the Bairro Alto, the Rua dos Condes, the Graça, and the Salitre Theatres, is however marginal to the field of this enquiry, which is mainly concerned with opera in the usually accepted sense of the term. It is nevertheless unfortunate that so little progress has been made in this area of research since the pioneering works of Teófilo Braga, José Ribeiro Guimarães, and António Sousa Bastos (notwithstanding the valuable contributions of Costa Miranda and Rossi quoted in my bibliography).

## The Bairro Alto Theatre (1760–71)

The public theatres were also destroyed by the earthquake of 1 November 1755. Five years later, in October 1760, a society was formed by the apothecary João Gomes Varela, with a 50 per cent share, in joint ownership with the wood-carver João da Silva Barros and the master mason Francisco Luís, with a 25 per cent share each, to rent the ruins of the palace of the Count of Soure for fifteen years, at 240$000 a year (later raised to 288$000), and erect an opera house there. The palace was situated where the Travessa do Conde de Soure and the Rua Luísa Todi now meet. It has been debated whether the location of this new Bairro Alto Theatre was the same as that of the earlier Casa dos Bonecos do Bairro Alto. The *Journal de littérature, des sciences et des arts* of 1781 seems to connect the two, when it considers the Bairro Alto Theatre to be the oldest there was in Lisbon. Whereas Júlio de Castilho[26] suggests that the two theatres were in the same place, both Ribeiro Guimarães[27] and Matos Sequeira[28] are of opinion that they were in different locations in the Bairro Alto.[29] The issue is further confused by the fact that the 1740 edition of the *Labirinto de Creta* by António José da Silva already refers to the 'Theatre of the new house in Bairro Alto' ('Theatro da nova casa do Bairro Alto').[30]

The best modern summary of the history of this theatre has been written by Mário Moreau.[31] Like the work of his predecessors, it is essentially based on a manuscript book containing the theatre accounts between 1761 and 1770.[32] Here only those facts which are more relevant to the history of opera will be mentioned (including several which have escaped Moreau's attention). The theatre's construction was directed by Nicolau Luís, the decoration by Lourenço da Cunha, and the stage curtain, which represented Apollo among the muses and also included an allegorical representation of the river Tagus, by Joaquim Manuel da Rocha. According to the *Journal de littérature* it had four tiers of boxes, twenty-seven of which were on the second and third floors.

In February 1761 the theatre had already been completed, at a cost of 6:023$853, and it was rented to João Pedro Tavares and José Duarte, the managers of a puppet opera company, who came from the Rua dos Condes Theatre, bringing with them all the stage props, which they later ceded to João Gomes Varela. Between St John the Baptist's day (24 June) of 1762 and Carnival of 1763 the theatre was rented out for 12$000 a day to a certain Mr Antonio, dancing-master, who presented an opera company.[33] Ninety-four performances brought a profit of 1:128$000, half of which went to Varela, who also received 112$800 out of the revenue of the theatre café ('botequim'). Between Easter of 1763 and Carnival of 1764 Mr Antonio's company brought in a profit of 1:050$000, and the theatre café 163$200. After a three and a half year loan the theatre and its belongings had been paid for, and there remained a profit of 21$198, being the difference between 3:473$845 gross income and 3:452$647 expenses. Thirty-six *balli* had been performed. In 1764, 46$271 were spent to enlarge the theatre and 111$200 on a house for the tailors and the costumes. By then Varela had bought a large number of costumes from the Italian opera of Fremunde (?), as well as musical scores, sets and stage props.

This was probably the same as Mr Antonio's company, of which little else is known. A 1762 edition of Goldoni's *L'amore artigiano*, with music by Gaetano Latilla, may be related to it.[34] Although it does not indicate the place of publication, Carvalhais[35] thinks that it may be been printed in Lisbon, in view of its numerous misprints. The same is probably the case with the libretto of '*O casamento de Lesbina*, drama jocozo para se representar em Musica no novo Teatro do Bairro Alto de Lisboa', which bears no date. Only a Portuguese version of the text is included, and the music is attributed to the 'Senhor Bonarelli, Mestre de Capela Veneziano', an obvious corruption of Buranello (Baldassare Galuppi), whose *Nozze di Dorina*, based on the same Goldonian libretto, was first performed in Bologna in 1755. The singers were Giovanni, Giuseppe and Rosa Ambrosini, and Gertrudes (Geltrude Pini?), and the dancers Nicola and Rosa Ambrosini, Giuseppe Conti and José Joaquim (Giuseppe Gioacchino?) Ricardino. The *balli* were by Giuseppe Conti.[36]

During the 1764–5 season the theatre-owners went into a fifty-fifty partnership with the manager of the Rua dos Condes Theatre, Agostinho da Silva, whereby two companies alternated in both theatres. There were 136 performances of plays and *balli*. The accounts also mention a performance for the benefit of a certain Cristiani, and another for the benefit of the singer Gertrudes, as well as a spectacle of acrobats. A list of debtors includes mainly noblemen who failed to pay for their tickets or boxes. One debt of 30$000 was considered lost, as the bill collector had gone to the debtor's house many times, and they had wanted to beat him up. Another debtor said that he did not remember. Even so the season's profit amounted to 1:227$938.

Meanwhile Agostinho da Silva and João da Silva Barros died, the latter being replaced by his son-in-law, the painter Bruno José do Vale. A new partnership was formed between the three partners and António José Gomes and Matias Ferreira da Silva. Between Easter and June 1765, there were twenty-nine performances of comedies and *balli*, and there was a 2:860$700 loss. Varela went to England to fetch an Italian opera company, and between 5 July 1765 and 5 July 1766 there were 135 performances of operas, comedies in Portuguese, and six comedies in Italian performed by the dancers, as well as oratorios during Lent. The singers were, according to the librettos, Giuseppe Giustinelli, Antonio Mazziotti, virtuoso of the King of Two Sicilies, Leopoldo Micheli, Gaetano Quilici, Angela Sartori, and Magdalena Tognoni Berardi. The settings were by Silvério Manuel Duarte, the combats by Francesco Rainoldi, and the *balli* by Innocenzo Trabattone. The dancers were the said Trabattone, Francesca Battini, Luigi Berardi, Baldassare Burretti or Barrettiere, Filippo and Rosa Boselli, Margarita Franco, Josézinho or Giuseppino, Rosa Petrai, Pasquale Trepani, and Carlo Vitalba.

The libretto of *Didone*, performed in the summer of 1765, is preceded by a letter from João Gomes Varela, presenting his opera and dance company. The opera was dedicated 'alle Ecc.^me Dame e Cavallieri della Capitale sudetta, ed agli rispettabilissimi Commercianti', a significant indication of the growing importance of the merchant class of Lisbon. In the following operas the Portuguese actress-singer Cecília Rosa de Aguiar replaced

Magdalena Tognoni Berardi, who had been taken ill. For *L'amore artigiano* of 1766 there were two new singers, Giovanni and Veronica G(h)erardi. The *balli* this time were by Antonio Ribaltone. The first performance was on 31 March to celebrate the Queen's birthday, according to the *Licenza*.

Between July 1765 and July 1766 the gross income was 9:403$666 and the expenses 12:326$866, resulting in a 2:923$200 loss. The accounts state that David Perez did not pay for his boxes, as three of the operas were his, and he had come to rehearse some of them. The King's dancing-master and choreographer, Andrea Alberti, *Il Tedeschino*, did not pay for his boxes either, as he rehearsed some of the *balli*.

Between July 1766 and Carnival 1767 the theatre was rented to the Portuguese actors, who published an advertisement in the *Hebdomadario Lisbonense* of 19 July 1766 announcing the performance of comedies, tragicomedies, operas, *entremezes*, etc. They gave 104 performances that brought a 1:112$000 profit, plus 112$000 from the theatre café. Meanwhile Francisco Luís sold his share in the society to Matias Ferreira da Silva for 1:200$000.

On 24 February 1767 an advertisement in the *Hebdomadario Lisbonense* by the managers of the Rua dos Condes and Bairro Alto Theatres announced that every day until 3 March there would be operas and other entertainments in both theatres. The accounts show that for the 1767–8 season, which started on 19 April and ended on 16 February, there were 150 performances of plays and *balli*. The gross income was 17:100$590 and the expenses 16:629$914, bringing a net profit of 470$676. In April João Gomes Varela was called by the general (the City Governor) of Oporto, to take up the impresarioship of the theatre there, but there is no indication that this project was carried out. He spent 47$500 on the journey.

The accounts for the 1767–8 season are much more detailed than for the previous ones. They show payments to seventeen Portuguese actors, including Maria Joaquina, who, with her father, received 500$000 for ten months, and the sisters Cecília Rosa and Luísa de Aguiar, who received 564$000 and 144$000 respectively, as well as a house which cost 60$000 a year. The remaining actors received between 288$000 and 110$000. There were eight dancers, including Paolo Orlandi, Giovanni Berardi and Pepa Olivares, who received between 800$000 and 277$000 plus houses paid for by the impresarios. Pedro António and his wife received 500$000 to act and dance.[37] The orchestra had fifteen members, comprising 7 violins, 1 cello, 1 double-bass, 2 oboes, 2 horns, and 1 bassoon (plus the conductor at the harpsichord). The violinists (one of whom at least probably played the viola) received between 1$600 and $900 each night they played. In some of the comedies boys and girls were employed at between $600 and $800 each night. Several payments also appear for arias and duets in the comedies and dramas, which were copied for Maria Joaquina, Cecília Rosa de Aguiar and other actors.

For the 1768–9 season José Gomes Varela and Bruno José do Vale rented the theatre to Matias Ferreira da Silva, and Italian operas were apparently performed. Between September and May Bruno José do Vale was in Italy to hire dancers and players. He heard operas in Genoa, Milan, Treviso and Venice, and brought back with him the Sabbatini dancers, brother and sister, and two violinists. His trip cost 2:375$345.

The gross income for the 1769–70 season was 15:978$000 and expenses amounted to 19:009$758, resulting in a loss of 3:031$758, to which was added the cost of Bruno José do Vale's voyage. There were 164 performances of Portuguese comedies, *balli*, and acrobats. The performance of *Demetrio na Russia* was forbidden by the authorities, for reasons which are not given in the theatre accounts.

Between 15 April and 30 June 1770 the gross income was 2:947$830 and the expenses were 3:908$939, resulting in a loss of 960$567 [*sic*]. A theatre-lover donated 16$000 to the society. Between 1766 and June 1770 the society's total profits were 2:207$789. After this date Varela rented the theatre to the other two partners, Bruno José do Vale and Matias Ferreira da Silva.

The singers who performed the 1770–1 operas were, according to the librettos: Cecília Rosa de Aguiar, Isabel Ifigénia de Aguiar (another sister of Cecília and Luísa), Pedro António, Angiola Brusa, Nicodemo Calcina, Maria Joaquina, Luísa Todi,[38] and Giuseppe Trebbi. The *balli* for the 1770 operas were by Vincenzo Sabbatini and performed by him and by Pedro António, Lucrezia Bettini, Betta Brigida, Luigi Lajè, Ricardo Giuseppe Maria, Pepa Olivares, Raniero Pazzini, Vittorio Perini, Francesca Pirotti, Anna Sabbatini, Carlo Sabbatini and Vittoria Varrè. The sets were by Simão Caetano Nunes, and the costumes by António Francisco.

The libretto of *Il viaggiatore ridicolo*, which was dedicated to the Count of Oeiras, indicates that the theatre manager was Bruno José do Vale. That of *Il bejglierbei di Caramania*, which was composed for Lisbon, was dedicated to the consul-general of Great Britain, 'il Cavaliere Giovanni Hort'. A rare review of this opera is included in a letter of 7 February written by the French officer Gaubier de Barrault to the Count of Oeiras, who was then with the court at Salvaterra:[39]

It is the nicest *buffo* opera that I have ever heard. The music is charming and in a new style. Scolari has used his ability to make the most of all the actors, and he succeeds in doubling their talents through his art by developing and accommodating the music to the quality and the range of their voices. Each of them finds himself in his proper setting. Louise has never sung so in tune and with such a strong voice. Maria Joaquina has two very beautiful arias which she sings well. Trebbi is a very handsome Turk. Calcini, the first eunuch, dressed himself in such a way that he resembles an old castrato from the Patriarcal; among others he sang one aria which is unique in its genre. Cécile is acceptable as a Turk. Isabelle has two light ariettas which she managed quite well, but Louise has one arietta in the second act which is magnificent and which she sang superbly. We are deprived of the pleasure of hearing Mlle Bruza in this opera. The finales are full, harmonious, proportioned, in short everything has pleased in this opera, even Pedro. For the audience, besides applauding the actors, redoubled their applause at each lovely piece, shouting *Vivat Maestre Scolari.*

In another letter of 11 February Gaubier de Barrault describes an incident in the theatre which originated in a dispute on *tempi* between the composer and conductor at the harpsichord Scolari, and the first violinist Todi. This description is worth transcribing here in full, in spite of its length, as it provides us with a rare glimpse into a Portuguese eighteenth-century opera house:[40]

It is too late for me to be able to give to Your Excellency a full account of the tragicomedy which went on yesterday at the Bairro Alto. I will only tell Your Excellency that the opera, which on that day was packed and magnificent, was interrupted by a quarrel which arose in the orchestra between Scolari and Todi about the pace of an arietta which Pedro sang. Scolari, who wanted it to go more presto, started to charge into the harpsichord accompaniment with all his might and main, and following his laudable custom inveighed against Todi, who did not apparently go along with his whim, calling him 'pig'. Todi answered back by calling him 'ass'; other compliments quickly followed and I saw the moment when Todi beside himself was about to throw his violin at Scolari's head; I was in the box of your lady mother,[41] who was at the opera that day. We could see very well that there was an argument going on but we could not tell why, for the music went on playing and the rumpus that this affair was causing in the stalls prevented us from distinguishing what was happening. Your lady mother sent me to see what it was all about. At the stage door I learned the names of the champions. I went immediately to Maria Joaquina's box, which overlooks the orchestra, and I had just gone in when I saw a corporal and two soldiers with bayonets on their rifles, who after having pushed their way past everyone in the stalls, climbed over into the orchestra pit. The corporal arrested Todi and told him to follow them. Todi stood up and obeyed. At the moment when Todi was coming out of the orchestra pit accompanied by the soldiers, Louise was coming onto the stage. In the twinkling of an eye she saw her husband being led away by the soldiers, gave a terrible cry, and ran after him. While this was going on on the stage, another scene was going on below, in the area through which one must pass to get out of the orchestra pit. No sooner had Todi found himself there in the darkness than, taking advantage of his knowledge of the place, he escaped the soldiers' hands, took the detours that he knew, went up on the stage, reached the small back door and was gone. A moment later the soldiers found their way again and ran after him. Louise knocked over everything she found in her way, the sentinel, men, women, nothing stopped her, she ran down the stairs four at a time and after her husband almost to the door of the large back court. I was asked to go after her, I ran there, and meeting one of the soldiers who told me that Todi had escaped I stopped her; the Count of Alvizan, who was on guard, and the Minister appeared and we made her come back up. She didn't cry, she howled; the most pleasant thing about it all was that through all this the opera did not stop for a moment, thanks to the ability of little Isabelle, who being on the stage at the moment of the catastrophe went on playing her part and sang it to the end of the act without the least mistake. I was nevertheless angry that Todi had run away, as that would necessarily stop the whole opera. Louise would certainly neither wish nor be able to continue playing her part. As I came back in the theatre I heard her shouting for her husband and asking me where he was. I answered immediately: 'Your husband is a fool; why did he have to run away?'[42] The moment I had said the word 'fool' she became furious with me: 'How dare you call my husband a fool in front of me?'[43] I feared she would rip off my eyes. I tried to appease her. There was no way. Someone came to summon me in the Marchioness' name and I decided to let her cry and leave her. We went back up, the Minister and myself, into your lady mother's box, where we found all the Foreign Ministers, Mr Manuel Bernardo de Melo and the Count of Alvizan, to whom your lady mother kept saying that Todi should be set free and the poor Count kept answering that he did not know where he was, but no matter how much he swore and protested, your lady mother would not believe him and had got it into her head that it was a slight on the part of the Count. In the middle of all this arrive Mme Todi in tears and Cécile all red with anger asking for mercy. The Count of Alvizan, who had sent everywhere in search of Todi, went out himself to see if there was any news of him, and while he was going one way, Todi appeared from another, brought by the corporal who had followed in his steps and had arrested him. Learning on arrival that he was free, he came immediately to your lady mother's box; the moment she saw him, his wife passed from extreme grief to extreme joy. It was a touching spectacle for the Marchioness and for all present. After the first moments of tenderness, Todi, Louise and Cécile all started to inveigh in chorus against Scolari but they were making such a noise that your lady mother told them to be quiet, scolded Todi and sent him back to the orchestra after advising him to go on performing his duty without saying anything, without the least rancour and as if nothing had happened. Then she called for Scolari, whom she told to be less impulsive and more prudent and whom she gave express recommendation that an end should be put to this affair. As a result order was restored and the opera went on better than ever until the end. In the midst of it all poor Bruno had the air of a criminal in the oratorio. 'I'm the one who'll have to pay for all these foolishnesses', he said sadly. The truth is that this is unfortunate for him; and the truth is also that although Todi is an arrogant fellow, on this occasion he was not the one to start the trouble. Scolari is an insolent chap who comes drunk to the theatre almost every day and who since he has been here has caused twenty such scenes. The same thing happened between him, the Sestini and the Falquini and every day he has some hard and obscene things to say to these poor girls, who do what they can. He is chapelmaster and is right in wishing that his work be performed as he wants, but this gives him no right to insult anyone. He is a very good musician but a very dangerous and very brutal person.[44]

This was apparently the last Italian opera to have been performed at the Bairro Alto Theatre, for reasons which will be discussed below.[45] Even if we take into account the ambiguous meaning with which the term opera was employed in this period, the half-dozen extant librettos from this theatre can hardly correspond to the total number of operas that were put on stage there. Mr Antonio's company, which appeared in the 1762–3 and 1763–4 seasons, seems to have been a true opera company. No details

Teatro da Rua dos Condes, demolido em 1882

(Desenho de M. de Ma...)

*Fig. 5 The Teatro da Rua dos Condes, demolished in 1882.*

are available either of the Italian operas performed during the 1768–9 season, unless they were the same which were produced at the Rua dos Condes Theatre.

Accounts preserved in the AHMF, Caixa 5, show that the royal family used to attend performances at the Bairro Alto. According to them, the royal boxes were decorated for their visit on the following dates:

| | |
|---|---|
| 1765 | 1 August, 8 September, 3 November, 4 December |
| 1766 | 20 April, 8 and 16 June |
| 1767 | 8 September |
| 1768 | 11, 25 October, 8 December |
| 1769 | 28 May, 24 August, 10 September, 15 October |
| 1770 | 2 and 23 September, 21 October, 27 December |
| 1774 | January |

## The Rua dos Condes Theatre (1762–75)

The Rua dos Condes Theatre was also built, or rebuilt, after the earthquake.[46] According to the *Journal de littérature* of 1781, it was smaller but more ornate than the Bairro Alto. It also had four tiers of boxes, but only twenty-four boxes in each. Judging by a late nineteenth-century drawing,[47] its external appearance was pretty shabby. Mention has been made of the 'opera' *Ciro reconhecido*, which was performed there in 1762, and also of its association with the Bairro Alto Theatre after 1764. The first librettos of Italian operas performed there after the earthquake are for 1765, and they do not indicate the names of the singers. Carvalhais' copy of *La contadina in corte* (which was dedicated to the Countess of Oeiras) had a few names added in pen, including that of Maria Joaquina in the role of Tancia.[48] *Il mercato di Malmantile* was dedicated to the Duke of Cadaval and its first performance was announced by the theatre managers for 28 July 1765 in the *Hebdomadario Lisbonense*. The *balli* for the three 1765 operas were written and directed by Angelo Giacomazzi.

The librettos of *Il ciarlone* and *La calamità de' cuori* of 1766 do not indicate the names of the singers either. Those of the next two operas, *L'olandese in Italia* and *Il proseguimento del ciarlone*, show that they were sung by Nicodemo Calcina, Salvatore Carobene, Geltrude Falchini, Giovanni Battista Gherardi, Veronica Gherardi, Rosa Scannavini and Giuseppe Secchioni. According to the librettos, the music of *Il ciarlone* was by Giuseppe Avossa (or Abbos) and that of *Il proseguimento* by Luigi Marescalchi, but it is interesting to note that in the summer of 1767 a version of *Il ciarlone* with music by Marescalchi was sung in Madrid at the Teatro de S. Ildefonso by a company which included the singers Fiorini, and Giovanni and Veronica Gherardi.[49] Marescalchi himself was also in Lisbon in 1766, as his signature appears in the register of the Irmandade de Santa Cecília on 28 July of that year.

The libretto of *L'olandese in Italia* bears a letter of dedication to the ambassador of the Low Countries, Baron Reinier de Haesten, dated September 1766. That of *Il proseguimento del ciarlone* is dedicated to the Marchioness of Louriçal, and includes a letter written by the librettist and singer Fiorini, where he says that, having seen *Il ciarlone* performed that year at the theatre of the Marquis of Louriçal, he had been inspired to work on the second part of the same play.[50]

The next librettos that survive from the Rua dos Condes are for 1768. *Demetrio* by Perez, performed in the autumn, was sung by Angiola Brusa, Geltrude Falchini, Gaetano N. N. (Quilici?), Anna and Giovanna Sestini, and Giuseppe Trebbi. The *balli* were by Paolo Cavazza, and performed by him and the following dancers: Luigi Antonio, Francesca and Giovanni Battista Falchini, Ranieri Pozzini, Rubbini, Regina and Rosa Tedeschini, Caterina Verga, and Angiola Zucchelli. The costumes for the opera were designed by Paolino Solenghi (the tailor of the royal theatres) and those for the *balli* by José António. The sets were painted by Simão Caetano Nunes. The theatre manager was one of the violinists of the Royal Chamber, Gonçalo Auzier Romero, who dedicated the libretto to the Marchioness of Tancos.

*La betulia liberata* by Scolari, performed in Lent, is described as an 'opera drammatica ... da rappresentarsi'. The singers included, besides the above named, Gaetano Scovelli, known as *Il biondino*. The libretto was dedicated to D. Maria Majer (Mayer?) while that of *Artaserse*, performed during Carnival, was dedicated to the Marchioness of Louriçal. A third work by Scolari that was probably performed in that year is *L'Arcifanfano*, whose undated libretto is dedicated to David Perez.

In 1771 an attempt was made to reorganise all theatrical activity in Lisbon. An extensive description of the facts surrounding it appears in a note to the 1816 edition of António Diniz da Cruz e Silva's heroic-comic poem *O hissope*,[51] which was attributed by Teófilo Braga to Timothée Lecusson Verdier.[52] Whoever its author may have been, he was certainly a contemporary or near contemporary of the facts he describes, which makes his testimony particularly valuable, even if remaining evidence shows it to be not entirely accurate. The note refers to the line in the poem which reads 'Si tu, oh estremada Zamperini', and is as follows:

*Zamperini* Venetian actress and singer who came to Lisbon in 1770, as *prima donna* of an Italian company that had been hired in Italy by Sr Galli, apostolic notary to the Nunciature and banker to the Roman Curia.

The Rua dos Condes theatre was given to this *virtuous* society. As *Italian opera* had not been heard for some time in Lisbon, the arrival of these *virtuosi* caused quite a stir, in particular the *Senhora Zamperini*, who along with her family was given splendid lodgings. This *Zamperini* family consisted of three sisters and their father, a robust and good-looking man, who, despite a large wig, with which he wished to defeat any clever guesses at his own age, showed however by his face that he was in a position to demand from *Senhora Zamperini* something less than pious and filial respect, and to grant her something more than his paternal blessing.

As it became necessary to fund this theatrical speculation, those who were interested in it had the idea of having recourse to the son of the Marquis of *Pombal*, the *Count of Oeiras*, who was then the President of the *Lisbon* City Senate. The latter was already a captive of the charming voice of the siren *Zamperini*, and he easily agreed to the plan which was proposed to him. Under his auspices a society was to be formed with a capital of 100,000 *cruzados* [40:000$000], divided into 100 shares of 400$000 each. In order to gather this amount promptly, a trick was played on some Portuguese and foreign merchants, who were summoned to come to the Senate on a certain date, at a certain hour, without being told the purpose of the meeting. There they heard from the mouth of the Count-President the conditions for the new theatrical Society. For some of them the fear of being thought ill of by the Government, for the others the wish to please the son of the Prime Minister, were the motives which made them all sign those conditions, of which the most grievous was the amount, which they immediately subscribed.

It seems that one of the odd aims of the inventors and agents of this Society was to impose a fine on the austere gravity of some of the old merchants; for in the list of shareholders, most of the names are those of aged persons, who had never been seen at a public entertainment.[53] This same meeting appointed four directors and theatrical inspectors, who with the utmost unselfishness rejected any commission or salary, being satisfied with the reward of a box in the theatre for all four of them. Those who were appointed *nemine discrepante* were *Inácio Pedro Quintela*, Purveyor of the Company of *Gran-Pará e Maranhão*, and uncle of the present Baron of *Quintela*, *Alberto Meyer*, *Joaquim José Estolano de Faria*, and *Teotonio Gomes de Carvalho*.

A few months after the theatre had opened under this management, the above-mentioned father of *Senhora Zamperini* died; the management gave him a costly funeral, and on the thirtieth day after his death magnificent exequies in the

Church of Loreto[54] where he was buried. Some critics with sharp tongues had spread the rumour that the funeral address at these exequies would be given by *Padre Macedo*,[55] a very good and justly credited preacher of those days, and a poet who had already written several sonnets, etc., in praise of the *Zamperini*. The Patriarch *D. Francisco de Saldanha*, fearing that this might happen called *Padre Macedo* to his presence and forbade him to preach in these exequies, to go to the *Opera*, or to write verses to *Zamperini*, and ordered him to wear a wig, instead of the way he wore his hair, *à italiana*, well-combed, and very powdered. *Padre Macedo* answered giving the example of the priests of the Nunciature, who all wore pomade and powders; and citing the fact that the wig was against canon law; for even those priests who wore it on account of disease, were obliged to ask for a dispensation from Rome, which was taxed at a *quartinho* [1$200] and was valid for a year. But all this was to no avail, for the Patriarch was unrelenting in this matter of the wig, and he only relaxed his order of not going to the *Opera*, on condition that he would not appear in the stalls, but only appear towards the rear of some box, such as that of the auditor of the Nunciature, *Antonini*, the secretary of the Cardinal *Conti*, *Padre Carlos Bacher*, and other Italian priests who like him attended the Opera and Zamperini's house.

*Padre Macedo* was not the only passionate admirer of *Zamperini*; many national and foreign poets offered her the obsequious inspiration of the Muses. Among them was the chargé d'affaires of France, the Chevalier de Montigny, whose verses were still remembered. In all states and all age-groups did this Siren find profitable admirers. On holy days she gathered a numerous and dazzling crowd at the last Mass at the Church of Loreto, which she used to attend.

In less than two years, immediately after the death of the director *Inácio Pedro Quintela*, the capital of the theatrical Society had been spent, and the revenue was so small that it scarcely covered the most essential expenses for the most ordinary things. The managers stopped paying the salaries of the artists and the members of the orchestra. Among them was a certain *Schiattini* [Innocenzo Schettini], a tenor-alto ['tenor acontraltado'], a jolly fellow and a poet, who, because he had asked his due in a style which did not please the managers, was lodged by them in the madhouse, from where he was taken to the theatre each time there was an opera. *Schiattini* took advantage of the privilege associated with the lodgings to which he had been assigned to take his revenge by parodying on stage his role in the drama, with spoken and sung satires that amused the audience at the cost of the managers. They grew even more angry, and poor *Schiattini*, seeing himself in a tighter spot, appealed to King José, who, after being informed of the injustice with which he was being treated, took him into his Chapel.[56]

It seems needless to say that this theatrical enterprise lasted only until mid-1774, when the Marquis of *Pombal* had *Zamperini* expelled from Lisbon, and even more needless to describe the causes of this Government order; I will only say that the shareholders did not receive anything from this society, for it was pawned and in debt to countless creditors. They did not have any other profit than that of not being bound by more than the capital, which each one of them had thought of as lost the moment they had subscribed to it.

I agree that this note is long enough; but I thought it necessary to give my readers a true fragment of the history of our theatre, and of this *Senhora Zamperini*, who is so well-praised in these eight lines of our Poet. He himself did not miss the chance to admire the gifts of this celebrated *virtuosa*, for as he was an intimate friend of Teotónio Gomes de Carvalho, he was frequently admitted to, and seen in, the management's box.

Several details in Verdier's narrative, and in particular the possible reasons behind the creation of the *Sociedade para a Subsistencia dos Theatros Publicos de Lisboa*, need to be corrected in the face of surviving documents. One of them is a list of contracts preserved in the Teatro Nacional de S. Carlos[57] that shows that the Zamperini family arrived in Portugal (at the border town of Elvas) only on 19 June 1772, one whole year after the Society had been created, and that therefore the Count of Oeiras' interest in the singer could hardly have had anything to do with it.

The original petition for the creation of the Society was presented to the King on 31 May 1771 and its statutes approved and published on 17 June of that same year.[58] The petition was presented by José Joaquim Estolano de Faria, Anselmo José da Cruz Sobral, Alberto Mayer and Teotónio Gomes de Carvalho, and was signed by forty Lisbon merchants. It uses very characteristic arguments to justify the establishment of public theatres, claiming that when these were well regulated they were the public school where the people learned the healthier maxims of politics, morality, love of their land, and the fidelity with which they should serve their sovereigns, and where they became civilised, thereby shedding the remnants of barbarism that the unhappy centuries of ignorance had left in them.

The statutes consisted of thirty-three articles, the first of which established that the Society's name would be *Instituição estabelecida para a subsistencia dos theatros publicos da corte*,[59] its capital being that mentioned by Verdier. The remaining articles established among other things that the Society would be run by a board of four directors, who would be annually elected in the presence of the President of the City Senate, and each of whom would have a key to the safe.[60] During the first six years no money could be drawn from the Society and no profits would be distributed, as the main end of the Society was not to make money, but rather to support the theatre, whose income was always very uncertain (articles v–viii). The Society would present its balance and accounts to the Government every year. It would cease when its capital had been exhausted. The shareholders' responsibility amounted only to their part in the capital (article vi).

The Society pledged to support at least two theatres, one for the operas and Italian comedies and the other for Portuguese comedies and dramas. No other theatres would be allowed in Lisbon. No one else in Lisbon could present *balli*, serenatas, operas, oratorios, dramas, comedies, fireworks, etc., under threat of jail and a fine of 200$000 that would be paid to the Royal Hospital (de Todos-os-Santos). Only the balls and *assembleias de nações estrangeiras* were exempted from this prohibition (articles viii and ix).

It was declared that the acting profession was not dishonourable. For the duration of their contracts artists could not be arrested for a civil or a criminal suit without an order of the theatre inspector, save if they were caught in the act. Their salaries could not be embargoed either, but the directors could ask the inspector to arrest any of the actors who did not fulfil their obligations. Their case would be immediately brought before the City Senate. Those actors who did not accept the Society's terms could not be hired by the provincial theatres for the same amount or lower than had been offered them (articles X–XII). Performances would be attended by an inspector or minister who would maintain order, assisted by a military officer. The contracts with the actors would be drawn up by the inspector (articles XIII–XV).

Decorations, costumes and sets for the theatres imported from abroad would be exempted from taxes, but they could not be sold to third parties (article XVI).

One of the directors was responsible for the accounting, administration and foreign correspondence, another for choosing the plays, distributing the parts, regulating rehearsals, etc., a third for the sets, decorations, lighting, etc., and a fourth for inspecting the construction and commodities, and for the archive, the storehouses, the actors' houses, etc. They would meet at least once a week on a Monday, and would determine the days and hours of performances and have billboards affixed. There would be no performances during Lent. One of the directors would always attend and direct each performance from the directors' box (articles XVII–XXIII).

Only two boxes and two *frisas* (boxes on the main floor) would be free: one for the directors, another for the President of the City Senate, and the other two for the inspector and the military authority. Admission tickets costing 240 rs would be issued to people with no fixed place. Women, as well as the equerry and servants of box owners had free entry. A special ticket would be issued to anyone wishing to go out of the theatre and in again during performances, or to circulate in the theatre. Yearly subscribers to the boxes and the stalls would benefit from a 10 per cent discount. Yearly subscribers to the boxes would be given an entry ticket, which they could give to whomever they pleased. Subscriptions would be paid at the end of each month. Failure to pay would entail the suspension of the right of admission, and debts would be collected through the courts. For performances other than operas or Portuguese comedies prices would be lower. Prices could only be raised with royal permission. Any of the decisions of the directors would be communicated to the President of the City Senate, who would bring them to the presence of the King when necessary (articles XXIV–XXXI).

Ticket prices would be as follows:

|  | Theatre for dramas and Portuguese comedies [Bairro Alto Theatre] | Theatre for operas and Italian comedies [Rua dos Condes Theatre] |
|---|---|---|
| **1st floor** | | |
| Proscenium boxes | 2$000 | 2$400 |
| Four boxes at the back | 2$400 | 3$200 |
| Remaining side boxes | 1$200 | 1$600 |
| **2nd floor** | | |
| Four proscenium boxes | 2$400 | – |
| Four boxes at the back | 3$000 | Two side boxes 3$200 |
| Remaining side boxes | 1$600 | 2$000 |
| **3rd floor** | | |
| Four proscenium boxes | 2$000 | 2$400 |
| Five boxes at the back | 2$400 | 3$200 |
| Remaining side boxes | 1$200 | 2$000 |
|  | Five verandas at the back | 2$400 |
|  | Four proscenium boxes | 1$600 |
| Upper stalls | $300 | $480 |
| Lower stalls | $240 | $400 |
| Verandas | $160 | $240 |

Benevides[61] comments that these same prices obtained in the S. Carlos Theatre for more than fifty years from its inauguration in 1793.

The Society borrowed 6:000$000 from the City Senate on 13 March 1773 and again 1:600$000 and 1:000$000 on 13 and 20 June.[62] A rough estimate shows that during the first operatic season of 1772–3 nearly 30:000$000 was spent on singers' and dancers' salaries alone. Notwithstanding the scandals involving Zamperini and her admirers, some echoes of which are mentioned below, the true reasons behind the financial failure of this theatrical venture are probably those that plagued most commercial opera enterprises in the eighteenth century, namely their excessive cost.

Table 3 gives the essential data contained in the list of contracts preserved at the Teatro Nacional de S. Carlos archive, with the names of the singers and dancers alphabetically reordered and corrected in accordance with the librettos. Some of the singers are classified according to the *Indice de' spettacoli teatrali per il carnevale dell'anno 1773*, published in Milan by Pietro Agnelli and quoted in Carvalhais.[63] Anna and Antonia Zamperini had received 500 zecchini as advance payment in Venice on 2 April 1771. Several other singers also received advance payments from Padre Bernardo, an associate of Padre Galli, between 21 March 1771 and 7 June 1772, in the following cities: Modena, Milan, Bologna, Florence, Mantua and Barcelona.

Sestini is identified in the *Indice* as Giovanna Stogler Sestini (she appears as D. Joana Sestini in several librettos). Burney[64] says of her that she came from Lisbon to London and that her voice was beautiful, clear and sweet-toned, her figure elegant, and her acting graceful. Of Zamperini he says that she was a very pretty woman, but an affected singer.

Carvalhais[65] notes that the Zamperini sisters created several of the roles that they later sang in Lisbon at the Teatro San Moisè in Venice, such as those in *L'anello incantato* by Bertoni (Autumn 1771), *L'isola di Alcina* by Gazzaniga and *La contessa di Bimbimpoli* by Astaritta (Carnival, 1772), a witness to the fact that in those days it was often the singers who were responsible for spreading the repertoire throughout Europe. For most of this period we do not know who the musical directors were either at the Rua dos Condes or the Bairro Alto Theatre, but it seems certain that, with the already mentioned exceptions of Scolari and Marescalchi, they were not opera composers. Another exception is that of Alberto José Gomes da Silva, the author of *Il Geloso* of 1775, the only Portuguese composer to have had an opera performed in the public theatres in the third quarter of the century.

Anna Zamperini became the pretext for a war between poets, those of the Arcádia Lusitana on one side and those of the group of the Ribeira das Naus on the other, which is preserved in two manuscript collections.[66] Alberto Pimentel has published a selection of this poetry, partly in praise of the singer, partly satirising her (some of it in an obscene vein).[67] He mentions the following coinages that her name gave rise to: *zamparinar* (to applaud or court the Zamperini), *enzamparinar-se* (to fall sadly in love with her) and *zamperino* used as an adjective. The way she used her hat tipped over her forehead and falling towards her right ear became a fashion known as *chapéu à Zamparina*.

Of the dancers included in the list of contracts, the following were also choreographers: Venceslao de Rossi, Alessandro Guglielmi, Giuseppe Magni, and Isidore Jean Gabriel Dupré. The sets were by Simão Caetano Nunes and Antonio Stoppani, and the costumes by Domingos de Almeida. The combats for *Il Cidde* were rehearsed by the King's fencing-master, Pietro Antonio Faveri. The contracts also show that the dancers Bardelli, Anna and Giovanni Battista Bedotti, Constantini, Dannunzio, and Dupré performed also at the Bairro Alto Theatre between December 1773 and January 1774. The *Indice de' spettacoli* says that besides *balli*, Portuguese tragedies and comedies were performed during the same season in that theatre.

Table 3 *Singers and Dancers at the Rua dos Condes Theatre, 1772–5*

| Singer | Period of contract and supplementary data | Yearly salary |
|---|---|---|
| *Nicodemo Calcina* | 26 June 1772–†3 June 1773<br>800 zecchini at 1$620     =<br>for houses: 20 zecchini     = | 1:312$000 [*sic*]<br>+ 32$000 |
| *Sebastiano Folicaldi*, first tenor | 26 June 1772–Carnival 1775<br>1,000 zecchini     =<br>for houses: 20 zecchini     =<br>Between October 1774 and Carnival 1775 received 168$000 a month. | 1:600$000<br>+ 32$000 |
| *Vincenzo Goresi* | 14 June 1772–(Carnival) 1775<br>1st year: 300 zecchini     =<br>for houses: 20 zecchini     =<br>2nd and 3rd years:<br>Brought his wife. Had debts to the Count of Oeiras, to Francesco [Antonio?] Lodi, and to Giuseppe Trebbi. | 480$000<br>+ 32$000<br>364$800 |
| *Massimo Giuliani*, second tenor; *parte seria* and *mezzo-carattere* in the *drammi giocosi* | Easter 1772–Carnival 1774<br><br>He had houses and received 50 zecchini at the end of his contract. | 480$000 |
| *Maria Joaquina* | 25 July 1773–28 February 1775<br>Hired for 60$000 a month.<br>Total received: | 1:033$545 |
| *Antonio Marchesi*[68] | Easter 1772–Carnival 1774<br>1st year:<br><br>2nd year: | 480$000<br>+160$000<br>500$000 |
| *Innocenzo Schettini*, 'tenor acontraltado' (see p. 93 above) | 8 March 1774–11 October 1774<br>7 months and 3 days<br>Hired for 700 zecchini + 30 zecchini for houses. Brought his wife. Became mad on October 11. | 662$667<br>+ 28$400 |
| *Anna Sestini*, *secondo uomo* in the *drammi serii*; *parte seria* and *mezzo-carattere* in the *drammi giocosi* | Easter 1772–Carnival 1774 | 400$000 |

## Table 3 (*cont.*)

| Singer | Period of contract and supplementary data | Yearly salary |
|---|---|---|
| *Giovanna Sestini, prima buffa*[69] | Easter 1772–Carnival 1774 | 2:000$000 |
| *Teresa Turchi Sestini* | Easter 1772–Carnival 1774 | 400$000 |
| *Antonio Tedeschi*, first tenor; *parte seria* and *mezzo carattere* in the *drammi giocosi* | 26 June 1772–4 June 1773<br>425 zecchini =<br>for houses: 20 zecchini =<br>Was probably dismissed, receiving 932$235. | 680$000<br>+ 32$000 |
| *Luísa Todi* | 1 June 1774–30 June 1775<br>On 4 October 1774, she received her part for *Calandrano* and started being paid. On 29 January 1775, she returned the part of the opera of Maestro Alberto [José Gomes da Silva] and did not want to go on performing, and on the 27th she refused to attend the rehearsal. | 1:200$000 |
| *Giuseppe Trebbi*, first tenor | 1 April 1772–5<br>1st and 2nd years<br>for houses<br>3rd year | 1:280$000<br>+ 32$000<br>1:552$000 |
| *Anna* and *Antonia Zamperini* | 19 June 1772–28 February 1775<br>1,000 zecchini each =<br>They had houses and from 23 November 1773, a carriage and two mules, which, with the chapelmaster (?) cost 32$400. They received 640$000 to return home. | 3:200$000 |
| Dancer | Period of contract and supplementary data | Yearly salary |
| *Beatrice Bardelli* | 14 June 1772–28 February 1775<br>1st year: 200 zecchini =<br>for houses: 20 zecchini =<br>2nd and 3rd years | 320$000<br>+ 32$000<br>288$000 |

## Table 3 (*cont.*)

| Dancer | Period of contract and supplementary data | | Yearly salary |
|---|---|---|---|
| *Anna Maria* and *Giovanni Battista Bedotti* (sister and brother) | 30 May 1773–5 750 zecchini for houses: 40 zecchini | = = | 1:200$000 + 64$000 |
| *Rosa Campora* | Easter 1772–23 February 1775 <br><br> for houses <br> Was dismissed, receiving 524$000. | | 480$000 28$000 |
| *Geltrude Cioli* | 14 June 1772–Carnival 1775 1st year: 182 zecchini for houses: 20 zecchini In the 2nd year she received 288 rs a month and no houses. | = = | 292$000 32$000 |
| *Giuseppe Constantini* | 14 June 1772–†(?)27 August 1774 1st year: 400 zecchini for houses 2nd year: 300 zecchini Had a fit on 27 August 1774, and in all probability died. | = = | 640$000 + 38$000 480$000 |
| *Pietro Dannunzio* | 14 June 1772–4 365 scudi romani for houses: 20 zecchini | = = | 313$900 + 32$000 |
| *Isidore Jean Gabriel Dupré* | 1 April 1772–5 £30,000 Was hired in Paris. | = | 2:800$000 |
| *Giovanni Ferraresi* | Easter 1772–Carnival 1773 | | 368$000 |
| *Luigi Grazioli, Il Schizza* | 15 June 1774–Carnival 1774 24$000 a month | = | 204$000 |
| *Geltrude Guadagnini* | Easter 1772–23 February 1773 <br><br> She received 245$311. | | 240$000 |

Table 3 (*cont.*)

| Dancer | Period of contract and supplementary data | Yearly salary |
|---|---|---|
| *Alessandro* and *Anna Guglielmi* (husband and wife) | 26 June 1772–16 May 1774<br>the husband: 700 zecchini    =<br>the wife: 300 zecchini    =<br>for houses: 30 zecchini    =<br>They received 160$000 to return home. | 1:120$000<br>480$000<br>+ 48$000 |
| *Eusebio Luzzi* | 26 June 1772–4<br>500 zecchini    =<br>for houses: 20 zecchini    = | 800$000<br>+ 32$000 |
| *Giuseppe Magni* | 14 June 1772–4<br>400 zecchini    =<br>for houses: 20 zecchini    = | 640$000<br>+ 32$000 |
| *Marie Hélène Flamant Mercadet*; her son, *Jean Rémige Mercadet*; her niece, *Marie Moissonier* | 1 April 1772–31 March 1773<br>They lived with Dupré. | ? |
| *Vittorio Perini* | Easter 1772–23 February 1773 | 600$000 |
| *Francesca Pirotti* | Easter 1772–Carnival 1773<br><br>She only received 17$280 in April 1772, because she fell sick. | 432$000 |
| *Teresa Rosignoli* | 14 June 1772–28 February 1775<br>300 zecchini giliati    =<br>for houses: 20 zecchini    = | 522$000<br>+ 32$000 |
| *Teresa Tizzoni Rossi* (wife of Venceslao de Rossi) | 28 March 1772–4<br>600 zecchini    =<br>for houses: 20 zecchini    =<br>She received 200 zecchini for the journey to and from Lisbon. | 960$000<br>+ 32$000 |
| *Venceslao de Rossi* | 26 June 1772–4<br>600 zecchini    =<br>for houses: 20 zecchini    = | 960$000<br>+ 32$000 |

Table 3 (*cont.*)

| Dancer | Period of contract and supplementary data | Yearly salary |
|---|---|---|
| *Anna* and *Carlo Sabbatini* (sister and brother) | Easter 1772–Carnival 1773<br>1:184$000 each<br>and houses | = 2:368$000 |
| *Michele Saraceni* | 26 June 1772–4<br>365 scudi romani<br>for houses: 20 zecchini | = 313$900<br>= + 32$000 |
| *Magdalena Tessaroli* | 26 June 1772–18 March 1773<br>300 zecchini giliati<br>for houses: 20 zecchini<br>and a mirror of good glass | = 522$000<br>= + 32$000 |
| *Peregrino Turchi* and his wife | Carnival 1775, ending 28 February<br>130 pesos duros<br>With carriages to take them to the rehearsals. They would not receive anything if on the first day they did not please the public. | = 104$000 |
| *Anna Zoccoli* | 22 June 1772–15 October 1773<br>550 zecchini<br>for houses: 20 zecchini<br>She was to be paid her return trip to Genoa, but she ran away on 15 October. | = 880$000<br>= + 32$000 |
| *Angiola Zucchelli*[70] | Easter 1772–Carnival 1774<br>1st year:<br>2nd and 3rd years: | 528$000<br>768$000 |
| Others | Period of contract and supplementary data | Yearly salary |
| *José Arsénio* [*da Costa*], extra and actor in the dances | May 1772–February 1773 | 106$000 |
| *Nicola Belleti*, prompter | 21 July 1772–30 July 1773 | 54$000 |

Table 3 *(cont.)*

| Others | Period of contract and supplementary data | | Yearly salary |
|---|---|---|---|
| *Gasparo Camilo Guedoti,* (dancer?) | 14 June 1772–28 February 1775 | | |
| | 14$200 a month | = | 170$400? |
| | for houses: 20 zecchini | = | + 32$000 |
| *Fernando António de Miranda*, prompter | March 1773–28 February 1775 | | |
| | 97$440 for 2 years | = | 48$720 |
| *Francesco Saverio Todi,* violinist | 7 July 1774–January 1775 He received 2$400 for each night he played. For thirty-four performances between September 1774 and January 1775 he received 81$600. | | |

Not included in this list, but appearing in the librettos, are the following names:

Lambert Beau, dancer (*Il barone di Rocca antica*, 1773; *Il geloso*, 1775)
Jean Baptiste Flambeau, dancer (*Il geloso*, 1775)
Giovanni Battista Luzzi, dancer (*L'anello incantato*, 1772)
Antonio Pesci, dancer (*Il disertore*, 1772)
Domenico Rosetelli, dancer (*Il Cidde*, 1773)
Cecilia Zamperini, singer (*La sposa fedele*, 1773; *Il geloso*, 1775)
Pietro Zoccoli, dancer (*Il geloso*, 1775)

A brief comparison between the above data and those available for the court theatres will show that top singers and dancers at the Rua dos Condes were paid as well, if not better, as those in the royal service.[71]

The royal family were also frequent visitors to the Rua dos Condes Theatre. Documents in the AHMF, Caixa 5, show that they visited the theatre on the following dates:

1765  29 September, 8 and 26 December
1766  11 and 19 May, 1 June, 5 and 13 July, 16, 21 and 30 November, 8 and 28 December
1767  2, 9, 16, 23 and 30 August, 6, 13, 20 and 27 September, 18 October, 27 December
1768  1 and 3 January, 2 June, 10, 17, 24 and 31 July, 7 and 14 August, 4, 11, 18, 25 and 29 September, 16 October, 6 November, 28 December
1769  1 January, 4 and 11 June, 2, 16 and 30 July, 13 and 20 August, 3, 17 and 24 September, 18 October

1770    3, 4, 5, 10, 14 and 17 June, 22 and 29 July, 5, 19 and 26 August, 8, 16
        and 29 September, 28 October
1771    1 January, 21 July, 4ᵃ, 11 and 18 August, 1 September
1772    31 May, 18 June, 2ᵃ, 9ᵃ, 16ᵃ, 23ᵃ, and 30ᵃ August, 6, 20 and 27
        September, 18 and 28 October, 8 November, 21 December
1773    23 and 31 May, 27 June, 18 July, 8ᵃ, 15ᵃ, 22ᵃ and 29ᵃ August, 5, 12, 19
        and 26 September
1774    October

[a] On these dates there was also a bullfight at the Terreiro do Paço.

Wraxall[72] has left an interesting description of those visits:

As soon as the Bull Feast ended, which was commonly about six o'clock, the King, Queen, and Royal family immediately repaired to the Italian Opera, which was at a very inconsiderable distance, in the same quarter of Lisbon. Such was the invariable Usage, or Etiquette, every Sunday. Yet, there, as at the Bull Feast, though seated in the front of the Theatre, they were supposed to preserve their Incognito. Joseph's dress, on these occasions, was always a full trimmed suit of silk, or of cloth; either quite plain, or embroidered with white silk; the sumptuary laws of Portugal prohibiting embroidery of gold or silver. He wore a flowing tye-wig ... and the Portuguese Order of Christ on his breast. The Queen and Princesses were covered with diamonds ... During the course of the performance, His Majesty never failed to go round to his private Box, close to the Stage, in order to view the Ballets, after each of which he returned to the Royal family. On these little excursions, which he always seemed to enjoy, and during which he generally made the best use of his time, with his Opera glas [*sic*], in contemplating the female part of the audience who filled the side Boxes, several Noblemen accompanied him.

## *The Rua dos Condes and Salitre Theatres (1778–93)*

Whatever the real reasons may have been, there was no public opera in Lisbon between 1775 and 1790. It has been said that after the Zamperini episode the Marquis of Pombal banned actresses from the Lisbon stages, but this ban can hardly have been total, or have remained in force for very long, if Cecília Rosa de Aguiar was still performing in 1780, as the already quoted article in the *Journal de littérature* of 1781 suggests. A number of booklets exist of plays performed in the Bairro Alto and the Rua dos Condes Theatres in the first years of Maria I's reign, namely in 1778, 1779 and 1780. Some problem seems to have arisen in this last year, as may be seen from a petition written on 15 December by Paulino José da Silva and Henrique Silva Quintanilha, respectively manager and owner of the Rua dos Condes Theatre.[73] In it they ask the Queen's permission to present comedies and tragedies in their theatre, performed *by men*, arguing that they had incurred expenses and that they were paying taxes on the theatre. They reminded the Queen that both her father and her grandfather frequently attended theatrical performances, approving by their presence an activity which did not offend propriety in any way.

Teatro do Salitre, demolido em 1879 para a construção da Avenida da Liberdade

*Fig. 6 The Teatro do Salitre, demolished in 1879.*

The opinion of the Intendent General of Police, Diogo Inácio de Pina Manique,[74] which is appended to this petition, is, if anything, amusing. In it he says that while it was true that the Church Fathers had forbidden Catholics to attend the theatres, this had been due to the obscenities of the Greek theatre. In modern times the theatre was a school of morality which censured vice. There were two theatres in Madrid, three in Paris, seven in Venice, two in Parma, and even the Empire of the World, the Head of all the Church, respectable Rome, had five. The petition should therefore be granted, especially since performances would all be given by men, and there would thus be no danger of disturbances occurring, which were unavoidable when many people of the opposite sex came together. And so as to prevent any abuses, no women should be allowed either backstage or in the set or costume rooms. There should be no curtains in the boxes, and no prostitutes allowed. All the plays would first have to be examined by the Tribunal da (Real) Mesa Censória.[75]

On 27 November 1782 João Gomes Varela opened a new theatre in the Rua do Salitre. Its architect and first manager was Simão Caetano Nunes, replaced in 1791 by Paulino José (da Silva?).[76] A note written by Pina Manique to the Home Secretary, José de Seabra da Silva, in 1792[77] says that the theatre had only one door. The stairs were not wide enough for two people to walk side by side. The corridors were such that if two people met, one of them would have to lean against the wall, to let the other pass with difficulty. He left to the consideration of the Minister what might happen in such a narrow place, where the two sexes met. The theatre foundations were made of wooden stakes.

The new theatre offered spoken drama and *balli*, as well as companies of acrobats and other attractions. Ticket prices for a concert given there by the violinist Antonio Lolli in 1787 were 9$600, 6$400 and 4$800 for the boxes, and 1$200 and $800 for the stalls, thrice as much as those established for the Rua dos Condes in 1771.[78] Even if these prices were probably exceptional, they suggest that the prices demanded at the Rua dos Condes may have been too low, as there was no significant rise in the cost of living between those two years, and may help explain the financial failure of the Sociedade para a Subsistencia dos Theatros Publicos.

This is how Beckford describes a performance at the Rua do Salitre in 1787:[79]

... the performance lasted above four hours and a half, from seven to near twelve. It consisted of a ranting prose tragedy, in three acts, called *Sesostris*, two ballets, a pastoral, and a farce. The decorations were not amiss and the dresses showy. A shambling, blear-eyed boy, bundled out in weeds of the deepest sable, squeaked and bellowed alternately the part of a widowed princess. Another hob-e-di-hoy, tottering on high-heeled shoes, represented her Egyptian Majesty, and warbled two airs with all the nauseous sweetness of a fluted falsetto. Though I could have boxed his ears for surfeiting mine so filthily, the audience were of a very different opinion, and were quite enthusiastic in their applause.

Speaking of the Rua dos Condes, Beckford says that Her Majesty's absolute commands having swept females off the stage, their parts were acted by calvish young fellows.[80] Murphy, writing in 1789–90, says:[81]

There are two theatres here for dramatic performances;[82] on Sundays they are much crowded. I could perceive but few ladies among the audience, and these with few exceptions, sat, not promiscuously in the company of men, as in other theatres, but apart. The music was excellent, the dresses and scenery tolerable, the acting indifferent, or rather bad. Of late years no females were allowed to perform on the stage; hence the men were obliged to assume the female garb. How provoking it was to see the tender, the beautiful Ignez de Castro represented by one of these brawny, artificial wenches ... instead of the delicate faltering accents of the fair victim he roared,

> – like the ocean when the winds
> Fight with the waves

Even though the reintroduction of actresses was timidly defended in the *Jornal encyclopedico* of August 1789 and January 1792[83] (with the proviso that those plays where they represented immoral passions, intrigues and other falsities should be abolished) this ban was only lifted in Lisbon in 1799. The ban does not seem to have been in force in Oporto.[84]

One minor genre which became very fashionable in this period is that of the *elogios dramáticos* performed to celebrate the anniversaries of members of the royal family, who again became visitors to the Rua dos Condes and Salitre Theatres, as is shown by several entries in the AHMF accounts. Thus in February 1782 Paulino José da Silva received 127$150 'for the expenses he incurred in rebuilding the room, boxes and stable in the Opera House at the Rua dos Condes, which are usually used by their Majesties.' He received further sums of money for the same purpose in May, August, September and October 1787.[85] In December 1787 Petronio Mazzoni also received 425$455 to prepare the Salitre Theatre so that the royal family could go there to see the opera and a further sum in May 1788 for both the Salitre and the Rua dos Condes Theatres.[86]

The French ambassador, the Marquis de Bombelles, describes some of those visits to the public theatres in 1787–8. He expresses surprise that such an austere Princess, who had been so reluctant to let the theatres in her capital be reopened, would allow herself to be led to one of the most indecent, which had attracted the condemnation of the Church.[87] His own opinion of the theatres generally confirms that of other foreign visitors.

The composer Marcos Portugal (1762–1830), who was to become quite popular in Italy and elsewhere after 1792, started his dramatic career at the Salitre Theatre in 1782. Only two of the several scores he wrote for the *elogios dramáticos*, *entremezes* and *dramas* performed there have apparently survived.[88] Among those lost, three were written for translations of Italian *burlette* which are also classified as such in the author's autograph catalogue,[89] and may have been sung throughout. These are *A noiva fingida* (or *Le trame deluse*) and *Os viajantes ditosos* (or *I viaggiatori felici*) of 1790, and *O Lunático iludido* (or *Il mondo della luna*) of 1791. The *aviso* printed in the libretto of *Os viajantes ditosos* is a curious defence of Portuguese vocal music:[90]

We are persuaded that the public is satisfied with the efforts we have made to demonstrate that our language is susceptible of all that soft and gentle harmony with which Music slowly and pleasurably penetrates those expressions that Poetry uses in the Theatre to instruct and entertain ... It is true that Italy has the right to give a more pleasant singing tone to the Theatres of all nations, not only on account of its pure language, which allows itself to be cut, extended, and accommodated to the measure of quavers, demi-semi-quavers, etc., but also because its old musical schools were always the first to have plenty of these pleasant compositions. But now that we see one such School established among us and protected by our august sovereigns, whence geniuses and talents emerge who are worthy of being set on a par with Jommelli, Perez, Paisiello, Cimarosa, and all the good Italians, why should we let them lose in idleness the fame that they might otherwise acquire? And why, having our own means of entertainment, should we always go and beg for foreign favours?

These *burlette* were performed by the same Portuguese actors who appeared in the remaining repertory of the theatre: Victor Porfírio de Borja (*terceira dama*), José Arsénio da Costa (*segundo gracioso*), José Felix da Costa, Custódio José da Graça (female roles), João Inácio, Victorino José Leite (*primeira dama*), Francisco Manuel Madeira (*segunda dama*), José Martins, José Procópio Monteiro, António Manuel Cardoso Nobre (*pri-*

*meiro galan*), José dos Santos (*primeiro gracioso de meio carácter*), António José da Serra (female roles), Diogo da Silva (*primeiro gracioso carregado*). The only Italian name connected with the Salitre Theatre is that of Nicola Ambrosini, who sang in the *Pequeno drama* of 1787.

The remaining information available for the last theatrical seasons in Lisbon before the inauguration of the S. Carlos Theatre stems from Formenti's *Indice de' teatrali spettacoli di tutto l'anno*[91] and from the librettos. On 21 August 1788 the drama *O prazer da Olissea* by Salvador Machado de Oliveira, with music by António da Silva Gomes e Oliveira, was performed at the Rua dos Condes, accompanied by a *ballo* directed by Alessandro Zucchelli. During the 1788–9 season, comedies and tragedies in Portuguese were performed at the Rua dos Condes, along with Italian *balli* directed by Antonio Marrafi.[92] For the 1789–90 season comedies and musical *entremezes* were performed by Portuguese actors, along with Italian *balli*, while another Italian dance company performed *balli* by Antonio Marrafi and Antonio Cianfanelli at the Salitre Theatre.[93]

In the 1790–1 season there was again opera at the Rua dos Condes, performed by a reduced company consisting of the following singers: Francesco Bartocci (*primo buffo, virtuoso di camera* of the Duke of Parma), Leonardo Martini (*prima donna*), Francesco Rossi (*seconda donna*) and Luigi Secchioni (who had also appeared in the same theatre as a dancer in the previous seasons). These were joined by Carlo Fidanza and António José da Silva in the *drammatica azione Il tempio della Gloria*, which the theatre manager Domingos de Almeida had ordered from Italy for the birthday of Queen Maria I on 17 December. Domingos de Almeida was also responsible for the costumes, while the architect, painter and theatrical machinist was Manuel da Costa. The *balli* were directed by Leopoldo Banchelli, Luigi Chiaveri and Pietro Pieroni. The musical director was António Leal Moreira.

In the 1791–2 season there were the following additions to the *buffo* company: Antonio Brizzi (*primo buffo*), Luigi Brizzi and Andrea Rastrelli (*primi mezzi-caratteri a vicenda*) and Antonio Soldati (*secondo mezzo-carattere*). Francesco Minola and Felice Cerliani from Milan were now theatre painter and machinist. The *balli* were by Leopoldo Banchelli, Carlo Bencini, Luigi Chiaveri and Pietro Pieroni. The music director was again António Leal Moreira, the first violinist in the operas was Estanislau Borges (Coelho), of the Royal Chamber, and that of the *balli* Giuseppe Filippi. The libretto for Gazzaniga's *Il Don Giovanni* indicates that the theatre manager was now Francesco Antonio Lodi. The repertoire for these two seasons was mainly centred on Paisiello, Cimarosa, and Gazzaniga.

During this season there were also a few concerts at the Rua dos Condes, which were announced in the *Gazeta de Lisboa*. The first was on 23 May, for the benefit of Pierre Gervais, a violinist in the Royal Chamber. Ticket prices were 6$400, 4$800 and 1$600 for the boxes, and $800 and $480 for the

*Fig. 7  The Teatro de S. Carlos.*

stalls, twice as much as those demanded in 1771. The programme, which was exceptionally announced in the *Gazeta*, was as follows:

1ª Huma Synfonia do célebre *Haiden*. 2ª Mr Rossi cantará huma Aria de *Cimarosa*. 3ª Mr. Gervais tocará na Rebeca hum Concerto de *Viotti*. 4ª Mr. *Bartozzi* cantará huma Aria de *Paesiello*. 5ª Huma Synfonia concertante de *Devienne* na qual executará os Solos de Fagote Mr. *Wettin*, e os de trompa Mr. *Wattmann*.[94] 6ª Mr. *Martini* cantará huma Aria de *Cimarosa*. 7ª Mr. *Gervais* com a Rebeca desafinada[95] executará huma Sonata de *Lolly*. 8ª Mrs. *Bartozzi*, *Martini*, e *Rossi* cantarão hum novo Terceto de *Guillelmi*. 9ª Acabará o Concerto com huma Arieta com variações executada por Mr. *Gervais*.

On 6 June there was a concert for the benefit of M. and Mme. Maréchal, who played the pianoforte and the harp, and at which several arias were also sung. On 14 November Wettin, alias Weltin, also gave a concert, where he played the bassoon, the oboe, and the flute, and Gervais performed a solo of his own composition.

The construction of the new S. Carlos Theatre began on 8 December 1792. The theatre was built on the initiative of the Intendent General of Police, Pina Manique, with funds supplied by a group of Lisbon capitalists: Joaquim Pedro Quintela (a nephew of the Inácio Pedro Quintela whom we have seen associated with the Sociedade para a Subsistencia dos Theatros Publicos), who gave the grounds, Anselmo José da Cruz Sobral, Jacinto Fernandes Bandeira, António Francisco Machado, João Pereira Caldas and João Ferreira Sola. The architect was José da Costa e Silva, who followed the plan of the S. Carlo Theatre in Naples, and the whole construction cost 165:845$196 (little more than the cost of the masonry work for the Ópera do Tejo in 1755).[96] The theatre was named S. Carlos in honour of Princess Carlota Joaquina, and incorporated in the property of the Casa Pia, a charitable institution directed by Pina Manique, but sixty years were to pass before the financial backers of the project and their descendants were fully reimbursed.

The S. Carlos Theatre was inaugurated on 30 June 1793 with *La ballerina amante* by Cimarosa. The managers were Francesco Antonio Lodi and Andrea Lenzi or Lence.[97] The music director was António Leal Moreira, but the opera company was a different one from that which had appeared at the Rua dos Condes. From then until the end of the century the S. Carlos was the only Italian opera house in Lisbon.[98]

## Opera in Oporto (1760–97)[99]

The only other city beside Lisbon that possessed a public opera house in our period was Oporto. The original motive behind its creation were the festivities promoted in 1760 by the City Senate, in honour of the wedding of Prince Pedro and his niece Princess Maria Francisca (the future Pedro III and Maria I). It was built in a stable belonging to the Duke of Lafões in the square of the Corpo da Guarda, and is thus sometimes called Teatro do Corpo da Guarda in contemporary documents.[100] Here the name Teatro Público, which is the one normally used in the librettos, will be retained.

Magalhães Basto[101] described the early history of this theatre based on documents preserved in the Gabinete Histórico da Cidade, among them a *Libro para servir de Receita e despeza q se faz na festividade dos despozorios da Snrᵃ Princeza com o Sor Hifante D. Pedro por ordem e conta do Senado*. The plan of the adaptation of the stable to a theatre was made by João Glama Strobel, who received 24$000. The whole construction cost 2:208$315. The opera company was hired in Lisbon by the Senate agent in that city, Lopo José de Azevedo Vargas. It had six singers, including the manager Nicola Setaro,[102] who would come to Oporto at their own expense to perform three *opere buffe*, of which two would be different. For this they would receive 288$000, and if the Senate was pleased with the operas they would perform them again for a further 288$000. If the Senate did not wish to do so, then Setaro might give these performances on his own initiative, with all expenses at his own cost, except the house and the stage. For the other operas the Senate would have the theatre ready at its own cost, including the lights and the orchestra. The first opera would be performed on 15 August.

The company arrived by land on 1 August, while nine boxes, a trunk and a bundle with the theatre props, as well as the company's personal luggage, arrived by sea. They gave four performances, the last of which, on 17 September, cost the Senate 96$000. There were at least two dancers. The orchestra had eighteen players, including two horns and one oboe, who received 266$000. The oboe player, Pasquale Marinaro, had also been hired in Lisbon and received 9$600. Augusto João Razel received 150$000 to compose (?) the opera and for its binding, and for accompanying the operas that were performed. He received a further 51$520 for unspecified reasons. An intriguing detail concerns the mention in the contract of the City Senate barns in the Alley of the Porta do Olival, where 'operas and *comedias* had been previously performed', but this is possibly just another broad use of the term opera in the sense alluded to at the beginning of this chapter. No traces exist either of any performances of the Setaro company in Lisbon prior to their coming to Oporto.

The next recorded performance of an opera in Oporto is that of the *dramma giocoso Il trascurato* (*O descuidado*) in 1762. According to a very rare libretto in Carvalhais' collection,[103] the singers were Alessandro Basili, Nicola Garsoni, Maria Giuntini, Lucia Paladini, Anna ('Aninhas'), and Nicola Setaro (who was also the manager), and Petronilla Trabò. The name Durel was added by hand. These are probably the same singers who appeared in 1760 and it is possible that they also performed in Oporto in 1761. Petronilla Trabò had sung at the Rua dos Condes Theatre in 1739–40.[104] The libretto was dedicated to D. Ana Joaquina de Lancastre, wife of the City Governor, Lieutenant-General João de Almada e Melo.

A review of this opera was published by Padre Francisco Bernardo de Lima in his *Gazeta literária* of June 1762.[105] It is the pretext for a long and very interesting essay on opera, by the pen of one of the most distinguished representatives of the Enlightenment in Portugal (whose literary journal was significantly banned at the end of two years). The author complains that (by then) the Senate did not contribute in the least towards the expenses of this necessary entertainment, which might distract the citizens from those indiscreet reflections on matters that only tended to contribute towards their ruin.[106] As a result the mime shows (*pantomimas*) had been suppressed, and the theatre sets consisted only of two rows of columns, whether the opera setting was a city, a square, a garden, a grove, a room, the seaside, etc.:

Considering the city's exorbitant expenses in other necessary things, the small amount to be added to the daily revenue of the theatre would be very inconsiderable. As everyone knows, Genoa, a Republic which exists only by its commerce, thinks it necessary to maintain two excellent theatres at either end of the city. Parma, with half the population of Oporto, and much less commerce, has theatres which could adorn the most famous capitals of Europe. In a word, in every city of some consideration, where it is known what is good for the state, everything necessary for this exquisite entertainment is provided, for it is known that the expenditure of a small amount of the country's available revenue produces the best imaginable results for the good of society. Still it should be said that this expenditure is made only after everything that is absolutely necessary to the same cities has been taken care of.[107]

Francisco Bernardo de Lima proceeds to describe the plot of the opera, and to make a few comments on two of the singers. He criticises the continuous battle that sometimes existed between the *prima buffa* (Giuntini), who had an excellent voice, and the orchestra:

we guess that the purpose of this was to see which of them would run out of breath first ... this would be a triumph like that of the singer Salvaia, who made the King of Sardinia's best Sicilian horn player burst his lungs ... If the first actress of the Oporto Theatre can do this, wouldn't it be better if she were to show the tunefulness of her voice clearly, rather than try with infinite variations to refine the beauty of arias by, for example, Pergolesi? And to use the art of breath control solely to perform difficult passages which are not even moving? This we call artificial music, which is nothing but a combination of difficult sounds, which may please the ear, but will never penetrate into the innermost part of the soul. It would be much better to employ the melody of the song to bring to life the images of the poetry, and to embellish the modulations of the voice through the pleasures of harmony, which is what we call expressive music.

The *buffo*, who is one of the best in Europe, makes his audience understand everything he sings, a quality that is common to most of the Italian *buffi*. They use certain sounds that epitomise hunger, cold, pain, joy, in short, they have expression, which is the true music of drama. They could almost be considered mime artists, although the Italians do not see them like that.

The beautiful performance of these two actors hides some of the infelicities of the composition ... But we must say something here about the opera as printed, and not as performed, and say that in publishing these works a man is needed who knows something about the art of writing drama. Had the publisher of this opera been such a man, he would not have placed after the recitative of Lisaura, beautifully performed by Giuntini:

Giusti Dei, v'è nel Mondo
Cotanta iniquità?

.......................................................................................................

Dove si cela, dove
L'empio, ch'il genitor tradire aspira?
Seco voglio sfogar lo sdegno, e l'ira.
Ma no femina imbelle,
Che dir, che far potri? etc.

As we were saying, he would not immediately follow this with an aria dedicated to
Nize, which even the most stupid person would realise does not follow that
recitative, and which ends:

Mentre folgori e baleni
Sarò teco amata Nise,
Quando il ciel si rassereni,
Nise ingrata, io partirò

It would be better to suppress this aria in the printed text, and then it could be sung
in the third or fourth performance, where this impropriety would be excused as an
abuse that reigns in almost all Italian theatres; for in the repetition of the operas a
new aria serves to excite with something new the attention of those who have seen
the first performances. After the recitative the polite audience expects to see in the
aria the arts of the Poet and the Musician combined, to make the actors express the
violence of the passions by which they are supposed to be moved; for those arias,
which are not serio-comic ['jocoserias'], are made in imitation of the choruses in the
Greek tragedies, and therefore they employ the most sublime images from Lyrical
poetry.

In spite of what we have said, it is true that these defects that may be found in the
Italian operas of Oporto are common to the operas of all nations, for they are not
usually performed as they should be: instead of following the rules dictated by good
reason, only an artificial music is practised, varied with equally artificial dances,
which should be nothing but the representation of exaggerated gesture, just as
music is the most potent expression of speech: but as the Princes and the powerful
are occupied with serious business, they prefer to rest from their toils with this type
of spectacle which does not need much concentration but remains the most
enjoyable thing in the world.

An objection which has commonly been voiced against this entertainment . . . is
that it is unrealistic to deal with ordinary things in song, such as giving an order to a
servant, consulting a friend, challenging an opponent, etc. To this we answer that
the opposite of verisimilitude is that which is humanly impossible. It all depends on
custom; and if this has meant that poetry has been adopted in the theatres because it
expresses better than prose what we wish to say, why should we not allow the same
of music, which adds so much more energy and strength to poetry?[108]

The author then proceeds to develop the classical doctrine of music as the
imitation of nature. The long passage here quoted is however sufficient to
show him as a rare, well-informed, and lucid critic of opera in eighteenth-
century Portugal.

It has already been mentioned that in April 1767 João Gomes Varela, manager of the Bairro Alto Theatre, was called to Oporto by the City Governor to take up the impresarioship of the theatre, but that this project seems to have failed.[109] The next recorded performance in the Teatro Público was that of *Il tempio dell'Eternità*, a one-act *componimento drammatico* celebrating José I's birthday on 6 June 1768. The libretto, which does not include the names of the singers, is dedicated to Lieutenant-General João de Almada e Melo. A letter from the consul in Genova, Piaggio, to the Director of the Royal Theatres, dated 13 September, says that the tenor Dominico Zappa from Milan had been hired to sing in the theatre by the City Governor.[110]

Cacciò's *Indice de' spettacoli teatrali di tutto l'anno*, quoted by Carvalhais,[111] says that in 1770 three *opere serie* and four *opere buffe* were performed in Oporto.[112] The singers were Maria Giuntini and Marina Giordani in the *parte serie*, and Rosa and Nicola Ambrosini, Alessandro Basili, Nicolina Giordani, and Domenico Zappa in the *parti buffe*. The *balli* were by Filippo Boselli and Francesco Giordani, and performed by Giuseppe, Marianno and Nicola Ambrosini, Filippo and Rosa Boselli, Elisabetta Brigida, Carmina and Gasparo Giuntini, Francesco Giordani, and Antonio Portoghesini.

On 6 June 1772 *Il Demofoonte* by David Perez was performed by the following singers: Rosa Ambrosini, Pedro António (Pereira), Alessandro Basili, Maria Giuntini, Anna Lauretti, Luísa Todi, and Giuseppe Vighi. The *balli* were by Filippo Boselli and performed by him and by Giuseppe, Marianno and Nicola Ambrosini, Antonia, Pedro António, Lucrezia Bettini, Rosa Boselli, Margaretta Franchi and Josefa (Giuseppa?). The sets were by João Glama Strobel and Domingos Teixeira, the machines and decorations by Joaquim António Teixeira, and the costumes by Lazaro Genovese. The English visitor Richard Twiss attended a performance of the opera and said of the theatre that it was 'the vilest in the two kingdoms, very old and shabby. It serves for Portuguese plays and for Italian operas. I saw the opera of *Demofoonte done*, suitably to the place it was done in'.[113]

Cacciò's *Indice* for 1776–7 records the performance of *opere buffe* in Oporto by a company composed of Giuseppe Biagi, Alessandro Boselli, Lucia Galassi, Claudio Jemmi, Alfonso Nicolini, Giuseppe Pinetti, Giuseppa Rossi, Anna Setaro, and Luísa Todi. The *balli* were by Filippo Boselli and performed by him and by Lucrezia Bettini, Rosa Boselli, Giovanni Ferraresi, Geltrude Guadagnini and six extras. Further details on this period may be gleaned from some rare documents belonging to the archive of the Real Mesa Censória.[114] One of them indicates that on 25 September 1776 Filippo Boselli was summoned before the circuit judge ('juiz de fora') on the charge that he had presented performances without the permission of the Real Mesa Censória. To this he replied that he had not done so since 1774, following an order of the Corregedor do Crime. His witnesses were Alfonso Nicolini, João de Sousa Coutinho, a former actor of the theatre, and Alessandro Basili, prompter.

On 25 January 1779 Boselli was again called before the Procurator of the Real Mesa Censória. This time he took refuge in the house of the City Governor, and the latter took the Procurator to task for trying to enforce the Queen's orders in a theatre which belonged to him. Boselli finally appeared before the Procurator, declaring that he was the director of the theatre, and not its manager. (According to his witnesses,[115] the theatre manager was a certain Manuel Loureiro de Miranda, a sergeant in the city's regiment.) He presented a list of the plays performed in the theatre between 24 April and 11 December 1778 that deserves to be quoted here:

### Comedias [?]

1  *Tamerlão na Persia* Apostolo Zeno
2  *A Esposa Persiana* P. Metastasio
3  *O Amor da Patria* Carlos Goldoni
4  *Os amantes Zelosos* Carlos Goldoni
5  *O Amante Militar* Carlos Goldoni
6  *Dido Desamparada* P. Metastasio
7  *O Mentirozo* Carlos Goldoni
8  *O Criado de dois amos* Carlos Goldoni
9  *O Convidado de Pedra* Carlos Goldoni
10 *A Peruviana* Carlos Goldoni
11 *Mayor ventura de Amor* Anonymo
12 *Disparates de hum acerto* Anonymo
13 *Acertos de hum disparate* Anonymo
14 *Industrias de Sarilho* Anonymo
15 *Adriano em Siria* Alex. Antonio
16 *Adolonimo em Sydonia* Alex. Antonio
17 *A Olimpiade* P. Metastasio
18 *A Criada mais generosa* Anonymo
19 *O precipicio de Faetonte* A. José
20 *A familia do Antiquario* Goldoni
21 *Demofoonte em Tracia* Metastasio

### Entremezes

1  *O Rustico desprezado* Anonymo
2  *O velho Peralta* Anonoymo
3  *O velho scismatico* Anonymo
4  *O criado astucioso* Anonymo
5  *A Saloya fingida* Anonymo
6  *A velha presumida* Anonymo
7  *A Floreira* Anonymo
8  *Os Amantes jocozos* Anonymo
9  *O cazam.$^{to}$ industrioso* Anonymo

Another document in the archive of the Real Mesa Censória is a poster announcing a performance in the theatre for the benefit of Teresa Joaquina on 24 September 1779.[116] It consisted of the play *Mafoma*, or *O fanatismo*, by Voltaire, with a flute concerto at the end of the first act and a symphony at the end of the second. At the end of the third act the actress sang an aria, and at the end of the fourth a quintet was performed, followed by an oboe concerto. The spectacle ended with the *entremez O esposo fingido*.

Three letters written in 1778 present us with a unique picture of the conditions surrounding opera in Oporto during this period.[117] Their author, Ricardo Raimundo Nogueira, was a professor of law at Coimbra University and a canon of Elvas Cathedral, besides holding many other public offices, among them that of member of the Regency Council between 1810 and 1820. It is curious to note that despite his obvious liberal leanings he was also a member of the Coimbra Inquisition and a Royal Censor.

Faced with the question whether both the companies of opera and drama which had performed alternately in the theatre should be kept, or, if only one of them, which, Nogueira expresses his preference for the Portuguese drama company, for reasons which he gives in his second letter:

The opera, more than any other form of theatre, demands excellent actors who can perform and sing to perfection, a superb orchestra, rich and elegant costumes, numerous and magnificent extras, a spacious and well-lit theatre, and finally everything that Poetry, Music, and Painting are capable of to produce a grand, magnificent and brilliant spectacle ...

To speak truly, my friend, I doubt that it will be possible to establish an opera house as it should be in your homeland. I will not discuss whether Oporto can, or cannot, support an Italian theatre; the truth is that if it can, it does not want to. While I lived there, I saw that in spite of the most attentive protection, no opera worth seeing was produced. Once or twice they dared to present heroic operas; but how were they performed? None of the actors knew how to play a serious part with decorum, the costumes were undignified and old, the sets were almost always the same; the extras poor and shabby. I do not know if you still remember the way we laughed to see a woman of no merit play the role of Aeneas in Dido despised.[118] These profane mouths unworthily defaced the divine compositions of the illustrious Metastasio, and of the great Masters who set to music his admirable operas. We should not however confuse good and bad. I know that in your theatre worthy figures have sometimes appeared to whom what I have said does not apply.[119]

The said actors were thus almost always forced to perform serio-comic Operas that the Italians call *Burlettas*, and even in those they stumbled quite a lot, for there was never more than one Act that was worth listening to, and for a long time not one of them was a master of his profession. I think besides that a *Burletta* theatre has no merit other than the music, when it is good, as the compositions of this kind are the most absurd and insipid that may be imagined; and therefore I think that it is better to hear an eminent Musician in a Room, than to go to the theatre to listen to preposterous things, some very badly sung.

All this brings me to the conclusion: that Oporto cannot, or does not want to, maintain two complete theatres, one Portuguese, and the other Italian, with the perfection that they deserve. That it is better to have only one good and perfect theatre than two bad ones, such as those that have existed so far. That therefore you should try to reduce them to one only, and with the same expense, or maybe less, with which you supported a bad Italian theatre, and a mediocre Portuguese one, you should establish a very good Portuguese theatre that will entertain and instruct you, do honour to your City, and show the good taste of its citizens.

In the third letter Nogueira criticises the way in which the theatre had been run in the past, showing that it had been a bizarre instrument of 'enlightened' despotism, and proposing a new liberal alternative to it:

I do not see the need to force the people to give money to actors, whom they do not wish to hear.

The abuses that were prevalent in Oporto in this respect are intolerable. Let me briefly point out to you the most noteworthy of them. Let us however be just, and without running the risk of being called ungrateful, let us recognise the benefits, and remember that the best intentions are often unsuccessful, when the means one uses are misguided ones.

Your theatre's illustrious patron was given by the heavens to Oporto, to make it happy[120] . . . Among many other measures which he has taken for the happiness and security of the citizens of Oporto, he justly decided that the establishment of a permanent theatre could be very useful in civilising that city, in instructing its inhabitants, and in adorning it and gaining for it the appreciation of foreigners. These ideas are so commendable, that for this alone Oporto should grant him eternal recognition, even if it had no other reasons for considering him its father and protector.

Having therefore so judicious an end in view, he believed that the theatre could not exist without regular funds, and, to establish them, he sent word every year to those persons whom he considered capable of supporting that expense, asking them to take out a yearly subscription on a stalls seat or box. I think one does not need much logic to realise that an earnest request from persons of such quality is tantamount to a command. And what man in Portugal would dare say no to such a message? To this was added a degree of protection for the actors, and quite extraordinary regulations for the theatre, where it was established that Peter should sit in this place, and Paul in that; that the person who took a seat for a year could not lend it to a friend for an evening, that the owner of a box could only lend it to a family as a favour in certain circumstances and with certain limitations, and other Laws of a similar nature. And as no Law can be maintained without Magistrates to enforce it, so this one had its enforcers, who, thinking they had the same power as their master, and not possessing in truth the same ideas, were responsible for many acts of rudeness, often insulting honest people, and disregarding whomever they wished. And as they were Ministers, against whom there was no appeal, there was no option but to obey all their rulings promptly.

From this procedure the following inconveniences resulted. (1) Many people, who could not afford it, and others who did not want it were forced to subscribe. (2) The theatre was much worse than it would have been, had there been more freedom. (3) The number of spectators was very small. Let me try to show you this.

I say 1. That many people who could not afford it, along with others who did not want such an expense were forced to subscribe. Some of the permanent opera subscribers were the Judges of the Court of Appeals, and others the City Ministers. You know very well that the net salary of an Oporto Judge is eighty thousand *réis*; I would guess that an Extraordinary [Judge] makes three hundred thousand *réis* a year with the rest of his emoluments. I leave it to your judgement how a Minister, who needs must live like an honest person, can eat, dress, pay his servants and house rent on such a small income, and still put aside six or seven *moedas* [28$800 to 33$600] to spend on the Opera. I shall not speak of the Military; they are poor by nature, and all the economy in the world is not enough to enable them to live only on their pay. Many people who live from their rents are often burdened with debts, and only through the most strict administration can they support their households. Finally, even businessmen probably do not possess the wealth that the world thinks they do, and often they would be forced to squander the money of their creditors in that way, so as not to lose face.

Here we have many people who cannot afford to subscribe; there are also many who do not want to. You may have heard countless of them say that they did not take any pleasure in spending that kind of money, and who have subscribed because they dared not say no; and many of them showed that they were not lying, for in spite of the fact that they paid for their seats, not once did they occupy them.

Secondly I say that the Theatre was much worse than it might have been, had there been more freedom. The reason is clear. The actors were extremely well protected: they were assured of an unfailing income, which covered their salaries, and the remaining theatre expenses. They therefore became independent of the spectators, who would pay punctually whether they performed well or badly. Provided with this independence they tried to enjoy these advantages whilst doing as little work as possible. They presented very few new Operas, they performed with negligence, they mutilated the plays horribly, and they omitted the best arias and the more interesting roles at will. If an actor knew by heart some recitative or aria that he had learned when he had studied music, he would introduce it whenever he fancied, even if it was as out of place as mentioning Pilate in the Credo. Sometimes there were dances between the acts, and sometimes not, and sometimes they were such that it would have been better if there had not been any. But the money was always the same, and the poor spectator did not dare open his mouth, and to look like a courtier he often saw himself obliged to praise all these absurdities...

I almost forgot the multitude of benefit performances that were allowed in your theatre not only to the first actors, but also to the most inferior members. I remember that one year there were over twenty such benefits. Most of these good beneficiaries had assured protection. A subscription was opened, and those from whom levies had been exacted, whether they attended or not, came promptly to hand in the portion allotted to them.

My friend, the principal motive behind a public entertainment must be freedom. If the actors expect results only from their merits, we shall see them try to please their public, and attract it to the theatre. Only then will they perform new plays frequently, and work to produce them with perfection. They will vary the costumes and the sets, and with these novelties they will finally try to conciliate the wishes of the people, on whom alone their hopes lie. Nor must the spectator be disturbed in the theatre; this is a pleasure that he buys with his money, and that he wants to enjoy to his own satisfaction. Therefore any constraints that do not contribute towards maintaining the peace and quiet which should reign there, are unjust, and cannot but keep him away, and make him lose interest in returning to such a place. In many civilised cities the freedom of the theatres can become excessive, and in London, Paris, or Venice, spectators can be found booing bad actors, and throwing oranges and apples at them. I do not wish for freedom to that extent, but in no way can I approve of the constraints which have existed in Oporto.

I know perfectly well that some of the citizens of Oporto wish to defend the justice, or at least the necessity of this system, which I condemn. They say that it would be impossible to maintain a theatre in that city, if it were left entirely to the discretion of the public; that in the Opera House very few people appeared besides the subscribers, and that even many of these, despite the fact that they paid for their seats for the whole year, did not attend one single performance.

But these reasons do not convince me. Oporto is a City with a large population, and its inhabitants are eager to attend public entertainments. They ran away from the theatre, not because they were bored by the performances, but because of the violence done to them in having to subscribe, and the little merit of what there was to be seen. I can prove this by [personal] experience. I saw many plays performed, which always had very little attendance. On benefit nights, when there was usually more variety, and greater effort was made to please the audience, the boxes and the stalls were filled.

It is not known whether Nogueira's recommendations had any influence on the subsequent history of the theatre, which is still unclear on many points. Formenti's *Indice de' teatrali spettacoli* for the 1779–80 season records performances of tragedies and comedies there, accompanied by musical *intermezzi* (*entremezes*?). *Balli* by Filippo Boselli were also performed by him and by Antonio Avor, Rosa Boselli, Leonora Boschi, Teresa Dovar, Nicola Ferraresi, Geltrude Guadagnini, José (a Portuguese), and four extras.

According to Rebelo Bonito[121] on 22, 23 and 24 May 1785 there were three spectacles to celebrate the wedding of Prince João and Princess Carlota Joaquina. On 8 November of that same year there was a performance for the benefit of Clemente Pereira, with the comedy *O cavalheiro e a dama* by Goldoni, followed by an *entremez*. Between the acts several arias were sung and there was also a dance. On 20 November there was another spectacle for the benefit of José Felix da Costa, 'primeiro comico do Theatro Nacional', and as will be recalled also a member of the Salitre company. The tragedy *D. Ines de Castro* was performed, followed by an *entremez*.[122]

The *Descripção topographica e historica da cidade do Porto*, published by Padre Agostinho Rebelo da Costa in 1789, states[123] that in 1788 comedies and operas were performed twice a week in the public theatre. According to José Pedro Martins,[124] who does not indicate his source, the oratorio *Salome, madre de sette martiri Maccabei*, by João Cordeiro da Silva, was performed there in 1791. According to Rebelo Bonito[125] *Il fanatico burlato* by Cimarosa was performed on 6 November of the same year. A scene where priests burned incense before an idol gave rise to the intervention of the Inquisition, and had to be modified. Again according to José Pedro Martins, the opera *Semiramide* was performed on 2 February 1792.

Even though they are already outside our period, the following data, included in Formenti's *Indice*, and referring to the last seasons before the inauguration of the S. João Theatre, may be quoted here. During the 1793–4 season Italian *opere serie* and *buffe* were performed, along with *balli*, and with comedies and tragedies performed by the Portuguese company. The singers were Carlo Barlassina (*primo buffo a vicenda*), Giovanni Barlassina (*prima donna buffa e seria*), Giuseppe Dorelli (*primo tenore e mezzo carattere*), Rocco Girolami (*primo soprano*), Michele Liberati, known as Bologna (*secondo tenore*), Antonio Marchesi (*primo buffo a vicenda*), Irene Marchesi (*seconda buffa e seria*), and Anna Vicchi (*terza buffa ed ultima parte seria*). The dancers were Sebastiano Ambrosini, Gasparo Braccesi, Antonio Cianfanelli, Margarita Citerni, Teresa Paladini, Luigi Secchioni, Luigi Tamagni, Rafaella Vicchi, and Francisco Xavier, plus twelve extras. The *balli* were by Antonio Cianfanelli.

During the 1797–8 season the following operas were performed, whose composers are not indicated: *Il credulo*, *Il disertore francese*, *Il Don Giovanni*, and *L'impresario in angustie*. The singers were Marianna Chabrand Albani (*prima buffa*), Teresa Ancinelli (*seconda buffa*), Giuseppe Caravita (*primo buffo a vicenda*), Antonio Chiaveri (*secondo tenore*), Leutar Chiaveri (*seconda buffa*), Luigi Pugnetti (*primo buffo a vicenda*), and Pietro Ricci (*primo mezzo-carattere*). The *balli* were by Luigi Chiaveri, and performed by him and by Maddalena Ancinelli, Antonio Chiaveri, and Leutar Chiaveri.

The construction of the new S. João Theatre began in March 1796 and its inauguration was on 13 May 1798. The original project dates from 1793, and is due to the initiative of Francisco de Almada e Mendonça, the son of the late Governor João de Almada e Melo.[126]

# CHRONOLOGY

The following chronology attempts to bring together for the first time all documented productions of operas, intermezzi, *zarzuelas*, oratorios, serenatas and serenata-type compositions before the inauguration of the S. Carlos Theatre in 1793. It also includes the titles of the *operas portuguezas*, *comedias* and other types of spoken dramas with music known to have been performed during the first half of the eighteenth century, and those performed in its second half for which the author of the music is known.

Only copies of the librettos and the scores preserved in the main Portuguese libraries have been listed, with the exception of certain unique librettos in Carvalhais' collection which he quotes in his 'Subsidios', and which are now preserved in the Conservatorio di Musica S. Cecilia in Rome (*I-Rsc*). A figure after a library's siglum indicates the number of extant copies of the libretto in that library. Original Italian titles have been adopted throughout.

Titles and other information not within quotation marks stem from the librettos and/or scores (quotation marks are also used for certain additional information in the scores and librettos). Square brackets are used either to indicate doubtful productions or attributions, or scores which cannot be directly related to the relevant productions. As a rule no authorship attributions other than those given in the librettos or in other contemporary documents have been included. Dates of operas are usually those of first performances. As indicated below (in the list of Doubtful productions), alternative production years of works for which no evidence exists have not usually been retained.

Only those serenata performances for which the libretto or the title is known have been systematically listed. Following is a list of birthdays and namedays of members of the royal family on which serenatas were usually performed (according to the *Gazeta de Lisboa* and the librettos):

| | |
|---|---|
| 9 March (1717) | nameday of the Infante D. Francisco, brother of João V |
| 19 March (1753–88) | nameday of Prince (later) King José, and of Prince José, son of Maria I |
| 21 March (1782–91) | St Benedict, nameday of Princess Maria Francisca Benedita, sister of Maria I and wife of Prince José |
| 31 March (1726–80) | birthday of Princess (later Queen) Mariana Vitória, wife of José I |
| 25 April (1789–91) | birthday of Princess Carlota Joaquina, wife of Prince João |
| ? May (1731) | birthday of the Infante D. Carlos, son of João V |
| 13 May (1783–91) | birthday of Prince João, son of Maria I |
| 6 June (1718–76) | birthday of Prince (later King) José |
| 24 June (1712–38) | nameday of João V |
| (1789–91) | nameday of Prince João, son of Maria I |
| 29 June (1765–84) | nameday of Prince (later King) Pedro |
| 5 July (1735, 1778–85) | birthday of Prince (later King) Pedro |
| 25 July (1778–91) | birthday of Princess Maria Francisca Benedita, sister of Maria I and wife of Prince José |
| 26 July (1709–35) | nameday of Queen Maria Anne of Austria, wife of João V |
| 21 August (1778–88) | birthday of Prince José, son of Maria I |
| 28 August (1728, 1735) | birthday of the Empress Elizabeth of Austria |
| 7 September (1716–39) | birthday of Queen Maria Anne of Austria, wife of João V |
| 23 September (1729, 1731) | birthday of Prince Ferdinand of Spain, husband of Princess Maria Bárbara |
| 1 October (1718, 1719, 1727) | birthday of the Emperor Charles VI |
| 22 October (1711–39) | birthday of João V |
| 25 October (1725, 1732) | birthday of the Queen of Spain |
| 4 November (1716–34) | nameday of the Infante D. Carlos, son of João V, and of the Emperor Charles VI |
| (1788–91) | nameday of Princess Carlota Joaquina, wife of Prince João |
| 19 November (1719, 1731) | nameday of the Empress Elizabeth of Austria |
| 4 December (1730–3) | nameday of Princess Maria Bárbara, daughter of João V |
| 17 December (1735–91) | birthday of Princess (later Queen) Maria |
| 18 December (1779–90) | Nossa Senhora do Ó (nameday of Maria I) |

| | |
|---|---|
| 19 December (1731) | birthday of Philip V of Spain |
| 27 December (1721–39) | nameday of João V |

*1708*

Paço da Ribeira
'*Eligir al inimigo*, comédia' (Nery, 40)
m: Frei Pedro da Conceição

*1709*

26 July

Paço da Ribeira
*Loa para la comedia*
l: anonymous (*P-Cug*)

*1711*

22 October

Paço da Ribeira
*Fabula de Acis y Galatea*, fiesta armónica
l: Julião Maciel (D.B. Machado, III, p. 921)
(*P-Ln* 2)

*1712*

24 June

Paço da Ribeira
*Fabula de Alfeo y Aretusa*, fiesta armónica
l: Luís Calisto da Costa e Faria (*P-Cul*)

*1713*

22 October

Paço da Ribeira
*El poder de la armonía*, fiesta de zarzuela
l: Luís Calisto da Costa e Faria (*P-Cug, Cul, Mp*)
m: Jayme de la Te y Sagau

*1716*

7 September
4 November

Paço da Ribeira
'serenata' (*Gazeta de Lisboa*)
'serenata' (*Gazeta de Lisboa*)
Convento de Santa Clara (for the election of its prelate)
*Fiesta de zarzuela*
l: anonymous (*P-Cug, Ln* 4)

*1717*

3 August

House of the Secretary of State, Diogo de Mendonça Corte Real (to celebrate the birthday of the Infante D. Manuel)
'*Atis & Cybelle*, Opera, ou Comedia em musica' (*Gazeta de Lisboa*)
Gardens of the French ambassador, Abbé de Mornay

25 August      '*Acis & Galatea*, Opera, com todas as decorações e perspectivas pertencentes a sua representação' (*Gazeta de Lisboa*)

Royal site of Pedrouços

12 October      'serenata' (*Gazeta de Lisboa*)

## *1718*

Palace of the Count of S. Vicente (to celebrate his birthday)

23 January      '*Acis & Galatea*, Comedia, em hum teatro com perspectivas' (*Gazeta de Lisboa*)

Palace of the Marquis of Valença (to celebrate his birthday)

25 January      '*El imposible mayor en amor, le vence amor*, Comedia'

[l: José de Cañizares

sc: Sebastián Durón, *P-EVp*]

Palace of the Spanish ambassador, Marquis of Capicilatro (to celebrate the birth of Princess Mariana Vitória)

April      '*Vengar con el fuego el fuego*, Comedia de musica' (*Gazeta de Lisboa*)

[sc: anonymous, Arquivo da Casa Cadaval in Muge; cf. M.S. Ribeiro, 'El-Rei D. João, o Quinto . . .', p. 81]

## *1719*

Lisbon cathedral

22 January      *Oratorio*

l: Julião Maciel (*P-EVp*)

m: António Líteres

Paço de Ribeira

24 September      'serenata, cantada pelos novos e excellentes musicos' (*Gazeta de Lisboa*)

22 October      '*Triunfos de Ulysses & Glorias de Portugal*, composição em versos italianos' for three voices, in the presence of all the court and the foreign dignitaries (*Gazeta de Lisboa*)

## *1720*

Lisbon cathedral

22 January      *Oratorio*

l: anonymous (*P-EVp*)

m: Antonio de Literes

Paço da Ribeira

| | |
|---|---|
| 7 September | *Contesa delle stagioni*, serenata |
| | l: anonymous (*P-Cul, Ln, Mp*) |
| | sc: Domenico Scarlatti (*I-Vnm*) |
| 22 October | *Trionfo delle virtù*, serenata |
| | l: anonymous (*P-Cul, Lan, Ln, Mp*) |
| 27 December | *Cantata pastorale*, serenata |
| | l: anonymous (*P-Cug, Cul, Lan, Ln, Mp*) |
| | m: Domenico Scarlatti (*Gazeta de Lisboa*) |

*1721*

Paço da Ribeira

| | |
|---|---|
| 24 June | *Componimento musicale* |
| | l: anonymous (*P-Cul*) |
| 7 September | *Serenata pastorale* |
| | l: anonymous (*P-Ln, Mp*) |
| 27 December | *Aci, e Galatea*, serenata |
| | l: anonymous (*P-Lan, Ln, Mp*) |
| | m: Baron d'Astorga (*Gazeta de Lisboa*) |
| 18 September | House of Pedro Melo de Ataíde (on his daughter's baptism) |
| | 'serenata' (*Gazeta de Lisboa*) |

Palace of the Spanish ambassador, Marquis of Capicilatro (to celebrate the marriage contracts of the Princes of Portugal and Spain)

| | |
|---|---|
| 18 December | '*Las nuevas armas de amor*, Zarzuela en musica' (*Gazeta de Lisboa*) |
| | [l: José de Cañízares |
| | sc: Sebastián Durón, *P-EVp*] |

*1722*

Lisbon cathedral

| | |
|---|---|
| 22 January | *Oratorio* |
| | l: Julião Maciel (*P-EVp*) |
| | m: Antonio de Literes |

Paço da Ribeira

| | |
|---|---|
| 24 June | *Gl'amorosi avvenimenti*, serenata |
| | l: anonymous (*P-Cug, Cul, Ln, Mp*) |
| 26 July | *Il sacrifizio di Diana*, componimento musicale |
| | l: anonymous (*P-Cul, Lan, Ln, Mp*) |
| | m: Baron d'Astorga ('ao presente nesta Corte', *Gazeta de Lisboa*) |
| 7 September | 'Serenata composta em Musica pelo Abbade Scarlatti' (*Gazeta de Lisboa*) |

| 22 October | *Gli amori di Cefilo e d'Endimione*, serenata |
| | l: anonymous (*P-Ln* 2, *Mp*) |
| 27 December | *Le nozze di Baco e d'Arianna*, serenata |
| | l: anonymous (*P-Lan, Ln*) |
| | m: Domenico Scarlatti (*Gazeta de Lisboa*) |

*1723*

Palace of the Spanish ambassador, Marquis of Capicilatro (to celebrate the nameday of the Prince of Asturias)

| 24 August | *'El estrago en la fineza*, Comedia nova com musica e mutaçoens no Theatro' (*Gazeta de Lisboa*) |
| | [l: José de Cañizares |
| | sc: Sebastián Durón, *P-EVp*] |

Paço da Ribeira

| 27 December | *Le ninfe del Tago*, serenata |
| | l: anonymous (*P-Cug, Cul, Lan, Ln, Mp*) |

*1724*

Paço da Ribeira

| 24 June | *Aci, e Galatea*, serenata |
| | l: (same as 27 December 1721) (*P-Cug, Cul, Ln*) |

House of the British envoy, Saunderson (celebrating the birthday of the Prince of Wales)

| 10 November | 'serenata' (*Gazeta de Lisboa*) |

*1725*

Paço da Ribeira

| 9 October | 'serenata' (on the publication of the marriage contracts of the Princes of Portugal and Spain, *Gazeta de Lisboa*) |
| 22 October | *La constanza gradita*, serenata |
| | l: anonymous (*P-Cug, Ln* 2, *Mp*) |
| 27 December | *Amor nasce da'un'sguardo*, serenata |
| | l: anonymous (*P-Cug, Cul, Ln, Mp*) |

*1726*

Paço da Ribeira

| 31 March | *Dramma pastorale* da cantarsi |
| | l: anonymous (*P-Cug, Ln* 2, *Mp*) |
| 6 June | *Il doppio amore vilipeso*, serenata |
| | l: anonymous (*P-Cul, Lan, Ln, Mp*) |
| 24 June | *Serenata* da cantarsi |
| | l: anonymous (*P-Cul, Lan, Ln, Mp*) |

| | |
|---|---|
| 26 July | *Andromeda*, serenata<br>l: anonymous (*P-Cul, Ln, Mp*) |
| 27 December | *Serenata* fatta cantare<br>l: anonymous (*P-Ln* 2) |

*1727*

Palace of the ambassador extraordinary, Marquis of los Balbases

| | |
|---|---|
| 1 May | *Festejo harmónico*, serenata (for the nameday of Philip V of Spain, 'em huma grande galeria em forma de Theatro', *Gazeta de Lisboa*)<br>l: anonymous (*P-Cug, Cul, Ln*) |

Palace of the ambassador extraordinary, Marquis of los Balbases (for the nameday of the Prince of Asturias)

| | |
|---|---|
| 30 May | *Endimión y Diana*, comedia famosa<br>*Baile de Filida y Menandro*<br>l: anonymous (*P-Cug, Mp*) |
| 19 November | 'Comedia' (*Gazeta de Lisboa*) |

Paço da Ribeira

| | |
|---|---|
| 27 December | *L'Aurora*, serenata<br>l: anonymous (*P-Cug, Ln, Mp*) |

*1728*

Paço da Ribeira

| | |
|---|---|
| 11 January | *Festeggio armonico*, nel celebrarsi il real maritaggio de' ... Signori D. Ferdinando di Spagna Principe d'Asturia, e D. Maria Infanta di Portogallo ... ('em hũa especie de theatro, que para este fim se fabricou', *Gazeta de Lisboa*)<br>l: anonymous (*P-Cug, Mp*)<br>m: Domenico Scarlatti |

Palace of the ambassador extraordinary, Marquis of los Balbases

| | |
|---|---|
| 18 January | *Amor aumenta el valor*, fiesta<br>l: anonymous (*P-Ln, Mp*)<br>m: Act I, José de Nebra; Act II, Felipe Falconi; Act III, Jayme Facco |
| January | *Las Amazonas de España*, melodrama al estilo italiano<br>('Comedia harmonica', *Gazeta de Lisboa*)<br>l: anonymous (*P-Cug, Mp*) |

Paço de Ribeira

| | |
|---|---|
| February during Carnival | *Il D. Chisciote della Mancia*, intermezzi a sei voci<br>l: anonymous (*P-Mp*)<br>Palace of the cardinal da Mota |
| 22 April | *Il trionfo della Virtù*, componimento poetico posto in musica ('serenata', *Gazeta de Lisboa*)<br>l: D. Luca Giovine (*P-Cul, Mp*)<br>m: Francisco António de Almeida<br>Country house of the Marquis of Fronteira |
| May | 'serenata' (*Gazeta de Lisboa*)<br>Paço da Ribeira |
| 22 October | *Gli sogni amorosi*, serenata<br>l: anonymous (*P-Cug, Ln 2, Mp*) |

*1729*

| | |
|---|---|
| January | Various serenatas, at Elvas, near the Spanish border (where the exchange of the Portuguese and Spanish Princesses took place)<br>House of the French consul, Monsieur de Montagnac (to celebrate the birth of the Dauphin) |
| 19 October | '*L'amore vuol somiglianza*, serenata' (*Gazeta de Lisboa*)<br>Paço da Ribeira |
| 27 December | *Il trionfo d'Amore*, scherzo pastorale<br>l: anonymous (*P-Ln, Mp*)<br>sc: Francisco António de Almeida (*P-VV*) |

*1730*

| | |
|---|---|
| | At Santos (a borough of Lisbon), by amateurs |
| January | '*Endimión y Diana*, Comedia quasi toda de musica' (Monfort, p. 568)<br>Paço da Ribeira |
| Carnival | *Il D. Chisciotte della Mancia* rpt (Montfort, p. 583; Beirão, p. 64) |
| 24 June | *L'amore ingannato*, serenata<br>l: anonymous (*P-Ln*) |
| 27 December | *Gl'incanti d'Alcina*, dramma per musica da cantarsi, 2 acts. ('serenata', Monfort, p. 584)<br>l: anonymous (*P-Ln, Mp*)<br>m: Francisco António de Almeida (Monfort, p. 584) |

**1731**

|  |  |
|---|---|
| | Paço da Ribeira |
| Carnival | *Il D. Chisciotte della Mancia* rpt (Beirão, p. 78) |
| 22 October | *Il vaticinio di Pallade e di Mercurio*, serenata<br>l: anonymous (*P-Ln, Mp*) |
| 13 December | 'serenata' (to celebrate the birthday of the Archduchess Marie Elisabeth Louise of Austria, *Gazeta de Lisboa*) |

**1732**

|  |  |
|---|---|
| | Palace of the Marquis of Fontes (sung by four ladies to celebrate his birthday) |
| 8 January | *Il sogno d'Endimione o l'indiscretezza punita*, scherzo pastorale<br>l: anonymous (*P-Ln*) |
| Carnival | Several serenatas at court and at the houses of the aristocracy (Brasão), including at the house of D. Antónia Joaquina de Lavre<br>*Gli sposi fortunati*, componimento da cantarsi<br>l: anonymous (*P-Ln*)<br>m: António Teixeira (Brasão, p. 112) |

**1733**

|  |  |
|---|---|
| | Paço da Ribeira |
| Carnival | *La pazienza di Socrate*, dramma comico da cantarsi<br>l: Alexandre de Gusmão (Brasão, p. 132), (*P-Cug, Cul, Mp*)<br>sc: Francisco António de Almeida (Act III *P-La* 47–II–14) |
| | Teatro (Casa dos Bonecos) do Bairro Alto |
| June–October (1st date in Brasão, p. 160) | *Vida do grande D. Quixote de la Mancha e do gordo Sancho Pança*, ópera, 2 parts<br>t: António José da Silva (*Theatro comico portuguez*, I)<br>m: [António Teixeira?] |

**1734**

|  |  |
|---|---|
| | Paço da Ribeira |
| Carnival | *La pazienza di Socrate* rpt (Beirão, p. 123)<br>*Il D. Chisciotte della Mancia*, intermezzi a sei voci<br>l: (see 1728) anonymous (*P-Cul*) |
| last day of Carnival | *Pastorale a tre voci*, da rappresentarsi, 3 acts<br>l: anonymous (*P-EVp, Ln*)<br>Teatro (Casa dos Bonecos) do Bairro Alto |

April
    *Esopaida ou vida de Esopo*, ópera, 2 parts
    t: António José da Silva (*Theatro comico portuguez*, 1)
    m: [António Teixeira?]

*1735*
    Paço da Ribeira

Carnival
    *La finta pazza*, dramma per musica, 3 acts
    l: anonymous (*P-Cug*)
    m: Francisco António de Almeida
    Covilhã (to celebrate the birth of the Princess of Brazil)

March
    'uma especie de Opera com apparencias e varios coros de musica' (*Gazeta de Lisboa* of 31 March)
    Teatro (Casa dos Bonecos) do Bairro Alto

May
    *Os encantos de Medeia*, ópera, 2 parts
    t: António José da Silva (*Theatro comico portuguez*, 1)
    m: António Teixeira (Monfort, p. 584)
    Academia da Trindade

December–January 1736
    *Farnace*, dramma per musica, 3 acts
    l: anonymous (*P-Cug, Ln, Mp*)
    m: Gaetano Maria Schiassi (see p. 15 above)
    (Monfort, pp. 584–5, mentions six operas, or more likely performances, until 27 December)

*1736*
    Paço da Ribeira

Carnival
    *La risa di Democrito*, dramma per musica, 3 acts
    l: anonymous (*P-Cug, Cul, Ln*)
    Teatro (Casa dos Bonecos) do Bairro Alto

May
    *Anfitrião ou Júpiter e Alcmena*, ópera, 2 acts
    t: António José da Silva (*Theatro comico portuguez*, 1)
    m: [António Teixeira?]

November
    *O labirinto de Creta*, ópera, 2 parts
    t: António José da Silva (*Theatro comico portuguez*, 1)
    m: [António Teixeira?]
    Academia da Trindade

January–February (Monfort, p. 586)
    *Alessandro nell'Indie*, dramma per musica, 3 acts
    l: Metastasio (*P-Cug, Ln* 2, *Mp*)

m: Gaetano Maria Schiassi
*Il marito giocatore*, intermezzi
l: anonymous (*P-Cug*)

**1737**

        Teatro (Casa dos Bonecos) do Bairro Alto

Carnival      *Guerras do alecrim e manjerona*, ópera joco-séria, 2 parts
t: António José da Silva (*Theatro comico portuguez*, 11)
pts: António Teixeira (*P-VV*)

May        *As variedades de Proteu*, ópera, 2 parts
t: António José da Silva (*Theatro comico portuguez*, 11)
pts: [António Teixeira] (*P-VV*)
Academia da Trindade
*Artaserse*, dramma per musica, 3 acts
l: Metastasio (*P-Cug, Cul, Ln, Mp*)
m: Gaetano Maria Schiassi
*Demofoonte*, dramma per musica, 3 acts
l: Metastasio (*P-Cug, Ln, Mp*)
m: Gaetano Maria Schiassi
*Eurene*, dramma per musica, 3 acts (1736 according to the libretto, but Monfort, p. 587, refers that it was being rehearsed in January 1737)
l: anonymous (*P-Lac, Ln, Mp*)
m: Gaetano Maria Schiassi
*L'Olimpiade*, dramma per musica, 3 acts
l: Metastasio (*P-Cug, Cul, Ln 2, Mp*)
*Livietta e Tracollo*, intermezzi
l: anonymous (*P-Ln, Mp*)
m: Giovanni Battista Pergolesi

Autumn (Monfort,     *Anagilda*, dramma per musica, 3 acts
pp. 588–9)      l: anonymous (*P-Ln, Mp*)
m: Gaetano Maria Schiassi
*Siface*, dramma per musica, 3 acts
l: anonymous (*P-Cug, Ln, Mp*)
m: Leonardo Leo

**1738**

        Paço da Ribeira

22 October    *L'asilo d'Amore*, serenata
l: anonymous (Carvalhais, 'Subsídios')

Palace of the Patriarch D. Tomás de Almeida
(on his being promoted to cardinal)
*Le virtù trionfanti*, serenata
l: D. Antonio Tedeschi (*P-Cug* 2, *Ln*)
m: Francisco António de Almeida
Convento de Nossa Senhora da Conceição
de Marvila

Christmas          *Festivo applauso*
l: Sóror Arcângela Maria da Assunção
(*P-Cug*)
Teatro (Casa dos Bonecos) do Bairro Alto

January            *Precipício de Faetonte*, ópera, 2 parts
t: António José da Silva (*Theatro comico
portuguez*, II)
m: [António Teixeira?]
Academia da Trindade

January (Monfort, p. 589)   *Sesostri, Re d'Egitto*, dramma per musica, 3
acts
l: Apostolo Zeno (*P-Cug*)
Academia da Trindade

March (Monfort, p. 590)   *Il Siroe*, dramma per musica, 3 acts
l: Metastasio (*P-Ln*)
[*Semiramide*, dramma per musica, 3 acts]
l: anonymous (*P-Ln*, title page missing)
Teatro Novo da Rua dos Condes

November (Monfort,   *La clemenza di Tito*, dramma per musica, 3
p. 591)            acts
l: Metastasio (*P-Cug, Cul* 2)
*L'Emira*, dramma per musica, 3 acts
l: Metastasio (*P-Cug, Lac, Ln*)

*1739*
Paço da Ribeira

Carnival           *La Spinalba ovvero il vecchio matto*, dramma
comico da rappresentarsi in musica, 3 acts
l: anonymous (*P-Cug, Ln*)
sc: Francisco António de Almeida (*P-La*
48–II–42)
mod. edn: Lisbon, Fundação Calouste Gulbenkian, 1969 (Portugaliae Musica XII: sc.,
pts., p.sc.)
rec: Philips 839710/12 LY
Teatro Novo da Rua dos Condes
*Carlo Calvo*, dramma per musica, 3 acts

l: anonymous (*P-Cug, Ln*)
*Demetrio*, dramma per musica, 3 acts
l: Metastasio (*P-Cul, EVp, Ln*)
m: Gaetano Maria Schiassi
*Merope*, dramma per musica, 3 acts
l: anonymous (*P-Cug*, 2, *Cul, Ln*)
*Siface*, dramma per musica, 3 acts, rpt (see 1737)
l: anonymous (Carvalhais, 'Subsídios')
m: Leonardo Leo
*Vologeso*, dramma per musica, 3 acts
l: anonymous (*P-Cug, Cul, Ln* 2, *Lt*)

*1740*

Carnival

6 June

Paço da Ribeira
*Madama Ciana*, dramma per musica, 3 acts
l: anonymous (*P-Cug, Ln*)
*L'Angelica*, serenata
l: anonymous (*P-Lac, Ln*)
Teatro (Casa dos Bonecos) do Bairro Alto
*Endimião e Diana*, ópera
t: Padre Frei Inácio Xavier do Couto (Ms *P-EVp* 2)
Teatro Novo da Rua dos Condes
*Alessandro nell'Indie*, dramma per musica, 3 acts
l: anonymous (Carvalhais, 'Subsídios')
*Catone in Utica*, dramma per musica, 3 acts
l: Metastasio (*P-Cug*)
m: Rinaldo di Capua
*Ciro riconosciuto*, dramma per musica, 3 acts
l: anonymous (*P-Cug, Cul, Ln;* Ms copy *P-Ln* Cód. 1387 '1793')
*Ezio*, dramma per musica, 3 acts
l: Metastasio (*P-Ln*)

*1741*

Carnival

Teatro (Casa dos Bonecos) do Bairro Alto
*A ninfa Siringa ou os amores de Pan, e Siringa*, ópera portugueza*
*Semiramis em Babilonia*, ópera portugueza*

Teatro (Casa dos Bonecos) do Bairro Alto
and Teatro da Mouraria
   *Adolonimo em Sidonia*, ópera portugueza\*
Teatro da Mouraria
   *Encantos de Merlim*, ópera portugueza\*
Teatro Novo da Rua dos Condes
   *Didone abbandonata*, dramma per musica,
   3 acts
   l: Metastasio (*P-Cug, Cul*)
   m: Rinaldo di Capua

[Autumn]–January 1742    *Ipermestra*, dramma per musica, 3 acts
(Monfort, p. 595)    l: anonymous (*P-Ln*)
   m: Rinaldo di Capua

\*Published in *Óperas portuguezas*, which also contains the following *óperas*, for which no date is given: *Adriano em Siria* (Bairro Alto); *Novos encantos de amor, Filinto perseguido e exaltado, Os encantos de Circe* (Mouraria).

*1742*

   Paço da Ribeira
31 March    *Corsira*, serenata
   l: anonymous (*P-Ln*)
   Teatro Novo da Rua dos Condes
January (Monfort, p. 595)    *Bajazet*, dramma per musica, 3 acts
   l: anonymous (*P-Ln*)

*1744*

   Vila Viçosa
7 February    '*Roubo do Velocino de Ouro, Ópera* que ... fizeram os Ministros da Real Capélla daquella Villa em aplauso das melhoras del Rey nosso Senhor' (*Gazeta de Lisboa*)

*1747*

   Nossa Senhora da Nazaré
9 September    'Opera intitulada Alecrim e Mãjerona reprezentada por bons coriozos com admiraveis instromentos e vozes bem ajustadas' (Monfort, p. 598)
   Oporto
13 September    'Oratório em musica de cinco vozes com recitados, e arias, na forma das operas: tudo composto em metro Portuguez ... e alusivo à melhoria do nosso Soberano' (*Gazeta de Lisboa*)

| | |
|---|---|
| *1750* | |
| | Death of João V on July 31 |
| *1752* | |
| | Paço da Ribeira |
| 6 June | 'serenata' (with Gizziello singing, *Gazeta de Lisboa*) |
| | Paço da Ribeira, Teatro do Forte |
| 12 September | *Il Siroe*, dramma per musica, 3 acts |
| | l: anonymous (*P-Cug, Cul, EVp, Lac*) |
| | sc: David Perez (*P-La* 45–v–41/3, 'Prima opera/Nell' apertura del nuovo Teatro nel Real Palatio [*sic*] per li 12 di 7.ʰʳᵉ 1752. Orig. ˡᵉ) |
| 4 December | *L'Ippolito*, serenata a sei voci |
| | l: D. Antonio Tedeschi (*P-Lan, Ln, Mp*) |
| | sc: Francisco António de Almeida (*P-Ln* CIC n° 17) |
| Autumn | *Il Demofoonte*, dramma per musica, 3 acts |
| | l: Metastasio (*P-Cul, Ln*) |
| | sc. & pts: David Perez (*P-La* 45–v–5/7, 54–I–80/2, 54–III–71 *90/99*; *P-Ln* CIC    n° 100) |
| *1753* | |
| | Paço da Ribeiro, Teatro do Forte |
| January | 'opera' (*Gazeta de Lisboa*) |
| | Teatro de Salvaterra |
| Carnival (21 January, score) | *Didone abbandonata*, dramma per musica, 3 acts |
| | l: Metastasio (*P-Ln* 2) |
| | sc. & pts: David Perez (*P-La* 45–v–26/8, 45–v–48/9, 54–III–71 *63/83*) |
| | *La fantesca*, intermezzi |
| | l: anonymous (*P-Cug*) |
| | m: Johann Adolf Hasse |
| | Paço da Ribeira |
| 19 March | 'serenata' (in the Queen's chambers, *Gazeta de Lisboa*) |
| | Paço da Ribeira, Teatro do Forte |
| 31 March | *L'Olimpiade*, dramma per musica, 3 acts ('serenata' in the King's chambers, *Gazeta de Lisboa*) |
| | l: Metastasio (*P-Cug*) |
| | sc: David Perez (*P-La* 45–v–57/8, 'Nel Real Teatro in Lisbona la primavera del 1753') |

| | |
|---|---|
| 6 June | *L'eroe cinese*, dramma per musica, 3 acts |
| | l: Metastasio (*P-Ln*) |
| | sc: David Perez (*P-La* 45–v–29/32) |
| 26 June | 'opera' (*Gazeta de Lisboa*) |
| 23 September | 'serenata' (*Gazeta de Lisboa*) |
| October | 'opera' (*Gazeta de Lisboa*) |

*1754*

Teatro de Salvaterra

| | |
|---|---|
| Carnival | *L'Adriano in Siria*, dramma per musica, 3 acts |
| | l: Metastasio (*P-La, Ln*) |
| | sc: David Perez (*P-La* 45–IV–39/41, 54–I–86/8; *P-Ln* CIC n° 95) |

Paço da Ribeira, Teatro do Forte

| | |
|---|---|
| 31 March | *L'Ipermestra*, dramma per musica, 3 acts |
| | l: anonymous (*P-Cug, Lac, Ln*) |
| | sc. & pts: David Perez (*P-La* 45–v–34/6, 54–I–77/9, 54–III–71 84/89) |
| 6 June | *L'Artaserse*, dramma per musica, 3 acts |
| | l: Metastasio (*P-Cug, Ln*) |
| | sc. & pts: David Perez (*P-La* 45–IV–51/3, 47–V–10, 54–I–74/6, 54–III–63; *P-Ln* CIC n° 97; IPPC) |
| 17 December | 'serenata' (in the King's chambers, *Gazeta de Lisboa*) |

*1755*

Paço da Ribeira, Casa da Ópera

| | |
|---|---|
| 31 March (–May, *Gazeta de Lisboa*) | *Alessandro nell'Indie*, dramma per musica, 3 acts |
| | l: Metastasio (*P-Cug, Cul 2, Ln*) |
| | sc: David Perez (*P-La* 45–IV–45/7, 45–IV–48/50, 'Milano … 1752', 54–I–83/5; *P-Ln* CIC n° 96) |
| 6 June | *La clemenza di Tito*, dramma per musica, 3 acts |
| | l: Metastasio (*P-Cug 2, Ln 3*) |
| | sc: Antonio Mazzoni (*P-La* 45–I–17) |
| Autumn | *Antigono*, dramma per musica, 3 acts |
| | l: Metastasio (*BR-Rn*; quoted in McClymonds, *Niccolò Jommelli*) |
| | sc: Antonio Mazzoni (*P-La* 45–I–9/11) |

*1760*

Oporto, Teatro Público

15 August–17 September
4 *opere buffe* by a company directed by Niccolà Setaro (see p. III above)

*1761*

Palácio de Queluz

[? August for the birth of Prince Joséph on 21 August]
*La vera felicità*, componimento drammatico da cantarsi, 3 acts
l: Marianno Bergonzoni Martelli (*P-Cug 2, Cul, Ln 3, Lt*)
m: David Perez

*1762*

Oporto, Teatro Público
*Il trascurato*, dramma giocoso per musica, 3 acts
l: anonymous (Carvalhais, 'Subsídios')

*1763*

Teatro de Salvaterra

Carnival
*Il mercato di Malmantile*, dramma giocoso per musica, 3 acts
l: Carlo Goldoni (*P-Cul, EVp, Ln 2, Lt*)
sc: Domenico Fischietti (*P-La* 44–VI–27/9)
*Il dottore*, dramma giocoso per musica, 3 acts
l: Carlo Goldoni (*P-Cul, Ln 2*)
sc: anonymous (*P-La* 47–I–26/8, 'Salvat. Carn. 1763', 47–I–29/31)

Teatro de Queluz

[? November, AHMF, CX.3, 'Novembro 1763, dezarmar a Caza da Opera de Queluz']
*L'amante ridicolo deluso*, farsetta per musica, 2 acts
l: Alessandro Pioli (*P-Cug, Cul, Lac, Ln, Lt*)
sc: Niccolò Piccinni (*P-La* 45–VI–18/19, 'Intermezzo primo e secondo', 47–V–7/8; *P-VV*)

*1764*

Teatro de Salvaterra

Carnival
*Amor contadino*, dramma giocoso per musica, 3 acts
l: anonymous (*P-Cug, Cul, Lac, Ln 2, Lt*)

sc: Giovanni Battista Lampugnani (*P-La* 47–I–14/16, 47–III–33)

*L'Arcadia in Brenta*, dramma giocoso per musica, 3 acts

l: Carlo Goldoni (*P-Cug* 2, *Cul, Lac, Ln* 3)

sc: João Cordeiro da Silva [anon: *P-La* 47–I–16/19]

Palácio de Queluz

*Gli orti esperidi*, dramma per musica da cantarsi, 2 parts

l: Metastasio (*P-Cug, Cul, Lac, Ln*)

m: Luciano Xavier dos Santos

Teatro da Ajuda

6 June
*Componimento drammatico* da cantarsi ... che serve d'introduzione ad una farsetta in musica

l: anonymous (*P-Cul* 2, *La, Lac, Ln, Lt*)

m: João Cordeiro da Silva

*Il cavaliere per amore*, farsetta per musica, 2 parts

l: anonymous (*P-Cug* 2, *Cul, Lac, Ln, Lt*)

sc: Niccolò Piccinni (*P-La* 45–VI–51/2, 'Intermezzi')

*1765*

Teatro de Salvaterra

Carnival
*Demetrio*, dramma per musica, 3 acts

l: Metastasio (*P-Cug, La, Ln*)

sc: David Perez (*P-La* 45–V–2/4, 48–III–48/9, 'Originale' *P–VV*)

–
*Il mondo della luna*, dramma giocoso per musica, 3 acts

l: Carlo Goldoni (*P-Cul, La, Lac, Ln, Lt*)

sc: Pedro António Avondano (*P-La* 44–II–22/4)

Teatro da Ajuda

6 June
*Gli stravaganti*, farsetta per musica, 2 acts

l: anonymous (*P-Cul, Lac, Ln, Lt*)

sc. & pts: Niccolò Piccinni (*P-La* 46–I–38/48, 54–III–72, 54–III–73 I/II)

Palácio de Queluz

29 June
*Ercole sul Tago*, dramma per musica da cantarsi, 1 act

l: Vittorio Amadeo Cigna-Santi (*P-Cug*)

sc: Luciano Xavier dos Santos [*P-La* 48–II–41, '1785']
Teatro da Ajuda

Autumn | *I francesi brillanti*, dramma giocoso per musica, 3 acts
l: Pasquale Mililotti (*P-Cug, Cul, Lac, Lcg, Ln, Lt*)
m: Giovanni Paisiello
Teatro do Bairro Alto

Summer | *Didone*, dramma per musica, 3 acts
l: Metastasio (*P-Cul, Ln*)
m: David Perez and others (see Salvaterra 1753)

[21 August? for the birthday of Prince José] | *Zenobia*, dramma per musica, 3 acts
l: anonymous (*P-Cug, Cul*)
sc: David Perez (*P-La* 45–V–55/6)
Oporto, Academia de Cirurgia Portuense

20 January | 'serenata' (*P-Ln* Res. 1559 P(7))
m: Giacomo Sartori
Teatro do Bairro Alto

Autumn | *La Semiramide riconosciuta*, dramma per musica, 3 acts
l: Metastasio (*P-Cug, Ln*)
sc: David Perez (*P-La* 45–V–52/4, 'La Semiramide'
Teatro da Rua dos Condes

28 July–(*Hebdomadario Lisbonense*) | *Il mercato di Malmantile*, dramma giocoso per musica, 3 acts
l: [Carlo Goldoni] (*P-Cug*)
sc: Domenico Fischietti [see Salvaterra 1763]

Autumn | *Le contadine bizzarre*, dramma giocoso per musica, 3 acts
l: anonymous (*P-Cug* 3, *Cul, Lcg, Ln* 2; Ms copy *P-Ln* Cód. 1393, '1789')
sc: Niccolò Piccinni [*P-La* 45–VI–59/61, 'Nel Teatro in S. Samuel. 1763. Venezia', 47–VI–31/3, 'Nel Teatro in S. Samuel. 1764']

— | *La contadina in corte*, dramma giocoso per musica, 3 acts
l: anonymous (*P-Cug, Lt*)

139

*1766*

|  |  |
|---|---|
|  | Teatro de Salvaterra |
| Carnival | *La cascina*, dramma giocoso per musica, 3 acts |
|  | l: Carlo Goldoni (*P-Cug* 2, *Lcg*, *Ln*) |
|  | sc: Giuseppe Scolari (*P-La* 46–v–52/4) |
|  | Teatro da Ajuda |
| 31 March | *L'incognita perseguitata*, dramma giocoso per musica, 3 acts |
|  | l: Giuseppe Petrosellini (*P-Cug*, *Cul*, *Lac*, *Lcg*, *Ln* 2) |
|  | sc: Niccolò Piccinni (*P-La* 46–1–13/15, 'S. Samuel. 1764') |
| 6 June (14 performances, AHMF, CX. 5) | *Le vicende della sorte*, dramma giocoso per musica, 2 acts |
|  | l: Giuseppe Petrosellini (*P-Cug*, *Cul*, *Lac*, *Lcg*, *Ln* 2, *Lt*) |
|  | m: Niccolò Piccinni |
| Autumn | *L'amore in musica*, dramma giocoso per musica, 3 acts |
|  | l: anonymous (*P-Cug*, *Lcg*) |
|  | sc: Antonio Boroni (*P-La* 44–III–72/4) |
|  | Palácio de Queluz |
| 29 June | *Il natal di Giove*, dramma per musica da cantarsi, 1 act |
|  | l: Metastasio (*P-Lan*) |
|  | m: Luciano Xavier dos Santos |
|  | Teatro do Bairro Alto |
| 31 March | *L'amore artigiano*, dramma giocoso per musica, 3 acts |
|  | l: Carlo Goldoni (*P-Cug* 2, *Cul*, *Lac*) |
|  | m: Gaetano Latilla |
|  | Teatro da Rua dos Condes |
|  | *La calamità de' cuori*, dramma giocoso per musica, 3 acts |
|  | l: anonymous (*P-Cug*, *Cul* 2, *Lcg*) |
|  | m: Baldassare Galuppi |
|  | *Il ciarlone*, dramma giocoso per musica, 3 acts |
|  | l: Antonio Palomba (*P-Cug* 2, *Cul* 2, *Lcg*) |
|  | m: Giuseppe Avossa (Abbos) |
| September | *L'olandese in Italia*, dramma giocoso per musica, 3 acts |
|  | l: Niccolò Tassi (*P-Cug*, *Cul* 2, *Lac*) |
|  | m: Giovanni Maria Rutini |

Autumn
*Il proseguimento del ciarlone*, dramma
giocoso per musica, 3 acts
l: Giacomo Fiorini (*P-Cug, Cul, Lt*)
m: Luigi Marescalchi

*1767*

Teatro de Salvaterra

Carnival
*Enea nel Lazio*, dramma per musica, 3 acts
l: anonymous (*P-Cug* 3, *Cul, Lac, Lcg, Ln, Lt*)
sc: Niccolò Jommelli (*P-La* 47–X–8/10)

–
*Notte critica*, dramma giocoso per musica, 3
acts
l: Carlo Goldoni (*P-Cug* 2, *Lac, Ln, Lt*)
sc: Niccolò Piccinni (*P-La* 46–I–24/6)

Teatro de Queluz
*L'isola disabitata*, componimento drammatico da rappresentarsi, 1 act
l: Metastasio (*P-Cug, Cul, Ln*)
sc: David Perez (*P-La* 45–V–33, 54–I–16)

Teatro da Ajuda

6 June
*Il ratto della sposa*, dramma giocoso per
musica, 3 acts
l: Gaetano Martinelli (*P-Cug* 2, *Cul, Lac,
Lcg, Lt*)
sc. & pts: Pietro Alessandro Guglielmi (*P-La*
44–VIII–59/61, 47–V–41/9, 54–III–57/9)

Autumn
*L'isola della fortuna*, dramma giocoso per
musica, 3 acts
l: Giovanni Bertati (*P-Cug* 2, *Cul* 2, *Lac, Ln*
2, *Lt*)
sc: Andrea Lucchesi (*P-La* 44–XI–27/9)

*1768*

Teatro de Salvaterra

Carnival
*Pelope*, dramma per musica, 3 acts
l: Mattia Verazzi (*P-Cug* 2, *Cul* 2, *Lac, Ln* 2)
sc: Niccolò Jommelli (Act 1 *P-La* 44–X–74)

–
*Le vicende amorose*, dramma giocoso per
musica, 3 acts
l: Pallavicino (*P-Cug* 2, *Cul, Lac, Ln*)
sc: Ferdinando Giuseppe Bertoni (*P-La*
44–III–7/8, 'Le vicende d'amore ... In San
Moisè ... 1760', 44–III–9/11)

Teatro da Ajuda

| | |
|---|---|
| 31 March, 6 June (12 performances, AHMF, CX. 5) | *Solimano*, dramma per musica, 3 acts<br>l: anonymous (*P-Cug* 2, *Cul, Lac, Lcg, Lt*)<br>sc: David Perez (*P-La* 45–V–44/6, 'Neli Gloriosi giorni de 31 di Marzo e 6 di Giugno', 47–VI–25/7) |
| Summer | *Le due serve rivali*, dramma giocoso per musica, 3 acts<br>l: anonymous (*P-Cug, Cul, La, Lac, Ln* 2)<br>sc: & pts: Tomaso Traetta (*P-La* 46–VI–41/54, 46–VII–28/9, 54–III–37/44) |

Palácio de Queluz

| | |
|---|---|
| | *Il sogno di Scipione*, dramma per musica da cantarsi<br>l: Metastasio (*P-Cug, Lac, Lt*)<br>m: Luciano Xavier dos Santos |

Teatro da Rua dos Condes

| | |
|---|---|
| Carnival | *Artaserse*, dramma per musica, 3 acts<br>l: Metastasio (*P-Cug* 3)<br>m: Giuseppe Scolari |
| Lent | *La Betulia liberata*, opera drammatica da rappresentarsi, 2 parts<br>l: Metastasio (*P-Cug*)<br>m: Giuseppe Scolari<br>[*L'Arcifanfano*, dramma giocoso per musica, 3 acts<br>l: anonymous (*P-Cug* 2, *Cul, Ln*, n.d., no names of singers)<br>m: Giuseppe Scolari] |
| Autumn | *Demetrio*, dramma per musica, 3 acts<br>l: anonymous (*P-Cug*)<br>sc: David Perez (see Salvaterra 1765) |

Oporto, Teatro Público

| | |
|---|---|
| 6 June | *Il tempio dell'Eternità*, componimento drammatico da rappresentarsi in musica, 1 act<br>l: Metastasio (*P-Cug, Cul*) |

*1769*

Teatro de Salvaterra

| | |
|---|---|
| Carnival | *La finta astrologa*, dramma giocoso per musica, 3 acts<br>l: anonymous (*P-Cug, Cul, La, Lac, Ln* 2)<br>sc: Niccolò Piccinni (*P-La* 45–VI–29/31, 'L'Astrologa') |

| | |
|---|---|
| – | *Il Vologeso*, dramma per musica, 3 acts<br>l: anonymous (*P-Cug* 2, *Lac*, *Lcg*, *Ln*)<br>sc: Niccolò Jommelli (*P-La* 44–X–57/9)<br>Palácio da Ajuda |
| 17 March | 'Oratória' (AHMF, CX. 257) |
| 19 March | 'Oratória da Paixão' (AHMF, CX. 257)<br>Teatro da Ajuda |
| 31 March–28 December (10 performances, AHMF, CX. 257) | *L'amore industrioso*, dramma per musica, 3 acts<br>l: anonymous (*P-Cug* 2, *Cul*, *Ln* 2)<br>sc. & pts: João de Sousa Carvalho (*P-La* 48–I–13/26, 54–III–48/55)<br>overture, mod. edn: Lisbon, Fundação Calouste Gulbenkian, 1960, 1964 (Portugaliae Musica II: sc. & pts.), ov. rec: Philips 835770 LY |
| 6 June (12 performances, AHMF, CX. 5) | *Fetonte*, dramma per musica, 3 acts<br>l: Mattia Verazzi (*P-Cug* 2, *Cul* 2, *La*, *Lac*, *Ln* 2, *Lt*)<br>sc: Niccolò Jommelli (*P-La* 44–X–14/16)<br>Teatro de Queluz<br>*Le cinesi*, componimento drammatico che introduce a un ballo, 1 act<br>l: Metastasio (*P-Cug* 2, *Lac*, *Lt*)<br>m: David Perez |

**1770**

| | |
|---|---|
| | Teatro de Salvaterra |
| 20 January–25 February (13 performances, AHMF, CX. 257) | *Il matrimonio per concorso*, dramma giocoso per musica, 3 acts<br>1: Gaetano Martinelli (*P-Cul*, *Lcg*)<br>sc: Niccolò Jommelli (*P-La* 44–X–24/6) |
| 18 January–24 February (13 performances, AHMF, CX. 257) | *Il Re pastore*, dramma per musica, 3 acts.<br>l: Metastasio (*P-Cug* 3, *Cul*, *Lac*, *Lcg*, *Ln*)<br>sc: Niccolò Jommelli (*P-La* 44–X–63/5)<br>Palácio da Ajuda |
| 19 March | 'serenata' (AHMF, CX. 5) |
| 31 March | 'serenata' (AHMF, CX. 5)<br>Teatro da Ajuda |
| April (for the Queen's birthday) | *La schiava liberata*, dramma serio-comico per musica, 3 acts<br>l: Gaetano Martinelli (*P-Cug*, *Cul*, *Lcg*)<br>sc: Niccolò Jommelli (*P-La* 44–X–48/50) |
| 6 June | *La Nitteti*, dramma per musica, 3 acts<br>l: Metastasio (*P-Cug*, *Cul*, *Lac*, *Lcg*, *Ln* 2, *Lt*) |

<table>
<tbody>
<tr><td></td><td>sc: & pts: Niccolò Jommelli (*P-La* 44–X–27/9, 44–X–30/47)</td></tr>
<tr><td></td><td>Teatro do Bairro Alto</td></tr>
<tr><td>Summer</td><td>*Il viaggiatore ridicolo*, dramma giocoso per musica<br>l: Carlo Goldoni (*P-Cug, Lac, Ln* 2)<br>m: Giuseppe Scolari (with arias by Antonio Mazzoni)</td></tr>
<tr><td>Autumn</td><td>*L'incognita perseguitata*, dramma giocoso per musica, 3 acts<br>l: Giuseppe Petrosellini (*P-Cug, Ln*)<br>m: Niccolò Piccinni [see Ajuda 1766]</td></tr>
<tr><td></td><td>Oporto, Teatro Publico (Cacciò, quoted in Carvalhais, 'Subsídios')<br>*L'Achille*<br>*La Didone abbandonata*<br>*Il Demetrio*<br>*Li francesi brillanti*<br>*La serva spiritosa*<br>*Il buovo d'Antona*<br>*Le due serve rivali*</td></tr>
</tbody>
</table>

## 1771

<table>
<tbody>
<tr><td></td><td>Teatro de Salvaterra</td></tr>
<tr><td>Carnival</td><td>*Il cacciatore deluso*, dramma serio-comico per musica, 3 acts<br>l: Gaetano Martinelli (*P-Cug, Cul, Lac, Ln, Lt*)<br>sc: Niccolò Jommelli (*P-La* 44–IX–62/4)</td></tr>
<tr><td>–</td><td>*Semiramide*, dramma per musica, 3 acts<br>l: Metastasio (*P-Cug, Cul, Lac, Lcg, Ln* 2, *Lt*)<br>sc: Niccolò Jommelli (*P-La* 44–X–66/8, 'Placenza 1753')</td></tr>
<tr><td>31 March</td><td>*idem*, at the Teatro da Ajuda (AHMF, CX. 5)</td></tr>
<tr><td></td><td>Teatro da Ajuda</td></tr>
<tr><td>6 June–18 December (10 performances, AHMF, CX. 5)</td><td>*La clemenza di Tito*, dramma per musica, 3 acts<br>l: Metastasio (*P-La, Lac, Lcg, Ln* 3, *Lt*; Ms copy *P-Lan* RMC no. 2210)<br>sc. & pts: Niccolò Jommelli (*P-La* 44–IX–65/84, 54–III–66)</td></tr>
</tbody>
</table>

| | |
|---|---|
| 25 June–21 December (8 performances) | *Il cacciatore deluso* rpt (AHMF, CX. 5) |
| 29 June | Palácio de Queluz |
| | *Il palladio conservato*, dramma per musica da cantarsi, 1 act. |
| | l: Metastasio (*P-Cug* 2) |
| | sc: Luciano Xavier dos Santos (*P-La* 48–III–7, '1783') |
| 31 August ('for the English duke') | *L'Imeneo in Atene* (AHMF, CX. 5) |
| | [*P-La* 47–I–38/9: *Imeneo in Atene* by Nicola Porpora, '1726, Venezia'] |
| | Teatro do Bairro Alto |
| Carnival | *Il bejglierbei di Caramania*, dramma giocoso per musica |
| | l: Girolamo Tonioli (*P-Cug*) |
| | m: Giuseppe Scolari |
| | House of L. G. Pientzenauer |
| Lent | *L'Isacco, figura del Redentore*, oratorio per musica da cantarsi nella privata Assemblea di Luigi Giuseppe Pientzenauer |
| | l: anonymous (*P-Lac*) |
| | m: José Joaquim dos Santos (performed by singers of the Royal Chapel) |

*1772*

| | |
|---|---|
| | Teatro de Salvaterra |
| Carnival | *La scaltra letterata*, dramma giocoso per musica, 3 acts |
| | l: Antonio Palomba (*P-Cug* 2, *Cul, Lcg, Ln* 2) |
| | sc: Niccolò Piccinni (*P-La* 46–I–35/7) |
| – | *Lo spirito di contradizione*, dramma giocoso per musica, 3 acts |
| | l: Gaetano Martinelli (*P-Cug, Cul, Lcg, Ln*) |
| | sc: Jerónimo Francisco de Lima (*P-La* 48–II–10/11) |
| | Palácio da Ajuda |
| 19 March | 'Oratória' (AHMF, CX. 5) |
| | [*Adamo ed Eva*, dramma sacro, 2 parts |
| | l: anonymous (*P-Cug*, '1772'; Ms copy *P-Lan* n° 2220) |
| | m: Pedro António Avondano] |
| | Teatro da Ajuda |
| 20 April–17 December (9 performances, AHMF, CX. 5) | *Ezio*, dramma per musica, 3 acts |
| | l: Metastasio (*P-Cug, Cul* 2, *Ln* 2) |
| | sc: Niccolò Jommelli (*P-La* 44–X–11/13, 48–III–47) |

6 June–18 December (9 performances, AHMF, CX. 5)

*Le avventure di Cleomede*, dramma serio-comico per musica
l: Gaetano Martinelli (*P-Cul, Lac, Lcg, Ln* 2, *Lt*)
sc: Niccolò Jommelli (*P-La* 44–IX–58/61)

29 September, 4, 25 October

*La scaltra letterata* rpt (AHMF, CX. 5)

29 June

Palácio de Queluz
*Issea*, serenata pastorale
l: anonymous (*P-Cug, Cul, Ln* 2, *Lt*)
sc: Giulio Gaetano Pugnani (*P-La* 47–IV–16)

Teatro do Bairro Alto
*D. Afonso de Albuquerque em Goa*, tragi-comédia (Sousa Bastos, *Carteira do Artista*, p. 721)
t: Antonio José de Paula
m: Frei Manuel de Santo Elias

Teatro da Rua dos Condes

Summer

*L'anello incantato*, dramma giocoso per musica, 3 acts
l: Giovanni Bertati (*P-Cug, Cul, Lt, Ln*)
m: Ferdinando Giuseppe Bertoni

–

*Il disertore*, dramma giocoso per musica, 3 acts
l: anonymous (*P-Cul, Lac, Lt*)
m: Pietro Alessandro Guglielmi

Autumn

*Antigono*, dramma per musica, 3 acts
l: Metastasio (*P-Cug* 2, *Cul, Lcg, Ln, Lt*)
sc: Gian Francesco di Majo (*P-La* 44–XI–36/8)

–

*L'isola di Alcina*, dramma giocoso per musica, 3 acts
l: Giovanni Bertati (*P-Cul, Ln* 2, *Lt*)
m: Giuseppe Gazzaniga

*La locanda*, dramma giocoso per musica, 3 acts
l: Giovanni Bertati (*P-Cul* 2)
m: Giuseppe Gazzaniga

Oporto, Teatro Público

6 June

*Demofoonte*, dramma per musica, 3 acts
l: Metastasio (Carvalhais, 'Subsídios')
sc: David Perez (see Paço da Ribeira 1752)

*1773*

| | |
|---|---|
| | Teatro de Salvaterra |
| Carnival | *La fiera di Sinigaglia*, dramma giocoso per musica, 3 acts<br>l: Carlo Goldoni (*P-Cug, Cul, Lcg, Ln* 2, *Lt*)<br>sc: Domenico Fischietti (*P-La* 44–VI– 24/6) |
| – | *Le lavandarine*, farsetta giocosa per musica, 2 parts<br>l: Francesco Mari (*P-Cug, Cul, Lcg, Ln* 2, *Lt*)<br>m: Francesco Zanetti |
| – | *La pastorella illustre*, azione testrale per musica, 2 parts<br>l: Tagliazucci (*P-Cug* 2, *Lcg, Ln*)<br>sc: Niccolò Jommelli (*P-La* 44–X–72/3) |
| | Palácio da Ajuda |
| 19 March | *L'imeneo in Atene* rpt (AHMF, CX. 5; see Queluz 1771) |
| | Teatro da Ajuda |
| 31 March | *Cerere placata*, festa teatrale, 2 acts (AHMF, CX. 5)<br>sc: Niccolò Jommelli (*P-La* 44–IX–85/6, 'Napoli 14 Settembre 1772. Dal Sig. <sup>r</sup> Duca d'Arcos') |
| 30 April–13 October (6 performances, AHMF, XX/Z/40) | *Armida abbandonata*, dramma per musica, 3 acts<br>l: anonymous (*P-Cug, Cul, Lac, Lcg, Ln* 2, *Lt*)<br>sc: Niccolò Jommelli (*P-La* 44–IX–46/8, 47–VI–19/21, 48–III–42) |
| 6 June–14 November (7 performances, AHMF, XX/Z/40) | *Eumene*, dramma per musica, 3 acts<br>l: Apostolo Zeno (*P-Cug* 2, *Cul, Ln, Lt*)<br>sc: João de Sousa Carvalho (*P-La* 48–I–38/40, 'dramma serio') |
| | Teatro de Queluz |
| 2nd performance: 9 August (AHMF, XX/Z/40) | *La finta ammalata*, farsetta per musica, 2 acts<br>l: Antonio Palomba (*P-Ln* 2)<br>m: 'diversi celebri Maestri di Capella' |
| | Teatro da Rua dos Condes |
| Carnival | *La contessa di Bimbimpoli*, dramma giocoso per musica, 3 acts<br>l: Giovanni Bertati (*P-Cug, Cul, Lt*)<br>m: Gennaro Astaritta |

| | |
|---|---|
| Lent | *La Betulia libertata*, dramma sacro, 2 parts<br>l: Metastasio (*P-Cul, Lt; A valerosa Judith ou Bethulia liberata*, drama que no idioma italiano se reprezentou no teatro da R. dos Condes: *P-Cul* 2, *Lt*, TNM) |
| Spring | *La finta semplice o sia il tutore burlato*, dramma giocoso per musica, 3 acts<br>l: anonymous (*P-Lcg, Ln*)<br>m: Giacomo Insanguine |
| – | *La molinarella*, dramma giocoso per musica, 3 acts<br>l: anonymous (*P-Ln, Lt*)<br>m: Niccolò Piccinni |
| Summer | *Il barone di Rocca Antica*, intermezzo per musica, 2 parts<br>l: anonymous (*P-Cul, Lcg*)<br>m: Carlo Franchi |
| – | *Le finte gemelle*, dramma giocoso per musica, 3 acts<br>l: Giuseppe Petrosellini (*P-Cul, Lt*)<br>m: Niccolò Piccinni |
| – | *La giardiniera brillante*, intermezzo per musica, 2 parts<br>l: anonymous (*P-Cul, Ln*)<br>m: Giuseppe Sarti |
| – | *Le orfane svizzere*, dramma giocoso per musica, 3 acts<br>l: Pietro Chiari (*P-Lcg*)<br>m: Antonio Boroni |
| Autumn | *Il matrimonio per concorso*, dramma giocoso per musica, 3 acts<br>l: anonymous (*P-Cul, Lcg, Ln* 2, *Lt*)<br>m: Felice Alessandri |
| – | *La sposa fedele*, dramma giocoso per musica, 3 acts<br>l: anonymous (*P-Cug, Cul, Ln, Lt*)<br>sc: Pietro Alessandro Guglielmi [*P-La* 44–IX–10/11, 'San Moisè. Carnevale 1767'; *VV*] |
| Winter [–January 1774?] | *Il Cidde*, dramma per musica, 3 acts<br>l: Gioacchino Pizzi (*P-Cul, Lcg, Lt*)<br>sc: Antonio Sacchini [*P-La* 47–IV–29, 'Argentina 1769', 54–III–35/6] |

*1774*

Carnival

Teatro de Salvaterra

*Creusa in Delfo*, dramma per musica …
misto di cori, e danze, 2 acts (4 dances)
l: Gaetano Martinelli (*P-Cug, Cul, La* 2,
*Lcg, Ln* 2, *Lt*)
sc. & pts: David Perez (*P-La* 45–V–22/5,
48–III–34, 54–III–56)

–

*L'inimico delle donne*, dramma giocoso per
musica, 3 acts
l: Giovanni Bertati (*P-Cug Cul*, 2 *Ln, Lt*)
sc: Baldassare Galuppi (*P-La* 44–VII–3/5)

–

*Il superbo deluso*, dramma giocoso per
musica, 3 acts
l: Marco Coltellini (*P-Cug* 2, *Cul, Lcg, Ln* 2)
sc. & pts: Florian Leopold Gassman (*P-La*
44–VII–74/91, 45–III–55 *20/28*, 54–III–60
*1/19*, 54–III–61 *1/26*)

Teatro da Ajuda

Spring

*L'Olimpiade*, dramma per musica, 3 acts
l: Metastasio (*P-Cug, Cul, Lan, Ln* 2, *Lt*)
sc: Niccolò Jommelli (*P-La* 44–X–69/71)

6 June

*Il trionfo di Clelia*, dramma per musica, 3 acts
l: Metastasio (*P-Cug*, 2, *Cul, La, Ln* 2, *Lt*)
sc: Niccolò Jommelli (*P-La* 44–X–54/6)

Teatro de Queluz

(For the birth of the
Infanta D. Maria
Clementina)

*Il ritorno di Ulisse in Itaca*, componimento
drammatico per musica da rappresentarsi, 1
act
l: Mariano Bergonzoni Martelli (*P-Ln*)
m: David Perez

House of the Marquis of Penalva

*O Numen reconhecido*, drama para se cantar
em louvor de Sua Majestade Fidelissima na
occasião dos novos estabelecimentos das
Escolas Publicas das Artes e Sciencias … no
dia em que seus filhos o Conde de Tarouca e
Jose Telles da Sylva fizeraõ exame de Logica
e Metafysica.
l: anonymous (TNM)

Teatro da Rua dos Condes

Spring

*L'impresa d'opera*, dramma giocoso per
musica, 3 acts

|  |  |
|---|---|
| | l: anonymous (*P-Cul, La, Ln, Lt*) |
| | sc: Pietro Alessandro Guglielmi [*P-La* 44–VIII–54/5] |
| – | *L'isola d'amore*, intermezzo per musica, 2 acts |
| | l: anonymous (*P-Cul, La, Lcg*) |
| | m: Antonio Sacchini |
| Summer | *L'amore senza malizia*, dramma giocoso per musica, 3 acts |
| | l: Pietro Chiari (Carvalhais, 'Subsídios') |
| | m: Bernardino Ottoni [*P-La* 45–III–28/9] |
| Autumn | *Calandrano*, dramma giocoso per musica, 3 acts |
| | l: Giovanni Bertati (*P-Cul, La, Ln, Lt, Pm*) |
| | m: Giuseppe Gazzaniga |

*1775*

Teatro de Salvaterra

|  |  |
|---|---|
| Carnival | *L'accademia di musica/La conversazione*, divertimenti per musica |
| | l: anonymous (*P-Cug* 2, *Lcg, Ln* 2, *Lt*) |
| | sc. & pts: Niccolò Jommelli (*P-La* 44–IX–27/42, 54–III–46) |
| – | *I filosofi immaginari*, dramma giocoso per musica, 3 acts |
| | l: anonymous (*P-Cug, Cul, Lcg*) |
| | sc: Gennaro Astaritta (*P-La* 44–II–12/14) |
| – | *L'incostante*, intermezzi per musica, 2 parts |
| | l: anonymous (*P-Cug* 2, *Cul, Lcg, Ln, Lt*) |
| | sc: Niccolò Piccinni (*P-La* 46–I–16/17) |
| – | *Lucio Papirio dittatore*, dramma per musica, 3 acts |
| | l: Apostolo Zeno (*P-Cug* 2, *Cul, Lcg, Ln, Lt*) |
| | sc: Giovanni Paisiello (*P-La* 45–IV–3/4) |

Teatro da Ajuda

|  |  |
|---|---|
| 31 March | *Li napoletani in America*, dramma giocoso per musica, 3 acts |
| | l: Francesco Cerlone(*P-Cug, Cul, Lcg, Ln* 2) |
| | m: Niccolò Piccinni |
| 6 June | *Demofoonte*, dramma per musica, 3 acts |
| | l: Metastasio (*P-Cul, Lcg, Ln, Lt*) |
| | sc: Niccolò Jommelli (*P-La* 44–IX–93, 44–X–1/5) |

|  |  |
|---|---|
|  | Casa da Alfândega, Sala do Selo |
| 7 June (on the inaugu-ration of the equestrian statue of José I) | *L'eroe coronato*, serenata per musica<br>l: Gaetano Martinelli (*P-Cug, Cul, Lac* 2, *Ln* 6; Ms copy *P-Lan* RMC n° 2282)<br>m: David Perez |
| 8 June (*idem*) | Sala do Tribunal da Junta do Comércio<br>*O monumento imortal*, drama para cantar-se<br>l: Teotónio Gomes de Carvalho (*P-Cug* 2, *Cul, La, Lac* 3, *Ln* 3 Ms copy *P-Lan* RMC n° 2202)<br>m: João de Sousa Carvalho (according to Frei Cláudio da Conceição, *Gabinete Histórico*, vol. XVII, p. 284, quoted in Vieira, II, p. 341)<br>Teatro da Rua dos Condes<br>*Il geloso*, dramma giocoso per musica, 3 acts<br>l: Girolamo Tonioli (Carvalhais, 'Subsídios')<br>m: Alberto José Gomes da Silva |

## 1776

|  |  |
|---|---|
|  | Teatro de Salvaterra |
| Carnival | *La cameriera per amore*, dramma giocoso per musica, 3 acts<br>l: anonymous (*P-Cul* 3, *Lcg, Ln* 2)<br>sc: Felice Alessandri (*P-La* 44–I–13/15) |
| – | *La contadina superba ovvero il giocatore burlato*, farsa per musica, 2 parts<br>l: anonymous (*P-Cug* 2, *Cul, Lcg, Lac, Ln* 2, *Lt*)<br>sc: Pietro Alessandro Guglielmi (*P-La* 44–VIII–43/44) |
| – | *Il filosofo amante*, farsa per musica, 2 acts<br>l: anonymous (*P-Cul* 2, *Lt*)<br>sc: Giambattista Borghi (*P-La* 44–III–62/63) |
| – | *Ifigenia in Tauride*, dramma per musica, 3 acts<br>l: Mattia Verazzi (*P-Cug, Lcg, Ln, Lt*)<br>sc: Niccolò Jommelli (*P-La* 44–X–17/19, 'L'Ifigenia, Roma 1751') |
| – | *Il tutore ingannato*, dramma giocoso per musica, 3 acts<br>l: anonymous (*P-Cug, Cul, Lac, Lt*)<br>sc: Luigi Marescalchi (*P-La* 44–XI–73/75) |

|  | Teatro da Ajuda |
|---|---|
| 6 June | *Alessandro nell'Indie*, dramma per musica, 3 acts<br>l: Metastasio (*P-Cul, Ln*)<br>sc: Niccolò Jommelli (*P-La* 44–IX–43/45) |

*1776/77*

Oporto, Teatro Público (Cacciò, quoted in Carvalhais, 'Subsídios')
*Opere buffe* and *balli*

*1777*

| 24 February | Death of José I |
|---|---|
|  | Palácio da Ajuda |
| 17 December | *La Pace fra la Virtù e la Belleza*, componimento drammatico per musica ('serenata', AHMF, xx/G/19, f. 43)<br>l: anonymous (*P-Cug, Lcg*)<br>sc: David Perez (*P-La* 45–V–40, 45–V–47) |

*1778*

|  | Palácio da Ajuda |
|---|---|
| 31 March | *Gioas, Re di Giudà*, sacro componimento drammatico per musica da cantarsi in camera, 1 act<br>l: anonymous (*P-Cug, Cul, Lt*)<br>sc: António da Silva Gomes e Oliveira (*P-La* 48–III–18, 48–V–21) |
|  | Palácio de Queluz |
| 5 July | *Alcide al Bivio*, dramma per musica da cantarsi, 1 act<br>l: Metastasio (*P-Cug, Ln*)<br>sc: Luciano Xavier dos Santos (*P-La* 48–II–38) |
| 25 July | *L'Angelica*, serenata per musica<br>l: Metastasio (*P-Ln*)<br>sc: João de Sousa Carvalho (*P-La* 48–I–34/35; *VV*) |
| 21 August | *Il natal di Giove*, serenata per musica<br>l: Metastasio (*P-Cug*)<br>sc: João Cordeiro da Silva (*P-La* 48–III–31/32) |

|  | Teatro de Queluz |
|---|---|
| 17 December | *Il ritorno di Ulisse in Itaca*, componimento drammatico per musica da rappresentarsi ('opereta', AHMF, xx/G/20, f. 55), 1 act<br>l: Marianno Bergonzoni Martelli (*P-Cug, Cul, Lac, Ln*)<br>m: David Perez (see Queluz 1774) |

*1779*

|  | Palácio da Ajuda |
|---|---|
| 5 April (AHMF, xx/G/20, f. 62) | *Gli orti esperidi*, serenata per musica<br>l: Metastasio (Carvalhais, 'Subsídios')<br>sc: Jerónimo Francisco de Lima (*P-La* 48–II–4/5) |
| 29 June | *L'ommagio de'pastori*, serenata (AHMF, xx/G/20, f. 66) |
|  | Palácio de Queluz |
| 5 July | *Perseo*, serenata per musica<br>l: Gaetano Martinelli (*P-Cug, Ln*)<br>sc: João de Sousa Carvalho (*P-La* 48–I–46/47) |
| 25 July | *Ati, e Sangaride*, serenata per musica<br>l: Gaetano Martinelli (*P-Cug, Lcg, Ln* 2)<br>sc: Luciano Xavier dos Santos (*P-La* 48–II–39) |
| 21 August | *La Galatea*, serenata per musica<br>l: Metastasio (*P-Ln*)<br>sc: António da Silva Gomes e Oliveira (*P-La* 48–III–16/17) |
| 17 December | 'Serenata' (*Gazeta de Lisboa*)<br>[*Per l'Augustissimo giorno natalizio* di Sua Maestà Fedelissima Donna Maria I, Regina di Portogallo<br>l: Luigi Godard (2 edns: one printed in Rome, 1779, in *P-Cug*; the other printed in Lisbon, n.d., *P-Cug, EVp*)<br>sc: Marcello Bernardini di Capua (*P-La* 47–II–35, 'Cantata a cinque voci', no title)] |
|  | Palácio da Ajuda |
| 18 December | *La Pace fra la Virtù e la Belleza* rpt (AHMF, xx/G/20, f. 73; see Ajuda 1777) |

*1780*

|  | Palácia da Ajuda |
|---|---|
| 19 March | 'Oratória da Paixão' (AHMF, xx/G/20, f. 79) |

| | |
|---|---|
| 31 March | *L'isola disabitata*, serenata per musica<br>l: Metastasio (*P-EVp, Ln*)<br>sc: Niccolò Jommelli (*P-La* 44–x–24)<br>Palácio de Queluz |
| 29 June | *L'Endimione*, serenata per musica<br>l: Metastasio (*P-Cug, Cul, EVp*)<br>sc: Niccolò Jommelli (*P-La* 44–x–6/7)<br>Teatro da Ajuda |
| 5 July | *Testoride argonauta*, dramma per musica da rappresentarsi, 2 acts (*P-Cug, Ln, Lt*)<br>l: Gaetano Martinelli (*P-Cug, Ln, Lt*)<br>sc: João de Sousa Carvalho (*P-La* 48–I–50/I) |
| 25 July | *idem*, rpt (AHMF, CX. 13)<br>Palácio da Ajuda |
| 17 December | *Edalide e Cambise*, dramma per musica, I act ('serenata', AHMF, xx/G/20, f. 96)<br>l: anonymous (*P-Cul*)<br>sc: João Cordeiro da Silva (*P-La* 48–III–23/4, 'serenata') |
| 18 December | *L'isola disabitata* rpt (AHMF, xx/G/20, f. 96)<br>Oporto, Teatro Público<br>Tragedies and comedies, with 'intermezzi in musica' (Cacciò, quoted in Carvalhais, 'Subsídios') |

**1781**

| | |
|---|---|
| 23 January | Death of Queen Mariana Vitória<br>Palácio da Ajuda |
| 29 June | *Amore e Psiche*, dramma per musica, 2 acts ('serenata', AHMF, xx/G/20, f. 107)<br>l: Marco Coltellini (*P-EVp*)<br>sc: Joseph Schuster (*P-La* 46–v–18/19)<br>Palácio de Queluz |
| 5 July | *Seleuco, Re di Siria*, dramma per musica da cantarsi, I act ('serenata', AHMF, xx/G/20, f. 108)<br>l: Gaetano Martinelli (*P-EVp, Ln, Lt*)<br>sc: João de Sousa Carvalho (*P-La* 48–I–48/9) |
| 25 July | *Il natal d'Apollo*, serenata per musica<br>l: Saverio Mattei (*P-Cug, Cul, EVp, Ln*)<br>sc: Pasquale Cafaro (*P-La* 44–IV–30/I) |

21 August
*Palmira di Tebe*, serenata per musica
l: Gaetano Martinelli (*P-Cug, Lac, Ln, Lt*)
sc: Luciano Xavier dos Santos (*P-La* 48–III–8)

Palácio da Ajuda

7 October
*Seleuco, Re di Siria* rpt (AHMF, xx/G/20, f. 112)

17 December
*Enea in Tracia*, dramma per musica, 1 act ('serenata', AHMF, xx/G/20, f. 116)
l: Gaetano Martinelli (*P-Ln*)
sc: Jerónimo Francisco de Lima (*P-La* 48–I–32/3)

18 December
*Perseo* rpt (AHMF, xx/G/20, f. 116; see Queluz 1779)

*1782*

Palácio da Ajuda

19 March
*Gioas, Re di Giudà* rpt (AHMF, xx/G/20, f. 123; see Ajuda 1778)

21 March
*Stabat Mater* by Haydn (AHMF, xx/G/20, f. 123)

Palácio de Queluz

29 June
*Il natal di Giove* rpt (AHMF, xx/G/20, f. 129; see Queluz 1778)

5 July
*Everardo II, Re di Lituania*, dramma per musica da cantarsi, 1 act ('serenata', AHMF, xx/G/20, f. 131)
l: anonymous (*P-Cug, Lan, Ln*)
sc: João de Sousa Carvalho (*P-La* 47–v–28, incomplete)

25 July
*Calliroe*, serenata per musica
l: Gaetano Martinelli (*P-Cug*)
sc: António da Silva Gomes e Oliveira (*P-La* 48–III–14/15)

21 August
*Bireno ed Olimpia*, serenata per musica
l: Gaetano Martinelli (*P-Cug* 2)
m: António Leal Moreira

Palácio da Ajuda

17 December
*Penelope nella partenza da Sparta*, dramma per musica, 1 act ('serenata', AHMF, xx/G/20, f. 139)
l: Gaetano Martinelli (*P-Cul, Ln* 2)
sc: João de Sousa Carvalho (*P-La* 48–I–44/5)

|  | overture, mod. edn: Lisbon, Fundação Calouste Gulbenkian, 1968 (Portugaliae Musica XIV: sc. & pts) |
|  | ov. rec: Philips stereo 198481 |
| 18 December | *L'Angelica* rpt (AHMF, XX/G/20, f. 139; see Queluz 1778) |

*1783*

|  | Palácio da Ajuda |
| 19 March | *La passione di Gesù Christo Signor Nostro*, oratorio sacro |
|  | l: Metastasio (*P-Cul, EVp*) |
|  | sc: Luciano Xavier dos Santos (*P-La* 48–III–9/10) |
| 21 March | *Salome, madre de sette martiri Maccabei*, oratorio sacro |
|  | l: Gaetano Martinelli (*P-Ln*) |
|  | sc: João Cordeiro da Silva (*P-La* 48–VI–14/15) |
| 13 May | *Il palladio conservato*, serenata per musica |
|  | l: Metastasio (*P-EVp, Lac*) |
|  | sc: Luciano Xavier dos Santos (*P-La* 48–III–7, '1783'; see also Queluz 1771) |
|  | Ajuda or Queluz |
| 29 June | *Penelope nella partenza da Sparta* rpt (AHMF, XX/G/24, f. 13; see Ajuda 1782) |
|  | Palácio de Queluz |
| 5 July | *Siface e Sofonisba*, dramma per musica da cantarsi, 1 act ('serenata', AHMF, XX/G/24, f. 15) |
|  | l: Gaetano Martinelli (*P-Cug, Lcg, Lt*) |
|  | sc: António Leal Moreira (*P-La* 48–II–22/3) |
| 25 July | *L'Endimione*, dramma per musica da cantarsi, 1 act ('serenata', AHMF, XX/G/24, f. 15) |
|  | l: Metastasio (*P-Cug, EVp, Lac, Ln* 2) |
|  | sc: João de Sousa Carvalho (*P-La* 48–I–36/7) |
| 21 August | *Teseo*, dramma per musica da cantarsi, 1 act ('serenata', AHMF, XX/G/24, f. 17) |
|  | l: Gaetano Martinelli (*P-Lcg, Ln, Lt*) |
|  | sc: Jerónimo Francisco de Lima (*P-La* 48–II–6/7, 'serenata') |
|  | Palácio da Ajuda |
| 17 December | *Tomiri*, dramma per musica, 1 act ('serenata', AHMF, XX/G/24, f. 23) |

l: Gaetano Martinelli (*P-Lcg, Ln, Lt*)
sc: João de Sousa Carvalho (*P-La* 48–1–28/9, 'Tomiri, Amazzona Guerriera')

18 December     *La pietà di Amore*, dramma per musica, 2 parts ('serenata', AHMF, xx/G/24, f. 23)
l: anonymous (*P-Lac*)
sc: Giuseppe Millico (*P-La* 45–1–23/4, 'Dramma'; *VV*)

*1784*

Teatro da Salvaterra

February (9 performances,     *Dal finto il vero*, dramma giocoso per
AHMF, CX. 257)     musica, 3 acts
l: Saverio Zini (*P-Cug* 2, *EVp, Lac, Lcg, Ln* 2, *Lt*)
sc: Giovanni Paisiello (*P-VV*)

Palácio da Ajuda

19 March     *Il ritorno di Tobia*, oratorio sacro
l: anonymous (*P-Cul, Lac, Lt*)
m: Franz-Joseph Haydn

21 March     *Gioas, Re di Giudà* rpt (AHMF, xx/G/24, f. 28; see Ajuda 1778, 1782)

Palácio de Queluz

29 June     *Everardo II, Re di Lituania* rpt (AHMF, xx/G/24, f. 34; see Queluz 1782)

5 July     *Adrasto, Re degli Argivi*, dramma per musica da cantarsi, 1 act ('serenata', AHMF, xx/G/24, f. 35)
l: Gaetano Martinelli (*P-Cul*)
sc: João de Sousa Carvalho (*P-La* 48–1–8/9)

25 July     *Il ratto di Proserpina*, dramma per musica da cantarsi, 1 act ('serenata', AHMF, xx/G/24, f. 36)
l: Gaetano Martinelli (*P-Cug, Lac, Lcg*)
sc: João Cordeiro da Silva (overture: *P-Em* n° 458)

21 August     *Cadmo*, dramma per musica da cantarsi, 1 act ('serenata', AHMF, xx/G/23)
l: Gaetano Martinelli (*P-Lt*)
m: António da Silva Gomes e Oliveira

Palácio da Ajuda

17 December     *Esione*, dramma per musica da cantarsi, 1 act ('serenata', AHMF, xx/G/23)
l: Gaetano Martinelli (*P-Lt*)

|                          |                                                                                                      |
| ------------------------ | ---------------------------------------------------------------------------------------------------- |
|                          | sc: Luciano Xavier dos Santos (*P-La* 48–III–3)                                                       |
| 18 December              | *Tomiri* rpt (AHMF, xx/G/24, f. 47; see Ajuda 1783)                                                   |
|                          | Teatro do Salitre                                                                                    |
|                          | *A casa de pasto*, pequena peça                                                                       |
|                          | l: José Daniel Rodrigues da Costa (*P-Cug*, TNM)                                                      |
|                          | m: [Marcos Portugal]                                                                                 |

*1785*

Teatro de Salvaterra

Carnival      *L'amor costante*, dramma giocoso per musica, 2 acts
l: anonymous (*P-Cug, Lcg, Ln*)
sc: Domenico Cimarosa (*P-La* 47–II–39/40, 'Alla Valle .. Intermezzi a cinque voci')
*Il conte di bell'umore*, dramma giocoso per musica, 2 acts
l: anonymous (*P-Cug, Cul, La, Lcg, Ln 2*)
sc: Marcello Bernardini di Capua (*P-La* 44–IV–44/6, wrongly attributed to Rinaldo di Capua in the catalogue)

–      *La vera costanza*, dramma giocoso per musica, 3 acts
l: anonymous (*P-Cug, Cul, Ln 2*)
sc: Jerónimo Francisco de Lima (*P-La* 48–II–8/9; *VV*)

Palácio da Ajuda

19 March      *Il trionfo di Davidde*, oratorio sacro
l: Gaetano Martinelli (*P-Cul, Ln*)
sc: Braz Francisco de Lima (*P-La* 48–I–30/1)

21 March      *Salome, madre de sette martiri Maccabei* rpt (AHMF, xx/G/24, f. 55; see Ajuda 1783)

28 March (for the wedding of Prince João and Princess Carlota Joaquina)      *L'imenei di Delfo*, serenata per musica
l: Gaetano Martinelli (*P-Lcg*)
sc: António Leal Moreira (*P-La* 48–II–20/1)

Teatro da Ajuda

9 June (*Gazeta de Lisboa*, 4 performances, 5th and 6th in December, AHMF, CX. 29)      *Nettuno ed Egle*, favola pastorale per musica da rapresentarsi, 2 acts ('opera', AHMF, xx/G/24, f. 58)
l: anonymous (*P-Cug, Cul, La, Lcg, Ln 2*)

|  |  |
|---|---|
|  | sc: João de Sousa Carvalho (*P-La* 48–1–41) Palace of the Spanish ambassador, Count of Fernan Nuñez |
| 13 April | *Le nozze d'Ercole ed'Ebe*, dramma per musica da cantarsi, 2 parts<br>l: anonymous (*P-Cug* 2, *EVp*, *Lac*, *Ln* 2; Mes copy *P-Lan* RMC nº 1106)<br>sc: Jerónimo Francisco de Lima (*P-La* 48–11–2/3<br>overture, mod. edn: Lisbon, Fundação Calouste Gulbenkian, 1973 (Portugaliae Musica XXIII: sc. & pts) |
| 15 June | *Il ritorno di Astrea in Terra*, dramma per musica da cantarsi, 2 parts<br>l: anonymous (*P-Cug* 3, *Cul*, *EVp*, *Lac*, *Ln* 2)<br>sc: José Palomino (*P-La* 45–IV–24/5, 'cantata li 15 de Giugno de 1785')<br>Palácio de Queluz |
| 5 July | *Ascanio in Alba*, dramma per musica da cantarsi, 2 parts ('serenata', AHMF, XX/G/24, f. 63)<br>l: Claudio Niccolò Stampa, with alterations by Giuseppe Parini (*P-EVp*, *Lcg*)<br>sc: António Leal Moreira (*P-La* 48–11–14/15) |
| 25 July | *Ercole sul Tago*, dramma per musica da cantarsi, 1 act, ('serenata', AHMF, XX/G/24, f. 63)<br>l: Vittorio Amadeo Cigna-Santi (*P-Cul*, *EVp*, *La*)<br>sc: Luciano Xavier dos Santos (*P-La* 48–11–41, '1785' see also Queluz 1765) |
| 21 August | *Archelao*, dramma per musica da cantarsi, 1 act ('serenata',, AHMF, XX/G/24, f. 66)<br>l: Gaetano Martinelli (*P-EVp*)<br>sc: João Cordeiro de Silva (*P-La* 48–III–19/20)<br>Teatro da Ajuda |
| 17 and 18 December | *Nettuno ed Egle* rpt (AHMF, XX/G/25, f. 60) |
| *1786* | Teatro de Salvaterra |
| February (9 performances, AHMF, CX. 258) | *La finta giardiniera*, dramma serio-comico per musica, 3 acts<br>l: anonymous (*P-EVp*, *Lcg*, *Lt*)<br>sc: Pasquale Anfossi (*P-La* 43–1–43/5, 'La Finta Giardiniera per Amore') |

| | |
|---|---|
| – (10 performances, *ibid.*) | *Li fratelli Pappamosca*, dramma giocoso per musica, 2 acts<br>l: anonymous *P-La, Lcg, Ln* 2)<br>m: Pietro Alessandro Guglielmi |
| – (5 performances, *ibid.*) | *Gl'intrichi di Don Facilone*, dramma giocoso per musica, 2 acts<br>l: anonymous (*P-Cul, EVp, Ln* 2)<br>sc: Pietro Alessandro Guglielmi (1st act: (*P-La* 44–VIII–47) |
| | Palácio da Ajuda |
| 19 March | *Ester*, oratorio sacro<br>l: Gaetano Martinelli (*P-EVp, Lac*)<br>sc: António Leal Moreira (*P-La* 48–II–18/19) |
| 21 March | *Il trionfo di Davidde* rpt (AHMF, xx/G/24, f. 80; see Ajuda 1785) |
| | Casa da Assembleia das Nações Estrangeiras |
| 28 March (benefit for Gonçalo Auzier Romero) | *La passione di Gesù Christo Signor Nostro*, oratorio sacro<br>l: anonymous (*P-Cul, EVp, Ln* 4)<br>m: Niccolò Jommelli |
| 25 May | Death of Pedro III |
| | Teatro do Salitre |
| | *Os bons amigos*, farsa or entremez<br>l: anonymous (TNM)<br>m: Marcos Portugal |
| | Academia Real das Ciências |
| 8 December | *Ecloga pastoril* com musica . . . para recitar-se na Academia celebrada em Louvor da Immaculada Conceição, no dia em que a Igreja celebra este . . . Mysterio<br>l: João Xavier de Matos (*P-EVp, Ln*)<br>m: José Joaquim dos Santos |
| | Real Casa Pia do Castelo de S. Jorge |
| 17 December | 'serenata' (*Gazeta de Lisboa*; see below doubtful productions, p. 174) |
| 18 December | 'serenata' (*Gazeta de Lisboa*) |

*1787*

| | |
|---|---|
| | Palácio da Ajuda |
| 25 July | *Alcione*, dramma per musica, 1 act ('serenata', AHMF, xx/G/24, f. 116)<br>l: Gaetano Martinelli (*P-Lcg*)<br>sc: João de Sousa Carvalho (*P-La* 48–I–6/7) |

| | |
|---|---|
| 21 August (Ajuda, according to Bombelles, p. 167) | *Telemaco nell'isola di Calipso*, dramma per musica, 1 act ('serenata', AHMF, xx/G/24, f. 119)<br>l: anonymous (*P-Cul, La*)<br>sc: João Cordeiro da Silva (1st part *P-Em* n° 451) |
| 17 December | *Artemisia, Regina di Caria*, dramma per musica da cantarsi, 1 act ('serenata', AHMF, xx/G/24, f. 127)<br>l: Gaetano Martinelli (*P-EVp*)<br>sc: António Leal Moreira (*P-La* 48–11–12/13) |
| 18 December | *Il ratto di Proserpina* rpt (AHMF, xx/G/24, f. 127; see Queluz 1784)<br>Teatro do Salitre<br>*A casa de café*, farsa or entremez<br>l: anonymous (TNM)<br>m: Marcos Portugal |
| 25 July | *Licença pastoril*<br>sc: Marcos Portugal (*P-La* 48–11–33) |
| 17 December | *Pequeno drama*<br>l: José Caetano de Figueiredo (*P-Cug, Cul 2, La,* TNM)<br>sc: Marcos Portugal (*P-La* 48–11–34)<br>Academia Real das Ciências |
| 8 December | *À Immaculada Conceição de Maria Santissima* ... cantata pastoril para representar-se na secção da Academia que se celebrou no dia em que se festeja este ... Mysterio<br>l: Domingos Maximiano Torres (Vieira, 11, pp. 275–6)<br>m: José Joaquim dos Santos |

*1788*

| | |
|---|---|
| | Teatro de Salvaterra |
| Carnival | *L'italiana in Londra*, dramma giocoso per musica, 2 acts<br>l: anonymous (*P-Cul, EVp, Lcg*)<br>sc: Domenico Cimarosa (*P-La* 47–11–42/4) |
| – | *Socrate immaginario*, dramma giocoso per musica, 2 acts<br>l: anonymous (*P-Cul 2, EVp, Ln, Lt*)<br>sc: Giovanni Paisiello (*P-La* 45–IV–15/18) |

|  | Palácio de Lisboa (Paço da Ribeira) (AHMF, CX. 36) |
|---|---|
| 25 July | *Megara tebana*, dramma per musica, 1 act ('serenata', AHMF, xx/G/27, f. 2) |
|  | l: Gaetano Martinelli (*P-Cul*) |
|  | sc: João Cordeiro da Silva (*P-La* 48–III–29/30; overture: *P-Em* n° 459) |
| 21 August | *Gli eroi spartani*, dramma per musica, 1 act ('serenata', AHMF, xx/G/26, f. 104) |
|  | l: Gaetano Martinelli (*P-Lcg*) |
|  | sc: António Leal Moreira (*P-La* 48–II–16/17) |
|  | Teatro da Rua dos Condes |
| 21 August | *O prazer da Olissea*, drama, 1 act |
|  | l: Salvador Machado de Oliveira (*P-Lac* 2) |
|  | m: António da Silva Gomes e Oliveira |
|  | Teatro do Salitre |
| 25 April | *Idílio* |
|  | l: José Procópio Monteiro (Carvalhais, *Marcos*, p. 133) |
|  | m: Marcos Portugal |
| 13 May | *Licença métrica* |
|  | m: Marcos Portugal (Carvalhais, *Marcos*, p. 137) |
| 25 July | *Idílio* |
|  | l: José Procópio Monteiro (*P-Cul*) |
|  | m: Marcos Portugal |
|  | *A Castanheira ou a Brites Papagaia*, entremez |
|  | m: Marcos Portugal (Carvalhais, *Marcos*, p. 42) |
| 11 September | Death of Prince José |
| *1789* |  |
|  | Palácio da Ajuda |
| 25 April | *Bauce e Palemone*, dramma per musica, 1 act ('serenata', AHMF, xx/G/27, f. 26) |
|  | l: Gaetano Martinelli (Carvalhais, 'Subsídios') |
|  | sc: João Cordeiro da Silva (*P-La* 48–III–21/2; overture: *P-Em* n° 454) |
|  | Teatro da Ajuda |
| 13 May | *La vera costanza*, dramma giocoso per musica, 2 acts |
|  | l: anonymous (*P-EVp, Lcg, Ln*) |
|  | sc: Jerónimo Francisco de Lima (see Salvaterra 1785) |

| | |
|---|---|
| 19 May | *La vera costanza* rpt (AHMF, CX. 258) |
| | Palácio de Lisboa (Paço da Ribeira) |
| 24 June | *Numa Pompilio II, Re de Romani*, serenata per musica |
| | l: Gaetano Martinelli (*P-EVp, Lac, Lcg*) |
| | sc: João de Sousa Carvalho (*P-La* 48–1–42/3, 'dramma per musica') |
| 25 July | *Alcione* rpt (AHMF, xx/G/27, f. 33; see Ajuda 1787) |
| | Real Casa Pia do Castelo de S. Jorge |
| 1 September | *Gli affetti del Genio lusitano*, dramma per musica da cantarsi, 2 acts |
| | l: Gaetano Martinelli (*P-Cug* 2, *Cul, EVp, La, Ln*; Ms copy *P-Lan* RMC n° 1048) |
| | sc: António Leal Moreira (*P-La* 48–11–35) |
| | Palácio da Ajuda |
| 4 November | *Megara tebana* rpt (AHMF, xx/G/27, f. 44; see Ajuda 1788) |
| | Teatro da Ajuda |
| 17 December | *Lindane e Dalmiro*, dramma serio-comico per musica, 2 acts |
| | l: Gaetano Martinelli (*P-Cug, EVp, Ln*) |
| | sc: João Cordeiro da Silva (*P-La* 48–III–25/8) |
| 18 December | *Lindane e Dalmiro* rpt (AHMF, xx/G/28) |
| 26 December | *La vera costanza* rpt (AHMF, xx/G/28) |
| | Teatro do Salitre |
| | *O amor da Patria*, pequeno drama |
| | m: [Marcos Portugal] (Carvalhais, *Marcos*, p. 30) |
| 25 April | *Gratidão*, drama |
| | l: João António Neves Estrela (*P-Cul*, TNM) |
| | m: Marcos Portugal |
| 13 May | *A inveja abatida*, drama |
| | l: José Procópio Monteiro (*P-Cul, La, Ln*) |
| | m: Marcos Portugal |
| 25 July | *O amor conjugal*, drama |
| | l: José Procópio Monteiro (*P-Cul*; Ms copy *P-Lan* RMC n° 1640) |
| | m: Marcos Portugal |
| 17 December | *Elogio* |
| | m: Marcos Portugal (Carvalhais, *Marcos*, p. 122) |

*1790*
                                        Teatro de Salvaterra
Carnival                                *L'amore ingegnoso*, dramma per musica, 2
                                        acts
                                        l: anonymous (*P-Cul, Lcg, Ln, Lt*)
                                        sc: Giovanni Paisiello (aria 'Un onesto gio-
                                        vinetto': *P-La* 48–III–47 *14*; full score:
                                        *P-VV*)
–                                       *La virtuosa in Mergellina*, dramma giocoso
                                        per musica
                                        l: anonymous (*P-Cug, Cul, Ln*)
                                        sc: Pietro Alessandro Guglielmi (*P-La*
                                        48–IX–19/20)
                                        Palácio da Ajuda
19 March                                'Oratória da Paixão, de Muzica de Jom-
                                        melli' (AHMF, xx/G/27, f. 56)
                                        Teatro da Ajuda
25 April and ? May                      *L'amore ingegnoso* rpt. (AHMF, CX. 259)
13 May; 18, 24, 29 June (CX.            *Le trame deluse*, dramma giocoso per
259)                                    musica, 2 acts
                                        l: anonymous (*P-EVp, Lcg, Ln* 2)
                                        sc: Domenico Cimarosa (*P-VV*)
                                        Palácio da Ajuda
25 July                                 *Numa Pompilio II, Re de Romani* rpt
                                        (AHMF, xx/G/27, f. 66; see Palácio de
                                        Lisboa 1789)
                                        Palácio de Queluz
4 November                              *Artemisia, Regina di Caria* rpt (AHMF,
                                        xx/G/27, f. 74; see Ajuda 1787)
                                        Teatro da Ajuda
17, 18 December (AHMF,                   *Axur, Re di Ormus*, dramma serio-comico
xx/G/28)                                per musica, 2 acts
                                        l: anonymous (*P-Cug, Lac, Ln* 2, *Lt*)
                                        sc: Antonio Salieri (*P-VV*)
26 December (AHMF,                      'récita que os Musicos Italianos do Theatro
CX.45, xx/G/27, p. 78)                  da Rua dos Condes vierão fazer ao de N.
                                        Sra. da Ajuda'
                                        Teatro da Rua dos Condes
25 July                                 *Sacrificio puro*, elogio (J.J. Marques,
                                        p. 139)
                                        l: Francisco Carlos de Oliveira (*P-Pa*)
                                        m: Frei Marcelino de Santo António
                                        ('mestre actual da Companhia do mesmo
                                        teatro')

*Il marchese di Tulipano*, dramma giocoso per musica, 2 acts
l: anonymous (*P-Lcg, Ln*; Ms copy: *P-Ln* Cód. 1395)
m: Giovanni Paisiello, rev. by António Leal Moreira
*I filosofi immaginari*, dramma giocoso per musica, 2 acts
l: anonymous (*P-Cug, Cul, Lcg, Ln* 2, *Lt*; Ms copies *P-Lan* RMC n° 1061, *P-Ln* Cód. 1385)
m: Giovanni Paisiello
*La serva padrona*, burletta in musica, 2 parts
l: anonymous (Carvalhais, 'Subsídios'; Ms copy: *P-Lan* RMC n° 1105)
m: Giovanni Paisiello

17 December    *Il tempio della Gloria*, drammatica azione per musica, 1 act
l: Eustachio Manfredi (*P-Cul, Lcg, Ln* 2; Ms copy: *P-Lan* RMC n° 1070)
m: Carlo Spontoni

Teatro do Salitre
*O amor artífice*, farsa
m: Marcos Portugal (Carvalhais, *Marcos*, p. 29)
*A noiva fingida*, drama jocoso em música, 2 acts
l: anonymous (*P-Cul, Ln*; Ms copy: *P-Ln* Cód. 1396)
m: Marcos Portugal
*Os viajantes ditosos*, dramma jocoso em música, 2 acts
l: anonymous (*P-Cug, Lt*)
m: Marcos Portugal

*1791*

Teatro de Salvaterra

Carnival    *La bella pescatrice*, dramma giocoso per musica, 2 acts
l: anonymous (*P-Cug* 2, *Cul, Lcg, Ln* 2)
sc: Pietro Alessandro Guglielmi (*P-VV*)

–    *Li due baroni di Rocca Azzurra*, dramma giocoso per musica, 2 acts
l: anonymous (*P-Cug, Cul, Lcg, Ln*)
sc: Domenico Cimarosa (*P-VV*)

|  | Palácio da Ajuda |
|---|---|
| 21 March | *Ester* rpt (AHMF, xx/G/27, f. 84; see Ajuda 1786) |
|  | Teatro da Ajuda |
| 25 April and 8 May | *Axur. Re di Ormus* rpt (AHMF, CX. 259; see Ajuda 1790) |
| 13 May | *La pastorella nobile*, dramma giocoso per musica, 2 acts |
|  | l: anonymous (*P-Cug, Cul, La, Lcg, Ln*) |
|  | sc: Pietro Alessandro Guglielmi (*P-VV* anon.) |
| ? June | *La pastorella nobile* rpt (AHMF, xx/G/29) |
| 24, 29 June | *Axur, Re di Ormus* rpt (AHMF, CX. 259) |
|  | Palácio da Ajuda |
| 25 July | *Megara tebana* rpt (AHMF, xx/G/27, f. 97; see Palácio de Lisboa 1788) |
|  | Teatro da Ajuda |
| 15, 24 August | *La pastorella nobile* rpt (AHMF, xx/G/29) |
| 5, 7 October | *Axur, Re di Ormus* rpt (AHMF, CX. 259) |
|  | Palácio de Queluz |
| 4 November | *Tomiri* rpt (AHMF, xx/G/27, f. 107; see Ajuda 1783) |
|  | Teatro da Ajuda |
| 17, 26, 29 December (AHMF, xx/G/29) | *Attalo, Re di Bitinia*, dramma per musica, 2 acts |
|  | l: anonymous (*P-Cug, Cul, EVp, Lcg, Ln, Lt*) |
|  | sc: Ferdinando Robuschi (*P-VV*) |
|  | Teatro da Rua dos Condes |
| Carnival | *L'italiana in Londra*, dramma giocoso per musica, 2 acts |
|  | l: anonymous (*P-Cug, Cul, La, Lcg, Ln, Lt*) |
|  | m: Domenico Cimarosa [see Salvaterra 1788] |
| Spring | *Il conte di bell'umore*, dramma giocoso per musica, 2 acts |
|  | l: anonymous (*P-Cug, La, Lcg, Ln, Lt*; Ms copy: *P-Ln* Cód. 1396) |
|  | m: Marcello Bernardini di Capua [see Salvaterra 1785] |
| – | *Giannina e Bernardone*, dramma giocoso per musica, 2 acts |
|  | l: anonymous (*P-Cug, Cul, Ln*) |
|  | sc: Domenico Cimarosa [*P-La* 44–v–6/7] |

| | |
|---|---|
| 25 April | *Dramma serio per musica* (2 recitatives, 2 arias, final duet)<br>l: anonymous (*P-La*; Ms copy: *P-Lan* RMC n° 1103) |
| 13 May | *Il puro omaggio*, dramma per musica, 3 scenes<br>l: Gaetano Martinelli (Carvalhais, 'Subsídios')<br>m: António Leal Moreira |
| Summer | *Il barbiere di Siviglia ovvero la precauzione inutile*, dramma giocoso per musica, 4 acts<br>l: anonymous (*P-Cug, Cul, Lt*)<br>sc: Giovanni Paisiello [*P-La* 45–IV–2; *VV*] |
| – | *La moglie capricciosa*, dramma giocoso per musica, 2 acts<br>l: anonymous (*P-Cug, Cul, La, Lcg, Ln*; Ms copy: *P-Lan* RMC n° 458)<br>sc: Giuseppe Gazzaniga [*P-La* 44–VIII–20/2; 47–V–40] |
| Autumn | *Li due supposti conti*, dramma giocoso per musica, 2 acts<br>l: anonymous (*P-Cul, La, Lcg, Lt*; Ms copies: *P-Lan* RMC n° 996, *P-Ln*, Cód. 1397)<br>sc: Domenico Cimarosa [*P-La* 47–II–47; *VV*] |
| – | *I zingari in fiera*, dramma giocoso per musica, 2 acts<br>l: anonymous (*P-La, Lcg, Lt*; Ms copy: *P-Lan* RMC n° 1365)<br>sc: Giovanni Paisiello [*P-La* 47–IV–5/6; 47–VII–20] |
| 17 December | *Il marito disperato*, dramma giocoso per musica, 2 acts<br>l: anonymous (*P-Cug, Cul, La, Lcg, Ln*)<br>m: Domenico Cimarosa<br>*La serva padrona*, burletta in musica, 2 parts<br>l: anonymous (*P-Cug, Cul, La, Ln*)<br>m: Giovanni Paisiello<br>*Un centone*<br>m: several composers (Formenti, quoted in Carvalhais, 'Subsídios')<br>Teatro do Salitre<br>*O amante militar*, entremez<br>m: Marcos Portugal (Carvalhais, *Marcos*, p. 29) |

*O lunático iludido*, drama adornado de música
l: anonymous (Ms copy: *P-Ln* Cód. 1393)
m: Marcos Portugal

*1792*

Teatro de Salvaterra

Carnival    *Il finto astrologo*, dramma giocoso per musica, 2 acts
l: anonymous (*P-Cul, Ln* 2)
sc: Francesco Bianchi (*P-La* 44–III–23/6, '1792')

–    *La modista raggiratrice*, dramma giocoso per musica, 2 acts
l: anonymous (*P-Cul, Lcg, Ln*)
sc: Giovanni Paisiello (Act I: *P-La* 47–IV–4, '1792'; complete score: *VV*)

–    *Riccardo Cor di Leone*, commedia per musica, 2 acts
l: anonymous (*P-Cul* 2, *Lcg, Ln*)
m: André Ernest Modeste Grétry

–    *La pastorella nobile* rpt (AHMF, xx/G/29)
Teatro da Rua dos Condes

Carnival    *Il Don Giovanni ossia Il convitato di pietra*, dramma per musica in un sol' atto
l: anonymous (*P-Cul, La, Lcg, Ln* 2, *Lt*; Ms copy: *P-Lan* RMC nº 106)
m: Giuseppe Gazzaniga

–    *Chi dell'altrui si veste presto si spoglia*, dramma per musica, 2 acts
l: Giuseppe Palomba (*P-La*; Ms copy: *P-Lan* RMC nº 2260)
sc: Domenico Cimarosa [1st act: *P–VV*; 2nd act: *P-La* 47–III–2]

–    *L'impresario in angustie*, farsa per musica, 1 act
l: anonymous (*P-Cug, Cul, Lcg, Ln, Lt*; Ms copy: *P-Lan* RMC nº 4)
sc: Domenico Cimarosa [*P-La* 47–II–46]

*1793*

House of Anselmo José da Cruz Sobral, for
the birth of Princess Maria Teresa

29 April
*Il natale augusto*, dramma per musica, 2 parts
l: Gaetano Martinelli (*P-Cug* 2, *Cul, EVp,
Ln* 2)
m: António Leal Moreira
Real Casa Pia do Castelo de S. Jorge, *idem*

14 May
*La preghiera esaudita*, oratorio
l: Giovanni Gerardo de' Rossi (*P-EVp*)
m: Giovanni Cavi

DATE UNKNOWN

*Astrea placata*, serenata
l: anonymous (*P-Cug*, bilingual)

*Reign of João V*

*Cantata a quattro, Grazia, Amore, Morte,
Timore*
(dedicated to João V and Queen Marie Anne)
l: anonymous (*P-Ln, Mp*)
*Clori e Fili*, dialogo cantato dalle Signore
Elena Maria e Angiola Paghetti
l: anonymous (*P-Ln*)
*Eco immortale*, applauso festivo all'augusto
nome di Giovanni Quinto, Re di Portogallo
l: anonymous (*P-Cul, Mp*)

See also note to 1741 above, p. 134.

*Reigns of José I and Maria I*

*L'asilo d'Amore*
l: Metastasio (*P-Cug*)
m: João Cordeiro da Silva
*O baile mascarado*, drama jocozo para representarse em musica
l: anonymous (*P-Cug*; Ms copy: *P-Ln* Cód.
1393 '1789')
m: António de Figueiredo (do Espírito
Santo Ramos) and others
*O templo de Hymeneu*, compozição dramatica para se cantar nos felices despozorios da
Excellentissima Senhora D. Maria Ignacia
de Saldanha Oliveira, e Daun; com o
Excellentissimo Senhor D. Luiz da Costa, e
Souza de Macedo, e Albuquerque.

l: anonymous (*P-Lac*)
Novo Teatro do Bairro Alto
*O casamento de Lesbina*, drama jocozo
para se representar em musica
l: anonymous (*P-Cug, Cul*; Ms copy: *P-Ln*
Cód. 1393, '1794')
m: Baldassare Galuppi
Teatro da Rua dos Condes

(see above 1768, p. 142)  *L'Arcifanfano*, dramma giocoso per musica,
3 acts
l: Carlo Goldoni (*P-Cug* 2, *Cul, Ln*)
m: Giuseppe Scolari

## PLACE UNKNOWN

*1728*
14 November (*Gazeta*)  *La Fama trionfante*, serenata fatta cantare
dal … Conte d'Harrach, Generale delle
Squadre della Religione Gerosolimitana, e
suo Ambascadore [*sic*] Estraordinario alla
Sacra Real Maestà di Giovanni V. Re di
Portogallo.
l: anonymous (*P-Mp*)

*1735*
*Li trionfi d'Amore*, serenata a sei voci con
instromenti
l: Raimondi (*P-Cul*, 'Lisboa')
m: Giovanni Giorgi

*1738*
*Componimento drammatico* da cantarsi in
occasione delle felicissime Nozze dell'Illust.
ed Eccelent. Signora D. Giovanna Perpetua
di Bargança [*sic*] coll'Illustrissimo, ed Eccel-
entissimo Signore Marchese di Cascais
D. Luigi di Castro
l: anonymous (*P-Ln*)
m: António Teixeira

*1762*
*L'amore artigiano*, dramma giocoso per
musica, 3 acts
l: Carlo Goldoni (*P-Cug*)
m: Gaetano Latilla

*1764*

(Palácio da Ajuda?)
*Le difese d'amore*, cantata per le felicissime Nozze degli Eccelentissimi Signori D. Enrico Giuseppe di Carvalho e Mello, Conte d'Oeiras, e D. Maria Antonia de Meneses
l: anonymous (*P-Cug*)
m: Pedro António Avondano

*1769*

*Alcide al Bivio*, componimento drammatico per musica
l: anonymous (*P-La*, 'Lisboa')
m: F. Em. E.
(cant. La Sig. * * *
       La Sig. * * *
       La Sig. * * *)

*1771*

(Casa da Assembleia das Nações Estrangeiras or Palácio da Ajuda?)
*Il voto di Jefte*, dramma sacro
l: Girolamo Tonioli (*P-Cug*)
m: Pedro António Avondano

*1773*

(Casa da Assembleia das Nações Estrangeiras or Palácio da Ajuda?)
*Adamo ed Eva*, dramma sacro, 2 parts
l: anonymous (*P-Cug*)
m: Pedro António Avondano

*1774*
4 March

*Ester*, oratorio a 5 voci da cantarsi in Lisbona ...
l: anonymous (*P-Cug, Ln*)
m: Antonio Sacchini

*1783*

*O Hymeneo*, pequeno drama para se cantar no dia dos faustissimos desposorios do illustrissimo e excelentissimo Senhor Joseph de Vasconcellos e Sousa com a illustr. e excellent. senhora Dona Maria Rita de Castello Branco

l: Matias José Dias Azedo and Anacleto da
Silva Morais (*P-Cug, Cul, EVp, Ln* 2)
m: Jerónimo Francisco de Lima

*1788*
8 December

*La purissima concezione di Maria Santissima,*
cantata scenica da rappresentarsi nell'Oratorio di S. Signoria il Sigr. * * *
l: Luigi Torriani (*P-Ln*)
m: Marcos Portugal

*1791*

*Il natale di Maria,* dramma sacro
l: anonymous (*P-Ln,* 'Lisboa')
m: Niccolò Jommelli

*1792*

*Sant'Elena al Calvario,* 2 parts
l: Metastasio (*P-Cug* 2, *Cul, La, Lcg, Ln, Lt,*
'Lisboa'; Ms copy: *P-Lan* RMC n° 1056
m: Gaetano Issola

## DOUBTFUL PRODUCTIONS

Most doubtful productions mentioned by Teófilo Braga and other earlier
writers are very clearly misinterpretations of dramatic texts published in
the 'teatro de cordel' or elsewhere, such as *A destruição de Cartago,*
supposedly performed at the Casa da Ópera (do Tejo) on 6 June 1755,
which is probably the same as *Dido desamparada, destruição de Cartago,*
published in 1766, 1782 and 1790. Only a small number of these misattri-
butions is recorded below. Alternative production years of works for
which no evidence exists, such as that of Perez' *Il Siroe* at Salvaterra in 1756,
have not usually been retained.

*1729*

*Amor vencido de amor,* sarzuela epithalamica
nas vodas dos Principes do Brasil
t: António José da Silva (D. B. Machado,
IV, p. 41)

*1740*

*Labirinto de Creta,* obra que se ha de fazer
no Theatro da nova casa do Bairro Alto
t: António José da Silva (Frèches, ed.,
António José da Silva, *El prodigío de Amarante,* pp. 40–1)

**1755**

Paço da Ribeira, Casa da Ópera

Summer     *L'Olimpiade* by Perez ⎫
Autumn     *L'Artaserse* by Perez ⎬ (C.V. Machado,
*Colecção de Memorias*, p. 188)

**1756**

Teatro de Salvaterra
*Ezio* by Perez (J. J. Marques, p. 100; probably the same as *Ezio em Roma, Comedia
nova* of 1765 and 1789; the court did not go to
Salvaterra that year)

**1759**

Teatro de Salvaterra
*Enea in Italia* by Perez (J. J. Marques, p. 101,
Vieira, 1, p. 541; probably the same as *Eneas
em Getulia, opera*, published in the 'teatro de
cordel' in 1767, 1786, 1791; Perez' opera is
otherwise unknown)

**1760**

*Demetrio* by Perez (Braga, p. 40)
*Divertimento musicale boschereccio* da cantarsi
a più cori, e voci
l: Marianno Bergonzoni Martelli (*P-Cug* 3)

**1761**

*Ulisses em Lisboa*, opera portuguesa desti-
nada a celebrar o parto de Sua Alteza Real
t: Francisco José Freire (Cândido Lusitano)
(*P-Cug*; Ms copy: *P-Ln* Cód. 1379, '1782')

**1762**

*Le Grazie vendicate*
sc: Luciano Xavier dos Santos (*P-La*
48–III–4, '1762')
Teatro de Salvaterra
*Giulio Cesare* by Perez (J. J. Marques, p. 101)
or by Luciano Xavier dos Santos (Vieira, 1,
p. 541; both otherwise unknown)

**1763**

*L'Isacco, figura del Redentore*
sc: Luciano Xavier dos Santos (*P-La*
48–III–5/6, 'Musica fatta e dedicata a …
D. Maria Vitoria Regina … 1763')

1766

*La danza*
sc: Luciano Xavier dos Santos (*P-La* 48–II–40, '1766')
Teatro da Ajuda
*La villegiatura* by Piccinni (Carvalhais, 'Subsídios', quoting the German libretto collector Schatz)

1772

Palácio de Queluz
*Il Parnaso confuso* by Gluck (Marquês de Resende, 'Descripções e recordações históricas do Paço e Quinta de Queluz', p. 214; quite probably a fictional choice of title and composer)

1773

Teatro de Queluz
*Gianni e Bernardi* by 'Diversos' (Vieira, 1, p. 543)

1783

Teatro de Queluz
*Alceste* by Gluck (Sequeira, *Teatro de outros tempos*, sc: *P-La* 44–VIII–28/30, Portuguese copy)

1786

*A ilha de Thetis*, poema dramatico para musica consagrado à Magestade Augusta da Senhora Dona Maria I ... em applauso de seu anniversario natalicio ... XVII de Dezembro
l: José Anastásio da Costa e Sá (*P-EVp*; see above Real Casa Pia do Castelo de S. Jorge 1786, p. 160)

1787

*Lisboa reedificada*, poema dramatico para musica em applauso do 13 de Maio de 1787
l: José Anastásio da Costa e Sá (*P-La*)

1790

Teatro da Rua dos Condes

17 December

*Il disegno del nuovo tempio*, dialogo nella ricorrenza del faustissimo giorno natalizio

di Sua Maestà Fedelissima D. Maria I ... di
xvii Dicembre
l: Dafni Trinacrino (*P-Ln*)

*1791*

Oporto, Teatro Público
*Salome, madre de' sette martiri Maccabei* by
João Cordeiro da Silva (J. P. Martins,
p. 107)
*Il fanatico burlato* by Domenico Cimarosa
(Bonito, p. 138)

*1792*

*Beneficencia de Jove*, drama piscatorio
baquico para musica
l: Luís Rafael Soye (*P-Lac, Lt*)
*Os lavradores*, drama campestre para
musica
l: Luís Rafael Soye (*P-Cul, Ln, Lt*)
Oporto, Teatro Público

2 February          *Semiramide* (J. P. Martins, p. 107)

*1793*

*Il Re pastore* by Luciano Xavier dos Santos
(Vasconcelos, ii, p. 159; sc: *P-La* 48–iii–ii/13,
3 acts, 'La Musica humilmente consacra
All'Augusta Principessa del Brazili la Sig.$^{ra}$
D. Carlotta Giov.$^{na}$ Nostra Signora suo
indegno servitore, e Fedele vassalo questo
di lui. Originale. Luciani X.$^{er}$ di Santi l'anno
1797.'; no indication exists of it ever having
been performed)

# Appendix
## Original texts of documents

1 (see pp. 11–12)

iere fit un mois de la mort de lenfant Don Carlos et je na tant que demain pour doner ma lecsion de musique car je nen puis plus avec ses impertinences de deuille.

je fais tout mon possible pour divertir ma melancolie puis que vous aves la bonte de le vouloir ensi encore quil soit tres dificile dans un pais ou il nia auquen divertisement ceulement je se lui dechanter qui et tres gran pour moi car jaime la musique pasionement. ce jours nous somes sortie beaucoup de fois mais a des eglises seulement...

je suis tres aise que vous vous divertisie a entendre farinello et quil vous ait parut si bien tout le monde dit quil nia aucun qui chante ausi bien que lui et on voit bien par les arias (car jen et chante quelques unes et entandu ausi dautres) la grande agilite quil a la Reyne me dit iere que la Princesse lui avoit ecrit quil na rivoit deja pas trop aut mais je ne sait pas coment cela puise entre car javois entendu dire quil arivoit jusque a la fin duclavesin jauroit bien du plaisir a le pouvoir entendre mais il faut prendre paciencie puis que Dieu la voulu ansi.

la faute de liberte se me fait tout les jours plus sensible et je ne sait pas come je pourois vivre si je ne vois tant de plaisir pour la musique jatents chaque jours can il lui deplait ausi et quils me privent de ce divertisement alors ce sera me desesperer tout a fait.

nous pasons bien tristement; car le deuille continue toujour avec la meme rigueur ce que tout le monde trouve bien ridicule et ausi nous navons aucune musique les jours de gala; seulement dans ma chambre je done ma lecsion mais il ni a point de serenates...

nous avons asteur ausi un autre grand deuille pour la mort de la soeur de la Reyne il semble que a cette cour ils nachevent jamais.

Dimanche nous entendimes chanter Reginelle qui me sembla admirablement le Roy lentendit ausi dune porte...

tout et auplus miserable etat du monde le Roy ne pense a rien que a la Patriarchal et la Reyne ne fait rien;... pour que vous voies jusque ou va l'impertinence de cette

Cours ici je des femmes elles feseit des petits bales particuliers; la Reyne leur en voia ordre que on en fit plus. ausi jus que asteur l'impertinence ne toit que pour nous asteur elle et pour tout le monde ces dames sons desesperes mais il nia point de remede que la paciense;
ici nous avons asteur des sermons tout les jours et nous navons pas les divertisemens

(Caetano Beirão, (ed.), *Cartas da Rainha D. Mariana Vitória para a sua família de Espanha*, I *(1721–1748)*, pp. 142, 156, 159, 161, 177, 212, 224, 243, 246.)

2 (see pp. 27–9)

Le roi entretient un opéra italien qui lui coûte deux millions par an. C'est un spectacle majestueux et véritablement pompeux dont il régale sa cour deux ou trois fois par semaine. Il a fait bâtir à cette occasion une salle de spectacle de toute beauté et de la plus grande magnificence. Elle est octogone à quatre rangs de loges. Celle du roi est dans le fond, ornée de colonnes en façon de marbre, revêtues de moulures de bronze doré. Deux autres loges dans le même goût sont placées à droite et à gauche au bord du théâtre. Les autres sont revêtues de balustrades dorées qui en forment les devants, savoir celles du premier et quatrième rang; celles du deuxième et troisième rang sont ouvertes en plein sur le devant et dorées magnifiquement d'un or brillant qui imite le diamant par le feu qu'il jette. La richesse, la délicatesse et le bon goût se disputent à l'envie. Le théâtre est superbe. Il a cent quatre-vingts pieds de long sur soixante de large. Le parterre occupe toute la longueur de la salle. On y est assis commodément; il n'y a point d'amphithéâtre comme en France. Quelque beau que ce soit ce morceau véritablement beau et digne d'un roi, il y a au milieu de sa magnificence de grands défauts. La salle n'est pas assez grande proportionellement au théâtre. Les colonnes à pilastres qui soutiennent les loges et se terminent par des figures de géants sont trop grosses pour la grandeur de la salle. Il n'y a que trois loges à chaque rang; il en faudrait d'avantage. Je la trouve trop petite pour une salle de représentation et de dignité, et trop grande pour un spectacle particulier. Eu égard au théâtre, elle devrait être trois fois ce qu'elle est. Nonobstant ces défauts, on ne peut nier qu'on ne soit frappé, en entrant dans cette salle, par l'or et la magnificence qui éclate et reluit de tous côtés.

Il y eut deux représentations pendant notre séjour à Lisbonne. Le roi nous y fit inviter chaque fois. Il avait recommandé aux principaux seigneurs de sa cour de nous faire les honneurs du spectacle et de nous céder de préférence les bonnes places. Les Portugais, naturellement polis et affables, s'acquittèrent à merveille de cet ordre. L'on joua la *Clémence de Titus* du célèbre maître Astasi, le Corneille du théâtre italien. Les décorations et le spectacle en sont superbes. Le théâtre immense, orné somptueusement, enchantait nos regards. La plupart de nous eurent également les oreilles affectées de la musique italienne. Il y en a eu d'autres à qui elle ne plut pas. Ce sont des chapons qui chantent et représentent indifféremment les rôles d'hommes et de femmes. Le récitatif me parut des plus ennuyeux. Le goût de la musique italienne déplut aux Français qui n'y étaient pas accoutumés. Je ne prétends pas que leur goût doive prévaloir sur celui de toute l'Europe qui préfère la musique italienne. Je me contente de dire qu'elle ne me plut pas beaucoup.

Il n'y a point de cour en Portugal comme en France. On ne voit jamais manger le roi ni la reine. Personne n'assiste au lever ni au coucher du roi. La reine n'a pas de toilette publique. Jamais de jeux, jamais d'appartements. Leurs Majestés vivent dans leur cour comme des particuliers. On [ne] les voit qu'à l'opéra et par audience quand on veut leur parler. Le roi a un bon usage, qu'on ne peut louer trop dans un monarque, d'en donner deux publiques par semaine, l'une pour le peuple, l'autre pour la noblesse, de sorte que ses sujets on la facilité de parler directement à leur maître.

(Albert-Alain Bourdon (ed.), 'Description de Lisbonne extraite de la Campagne des Vaisseaux du Roy en 1755, par le Chevalier des Courtils', pp. 162–3.)

3  (see pp. 41, 43–7)

Chi crederebbe mai, caro Sig[re] Jommelli, che in vece di ricever il resto di tutta l'opera dell'Ezio, m'aveva di trovar con soli i recitativi dell'atto 2° e 3° della sud[a], che Lei adesso mi manda, senza veruna delle arie rispettive? Chi non aveva d'aspettare un simile mancamento, per cause delle sue deplorabili malatie accennate da Lei, se si vedono tre opere fatte in Italia, per altri teatri? Chi potea immaginare, che il Sig[r] Jommelli aveva da preferire il Teatro [ve]nale di Roma, al Teatro reale di S.M.F. da cui è lei proveduto d'una annua pensione di quatro cento zecchini, che gli furono accresciuti dopo di contentarsi da trecento? A chi non sarà più che strano il sentir dire a desso al Sig[re] Jommelli, in questa sua Lettera, che il gran guadagno dell'Opera di Roma Le sedusse, senza ricordarsi della sua privata scritura del 20 Agosto 1769 ibi ...

Passa Lei, nella sua Lettera, a domandar il perdone avanti di far l'opera di Roma, che feci poco dopo. Domandar perdono, e seguitar il fallo è una nuova idea di pentimento. Ne la mia amicizia, ne la mia protezione, e buon cuore a che Lei si racomanda adesso, possono giovargli; perche l'amicizia richiede una vera corrispondenza; e la protezione e buon cuore domandono sincerità, e vere scuse ...

Ho gran paura che l'opera degli anni di S.M.F., il nostro augusto sovrano, abbia di correr l'istessa fortuna dell' Ezio; perchè il Sig[re] Jommelli non conta il tempo che tardano i corrieri, quello che passa per lo studio de'cantanti, le soverchie prove che se bisognano, e che soglino farsi per acquistar quella accurata perfezione, con la quale s'eseguiscono qui le di Lei opere.

In occasione che il di 6 Giug. 1770 si festeggierà il giorno natalizio di S.M.F. nostro commune ed adorabile Padrone, si rappresenterà l'Opera = *La Nitteti*, per la quale sono necessari li qui appresso nuovi componimenti di musica per cui se ne forma la presente intenzione. La parte di Sammete sarà rappresentata dal Sig[r] Carlo Reina, per il quale necessitano che siano composte di nuovo tutte le 4 arie, et il Duetto. Cioè l'aria

| | |
|---|---|
| Sono in mai: non vego sponde | ⎫ del I° atto |
| Se d'amor, se di contento | ⎭ |
| Mi sento il cor trafiggere | dell II atto |
| Decisa è la mia sorte | dell III atto |

tenore dell'esemplare di sue corde, che qui annesso gli si acclude.

Secome la 2.[da] sud[a] aria = *Se d'amor se di contento* non è framezzata della prima che da una sola aria, così questa se desidera corta in forma che l'internandosi la seconda parte con la prima venisse quasi a formare una cavatina, è sconsar quasi l'obbligo di principiar da capo.

Le quattro sudette arie si desiderano come quella del Vologeso con il segno al mezzo dell'aria ad efetto non rieschino longhe.

*Appendix*

La Scena X del primo atto, che precede al Duetto si desidera, che in qualche sito, che lei ritroverà opportuno, principi ad essere il recitativo istromentato, talmente che possa su quello attacare il Duetto; quale /non meno che gli altri pezzi di musica/ si desidera che sia di quel calibro con cui si distingono le note del maestro Jommelli.

Per il sud° Duetto il p° soprano deve farlo il Battistino quale si averte di non sfogarlo molto giungendo il medesimo sino all *Amirè* e *Bemi* non sostenendole / ed il Reina deve essere il 2° soprano per il quale potrà regolarsi in conformità del già detto esemplare che si trasmette. La Parte di Beroe sarà rappresentata dal Sigʳ Battistini Vasquez, per il quale si desidera un nuovo componimento per l'aria che dice

Per costume o mio bel Nume

Questo sogetto avendo cantate tutte l'arie del Vologeso con molta abilita, ed applauso, si sono ritrovate ottime per il suo stile e modo di cantare. Il med° ha la sua giusta essecuzione. Ha poca voce, ma buona graziosa, ed espressiva. Finalmente è musico, per cui gli può scrivere, essendo certo della buona essecuzione.

Si regolerà per quest'aria come per le quattro sopraccennate del Rejnino, cioè con il segno al mezzo dell'aria.

La Musica della marcia che si accenna nel Libr. alla Scena VI del Primo atto nello Spartito non v'è; ma solo si è ritrovato il Basso senza gl'Istromenti; cosicche se ne fà istanza, e si desidera che non sia molto corta.

(Letter of the Director of the Royal Theatres to Niccolò Jommelli of 5 March 1771, *intenzione* for *La Nittetti* AHMF, Livro XX/Z/45, ff. 31v–32v, 21v–22.)

4  (see pp. 82)

| | |
|---|---|
| *Cláudio* | Foste enfim ao Bairro Alto? |
| *Júlio* | Nisso gastava o meu tempo! |
| | Não vou lá para esses bairros, |
| | meu amigo, em não havendo |
| | dous dedos de italiano |
| | não aturo. |
| *Matilde* | Ora isto é belo! |
| (aparte) | E no cabo entende-o tanto |
| | Como eu entendo o grego. |
| *Júlio* | Bairro Alto! nem por sombras. |
| *Cláudio* | Ora não sejas camelo: |
| | o nosso tablado hoje |
| | não inveja os mais perfeitos |
| | da Europa. |
| *Júlio* | Tenho dito |
| | si non habemo de quello, etc. |

(From the *Incisão anatomica ao corpo da Peraltice* (1771) transcribed in T. Braga, *Historia do theatro protuguez*, p. 219.)

5  (see pp. 87–9)

C'est le plus joli opéra bouffon que j'ai jamais entendu. La musique est charmante et dans un gout nouveau. Scolari a eu l'addresse de tirer tout le parti possible de tous les acteurs, et a doublé leurs talents par l'art qu'il a eu de les développer et de proportionner la musique à la qualité, et à l'étendue de leurs organes. Chacun d'eux se trouve dans son quadre. Louise n'a jamais chanté si juste ni avec autant de voix. Maria Joaquina a deux très beaux airs qu'Elle exécutent bien. Trebi est un très beau Turc. Calcini premier eunuque, s'est habillé de façon qu'il ressemble un vieux chatré de la Patriarcale; il chanta entre autres un air qui est unique dans son genre. Cécile en Turc est passable. Isabelle a deux arriettes légères dont Elle se tire fort joliment, mais Louise a dans le second acte une arriette qui est magnifique et qu'Elle a chanté superieurement. Nous sommes privés dans cet opera du plaisir d'entendre M.^lle Bruza. Les finales sont pleines, harmonieuses, bien coupées, enfin tout a plu dans cet opera, jusqu'à Pedro. Aussi n'ai je jamais rien vu de si bien reçu. Car le public non content d'applaudir les acteurs redoubloit ses battements de main a chaque beau morceau de l'ouvrage en criant *Vivat Maestre Scolari*.

Il est trop tard pour que je puisse donner a V.E. un détail bien complet de la tragicomédie qui s'est passée hier au Bairro Alto. Je me borne donc à dire a V.E. que le spectacle qui étoit ce jour là nombreux et magnifique fut troublé par une querelle qui s'éleva a l'orchestre entre Scolari et Todi, sur le mouvement d'une ariette que chantoit Pedro. Scolari, qui vouloit qu'elle marche plus ›presto‹, se mit a charger l'accompagnement de clavecin de toute sa force et selon sa louable coutume apostropha Todi, qui n'alloit pas aparement a sa fantaisie, de l'epithete de *Porco*, Todi lui repondit par *asno*, d'autres gentillesses se suivirent rapidement et je vis le moment que Todi hors de lui alloit jeter son violon a la tête de Scolari; j'étois dans la loge de M^de Votre mere, qui étoit ce jour là à l'opera. Nous entendions bien que l'on se disputoit mais nous ne pouvons par savoir pourquoi, parce que la musique continuoit toujours et le bruit que cette affaire excitoit dans le parterre nous empechoit de rien distinguer. M^de Votre mere m'envoia voir ce que c'étoit. J'appris à la porte du théâtre quels étoient les deux champions. Je passai tout de suite dans la loge de Maria Joaquina qui est sur l'orchestre et à peine y entrois-je que j'apperçus un Caporal et deux soldats baionette au bout du fusil, qui après avoir traversé le parterre pardessus tout le monde, ajambèrent l'orchestre. Le Caporal areta Todi et lui dit de le suivre. Todi se leva e obéit. Dans le moment que Todi sortoit de l'orchestre accompagné des Soldats, la Louise entroit sur la scène; voir son mari conduit par des Soldats, jetter un cri terrible et voler après son mari fut l'affaire d'un clin d'oeil. Tandis que cela se passoit sur la théâtre, il se passoit une autre scène dessous, par où il faut passer pour sortir de l'orchestre. Todi ne s'y étoit pas plutôt vû à l'obscurité que profitant de la connoissance qu'il a du local, il s'échappe d'entre les soldats, prends les détours qu'il connoissoit, monte au théâtre, gagne la petite porte de derrière et se sauve. Un moment après, les Soldats retrouvent leur chemin et court après lui. Louise renverse tout ce qui se trouve sur son passage, sentinelle hommes, femmes, rien ne l'arrete, elle saute les escaliers quatre a quatre et court après son mari presque jusqu'à la porte de la grande cour de derrière. La on me conjure de la suivre, j'y cours, et rencontrant un des soldats qui me dit que Todi s'étoit échappé j'atrappe; survient le Comte d'Alvizan qui étoit de garde et le Ministre nous la faisons remonter. Elle ne pleuroit pas, elle hurloit; ce qu'il ya eû de plus plaisant c'est que pendant tout ce tapage l'opera n'a pas arrêté un instant, par l'habileté de la petite Isabelle, qui se trouvant sur le théâtre au moment de la catastrophe a continué le role de sa scene et l'a chanté jusqu'à la fin de l'acte sans la moindre erreur. J'étois pourtant fâché que Todi se soit enfui, parce que cela arretoit par force tout l'opera. Louise n'auroit certainement ni voulu ni même pu continuer son role. En rentrant au théâtre je la trouvai qui demandoit son mari a tue-tête et qui me crie en me voyant *o meu marido*. Moi je répondit aussitot *Seu marido é hum tollo; para que fugir?* A peine ai-je lâché le mot de *tollo* qu'elle entre en fureur contre moi *V.M. tem o atrevimento de chamar o meu marido tollo adiante de min?* J'ai eu ma foi peur qu'elle m'arracha les yeux, je voulois l'appaiser, il n'y avoit pas moien, on vint m'appeler de la part de M^de la Marquise et je pris le parti de la laisser crier et de m'en aller. Nous rentrames, le Ministre et moi, dans la loge de M^de votre mere, ou nous trouvames tous les Ministres Étrangers, M^r Manuel Bernardo de Melo et le Comte d'Alvizan a qui M^de se tuoit de dire qu'il falloit relacher Todi et le pauvre Comte se tuoit de reponder qu'il ne savoit pas ou il étoit, mais il avoit beau juré et protesté. M^de Votre Mere n'en vouloit rien croire, et s'étoit mis dans la tête que c'étoit une défaite du Comte. Au milieu de tout cela arrive la Todi en larmes, la Cecile toute bouffie de colère demandant grace. Le Comte d'Alvizan qui avoit envoié de touts cotéz a la suite de Todi, sort lui même pour savoir si on en avoit des nouvelles, et dans le tems qu'il alloit par un endroit, Todi arrive par un autre, amené par le Caporal qui l'avoit suivi de près et l'avoit arretté. Sachant, en arrivant, qu'il étoit libre, il vint tout de suite à la loge de M^de Votre mere; la femme aussitôt qu'Elle le vit passa de l'extrême douleur à l'extrême joie. Ce fut un spectacle touchant pour M^de La Marquise et pour tous les assistants. Après les premiers mouvements de tendresse, Todi, la Louise et la Cécile se réunirent pour crier tous les trois en choeur contre Scolari mais ils faisoient un tel tapage que M^de Votre Mere les fit taire, fit une leçon a Todi et le renvoia a l'orchestre après lui avoir recommandé de continuer a faire son devoir sans dire mot, sans la moindre rancune et comme si rien ne fut arrivé. Ensuite Elle fit appeler Scolari, a qui elle dit d'être moins vif et plus prudent et lui recommanda très expressement qu'il ne fut plus question de cette affaire. Tout a en conséquence rentré dans l'ordre accoutumé et l'opera a continué on ne peut pas mieux jusqu'à la fin. Le Pauvre Bruno, au milieu de tout cela, avait l'air d'un criminel qui est dans l'*oratório*. C'est moi qui paierai toutes ces sottises la, disoit-il tristement. La verité est que cela est malheureux pour lui; et la verité est aussi que, quoique Todi soit un crâne il n'avoit cependant pas le premier tort dans cette occasion. Scolari est un insolent qui vient presque tous les jours ivre au theatre, qui depuis qu'il est ici a fait vingt de ces incartades. La même chose lui est arrivé avec la Sestini et la Falquini et tous les jours ici, il a quelques duretés obscènes a dire a ces pauvres filles qui font ce qu'elles peuvent. Il est maitre de chapelle et a raison de vouloir que son ouvrage soit exécuté comme il le veut, mais cela ne lui donne aucun droit d'outrager personne. C'est un fort bon musicien mais c'est un fort dangereux et fort brutal personnage.

(Letters of Gaubier de Barrault to the Count of Oeiras in *P-Ln* Cód. 619, ff. 335–6, 342v–3v.)

6

*Zamperini* Comica cantora, Veneziana, que veiu a Lisboa em 1770, com a qualidade de *prima Donna*, e á testa de uma companhia de comicos italianos, ajustados e trazidos de Italia pelo Sr. *Galli*, notario apostolico da Nunciatura, e banqueiro em negocios da Curia *Romana*.

Entregou-se a essa *virtuosa* sociedade o theatro da rua *dos Condes*. Como havia tempos que não se ouvíra *opera italiana* em Lisboa, foi grande o alvoroço que causou a chegada de tantos *virtuosos*, mormente da Senhora *Zamperini*, que logo com sua familia foi grandiosamente alojada. Esta familia *Zamperini* compunha-se de tres irmãas, e de un Páe, homem robusto e bem apessoado que, a pezar de uma enorme cabeleira com que debalde pretendia dar quinau aos espertos alvidradores de idades, mostrava todavia, no semblante, poder exigir da Senhora *Zamperini* menos alguma cousa, que piedoso e filial respeito, ou dever lhe outorgar alguma coisa mais que a sua paternal benção.

Sendo forçoso custear esta especulação theatral, os Agentes, interessados n'ella, lembrárão-se de recorrer ao filho do Marquez de *Pombal*, o *Conde d'Oeiras*, então Presidente do Senado da Camara de *Lisboa*, que, já prézo e pendente da encantadora voz da Sirêa *Zamperini*, annuiu sem difficuldade ao plano que lhe foi proposto. Sob os seus auspicios, ideou-se uma sociedade, com o fundo de 100 mil cruzados, repartido em 100 acções de 400 mil reis cada uma. Para alcance prompto d'esta quantia, lançou se uma finta sobre alguns negociantes nacionaes e estrangeiros, que em dia assignalado, e a horas fixas sendo juntos no Senado, sem saberem a que erão chamados, ouvirão da boca do Conde Presidente as condições d'essa nova Sociedade theatral. N'uns, o recêo de serem malvistos do Governo, n'outros, a vontade de agradar ao filho do primeiro Ministro, forão as poderosas considerações, que os arrastrárão todos a assignar as ditas condições, das quaes a mais penosa era a da somma, que logo preenchêrão.

Parece que os inventores e agentes desta Sociedade tivérão por alvo singular, o de mulctar a austera sisudesa de alguns negociantes velhos; pois no rol dos Assignantes, a maior parte dos nomes éra de pessoas idosas, que nunca haviao sido vistas em publicos divertimentos. Em essa mesma Junta forão logo nomeados quatro Administradores inspectores do theatro, os quaes, com o maior desinteresse, regeitando commissão e ordenado, se dérão por pagos e satisfeitos com a simples e modica retribuição de um camarote commum a todos quatro. *Ignacio Pedro Quintella*, Provedor da Companhia do *Gran Pará e Maranhão*, e tio do Illmo. actual Barão de *Quintella*, *Alberto Mayer*, *Joaquim José Estolano de Faria*, e *Theotonio Gomes de Carvalho* forão os nomeados Inspectores Administradores, *nemine discrepante*.

Poucos mezes depois da abertura deste theatro, assim montado e administrado, morreu o já indicado Pae da Senhora *Zamperini*: a Administração fez lhe um sumptuoso funeral, e no trigesimo dia, apoz o obito, magnificas exequias na Igreja do Loreto onde fôra sepultado. Alguns criticos de má lingua havião espalhado o boato de que, nessas exequias, havia de recitar a Oração funebre o Padre *Macedo*, a esse tempo muito bom, e justamente accreditado pregador, e poeta que já comprimentára a *Zamperini* com varios Sonetos, etc. O Patriarcha D. *Francisco de Saldanha*, receando que assim succedesse, mandou vir à sua presença o Padre *Macedo*, prohibiu lhe de orar em essas exequias; de ir a *Opera*; de fazer versos a *Zamperini*; e ordenou lhe de substituir por uma cabeleira o cabello que trazia, *á italiana*, bem penteado, e muito apolvilhado. Em vaõ allegou o P. *Macedo* com o exemplo dos clerigos da Nunciatura, que todos usavão de pomada e pós; e que a cabeleira offendía os canones; pois até os Padres, que délla usavão por causa de molestia, érão obrigados a impetrar *Breve de Roma*, que na Nunciatura éra taxado em um quartinho, por tempo de um anno de indulto. O Patriarcha foi inexoravel sobre este ponto da Cabeleira, e somente moderou a ordem de não ir á *Opera*, com o preceito unico de não apparecer na platêa, e com a faculdade de acantoar-se em fundo de algum Camarote, ou em frizura pouco aparente, como a do Auditor da

Nunciatura, *Antonini*, e do Secretario do Card. *Conti*, o P. *Carlos Bacher*, e outros P.P. italianos, que como elle, frequentavão a *Opera*, e a casa da *Zamperini*.

Não foi o P. *Macedo* o unico apaxonado admirador da *Zamperini*; muitos Poetas nacionáes e estrangeiros tributárão lhe obsequiosas inspirações das suas Musas. Entre elles distinguiu-se o Encarregado dos negocios de França, O *Chevalier de Montigny*, cujos lindos versos ainda são lembrados. Em todos os estados e em toda a idade, encontrou essa Sirêa rendidos e rendosos adoradores. Em Dias Santos, á ultima Missa a que ella costumava assistir, na Igreja do Loreto, éra o concurso que apoz si chamava, numeroso e luzidissimo.

Antes de findos dous annos, e logo depois da morte do administrador *Ig[nacio] P[edro] Quintella*, o fundo da Sociedade theatral achava se exhausto, e as receitas montando a tam pouco, que mal cobrião as despezas indispensaveis do serviço mais ordinario, os Administradores deixárão de pagar os salarios dos Comicos e dos musicos da Orchestra. Entre os primeiros havia um chamado *Schiattini* [Innocenzo Schettini], tenor acontraltado, homem jovial, e poeta, que, por haver pedido o que lhe era devido, em estylo que não agradou aos Administradores, foi por estes aquartelado na casa dos Orates, donde éra conduzido ao theatro, todas as vezes que havia Opera. *Schiattini* valendo se então do privilegio analogo ao alojamento a que fôra condemnado, vingava se em parodiar sobre a scena a parte, que no Drama lhe toccava, com satyras recitadas e cantadas, que divertião os espectadores á custa dos Agentes da Administração. Recresceu a provocada raiva destes, e o pobre *Schiattini*, vendo-se em maior aperto, recorreu a El Rei D. José que, informado da injustiça com que era tratado, o admittiu na sua Capella.

Excusado é, parece-me, dizer que esta negociação theatral apenas durou até meado de 1774, que o Marquez de *Pombal* fez sahir de Lisboa a *Zamperini*; e ainda mais excusado relatar as causas désta ordem do Governo; direi somente que os Accionistas não colhérão cousa alguma déssa empreza; pois achando-se empenhada e devedora a infinitos credores, não tiverão outro beneficio, que o que lhes resultava do privilegio especial de não serem obrigados a mais do que o fundo, que cada um julgou perdido, logo que com elle contribuiu.

Convenho que esta nota é sobejamente extensa; mas julguei necessario dar aos Leitores um fragmento, tal qual, da historia do nosso theatro, e desta Senhora *Zamperini*, tão louvada em estes outo versos do nosso Poeta, que não perdia a occasião de admirar as prendas de tam celebre *virtuosa*; pois, como amigo intimo de *Theotonio Gomes de Carvalho*, éra admittido e frequentes vezes visto no Camarote da Administração.

(Note 17 to António Diniz da Cruz e Silva, *O Hyssope, Poéma Heroi-Comico*, Paris, 1817, pp. 129–34)

## 7

*IL TRASCURATO, DRAMMA GIOCOSO PER Musica da rapresentarsi nel Teatro della molto illustre cità del Porto: nell' anno 1762*

Isto he:

O DESCUIDADO, OPERA COMICA PARA SE representar no Teatro publico da cidade do Porto. Dedicada á illustrissima e Excellentissima Senhora Dona Anna Joaquina de Lancastre. Porto na Officina do Capitaõ Manoel Pedroso. 1762.

## *Extracto desta opera com reflexoens sobre os Dramas em musica*

Todas as bellas artes dependem da vista, e do ouvido. E he sem duvida que nas operas Italianas, ou estas sejaõ heroicas, ou comicas, se acha o que mais lizongea estes dous sentidos, e o que ao mesmo tempo diverte o entendimento, quando a composição, ou ficção he boa, ou bem ideada. Naõ saõ as operas se naõ ficçoens representadas em musica vocal, e instrumental: as heroicas se chegaõ ás Tragedias como as de Apostolo Zeno, e Metastasio; e as comicas saõ verdadeiras comedias cantadas para fazer maior impressaõ nos ouvintes, as quaes, tendo por fim o ridiculizar algum vicio geral, e civilizar os habitantes de huma grande cidade, se achaõ estabelecidas para este fim nas cidades mais populozas da Europa, concorrendo os Monarcas ou os Senados com algum contingente extraordinario para poder supprir as dispezas que necessariamente se devem fazer naõ só com os Actores, mas com as decoraçoens dos Theatros, que he o que agrada á vista, e por isso huma das partes essenciaes da opera; e tambem com as danças dos intermedios para excitar a attençaõ dos espectadores, que sem isto com razaõ se infastiariaõ no segundo acto, por naõ poderem tolerar no espaço de quatro horas a continuaçaõ da musica vocal, por melhor que seja, sem alguma interrupçaõ agradavel, mas differente dos recitados, e arias.

Como o Senado do Porto naõ concorre hoje com a menor porçaõ de dispeza para este necessario divertimento, que pode interter os cidadoens na mais viva alegria, livrando os quando menos daquellas indiscretas reflexoens sobre materias, que só tendem a procurar-lhes a sua ruina, dizem os amantes das representaçoens theatraes, que a opera publica he por esta falta defeituosa; porque, sem embargo de serem imperfeitas as primeiras pantomimas, até estas se supprimiraõ por falta de meios, e que por este mesmo motivo as vistas do theatro apenas saõ duas de columnatas, ou a scena da opera se finja em huma cidade, ou em huma praça, ou em hum jardim, ou em hum bosque, ou em huma salla, ou nas margens do mar &c. As dispezas exorbitantes da cidade em outras cousas necessarias fazem que seja muito inconsideravel huma pequena somma que se acrescentasse ao producto quotidiano do theatro. Todos sabem que Genova, que he uma Republica que só subsiste pelo seu negocio de economia, julga necessaria a conservação de dous theatros excellentes nas duas extremidades da cidade. Parma com a metade do povo do Porto, e muito menos commercio tem theatros que podiaõ decorar as mais famosas capitaes da Europa. Em huma palavra, em todas as cidades de alguma consideraçaõ, em que se sabe o que convém ao estado, se promove tudo o que diz respeito a este exquisito divertimento, por se conhecer que a dispeza de huma pequena somma, que circula no mesmo paiz, produz os melhores effeitos que se podem imaginar para o bem da sociedade. Mas com tudo devemos dizer que estas dispezas se fasem despois de se cuidar, e executar o que he absolutemente preciso ás mesmas cidades.

A opera, de que damos noticia, tem por fim o mostrar as funestas consequencias, que resultaõ a hum particular, quando inteiramente se descuida dos negocios, de cujo bom exito depende a felicidade de sua caza. Tinha o descuidado, negligente Filisberto, que he a primeira personagem desta composiçaõ dramatica, hum litigio com hum Conde sobre a somma de trinta mil ducados, que era a maior porçaõ do seu capital; mas elle, só com o sentido na sua commodidade particular, hia perdendo o seu negocio, ao mesmo tempo que o roubava hum procurador em quem tinha confiado a demanda. Toda a familia de Filisberto fazia o mesmo que o procurador;

porque Aurelia orfa, que assistia na caza do descuidado namorando-se do ambicioso Cornelio, que só a pertendia pelo dote, juntamente com o procurador fizeraõ assignar hum papel a Filisberto, que por preguiça o naõ quiz ler, no qual se obrigou este a dar-lhe trinta mil ducados, dizendo-se-lhe que este papel era necessario para sahir bem a sua demanda; mas antes disto Lisaura filha de Filisberto lhe tinha feito assignar outro papel em que lhe deixava todos os seus bens a fim que ella se casasse com o seu amante Dorindo. O creado Pasquino, e a criada Purpurina aproveitaraõ-se da mesma negligencia para da mesma sorte se casarem. Despois de alguns episodios, em que Filisberto conserva sempre o caracter de hum homem amigo só do seu descanso, e inteiramente inimigo do trabalho, se declara Cornelio por amante de Aurelia, e mostra a Filisberto a obrigaçaõ que este lhe tinha feito; mas ao mesmo tempo mostra Dorindo o seu papel, que se prefere ao outro por estar feito antes do de Cornelio. Perdoa a todos Filisberto, que até se contenta de que cazem os criados, que tambem tinhaõ abuzado do bom, e culpavel genio de Filisberto. Este logo no principio do primeiro acto falando com sua filha mostra o seu caracter dizendo:

> *Possibile ch'un giorno*
> *Non posso star senza pensar a niente?*
> *Con questo tutto il di rompermi il capo*
> *Figlia troppo crudele*
> *Mi farete morir, voi lo sapete:*
> *Io bramo la mia pace,*
> *Faticare pensar m'annoja, e spiace.*

Assim pouco mais ou menos se vai continuando o mesmo caracter do descuidado, como tambem das mais personagens, ainda que com algumas improbriedades, que com tudo naõ fazem desmerecer os encantos da excellente voz da primeira cantarina. Tem-se admirado commumente aquelle continuo combate que algumas vezes havia entre esta, e a orchestra; e suppomos que o fim disto naõ era outro senaõ ver quem perderia primeiro o alento. Sabemos que este uso he quasi geral em todas as operas da Europa; mas nem por isso se segue que seja cousa optima, porque admira mais, do que internece. O maior bem, que daqui pode resultar, será hum infeliz triunfo, como o da Cantarina Salvaia, que com esta competencia fez arrebentar o mais perfeito trompa Siciliano do Rei de Sardenha; o que deu huma grande honra áquella mulher. Se isto pode executar a primeira actriz do theatro do Porto, naõ será melhor que mostre claramente a melodia da sua voz, do que querer requintar a belleza das arias v.g. de Pargolesi com variaçoens infinitas? e do que usar só da arte de economizar o alento unicamente para executar depois passagens difficeis que pouco ou nada movem? A isto chamamos musica artificial, que naõ consiste mais do que em huma combinaçaõ de sons difficeis, que poderaõ agradar ao ouvido, mas nunca penetrar até o intimo da alma. Muito melhor seria empregar a melodia do canto para animar as imagens da poesia, e embellecer as modulaçoens da voz pelos agrados da harmonia, que he o que chamamos musica expressiva.

O Bufám, que he dos melhores da Europa, dá a conhecer ao auditorio tudo o que canta, qualidade que he commua á maior parte dos bufoens Italianos. Tem estes sons particulares que caracterizaõ a fome, o frio, a dor, a alegria, em fim tem a expressaõ, que he a verdadeira musica de hum Drama, e se podem considerar quasi como pantomimos, que he o que naõ consideraõ os Italianos.

A bella execuçaõ destes dous actores, fazendo desculpar algumas impropriedades da composiçaõ, se pode com razaõ dizer aos que censuraõ os defeitos do papel, e estaõ surdos ás bellezas da musica, o mesmo que se disse em Pariz de hum que naõ sabia a differença de todas as composiçoens dramaticas: *Que era taõ estupido, que ia á opera para ver o enredo.* Mas como aqui devemos dar noticia da opera impressa, e naõ da representada, será preciso advertirmos que para a ediçaõ das obras se procura algum homem intelligente na arte da composiçaõ dos Dramas. Se o editor desta opera o fosse, naõ poria depois do recitado de Lisaura, bellamente executado por Giuntini:

> *Giusti Dei, v'è nel Mondo*
> *Cotanta iniquità?*
> .................................................
> *Dove si cela, dove*
> *L'empio, ch'il genitor tradire aspira?*
> *Seco voglio afogar lo sdegno, e l'ira*
> *Ma no femina imbelle,*
> *Che dir, che far potrei? &c.*

Naõ poria, como dizemos, immediatamente huma ária feita a Nize, que ainda o mais estupido conhece claramente naõ se seguir áquelle recitado, a qual ária acaba:

> *Mentre folgori e baleni*
> *Saró teco amata Nise,*
> *Quando il ciel si rassereni,*
> *Nise ingrata, io partirò.*

Seria melhor supprimir-se na impressaõ esta ária, que se podia cantar na terceira ou quarta representação, na qual se desculpa a impropriedade por ser abuso que reina quasi em todos os theatros Italianos; pois na repetiçaõ das operas serve huma nova ária de excitar a attençaõ com alguma cousa de novo aos que viraõ as primeiras representaçoens. Despois do recitado espera o auditório polido ver na aria unida toda a arte do Poeta, e do musico, para fazer exprimir aos actores a violencia das paixoens com que se suppoem estarem animados; porque as arias, que naõ saõ jocosserias, saõ feitas á imitação dos coros das tragedias Gregas, e por isso se empregaõ nellas as imagens mais sublimes da poesia Lyrica.

Naõ obstante o que dizemos, he certo que algumas impropriedades, que se podem achar nas operas Italianas do Porto, saõ comuas ás operas de todas as naçoens, porque naõ se representaõ ordinariamente como devem ser: em lugar de se seguirem as regras dictadas pela boa razaõ, só se observa huma musica artificial variada com danças tambem artificiaes, naõ devendo ser estas senaõ a representaçaõ do gésto exaggerado, assim como a musica he a expressaõ mais forte da declamaçaõ: mas como os Principes, e Grandes estaõ occupados de negocios serios, preferem para descansar das suas fadigas este genero de espectaculos que naõ pede muita attençaõ, sem que por isso deixem de ser estes espectaculos os mais divertidos do mundo.

A objecçaõ, que commumente se faz contra este divertimento, ou, para melhor dizer, o pretexto de que se servem muitos para mostrarem que tem razaõ de se desgostarem das operas Italianas, ainda sendo bem executadas, consiste em dizer, o que infinitas vezes está repetido, e vem a ser que he contra a verosimilhança o tratar as cousas ordinarias cantando, como v.g. o dar hum recado a hum criado, o consultar com hum amigo, o desafiar cantando &c. Respondemos a isto, que o contrario á verosimilhança consiste no que he humanamente impossivel. Tudo depende do costume; e se este fez adoptar os versos nos theatros por exprimir o que queremos, melhor do que a prosa, porque naõ se ha de admitir a Musica que dá muito maior energia, e força á Poesia? Diz um judicioso crítico moderno [*Lettres sur quelques écrits modernes*] que naõ he impossivel haver hum povo inteiro que fale sempre em verso, ou em musica: se logo na infancia nos costumarem a falar em ambas estas linguas, as podemos fazer falar taõ familiares como a prosa; e he-nos facil de fazer, sem offender a razaõ commua, e supposiçaõ que levamos, aos theatros de que os sujeitos, que os Actores representaõ, conversaõ entre si mutuamente.

Que a Musica, geralmente falando, he mais efficaz do que a declamaçaõ, e que dá mais força aos versos do que esta, he huma verdade, que só pode negar o que tem o ouvido muito longe do coraçaõ, ou naõ tem absolutamente instincto algum. Assim como o pintor imita as cores da natureza, da mesma sorte o musico imita os tons, os accentos, os suspiros, as inflexoens de voz e todos os sons, com que a natureza exprime os sentimentos, e as paixoens. A mesma natureza nos mostra os cantos que saõ proprios para exprimir os sentimentos, de sorte que, quando recitamos huma poesia terna, insensivelmente lhe vamos dando certos tons, accentos, e suspiros proprios, á proporçaõ de cada sentimento. Todos estes sons ou vozes inarticuladas tem huma força maravilhosa para nos mover, porque saõ os signaes das paixoens instituidos pela natureza, de que aquelles receberaõ a sua energia, e se conhecem em todo o mundo, ao mesmo tempo que as palavras articuladas saõ signaes arbitrarios das paixoens, instituidos pelos homens, e conhecidos em hum só paiz. Os signaes naturaes das paixoens, que a musica ajunta, e emprega com arte para augmentar a energia das palavras, tem huma força maravilhosa para nos mover; e esta, que he derivada da mesma natureza, faz que o recreio do ouvido venha a ser recreio do coraçaõ, como já advertio Cicero, hum dos maiores observadores dos affectos humanos.

As paixoens dos homens naturalmente se exprimem pela acçaõ, pela voz, e pelos sons articulados [*A Dissertation on the rise, union and power &c. of Poetry and Music*]. Nos seculos incultos parece que o gésto seria grosseiro, e horrivel, a voz só bramidos, e a lingua ou sons articulados seriaõ á similhança do grasnar dos patos, como ainda hoje vemos na lingua dos Hotentotes, que naõ admittio cultura alguma. Pelo decurso do tempo, em que se foi observando o mais agradavel, pela natural inclinaçaõ que temos á melodia, mudou-se a voz em som, o gésto em dança, e a fala em verso, seguindo-se naturalmente por frequentes experiencias os instrumentos musicos á imitaçaõ da voz humana. Tal he a origem, e uniaõ da musica, dança e poesia, que achamos ainda há poucos seculos continuada nas tribus selvagens de todos os climas, como nos Iroquezes, nos Huroens, nos habitantes do Perú &c., e o mesmo vemos na Grecia, se examinarmos bem esta origem. O judicioso Brown, que fez huma enumeraçaõ das consequencias naturaes de huma supposta civilizaçaõ entre as naçoens selvagens quando entrassem a cultivar as artes, diz que os seus Legisladores seriaõ os principaes musicos, que os seus mais antigos Heroes, e Deidades seriaõ louvados por serem eminentes na musica e dança, e que as suas primeiras historias seriaõ compostas em verso, e cantadas, assim como as suas maximas, proverbios, leis e ritos religiosos. Estas deducçoens se realizaõ mostrando-se que taes consequencias se seguiraõ de facto na antiga Grecia; e se provaõ com o testimunho de Plataõ, Luciano, Strabáõ, Plutarco, Homero, Hesiodo, e outros antigos escritores.

Quanto mais examinarmos a origem das primeiras representaçoens Gregas, mais veremos que estas procederaõ da natureza, e uniaõ, e progresso da melodia, dança, e naõ de causas meramente accidentaes, como suppozeraõ muitos escritores limitandoa á simples aventura de Thespis que casualmente cantou os louvores de Bacco em huma vindima. Da similhança das causas, e effeitos que achamos nas naçoens barbaras, principalmente da America, podemos concluir que as representa- çoens cantadas naõ tiveraõ huma origem accidental, mas sim huma origem certa derivada da natureza. Além disto, lendo attentamente os antigos escritores, vemos que muito antes de Thespis havia estas representaçoens. Plataõ diz expressamente que a Tragedia era muito antiga em Athenas, e praticada muito antes de Thespis. Suídas menciona Epigenes muito anterior a Thespis. Muitos escritores antigos nos dizem que havia na Grecia huma tradiçaõ de que alguns poetas tragicos em tempos muito antigos contendiaõ no tumulo de Theseu. Strabáõ diz que nos tempos antigos houve certames, ou representaçoens de poetas musicos, que cantavaõ peans ou triunfos para celebrar Apollo; o que foi estabelecido pelos habitantes de Delphos depois da guerra Chrissea. Timosthenes compoz hum poema, cujo assumpto era a victoria de Apollo contra a Serpente: a primeira parte era o preludio á batalha: a segunda o principio do combate: a terceira a mesma batalha: a quarta o pean ou triunfo sobre a victoria: a quinta huma imitaçaõ das angustias, e sibilaçaõ da Serpente que morria; e aqui temos a fórma, e substancia das primeiras tragedias compostas de narraçaõ, e sons correspondentes do triunfo. Dizem outros Auctores que o mesmo Apollo foi o fundador destes certames, e o primeiro que cantou as suas acções; e que huma parte do certame consistia em huma imitaçaõ de Apollo dançando depois da victoria; e em toda esta scena do chamado Deos da Musica, cantando, dançando, e applaudindo as suas proprias acções, temos huma pintura natural de hum Legislador nas naçoens barbaras. Estas nos mostraõ, assim como a Grecia no seu principio, que o canto das representaçoens se fundou na razaõ, e natureza, em lugar de ser contra a razaõ, e contra a verosimilhança, como hoje pertendem os que naõ examinaõ fundamentalmente esta materia.

Que as paixoens ternas naturalmente se fazem intender melhor por huma especie de canto, como por exemplo a irresoluçaõ de huma alma combatida com diversos movimentos, até o concedem todos aquelles, que naõ admittem os colloquios ordinarios em musica; sem advertirem que a arte sabe fazellos agradaveis imitando a bella natureza, isto he, o melhor que a natureza se pode imaginar, que he o fim das artes imitativas. Quando conversamos, diz o Abbade Orsei, [*Reflessioni sopra i Drami per musica*] empregamos, para dar força ao que dizemos, diversas inflexoens de voz: isto, que nos succede na vida ordinaria, tem mais lugar nos theatros onde a exageraçaõ pede que esta expressaõ seja mais forte, e por isso se usa com felicidade do verso. Mas como esta exaggeraçaõ deve mostrar-se mais nos poemas Lyricos, vem por fim a ser a mesma exaggeraçaõ necessariamente musica; e na verdade assim como na harmonia do discurso o verso he a exaggeraçaõ da proza, he tambem a musica a exaggeraçaõ do verso. Commummente huma obra em verso agrada mais que outra feita em proza, porque imprime mais vivamente a compaixaõ, a tristeza, o horror; da mesma sorte huma obra em verso pode adquirir maior força com o soccorro da expressaõ musica, e pintar melhor as paixoens. Se no Venceslau de Zeno vissemos que Casimiro cheio de remorsos falasse em proza: *De ti parto, e parto afflicto ah meu Juiz, e meu Rei, que naõ me atrevo a chamar pai*: produziria isto pouca commoçaõ no auditorio; mas esta se aumenta com a poesia dizendo:

> *Da te parto, e parto afflitto,*
> *O' mio Giudice, ó mio Re,*
> *Volea dir* mio genitor.

Accrescentando-se a Musica á Poesia, augmenta-se ainda mais a expressaõ de sorte, que a declamaçaõ, querendo adquirir maior energia com inflexoens de voz mais fortes, se converte em musica que excede, e agrada mais por este modo, do que a declamaçao ordinaria.

A exaggeraçaõ, como diz o Abbade Orsei, agrada em todas as representaçoes theatraes; e he tanto mais agradavel, quanto he mais forte. Assim nenhuma representaçaõ pode agradar tanto como os espectaculos lyricos, ou sejaõ tragicos ou comicos, pois para produzir o comico e ridiculo em huns, e o maravilhoso em outros, se eleva a exaggeraçaõ ao ponto mais alto. He verdade que por esta razaõ o bom successo de huns, e outros he tanto mais incerto, quanto he mais difficil sustentar huma exaggeraçaõ forte, do que huma menor; e daqui procede que estas representaçoens quasi nunca chegaõ á sua perfeiçaõ; de tal sorte que, perdendo os Auctores a esperança de ter bom successo em similhantes composiçoens, deraõ aos seus poemas huma fórma differente da que deviaõ ter naturalmente. O ponto principal, continúa o dito Abbade, he o distribuir bem a *caricatura*, isto he aquella exaggeraçaõ que deve haver tanto no nobre, como no burlesco para todas as circumstancias da representaçaõ, as quaes circumstancias se podem reduzir a quatro que saõ o *sujeito* ou assumpto dado para Poesia; a *expressaõ* que pertence à Musica; *a acçaõ* executada pela dança, e as *decoraçoens* ministradas pela pintura. Estas quatro partes bem combinadas, ainda que cada huma mediocremente em particular faráõ maior effeito do que huma das duas destas partes tractada de hum modo superior, em quanto se naõ fizer caso das outras. O sujeito que fica sendo extraordinario, e prodigioso, quanto for mais carregado, e cheio, produzirá transformaçoens, encantos, appariçoens &c. Mas pouco importa que estas maravilhas sejaõ incriveis, com tanto que sejaõ fundadas sobre a paixaõ que se quer excitar; e este he o ponto importante. O povo gosta destas extravagancias; e o Filosofo naõ se offende desta falta de verosimilhança, vendo que o povo naõ as desapprova, antes se agrada dellas; porque parece que a musica encobre estes defeitos.

Tal he o poder da musica nos Dramas, que até faz agradavel huma ficçaõ desordenada, seguindo com tudo o que parece dictar a razaõ, como se fossem verdadeiras ou verosimeis essas ficçoens. Com tudo naõ podemos approvar todas as cantatas, sonatas, e sinfonias dos dramas Italianos em musica, as quaes podemos chamar ridicularias sonoras. Para isto he necessario bom gosto, razaõ, e filosofia. Devem as sinfonias imitar naturalmente alguma couza que já ouvimos, como v.g. huma tempestade, huma batalha &c., ou dar a intender naturalmente o que naõ ouvimos, como o silencio v.g. de Armida, o ruido que se suppoem fazer huma sombra sahindo do tumulo &c., onde deve haver huma verdade de conveniencia. Como a sinfonia deve ter huma verosimilhança, assim como na poesia encontramos esta verosimilhança quando as sinfonias fazem o effeito quasi igual ao que os estrondos imitados podiaõ fazer, e quando nos parecem conformes a estes estrondos inauditos de que temos huma idéa confusa pela comparaçaõ que fazemos com outros estrondos, ou sons que temos ouvido; e assim dizemos que estas sinfonias imitaõ bem o natural, ainda que nunca vissemos a natureza nas circunstancias que a musica instrumental pertende copiar. Os principios da Musica saõ os mesmos que os da Poesia, e Pintura, que saõ huma imitaçaõ da natureza. Assim a musica naõ pode ser boa, se naõ for conforme as regras geraes destas duas artes, no que pertence á escolha das materias, á verosimilhança &c. Assim como as bellezas da execuçaõ devem servir na Poesia, e Pintura para pôr em praxe as bellezas da natureza que se imita: da mesma sorte a riqueza, e variedade dos accentos, e a novidade dos cantos naõ devem servir na musica se naõ para embellecer a imitaçaõ, por assim dizer, da lingua da natureza. Como o poeta naõ deve ser escravo dos consoantes para imitar o verdadeiro, ou o verosimil; assim o musico naõ deve ser escravo da harmonia para imitar agradavelmente a natureza, e as paixoens.

Nisto estaõ os Francezes muito superiores aos Italianos despois do famoso Lulli. A sinfonia de Mr. des Touches, que precede o oraculo das arvores de Dodone, em que o estrondo das folhas destas arvores saõ imitadas pelo canto, pela harmonia; e pelo rithmo musico dispoem o auditorio a achar a verosimilhança, fazendo crivel que hum som como aquelle devia preceder, e preparar os sons articulados do oraculo. As sinfonias do silencio de Armida, e os sons da guerra de Theseu por Lulli, a sinfonia que imita huma tempestade na opera de Alcyone de Marais &c. fizeraõ criveis todos os effeitos da musica antiga, em que se imitava o natural, e naõ se fazia caso do que he só difficil. A expressaõ do pensamento, do sentimento, das paixoens &c., deve ser, como diz o famoso Rameau no seu Codigo de Musica pratica, o verdadeiro fim da Musica: cuidamos só até agora em divertirmonos com esta arte contentando-se o ouvido com algumas flores diversamente dispersas, e com a variedade de movimentos, e acçaõ da pessoa que canta, a qual faz algumas vezes hum sentimento, que de nenhuma sorte se exprime pela musica.

Quanto ás decoraçoens, em que se deve comprehender todo o ornato exterior da scena, devem seguir a mesma regra; e para corresponder á exaggeraçaõ das outras partes, he necessario que os vestidos, e as vistas dos edificios, jardins, &c. sejaõ superiores aos vestidos, e edificios communs quanto a musica he superior ao discurso ordinario. A boa disposiçaõ das luzes, e dos mais ornatos do theatro acompanhadas da musica lizonjeaõ ao mesmo tempo os dous sentidos, vista, e ouvido do espectador, que naõ procurando nesta mistura de musica, e danças artificiaes se naõ hum alivio á sua melancolia, insensivelmente se vai corrigindo daquelles perniciosos defeitos que vê ridiculizados no theatro.

Os Athenienses, que foraõ, e seraõ sempre os nossos mestres, empregavaõ naõ só a musica, mas a riqueza, e magnificencia nas decoraçeons, como se pode ver principalmente em Franklin [*Dissertation on the Greek Theatre*] de tal sorte, que só a representaçaõ de huma tragedia lhes custou mais do que a guerra do Peloponneso. Este bom gosto dos Athenienses, ao mesmo tempo que procedia de huma grande politica para divertir o povo, ou trazendo-lhes á memoria as grandes acçoens dos seus antepassados, para as imitar, ou mostrando-lhes a fealdade dos vicios, e maus costumes para os evitar, fez nascer os Sófocles, os Euripides, e os Aristófanes, os Menandros, e os Filemons que illustraraõ a Grecia, e viviráõ sempre na memoria dos homens em quanto houver juizo no mundo. Todas as naçoens polidas procuraõ imitar esta politica, a pezar das declamaçoens com que alguns escritores, aliàs bem intencionados, querem desterrar da Republica as composiçoens Dramaticas que se cantaõ, ou recitaõ naturalmente: mas dizem os defensores do theatro que a causa procede de confundirem as representaçoens, que os Santos Padres condenavaõ, com as que hoje se executaõ na Europa: e respondem aos que dizem que, sendo a França a naçaõ que passa pela mais polida do mundo, foi o paiz em que mais se declamou contra as representaçoens: que os declamadores Francezes, que eraõ dez contra mil que as defendiaõ, naõ faziaõ idéa verdadeira dellas; pois, sem as ver, suppunhaõ-lhes hum fim diametralmente opposto ao que as representaçoens executaõ: que o Rei Christianissimo conhecendo até onde chegava esta espécie de rigorismo mal intendido, deu a direcçaõ da opera Italiana, e comedia Franceza a quatro dos principaes, e mais judiciosos senhores da sua Corte, e fez passar a Academia Real da Musica a pessoas que sabiaõ unir o bom gosto á filosofia: e que ainda concedendo que naõ haja cousa indifferente no mundo, e que tudo tem hum fim ou bom, ou mau, devem os homens naõ só admittir, mas promover tudo o que diz respeito ás representaçoens theatraes modernas, porque o seu fim he reformar agradavelmente os maus costumes e vicios, ao menos divertir-nos innocentemente evitando maiores desordens. Despreze-se, dizem elles, o compositor quando naõ tem o talento de exercitar este fim; mas naõ se censurem os theatros que estaõ prontos a receber as composiçoens, que se dirigem a executar os fins a que se destinaõ.

(Francisco Bernardo de Lima, *Gazeta litteraria*, Julho 1762, pp. 96–109. Footnotes in original have been incorporated into text – indicated by square brackets.)

8
## REFLEXOENS SOBRE O RESTABELECIMENTO DO THEATRO DO PORTO. EM TRES CARTAS. DE RICARDO RAIMUNDO NOGUEIRA. *1778*

### Segunda Carta

Meu presado amigo. Procurei mostrar na minha Carta do correio passado, que o Porto necessitava de hum theatro; segue-se vermos, que genero de peças se devem representar n'elle; quero dizer, se serà util conservar as duas companhias de Opera, e Comedia, que ahi representavaõ alternadamente; ou se bastarà que fique huma só, e qual ha-de ser esta?

Se convem a huma Cidade populosa, que haja n'ella hum theatro, como creio, que jà mostrei, he sem questaõ, que sempre se deve começar pelo theatro Nacional: e sò depois de termos boas representaçoens na nossa lingoa, nos poderemos lembrar de pôr na scena obras escritas em hum idioma estrangeiro, e ajudadas com as bellezas da Musica.

Digo pois, que no Porto deve haver hum theatro Portuguez. Mas naõ me satisfaço, que elle seja destinado unicamente para Comedias: quizera que taõ bem ahi se representassem Tragedias, as quaes arrancassem aos espectadores lagrimas de compaixaõ, e lhes mostrassem a belleza, e majestade da virtude no meio das calamidades. Se a Comedia nos aponta os deffeitos da vida commua, que fazem os homens ridiculos na Sociedade, representando-nos esses vicios com cores, que nos provocaõ a riza; a Tragedia offerecendo-nos em espectaculo, humas vezes o preverso abattido e atterrado pela maõ de huma Providencia, que zomba dos vaõs projectos da iniquidade; e outras o homem justo lutando com a desgraça, e sempre firme entre a universal ruina; grava altamente em nossos peitos o amor da virtude, o horror do vicio, a constancia nos infortunios, a moderaçaõ na prosperidade. Admirem pois os espectadores os funestos effeitos de huma ambiçaõ desordenada, e de hum espirito de vingança na Rodeguna; contemplem o merecido castigo da tyrannia na Athalia; tremaõ de horror ao ver o fanatismo induzir hum filho a cravar o punhal no peito de seu mesmo pay no Mahomet; estremeçaõ, vendo a enganada Merope levantar o braço para tirar a vida a aquelle filho, a quem tanto amava, e por cujo respeito unicamente queria viver; deplorem o infortunio da triste Zayra victima infeliz dos injustos zelos de hum amante, de quem apenas as ordens de seu pay, e de seu Deos a podem separar. Volte o espectador sensivel para caza com os olhos ainda mal enxutos d'aquellas lagrimas, que fazem honra à humanidade, e do que ouvio no theatro colha maximas uteis, e saudaveis, que lhe ensinem a naõ se desviar da estrada direita da honra, e da virtude tanto na prospera, como na adversa fortuna.

Mas parece-me que o estou ouvindo perguntar-me, para que gasto o tempo em persuadir a utilidade das Tragedias, se em Portuguez naõ ha composiçoens d'esse genero, que possaõ pôr-se no theatro? Porem, meu amigo, a difficuldade naõ he invencivel: Assim he, que os nossos Poetas se naõ applicàraõ a escrever semelhantes dramas, e se exceptuarmos a Castro do nosso immortal Antonio Ferreira, podemos dizer afoitamente, que naõ ha Tragedia Portugueza comparavel com as dos Mestres assim antigos, como modernos. Porem nòs temos jà na nossa lingoa algumas versoens muito sofriveis de varias Tragedias Francezas, e ahi no Porto vi representar algumas das de Voltaire assaz bem traduzidas. Se o publico entrasse a interessar-se por estas representaçoens, estou certo, que brevemente veriamos outras muitas traducçoens; e se os Directores do theatro recompensassem dignamente a fadiga dos traductores, assento que teriaõ muito, com que suprir a todas as representaçoens. Finalmente, he bem provavel, que esta proteçaõ viesse a avivar os engenhos Portuguezes, com quem a natureza certamente naõ foi escassa; e quem sabe se Portugal poderia algum dia jactar-se de ter taõ bem os seus Corneilles, e os seus Racines?

Mas pergunto: e que Comedias temos Portuguezas de origem capazes de se pôrem nos Theatros? Eu cuido que a falta he igual à das Tragedias; e bem que o numero das Comedias traduzidas seja mais consideravel, com tudo a maior parte d'ellas estaõ taõ desfiguradas nas versoens, que seria de desejar se traduzissem novamente em lingoagem mais pura, para que os espectadores naõ vaõ ao theatro aprender a falar com termos improprios, e a servir-se de expressoens barbaras, e alheas da nossa lingoa.

Haja pois no Porto hum Theatro Portuguez em que se façaõ Tragedias, e Comedias escolhidas: procurem-se Comicos excellentes, que as representem com propriedade e decencia; as scenas sejaõ do melhor desenho; os vestidos accommodados aos papeis, e nas Tragedias especialmente sejaõ ornados com a riqueza, e magnificencia, que os caracteres Tragicos demandaõ.

Mas que diremos do Theatro Italiano? As Operas certamente tem muitos apaixonados; e qual he o homem sensivel que se naõ interessa por huma boa musica? O Theatro Italiano parece taõ bem ter n'essa Cidade a preferencia, em razaõ da sua antiguidade. Mas a pezar de todas estas razoens, direi o que entendo: No Porto naõ deve haver Theatro de Operas Italianas. Naõ duvido, que muitos dos seus patricios se escandalizem de ouvir proferir esta proposiçaõ; que huns zombem do meu mao gosto; e outros se compadeçaõ da minha ignorancia. Mas antes que pronunciem a Sentença, peço-lhes que oiçaõ as razoens, que me movem a sentir assim, e pode ser que entaõ mudem de conceito.

*Appendix*

A Opera he de todos os espectaculos theatraes o mais magnifico, e luzido. Deixemos a questaõ, se ella he, ou naõ, huma composiçaõ monstruosa, e irregular, pois que naõ he este o ponto que agora tratamos. O certo he que o incomparavel Metastasio nos deixou Composiçoens de indizivel merecimento neste genero, as quaes eternisaraõ o seu nome em quanto a Poesia tiver estimaçaõ entre os homens. As Operas d'este grande Mestre saõ maravilhosas em todo o sentido: ellas estão chêas de maximas de virtude, e probidade, e ainda as mesmas scenas amorosas respiraõ sempre hum amor puro, e innocente. Mas naõ basta sò a bondade do drama. A Opera, mais que todas as outras representaçoens, demanda hum apparato de grande custo, e de extraordinaria magnificencia. Actores excellentes, que representem, e cantem com toda a perfeiçaõ, orquestra soberba, vestuario rico, e elegante, comparsas magnificas, e numerosas, hum theatro espaçoso, e bem illuminado e finalmente tudo quanto a Poesia, a Musica, e a Pintura tem mais capaz de fazer hum espectaculo grande, magnifico, e brilhante.

Supposto isto; se os Portuenses tem possibilidade, e valor para sustentarem huma Caza de Opera com todas estas circunstancias, digo que me parece m.^{to} bem que elles a estabeleçaõ. Este divertimento tem razoens, que o fazem recommendavel. A magnificencia do espectaculo arrebata os olhos; a suavidade da musica encanta os ouvidos; o grande numero de Professores de musica de todo o genero, que as Operas demandaõ, introduz o bom gosto d'esta Arte, e facilita aos curiosos os meios de a aprenderem.

Mas a dizer a verdade, meu amigo, duvido muito, que na sua patria possa estabelecer-se huma Caza de Opera, como ella deve ser. Naõ me metto a averiguar, se o Porto pode, ou naõ pode sustentar hum Theatro Italiano; o certo he que se pode, naõ quer. No tempo, em que eu ahi estive, vî que a pezar da protecçaõ mais empenhada, naõ se fazia huma Opera digna de se ver. Alguma vez se arrojaraõ a representar Operas Heroicas; mas como as executavaõ? Nenhum dos Actores sabia sustentar com decencia hum papel serio; o vestuario era indigno e velho; as scenas quasi sempre as mesmas; as comparsas pobres, e miseraveis. Eu naõ sei, se V.M. se lembra ainda do muito que nos provocou a risa ver huma mulher de nenhum merecimento fazer o papel de Eneas na Dido desprezada. Essas bocas profanas desfiguravaõ indignamente as divinas composiçoens do insigne Metastasio, e dos grandes Mestres que reduziraõ a musica suas admiraveis Operas. Naõ confundamos com tudo o bom com o mao. Eu sei que no seu theatro tem huma, ou outra vez apparecido figuras de merecimento, das quaes se naõ deve entender o que tenho dito.

Viaõ-se pois os taes Comicos obrigados a representar quasi sempre Operas jocoserias, a que os Italianos chamaõ Burlettas, e ainda nessas manquejavaõ summamente, porque nunca havia mais de hum Actor digno de se ouvir, e houve m.^{to} tempo, em que nenhum d'elles sabia do seu officio. Alem do que hum theatro de Burlettas assento que naõ tem outro merecim. ^{to} mais que o da musica, quando ella he boa, porque as composiçoens d'este genero saõ as mais absurdas, e insipidas, que se podem imaginar; e por consequencia parece-me, que he melhor ouvir em huma Sala a hum Musico eminente, do que ir ao Theatro ouvir cantar desproposi-tos, e alguns d'elles muito mal cantados.

De tudo venho a concluir: Que o Porto naõ pòde, ou naõ quer, sustentar dois theatros completos, hum Portuguez, e outro Italiano com a perfeiçaõ, que deve ser; Que he melhor ter hum sò theatro bom, e perfeito, do que dois maos, quaes eraõ os que atè agora ahi havia. Que por consequencia, devem V.M.<sup>es</sup> cuidar em os reduzir ambos a hum sò, e com a mesma despeza, com que até agora sustentavaõ hum mao theatro Italiano, e hum Portuguez mediocre, ou talvez com menos, devem estabelecer hum theatro Portuguez optimo, que os divirta, e instrua, que faça honra à sua Cidade, e mostre o bom gosto de seus Cidadaõs. Mas agora vejo que já escrevi mais do que queria: fiquemos aqui. Deos guarde a V.M. Ill.ª

## Terceira Carta

Meu presado amigo. Somos chegados à ultima parte das nossas reflexoens sobre o Theatro do Porto, e temos hoje para ver; =Como este theatro deve ser regulado? N'este ponto, meu amigo, de nenhum modo posso accomodar-me ao systema, que ahi atè agora se tem praticado. A liberdade he privilegio taõ essencial ao homem, que sò lhe pode ser coarctada quando assim o demanda huma necessidade inevitavel, e sò quanto esta necessidade o pede. Ora eu naõ vejo, que haja necessidade alguma de obrigar a gente a dar dinheiro a Comediantes, a quem naõ tem vontade de ouvir.

Os abusos, que se praticavaõ no Porto a este respeito, saõ intoleraveis. Deixe-me appontar summariamente os mais notaveis. Façamos porem justiça, e sem incorrermos na censura de ingratos, saibamos reconhecer os benefícios, e advirtamos, que as melhores intençoens saõ muitas vezes mal succedidas, por se quererem alcançar por caminhos errados.

A illustre pessoa, que protegia o seu theatro foi dada pelo Ceo ao Porto, para o fazer feliz. Elle naõ tem outro disvelo mais que o bem de seu povo, a quem ama como filhos. Entre outras muitas providencias, com que tem trabalhado na felicidade, e segurança dos Portuenses, justamente assentou que o estabelecimento de hum theatro fixo podia ser de grande utilidade para civilizar essa Cidade, para instruir os seus moradores, e para a condecorar, e fazer estimavel aos estrangeiros. Estas idêas saõ taõ louvaveis, que o Porto sò por isto lhe deveria hum agradecimento eterno quando naõ tivesse mais relevantes motivos para o considerar como seu pay e protector.

Tendo pois diante dos olhos hum fim taõ acertado, persuadio-se que o theatro nunca poderia conservar-se sem hum fundo certo, e para lho estabelecer, mandava todos os annos falar a aquellas pessoas, que lhe pareciaõ capazes de poder supportar essa despeza, e lhes pedia tomassem lugares fixos por anno de Cadeira, ou Camarote. Cuido que naõ he necessario muita Logica, para conhecer, que as pessoas d'aquella qualidade, quando pedem com empenho, mandaõ. E qual seria em Portugal o homem, que se atrevesse a dizer que naõ a semelhante recado? A isto accrescentava huma singular protecçaõ para com os Comicos, e hum Codigo de regulamentos muito extraordinarios para o Theatro, no qual estava disposto, que Pedro se devia sentar n'aquelle lugar, e Paulo n'este; que o que tomava huma Cadeira por anno a naõ poderia emprestar huma noite ao seu amigo; que o dono de hum Camarote naõ poderia brindar com elle huma familia, a quem desejava obsequiar, se naõ em certas circunstancias, e com certas limitaçoens, e outras Leis d'esta natureza. E como nenhuma Legislaçaõ pòde subsistir sem magistrados, que a façaõ executar, tinha esta taõ bem os seus executantes, os quaes julgando-se com hum poder igual ao de seu amo, e naõ tendo na realidade as mesmas idêas, praticavaõ mil insolencias, insultando muitas vezes as pessoas de bem, e desattendendo quem muito lhes parecia. E como eraõ Ministros, de quem naõ havia apellaçaõ, nem aggravo naõ havia remedio se naõ obedecer promptamente a todas as suas Sentenças.

D'este procedimento resultavaõ os inconvenientes seguintes – 1. Eraõ obrigadas a assinar muitas pessoas, que naõ podião, e outras, que naõ querião. 2. O theatro era muito pior do que havia de ser, se houvesse liberdade. 3. O numero dos espectadores era pouquissimo. Deixe-me ver se lhe mostro isto.

Digo 1. Que eraõ obrigados a assinar muitos, que naõ podião, e outros que naõ querião fazer esta despeza. Huns dos assinantes certos da Opera, eraõ os Desembargadores d'essa Relaçaõ, e os outros Ministros da Cidade. V.M. sabe muito bem, que hum Desembargador do Porto tem cento e oitenta mil reis de ordenado liquido; quero que hum Extravagante com o resto de seus emolumentos faça em tudo trezentos mil reis annuaes. Como he possivel, que hum Ministro, que necessariamente se ha-da tratar como homem de bem, com hum redito taõ pequeno, coma, vista, pague a criados, e aluguel de caza, e lhe sobejem seis ou sete moedas, para gastar na Opera, beneficios &c. Naõ falemos dos Militares; esses saõ pobres por natureza, e toda a economia do mundo naõ basta para os fazer subsistir sò com o soldo, que recebem. As pessoas, que vivem de suas rendas, muitas vezes estaõ carregadas de grandes dividas, e sò por meio do governo mais exacto podem sustentar as suas cazas. Finalmente os mesmos homens de negocio naõ tem talvez a opulencia, que o mundo julga; e quantas vezes, por naõ ficarem mal desperdiçariaõ d'esta sorte o dinheiro de seus credores?

Aqui temos muita gente, que naõ pode assinar; ha outra muita, que naõ quer. V. M. ouviria a infinitos dizerem que naõ fazião gosto algum de gastarem semelhante dinheiro, e que assinavaõ por naõ se atreverem a dizer que naõ; e com effeito muitos d'estes mostravaõ, que naõ mentiaõ, pois que a pezar de serem obrigados a pagar o lugar, nem huma só vez o iaõ occupar.

Digo em segundo lugar; Que o Theatro era muito pior do que havia de ser, se houvesse liberdade. A razaõ he clara. Os Comicos estavaõ altamente protegidos: logo no principio do anno tinhaõ a certeza de hum fundo infallivel, que supria os seus salarios e as mais despezas do theatro. Ficavaõ por consequencia independentes dos espectadores, os quaes, ou elles representassem bem, ou mal, lhes haviaõ de pagar ponctualmente. Postos nesta independencia cuidavaõ em desfrutar o beneficio com o menor trabalho possivel. Faziaõ pouquissimas Operas novas; representavaõ com negligencia; mutilavaõ as peças miseravelmente, e quando lhes parecia omittiaõ as melhores Arias, e os papeis mais interessantes. Se hum Actor tinha de memoria algum recitado ou aria; que aprendera, quando estudava musica, mettia-o aonde quer que se lhe antojava, ainda que entrasse ali como Pilatos no Credo. Humas vezes havia danças entre os actos, e outras naõ, e às vezes as faziaõ taes, que melhor seria as naõ houvesse. Mas o dinheiro era sempre o mesmo, o pobre espectador naõ ousava abrir a boca, e para parecer homem da Corte viasse muitas vezes na necessidade de elogiar todos estes despropositos. Porem vamos adiante.

Digo ultimamente; Que o numero dos espectadores era pouquissimo. Nem podia deixar de acontecer assim. O pouco merecimento das representaçoens desanimava a huns; outros naõ podiaõ levar à paciencia a falta de liberdade, que havia no theatro, taõ opposta ao que sabiaõ se praticava em outros theatros mais polidos; outros receavaõ ser insultados, e a muitos ouvi referir cazos sucedidos na Caza da Opera a pessoas de bem protestando, que nunca iriaõ là expôr-se a ser descompostos publicamente; outros finalmente, que talvez frequentariaõ o theatro, se os deixassem em liberdade, faziaõ timbre de là naõ entrarem, por isso mesmo que os tinhaõ obrigado a assinar.

Eis aqui as màs consequencias, que nasciaõ d'aquelles meios violentos, naõ obstante dirigirem-se estes a hum fim taõ justo, e acertado. Mas espere que ainda me esquecia a chusma de beneficios, que no seu theatro se concediaõ naõ sò às figuras, mas ainda aos mais inferiores membros d'elle. Lembro-me, que hum anno foraõ vinte, e tantos. A maior parte d'estes bons beneficiados tinhaõ protecçoens efficazes. Fazia-se o lançamento, e os que haviaõ sido multados, fossem ou naõ fossem à funcçaõ, vinhaõ promptamente entregar a porçaõ, em que os tinham taxado. E como era possivel, que hum theatro semelhante tivesse jamais frequencia de espectadores?

Meu amigo, o primeiro movel de hum divertimento publico deve ser a liberdade. Esperem os Actores todo o lucro do seu merecimento, e logo veremos como elles procuraõ agradar ao publico, e traze-lo ao theatro. Entaõ representaràõ frequentemente peças novas, trabalharàõ pelas executar com perfeiçaõ, variaràõ de vestidos, e de scenas, e finalmente procuraràõ com a novidade conciliar a vontade do povo, em quem unicamente tem toda a esperança. O espectador naõ deve taõ bem ser incommodado no theatro; este he hum prazer, que elle compra com o seu dinheiro, e de que quer gozar à sua satisfaçaõ. Pelo que todas as vezes que naõ perturbar o socego, e boa ordem, que ahi deve reinar, qualquer outro constrangimento he injusto, e naõ pòde deixar de o afugentar, e fazer-lhe perder o gosto de voltar a semelhante lugar. A liberdade dos Theatros em muitas Cidades civilizadas passa a excesso, e em Londres, París, Veneza, se vem todos os dias os espectadores dar pateadas aos Actores maos, e atirar-lhes com laranjas, e maçaãs. Eu naõ quero tanta liberdade porem de nenhuma sorte posso approvar o constrangimento, que no Porto se praticava.

Sei perfeitamente, que alguns dos Portuenses querem defender a justiça, ou ao menos a necessidade do systema, que reprovo. Dizem que n'essa Cidade seria impossivel conservar-se hum theatro, se o deixarem inteiramente à discriçaõ do publico; que na Caza da Opera apparecia muito pouca gente, alem dos assinantes, e que ainda muitos d'estes, naõ obstante pagarem os lugares por anno, naõ assistiaõ a huma sò representaçaõ.

Mas estas razoens naõ me convencem. O Porto he huma Cidade muito populosa, os seus moradores correm facilmente aos divertimentos publicos; e se fogiaõ do theatro, naõ era porque aborrecessem os espectaculos, era sim pela violencia, com que assinavaõ, e pelo pouco merecimento do que là havia que ver. Provo isto com a experiencia. Vi representar ahi muitas peças, que tiveraõ sempre hum concurso innumeravel. Nas noites de beneficio, em que havia de ordinario mais variedade, e maior cuidado em agradar, enchiaõ-se os Camarotes, e a platêa. E qual era a razaõ d'isto? Nenhuma outra mais do que achar o povo divertimento n'essas occasioens, e naõ o achar nas Operas, e Comedias, que ordinariamente se representavaõ.

Haja pois no theatro hum Director, ou Impresario de juiso, que saiba conhecer o gosto do publico, e lisongea-lo; esforcem-se os Actores, trabalhem por agradar; conceda-se huma liberdade raccionavel; desterrem-se as acçoens despoticas; e eu lhe prometto que o theatro se encha, que os espectadores se interessem, e que os Comediantes ganhem dinheiro.

Se depois de se praticar tudo isto, mostrar ainda assim a experiencia que o theatro se naõ pode sustentar sem essa violenta protecçaõ; (o que me parece impossivel) eu diria entaõ que he melhor naõ haver no Porto tal divertimento, do que ser sustentado pela força e pelo constrangimento. Porque naõ sei que pessoa alguma tenha o direito de pôr hum tributo ao povo para sustentar huma tropa de Comediantes, de que elle naõ gosta. Alem do que, se os espectaculos do Theatro naõ saõ de paixaõ dos seus patricios, o mais a que os poderàõ obrigar he a que paguem, mas naõ a que frequentem: e por consequencia semelhante theatro opprimiria o publico, naõ lhe causaria utilidade alguma, e sò seria bom para os Comicos, a quem naõ pezaria ganhar dinheiro com pouco trabalho. Naõ cesso pois de insistir em que a liberdade deve ser a primeira regra neste caso: por força ninguem se instrue, nem se diverte.

Eis aqui, meu amigo, o que me lembra dizer-lhe a respeito do restabelecimento do theatro d'essa Cidade. O Porto tem sujeitos muito doutos, e prudentes, que discorreràõ sobre este ponto infinitamente melhor. Eu disse-lhe ingenuamente o que sentia com aquella lizura, e sem ceremonia, que pede a nossa amisade. Estimarei, que as minhas reflexoens mereçaõ a sua approvaçaõ, pois sò entaõ teraõ para mim algum valor. Deos guarde a V.M.Ill.[a]

(*P-Cul* J.F. 4–9–5, pp. 98–118.)

# NOTES

## 1 OPERA DURING THE REIGN OF JOÃO V (1708–50)

1 The marriage had been effected by proxy on 9 July of the same year.
2 J. S. Silva, *Gazeta em forma de carta*, p. 178.
3 *P-Ln* Cód. 8942, published in R. V. Nery, *Para a história do barroco musical português*, p. 40.
4 *Dicionário biográfico de músicos portugueses*, p. 37.
5 J. S. Silva, *Gazeta em forma de carta*, p. 178.
6 *Ibid.*, entry for 15 May 1709, pp. 196–7.
7 R. Bluteau, *Vocabulário português e latino*. Although published in 1712–21, the first licence for its publication dates from 1698, which would put back its actual writing to the last decades of the seventeenth century. Bluteau had been in Italy and had probably had first-hand acquaintance with Italian opera.
8 According to J. J. Marques, *Cronologia da ópera em Portugal*, pp. 59–60.
9 Cf. R. Stevenson, *Vilancicos portugueses*, pp. XLVI–XLVII.
10 Further on the subject see M. C. de Brito, 'Vestígios del teatro musical español en Portugal a lo largo de los siglos XVII y XVIII'.
11 J. M. A. Nogueira, 'Memórias do teatro português', pp. 41–55.
12 G. M. Sequeira, *Teatro de outros tempos*, pp. 97ff.
13 *Origenes y establecimiento de la ópera en España*, pp. 68–9.
14 *Ibid.*, chs. II and III.
15 They were replaced in 1716 by another company which was also known as *de los Trufaldines*.
16 This is a different work from the *Acis y Galatea*, libretto by José de Cañizares, music by Antonio de Literes, performed at the Madrid court on 19 December 1708 and mentioned in Cotarelo y Mori, *Origenes y establecimiento de la ópera en España*, p. 42, for which the score and parts exist in *P-EVp*. The first record of a *zarzuela* performed in Portugal is that of *Hazer cuenta sin ia huespede zarzuela que se representa actualmente en Villa Viciosa de Portugal, recreo del Rey*

198

*D. Pedro, Impreso in Zaragosa, año 1704* (l: *BR-Rn*; private communication of
Manuel Ivo Cruz).

17  The librettist was Julião Maciel, a canon of Lisbon cathedral, according to D. B.
Machado, *Bibliotheca lusitana*, III, p. 921.

18  See p. 8.

19  *E-EVp* Cód. CLI/I–I nos. 3 and 9. They belong to a collection of over 100
*villancicos*, 15 of which are by Lésbio.

20  R. Bluteau only registers oboes (*boaz* or *boazes*) in the supplement to his
*Vocabulário português e latino.*

21  (1679–1759); he wrote several plays and poetry in Spanish.

22  He was a Spaniard who owned a musical press in Lisbon, where he printed
among other things seventy-seven of his own *Cantatas a solo* and one *a duo* for
voice and basso continuo. He was also the author of the music for several
*villancicos* for the feasts of Saint Cecilia and Saint Vincent performed in 1721, 1722
and 1723 (cf. E. Vieira, *Diccionario biographico*, II, p. 268).

23  'Esta Comedia foy representada pela Sñra Infante D. Francisca e pelas Damas do
Passo e faziaõ os papeis seguintes Ino – A Sñra Infante D. Francisca. Anfion – A
Sñra D. Ines Antonia da Sylva. Niobe – A Sñra D. Luisa Maria do Pilar. Dirce –
A Sñra D. Theresa Barbara de Meneses. Polidoro – A Sñra D. Ines Francisca de
Noronha. Porsidas – A Sñra D. Victoria Josefa de Borbon. Iris – A Sñra
D. Lorença Francisca de Mello' (R. V. Nery, *Para a história do barroco musical
português*, p. 79).

24  Cf. R. Mitjana, 'Espagne' in *Encyclopédie de la Musique et Dictionnaire du
Conservatoire*, IV, p. 2070.

25  *História de Portugal*, I, p. 554.

26  *Ibid.*, p. 529.

27  J. H. Saraiva, *História concisa de Portugal*, p. 220.

28  *Ibid.*, p. 221.

29  *Histoire de mon temps*, vol. I, ch. I, p. 13.

30  'Landed wealth remained in the hands of Church and Nobility. Out of
Portugal's 2 m. people, over 25,000 were members of religious orders and
over 30,000 were priests – that is, one in approximately every 36 inhabitants
(as compared with 1 in 33 in Spain). The number of convents rose from 396 in
1600 ... to 477 by 1739. It has been estimated that a third of the land in the
kingdom belonged to the Church, which also enjoyed a tithe of all agri-
cultural produce.' (V. M. Godinho, 'Portugal and her empire, 1680–1720',
p. 537).

31  'The King determined to convert his Royal Chapel into a See, and he has
appealed to the Pope, and in the meantime he is having it repaired with a new
main chapel and another thousand changes' (J. S. Silva, *Gazeta em forma de carta*,
entry for 15 February 1707, p. 98).

32  Probably in return for Portugal's help in the war against the Turks.

33  *Description de la ville de Lisbonne*, p. 40 of the Portuguese translation.

34  *Ibid.*

35  Cf. E. Vieira, *Diccionario biographico*, I, p. 534.

36  *Ibid.*, p. 547.

37  D. B. Machado, *Bibliotheca lusitana*, IV, p. 55.

38  Cf. J. Mazza, *Dicionário biográfico de músicos portugeses.*

39 Reproduced in M. C. de Brito, 'Um retrato inédito do compositor Francisco António de Almeida'.

40 To celebrate the birthday of the Infante D. António, brother of the King, on 6 June. During the first quarter of the eighteenth century, several serenatas, with music by Nicolà Porpora, Alessandro and Domenico Scarlatti, and Francesco Gasparini, were sung at the Portuguese embassy in Rome and at the Teatro Capranica, to celebrate royal births or birthdays, or the election of Pope Innocent XIII. The librettos of some of the operas by Antonio Bononcini, Giuseppe Orlandini and Alessandro Scarlatti that were performed in Venice and in Rome in this period were also dedicated to the Portuguese ambassador and to the Portuguese Cardinal da Cunha (cf. M. C. de Brito, 'Domenico Scarlatti e a música em Portugal no tempo de D. João V').

41 R. Kirkpatrick, *Domenico Scarlatti*, p. 59, quoting *Celani, I Cantori della Cappella Pontificia nei secoli XVI–XVIII*, p. 69.

42 *Gazeta de Lisboa*, 28 September 1719.

43 Cf. R. Pagano, *Scarlatti, Alessandro e Domenico: due vite in una*, pp. 354–63, and the same author's 'Le origine ed il primo statuto dell'Unione dei Musici intitolata a Santa Cecilia in Palermo'.

44 One of them, *Le nozze di Baco e d'Arianna* of 27 December 1722, is here identified for the first time as belonging to him (cf. Chronology, p. 126).

45 C. Beirão, *Cartas da Rainha D. Mariana Vitória*, p. 135.

46 *Musikalisches Lexicon, oder musikalische Bibliothek*, art. 'Portugal', p. 489.

47 Floriano or Floriani had been in the service of Prince Ruspoli between the years 1710 and 1711. Mossi is probably Gaetano Mossi, Mozi or Mozzi, who sang in Vivaldi operas between the years 1713 and 1718, and of whom several compositions are preserved in *P-Lf*. He was a member of an important musical clan to whom belonged also Caterina Leri or Leli Mossi, who sang in all the operas at the Teatro S. Bartolomeo in Rome between 1723 and 1725, and is identified in the librettos as 'virtuosa dell' ambasciatore di Portogallo' (private communication of Professor Reinhard Strohm). The score of the first part of *La contesa delle stagioni* of 1720, the only extant source of Scarlatti's serenatas for Portugal, which is preserved in *I-Vnm*, also lists the names of the soprano Cristini and the contralto D. Luiggi (cf. M. Boyd, *Domenico Scarlatti – Master of Music*, p. 108). Some of the players' names, such as Avondano and Thomas, introduce dynasties of court players up to the end of the eighteenth century (cf. J. Scherpereel, *L'orchestre et les instrumentistes de la Real Câmara à Lisbonne de 1765 à 1834*).

48 José António Carlos de Seixas (1704–42), vice-chapelmaster and organist, is mainly famous as a composer of keyboard music. He is not known to have written any operatic works.

49 *Gazeta de Lisboa*, 29 January.

50 According to A. Rodrigues Villa, 'Embajada extraordinaria del Marques de los Balbases a Portugal en 1727', *Revista de Archivos, Bibliotecas y Museos*, 11 (1872), p. 192, expenses with actors and players, etc., for this 'melodrama' amounted to 898$000 rs. The 'fiesta' *Amor aumenta el valor*, performed on 18 January, cost 1:025$400 rs (quoted in C. Beirão, *Cartas da Rainha D. Mariana Vitória*, pp. CIX-CX).

51 The music for all but two of them (*La risa di Democrito* and *Madama Ciana*, which are anonymous) was by Francisco António de Almeida. *Gl'incanti d'Alcina* of 1731 was a serenata according to J. Monfort, 'Quelques notes sur l'histoire du théâtre portugais (1729–1750)', p. 584. *La Spinalba* was successfully revived in recent years in Lisbon, Badajoz, Paris, Rome and London.

52 On 12 February 1728 and 8 February 1736.

53 Frei J. da Natividade, *Fasto de Hymeneo...*, mentions several serenatas performed in Elvas in January 1729, during the meeting between the Portuguese and Spanish Royal families.

54 *P-EVp* Códs. CIV/1–5 to 21d, published in J. Monfort, 'Quelques notes sur l'histoire du théâtre portugais (1729–1750)'; E. Brasão, *Diário de D. Francisco Xavier de Meneses, 4º Conde de Ericeira*.

55 C. Beirão, *Cartas da Rainha D. Mariana Vitória*.

56 *P-EVp* CIV/1–5 d, ff. 52v, 88v.

57 E. Brasão, *Diário de D. Francisco Xavier de Meneses, 4º Conde de Ericeira*, p. 132.

58 He was born in Brazil, studied law at the Sorbonne, and was agent to the Crown in Rome (where he may have met Francisco António de Almeida), before becoming the King's secretary in 1730. One of the most brilliant and progressive minds of his time, he is the author of a translation of *Georges Dandin (O marido confuso)* by Molière. It is possible that the above-mentioned librettos may have been adapted and not originally written by him.

59 On the Paghetti sisters (called the Paquetas in the diary), see p. 14.

60 CIV/1–6 d, ff. 17.

61 E. Brasão, *Diário de D. Francisco Xavier de Meneses, 4º Conde de Ericeira*, pp. 139, 140–3.

62 [Merveilleux], *Mémoires instructifs*, pp. 182–3 of the Portuguese translation. This is also confirmed by Princess Mariana Vitória in a letter of 21 February 1744: 'On Shrove Tuesday I danced with the little girls and three or four women because men are not allowed here' (C. Beirão, *Cartas da Rainha D. Mariana Vitória*, p. 229).

63 Gamekeepers.

64 J. Monfort, 'Quelques notes sur l'histoire du théâtre portugais (1729–1750)', pp. 584, 586.

65 *Ibid.*, p. 592. I have not found any evidence of *La Spinalba*'s having been sung for the inauguration of a new theatre at the royal farm of the Ajuda on 4 November 1739, as stated in P. von Waxel, 'Portugiesische Musik', p. 523.

66 C. Beirão, *Cartas da Rainha D. Mariana Vitória*, p. 46.

67 *Ibid.*, letter of 12 October 1730, p. 75. U. Prota-Giurleo, *Musicisti napoletani alla corte di Portogallo nel 1700*, pp. 5–6, mentions that King Charles of Bourbon used to send copies of the operas performed at the S. Carlo Theatre in Naples to his sister, Princess Mariana Vitória. In 1741 Leonardo Leo wrote for the Princess 'dodici arie nel più moderno stile con idee ben ritrovate e nuove'. All these works were lost in the 1755 earthquake.

68 C. Beirão, *Cartas da Rainha D. Mariana Vitória*, letter of 1 May 1736, p. 142. The original of this and other major historical texts is given in the Appendix, pp. 176–97.

69 *Ibid.*, letter of 28 July 1737, p. 156.

70 *Ibid.*, letter of 24 August 1737, p. 159.

71  *Ibid.*, letter of 13 May 1738, p. 161.

72  *Ibid.*, letter of 10 April 1741, p. 177.

73  *Ibid.*, letter of 22 June 1743, p. 212.

74  *Ibid.*, letter of 16 January 1744, p. 244. Nothing else is known of this singer.

75  *Ibid.*, letter of 1 March 1745, p. 243.

76  *Ibid.*, letter of 26 March 1745, p. 246.

77  C. de Saussure, *Voyage de Mons.*<sup>r</sup> ... *en Portugal*, p. 276 of the Portuguese translation.

78  This is the probable origin of the Assembleia das Nações Estrangeiras mentioned on p. 78.

79  These diaries themselves seem to be a symptom of these changes. An entry in *P-EVp* CIV/1–5 d, f. 127, suggests that the author of this diary may also have been the Count of Ericeira. He states that he wrote this news for the benefit of his absent friends and relatives.

80  J. Monfort, 'Quelques notes sur l'histoire du théâtre portugais (1729–1750)', p. 582.

81  This point is further developed in M. C. de Brito, 'Le rôle de l'opéra dans la lutte entre l'obscurantisme et les Lumières au Portugal (1731–1742).'

82  J. Monfort, 'Quelques notes sur l'histoire du théâtre portugais (1729–1750)', p. 582; *P-EVp* CIV/1–5 d, f. 16.

83  Transcribed in V. Ribeiro, 'O Pateo das Comédias e as representações teatrais (1729).'

84  *P-EVp* CIV/1–5 d, f. 42.

85  E. Brasão, *Diário de D. Francisco Xavier de Meneses, 4° Conde de Ericeira*, pp. 13, 16; *P-EVp* CIV/1–5 d, ff. 84, 100.

86  *Ibid.*, p. 72.

87  *Ibid.*, p. 94, 112; *P-EVp* CIV/1–5 d, f. 7v.

88  *Ibid.*, pp. 129, 135, 147; *P-EVp* CIV/1–6 d, f. 17v. The *presépios* were popular theatrical performances on the theme of the Nativity. The composer Francisco António de Almeida did not disdain writing music for them (cf. J. Monfort, 'Quelques notes sur l'histoire du théâtre portugais (1729–1750)', p. 584).

89  J. Monfort, 'Quelques notes sur l'histoire du théâtre portugais (1729–1750)', p. 570. This was approximately where the present Teatro da Trindade now stands (cf. G. M. Sequeira, *O Carmo e a Trindade*, II, pp. 32–5, and maps, pp. 48–9).

90  E. Brasão, *Diário de D. Francisco Xavier de Meneses, 4° Conde de Ericeira*, pp. 208, 215. Lázaro Leitão was one of the richest canons of the Patriarcal. He had been the Marquis of Fontes' secretary during the latter's embassy in Rome.

91  *I-Bc* L.117. Michel Corrette, in the preface to his *Mèthode théorique et pratique pour apprendre ... le violoncelle...*, Paris, 1741, p. A, states that Bononcini was chapelmaster to the King of Portugal, but this was certainly a confusion (communication from Professor Pilar Torres, of Lisbon).

92  *F-Pn* Vm.<sup>4</sup>, quoted by L. E. Lindgren, *A Bibliographical Scrutiny of Dramatic Works by Giovanni and his Brother Antonio Maria Bononcini*, p. 799.

93  *Origenes y establecimiento de la ópera en España*, pp. 38–9.

94  Letter of G. M. Schiassi to Padre Martini in *I-Bc* L.117, ff. 165–6. J. Mazza, *Dicionário biográfico de músicos portugueses, s. v.* 'Romão Mazza', p. 39.

95 This mistake is also made in M. C. de Brito, 'Le rôle de l'opéra dans la lutte entre l'obscurantisme et les Lumières au Portugal (1731–1742)'. Clerici had worked with Handel in London during the Royal Academy period.

96 J. Monfort, 'Quelques notes sur l'histoire du théâtre portugais (1729–1750)', pp. 584–5.

97 Letter of G. M. Schiassi to Padre Martini of April 1736 in *I-Bc* 1–4, f. 20. On António José da Silva's operas at the Bairro Alto see p. 20–2.

98 J. Monfort, 'Quelques notes sur l'histoire du théâtre portugais (1729–1750)', pp. 585–6.

99 *Ibid.*, p. 587.

100 C. H. Frèches, Introduction to António José da Silva, *El prodígio de Amarante*, pp. 26–9.

101 J. Monfort, 'Quelques notes sur l'histoire du théâtre portugais (1729–1750)', p. 587.

102 *Ibid.*, p. 589. The libretto of *Sesostri, Re d'Egitto* mentions the following dancers: Gabriele Borghesi from Bologna, Bernardo Gavazzi from Venice, and Giuseppe and Lorenza Fortini from Livorno.

103 And also to António Ferreira Carlos, according to C. H. Frèches, 'António José da Silva (O Judeu) et les Marionettes', p. 332.

104 He appears as manager of the Rua dos Condes Theatre in 1764 (see chapter 4, p. 85).

105 J. Monfort, 'Quelques notes sur l'histoire du théâtre portugais (1729–1750)', pp. 589–90.

106 The theatre was approximately where the Condes Cinema now stands.

107 Translations and adaptations from Metastasio and other authors, which became very popular in eighteenth-century Portugal. The diaries seem to imply that the nobles themselves were involved in their dissemination.

108 Her later affair with João V has been mentioned by modern authors, who do not generally indicate their source of information.

109 J. Monfort, 'Quelques notes sur l'histoire du théâtre portugais (1729–1750)', pp. 591–4.

110 *Ibid.*, pp. 594–5.

111 Cf. the list of Singers in the Public Theatres 1735–42 on p. 19.

112 According to E. Cotarelo y Mori, *Orígenes y establecimiento de la ópera en España*, pp. 88–90, 111, 115, 116.

113 According to C. V. Machado, *Colecção de Memorias*, p. 150.

114 Letter of G. M. Schiassi to Padre Martini of 6 May 1751 in *I-Bc* 1–4, f. 29. Further on Annibale Pio Fabri cf. article in *The New Grove Dictionary*.

115 Cf. 'Rinaldo di Capua' in *The New Grove Dictionary*.

116 'Subsidios para a historia da opera e da coregraphia italianas'.

117 J. M. A. Nogueira, 'Memórias do teatro português', p. 42.

118 E. Brasão, *Diário de D. Francisco Xavier de Meneses, 4° Conde de Ericeira*, p. 160.

119 A. J. Silva, *Obras completas*, IV, p. 61.

120 Of the existing literature on A. J. Silva only C. H. Frèches' above-mentioned articles have been found relevant for the purpose of the present study.

121 J. Mazza, *Dicionário biográfico de músicos portugueses*, p. 18, says that he was the author of seven operas. Recently new musical sources for *Anfitrião*,

*Guerras do alecrim e manjerona* and *As variedades de Proteu*, by (an) anonymous composer(s), have been discovered in Brazil (cf. M. I. Cruz 'Ópera portuguesa no Brasil do século XVIII').

122  J. Monfort, 'Quelques notes sur l'histoire du théâtre portugais (1729–1750)', p. 588.

123  Cf. T. Braga, *Historia do theatro portuguez*, pp. 191–2.

124  Cf. pp. 133–4.

125  Cf. e. g. M. I. Cruz 'Ópera portuguesa no Brasil do século XVIII'.

126  Cf. E. Brasão, *Diário de D. Francisco Xavier de Meneses, 4° Conde de Ericeira*, p. 141.

127  C. H. Frèches, 'António José da Silva (O Judeu) et les Marionettes', p. 334.

128  Like the one that is attempted by M. V. de Carvalho in 'Die Sinnentleerung des gesungenen Wortes: Zur Musik- und Theaterentwicklung in Portugal bis zur Entstehung des São-Carlos-Theater (1793)', ch. 1 of his thesis *'Denken ist Sterben ...'* As he admits himself in his *Vorwort* (p. 3), this chapter is not based on first-hand research, consisting rather on a critical evaluation of existing literature on the subject. Unfortunately some of his conclusions concerning the first half of the eighteenth century are either based on a less attentive reading of his sources, or on insufficient evidence. Thus he states that what the court permitted in private – Italian comic opera 'live' on the stage – was forbidden in public performances (p. 24), and further on (p. 25) that for the aristocracy and naturally for the church dignitaries, who also attended the *opera seria*, the propriety of the performances must be kept. He questions the present author's opinion (in 'Le rôle de l'opéra dans la lutte entre l'obscurantisme et les Lumières au Portugal (1731–1742)'), according to which the introduction of Italian opera in Portugal is also connected with the interests of a small intellectual elite, who wished to see Portugal re-enter the Common Market of European culture. There cannot be any doubt that such an elite existed, and that the Count of Ericeira was one of its most eminent members. On the other hand M. V. de Carvalho's own interpretation of António José da Silva's operas as a possible manifestation of the spirit of the Enlightenment (pp. 28–35) is certainly open to criticism, while his characterisation of the extant music to them as a parody of Italian operatic style betrays an inadequate knowledge of the history of eighteenth-century Italian opera. His list of operatic performances in Portugal 1711–93 (pp. 449–66) reproduces the numerous errors present in earlier chronologies.

129  J. Monfort, 'Quelques notes sur l'histoire du théâtre portugais (1729–1750)', p. 590.

130  *Ibid.*, p. 595.

131  J. M. A. Nogueira, 'Memórias do teatro português (1588–1762)', p. 43.

132  See p. 12.

133  J. B. de Castro, *Mappa de Portugal antigo, e moderno*, I, p. 372.

134  J. Monfort, 'Quelques notes sur l'histoire du théâtre portugais (1729–1750)', p. 596–9.

135  *I-Bc* 1–4, f. 23.

136  C. H. Frèches, 'Le théâtre aristocratique et l'évolution du goût au Portugal d'après la «Gazeta de Lisboa», de 1715 à 1739', pp. 100–1.

137 *Ibid.*, p. 106.
138 *Gazeta de Lisboa*, 18 September 1747.

## 2 COURT OPERA DURING THE REIGN OF JOSÉ I (1750–77)

1 Letter of 6 April in C. Beirão, *Cartas da Rainha D.Mariana Vitória*, p. 203.
2 Published in M. C. de Brito, 'A contratação do castrato Gizziello'. I have found no trace of Gizziello's previous stay in Lisbon in 1743, which is still mentioned in *The New Grove Dictionary*.
3 This secrecy was to be extended to the court of Lisbon, for reasons which Sebastião José does not give (letter of 16 June).
4 He is referred to as 'Virtuoso di Camera in attual Servizio di S.M.F.' in the librettos.
5 £4,000 according to C. Burney, *A General History*, IV, p. 395. 36,000 *cruzados* (14:400$000 rs!) according to Frei J. de S. José Queiroz: 'Let there be music; but I think that a musician such as Egipcielli was, with a salary of 36,000 *cruzados*, besides other very large benefits, does not seem right in a kingdom that His Majesty found to be in a state of utter misery, almost in the Iron Age; when under his father it had been possible to live in a Golden Age. When there is not enough gold available, one cannot and should not maintain the magnificence, splendour and exquisite taste of a theatre with a superb orchestra, considered by foreign ambassadors to be the best in the world. I was told as much by the Count of Perelada, who was at the *Favorita* in Vienna, in Naples, in Italy, and who finally saw the Spanish theatre after it was refined during the government of King Ferdinand and Queen Maria Bárbara. Let there be music; but if one cannot have an orchestra of forty-eight instruments make it one of sixteen, and as for operas, let those of scrupulous tastes content themselves with Bossuet. Since I have never seen any, I can do without them' (*Memórias*, pp. 184–5).
6 Anton Raaff was certainly not a lesser singer. Two letters that he wrote from Lisbon to Padre Martini in Bologna in 1753 and 1754 were published by P. Petrobelli in 'The Italian years of Anton Raaff', pp. 250–1. They do not however shed any light on this period, except to confirm the departure of Anna Peruzzi, who had come to Lisbon from Madrid in the hope of getting a place as a court singer.
7 Letter from G. M. Schiassi to Padre Martini, written on 29 May 1752. Perez received 2:000$000 rs a year according to a document in AHMF, CX. 2 (£2,000 according to C. Burney, *A General History*, IV, p. 572).
8 *Colecção de Memorias*, p. 188.
9 Bibiena earned 2:109$000 rs a year (AHMF, CX. 1). He married a Brazilian, Rosa Maria de Jesus, in 1755 and died in Lisbon on 20 November 1760. On Azzolini see p. 38.
10 *Gazeta de Lisboa*, 20 June.
11 *Gazeta de Lisboa*, 14 September. This was roughly where the tower in the Ministério do Exército building on the western side of the Praça do Comércio, formerly Terreiro do Paço now stands (see frontispiece). Nothing further is known about this temporary theatre.

12 *Gazeta de Lisboa*, 1 and 8 March. The theatre was built beside the country palace some forty miles north of Lisbon, where the court used to go hunting between mid-January and the end of February or sometimes mid-March. A plan exists of both the palace and the theatre in the Arquivo Histórico do Ministério das Obras Públicas. Drawings by Bibiena for *Didone abbandonata* are preserved in the Museu Nacional de Arte Antiga (nos. 304–6; see Fig. 1). Several other drawings by Bibiena and Inácio de Oliveira Bernardes preserved in the same collection have been related with other court productions by J. da Silva Correia in 'Teatros régios do século XVIII' (unfortunately I was not allowed access to the forthcoming posthumous work by the same author *Salvaterra de Magos. O Paço Real, a Ópera e a Falcoaria*). Cf. also M. S. Ribeiro, 'À margem da Exposição de Desenhos da Escola dos Bibiena'.

13 The initial contract between the master masons and João Pedro Ludovice (or Ludwig), who was in charge of the construction, is dated 7 July 1752 (*Certidão de Medição da ... Caza da Opera* in *P-Ln*). The total cost of the masonry work was 152:611$364 rs.

14 Fig. 3. Cf. J. de Figueiredo, 'Teatro Real da Ópera'. This attribution was disputed by A. V. da Silva, *As muralhas da Ribeira de Lisboa*, pp. 176–8, based on the fact that the dimensions of the theatre given in the Tombo (City Register) of Lisbon of 1755 do not agree with those in the plan. M. A. Beaumont, however, in 'Stage sets by the Bibiena', has published them again as belonging to the Casa da Ópera, and more recently S. Infante has reached the same conclusion ('Leitura arquitectónica da iconografia atribuída à Ópera do Tejo', in *Desenhos dos Galli Bibiena. Arquitectura e Cenografia. Exposição temporária*, pp. 39–43).

15 A. A. Bourdon ed., 'Description de Lisbonne', pp. 162–3. The original text is reproduced on pp. 177–8.

16 'Underneath the four tiers of boxes, of which there were thirty-two, there were ground-floor boxes [*frisas* or *baignoires*]' (editor's note 72, p. 179; see Fig. 2).

17 They may have been real marble, which is a very common stone in Portugal.

18 'These measurements agree with the scale of Bibiena's plan. The 180 feet correspond to the whole length of the room and the stage' (editor's note 74, p. 180).

19 'There were in reality four boxes on either side on each floor. But the Chevalier des Courtils, who must have had his eyes fixed on the stage during the whole performance, did not count those that were placed on both sides of the royal box.' (editor's note 74, p. 180; see Fig. 2).

20 Sunday 29 June and Saturday 5 July, according to the *Gazeta de Lisboa*.

21 M. de Figueiredo, *Teatro de...*, XIV, pp. 412–13.

22 *P-Ln*, Colecção Pombalina, Cód. 651, f. 78. It was published by G. M. Sequeira, *Teatro de outros tempos*, pp. 286–7, who also says that the theatre had a total capacity of 600 seats, based on a ms. 'Historia politica e economica do reinado do Senhor D. José' in his possession.

23 Probably quoting from the above ms. Many other details that he gives cannot be relied upon or quoted here, as they are based on sources which he does not identify.

24 G. M. Sequeira, *ibid.*, says that as this date fell during Holy Week, the opening was postponed until 2 April. The first date however is the one given by the *Gazeta de Lisboa* and in the libretto, and it is also confirmed in the French ambassador's dispatch to his court of 1 April (Paris, Archive of the Ministère des Affaires Etrangères, *Correspondence politique Portugal*, vol. 87, ff. 2–6, *Dépêche du comte de Baschi du 1er Avril*). The same dispatch indicates that the theatre director was the singer Francesco Feracci: 'They have tried to make this spectacle quite magnificent, but they are still far from the courts of Madrid and Dresden; the director here is a castrato called Feracci who has neither Farinelli's taste nor any of his talents, who is totally incapable of a similar task but who, in compensation, is considered to be one of the greatest scoundrels alive, and who does not spare the gold from Brazil. The performance lasted until two in the morning and it would be very trying to find oneself obliged to attend twice a week. I have thought therefore that the King would not disapprove if, in my absence, I sometimes left the field to the Spanish ambassador (coded passage).

25 *A General History*, IV, p. 571. His informant was Gerard de Visme, Esq., 'a gentleman long resident in Lisbon'.

26 This is in fact a very different version from the Milan 1752 version kept in *P-La* 45 IV–48/50 (cf. Chronology, p. 136). See Fig. 3.

27 According to G. M. Sequeira, *Teatro de outros tempos*, p. 290, the riding-master Carlos António Ferreira rode *Faca-Cega* or *Embaixador* at the head of twenty-five riders; 400 riders represented a phalanx of Lacedemonians according to C. V. Machado, *Colecção de Memorias*, pp. 150–1 (an obviously hyperbolic figure).

28 A short letter from him to Padre Martini dated from Lisbon, 15 March 1755, is preserved in *I-Bc* 1.18.41. It was carried by the singer Tommaso Guarducci, who was returning to Italy.

29 *Colecção de Memorias*, pp. 150–1. The only other opera that is documented, however, is *Antigono* by A. Mazzoni, for which a rare libretto exists in *BR-Rn*. It was performed in the autumn and included Gregorio Babbi and Gaetano Guadagni among the cast. The production was directed by Giuseppe Bonechy, 'Poeta di S. M. Fidelissima, et in attual Servizio delle Corte di Vienna, e di Pietroburgo', who was also the author of the *licenze* for all the operas performed at the Casa da Ópera.

30 A. A. Bourdon ed., 'Description de Lisbonne', pp. 162–3.

31 *Ibid.*, p. 149. The *Gazeta de Lisboa* records several serenatas performed in the royal palace that forms part of the monastery, during a visit of the royal family in October 1752, in which Gizziello, Raaff and Ciucci sang.

32 J. A. França, *A reconstrução de Lisboa e a arquitectura pombalina*, pp. 11–12.

33 Among others, the painter Giovanni Berardi returned to Rome at the end of 1755 (AHMF, CX. 2).

34 *The Private Correspondence of Sir Benjamin Keene*, Cambridge, 1933, p. 437, quoted in R. Kirkpatrick, *Domenico Scarlatti*, p. 126.

35 E. Cotarelo y Mori, *Orígenes y establecimiento de la ópera en España*, pp. 170, 176, 180 (note 3).

36 *Ibid.*, pp. 141–2, 169 (note 1).

37 *Ibid.*, pp. 141–2, 161 (note 1).

38 *A General History*, IV, p. 395.

39 Letter of the chargé d'affaires in Rome, José Pereira Santiago, of 2 February 1791, in AHMF, CX. 260; letter of the consul Giovanni Piaggio of 21 March 1791 in AHMF, CX. 261.

40 H. Abert, *W. A. Mozart*, I, p. 464.

41 I, p. 278.

42 In the absence of the librettos or any other documents, the performances of *Ezio*, *Siroe*, *Solimano* and *Enea in Italia* by Perez at Salvaterra in 1756, 1757 and 1759, mentioned in J. J. Marques, *Cronologia da ópera em Portugal*, pp. 100–1, are to be regarded as very doubtful. *La vera felicità*, performed at Queluz in 1761, is a serenata.

43 See pp. 61ff. As is shown below, the Ajuda and Queluz Theatres, and probably also the one at Salvaterra, were much smaller than the Ópera do Tejo. A mercantilist spirit presided over the reconstruction of Lisbon under the direction of Sebastião José de Carvalho e Melo, which had its symbolic expression in the renaming of the Terreiro do Paço as Praça do Comércio. Neither the Ópera do Tejo, nor the Royal Chapel and Patriarchal See, secular and religious expressions of absolutist power, were included in this reconstruction. The court moved to the Ajuda, in the suburbs of Lisbon, away from the economical and social centre of the city and the country.

44 Correspondence relating to the purchase of two Stainer violas and two oboes by the Turin maker Palanca has been published in M. C. de Brito, 'Alguns dados inéditos sobre instrumentos musicais em Portugal no século XVIII'. This article also discusses the possibility that the high pitch or 'tom natural' used by the Royal Chamber may have been slightly higher than modern pitch, based on the pitch of twenty court trumpets preserved in the Museu Nacional dos Coches, Lisbon, and on the fact that imported E violin strings were liable to frequent breaking. Music paper with ten staves, both in oblong and tall format (for motets and other church music) was ordered from a dealer dwelling under the clock in the Piazza S. Marco, in Venice, in 1773 (AHMF, Livro XX/Z/45, f. 39v).

45 Letters of 26 February and 22 October 1771, *ibid.*, ff. 31, 37.

46 He was also Music Inspector, according to G. M. Sequeira, *Teatro de outros tempos*, and his name occasionally appears in connection with other operatic dealings.

47 A list of court copyists is given in chapter 3, p. 62.

48 AHMF, Livro XX/Z/45, ff. 34v–35. For more about this letter see p. 44.

49 Four examples of these bindings are reproduced in M. A. M. Santos, *Biblioteca da Ajuda. Catálogo de música manuscrita*, IX.

50 Quoted by L. F. Tagliavini in W. A. Mozart, *Mitridate, Re di Ponto*, p. XII, note 23.

51 AHMF, Livro XX/Z/46, ff. 10v–12, 24.

52 Those for *Demofoonte* cost 1:272$200 rs according to Livro XX/Z/46, f. 23. Those for *Enea nel Lazio* cost 427$275 rs according to the accounts in *P-La* 52–XIV–35 (no. 79). Those for *Fetonte* were originally accompanied by miniature drawings with the identification of the characters, according to a letter from Piaggio dated 17 October 1768 in AHMF, CX. 260.

53 Livro xx/z/45, f. 5.
54 'glacés de prata falça, o que aqui chamaõ velilho, dito ordinario, galoens, rendas de varias larguras, franginhas estreitas e largas, velilho de ouro & glace ... veo de Bolonha fino para os peitos dos Muzicos de mulher, volante Lizo e Lavrado ... folhas encarnadas, palhetas largas e estreitas, canutilhos, trancinhas e tudo o mais que pertence ao Teatro.'
55 Letter of Pinto da Silva dated 28 February 1774 in AHMF, Livro xx/z/46, ff. 8v–9.
56 Copy of a letter from the Milan agent Antonio Zucchi, dated 30 March 1774 in xx/z/77 (II).
57 Letter of 28 December 1773 in AHMF, Livro xx/z/46, f. 5. In general Pinto da Silva seems more economically minded than his predecessor. He was also concerned with putting some order into his accounts as Director of the Royal Theatres and Keeper of the King's Privy Purse, as he states himself in a letter to the Prime Minister, Marquis of Angeja, as late as 1782 (Livro xx/z/47, ff. 83v–84, 86v).
58 Letter of Silva Botelho dated 1 March 1768 in Livro xx/z/45, ff. 2v–3.
59 'after the earthquake our August Sovereign did not want to hire any musicians for his theatre besides those who could be employed in his cathedral or royal Chapel' (Letter of the Director of the Royal Theatres to Niccolò Jommelli of 18 March 1771 in AHMF, Livro xx/z/45, f. 34). In fact, according to the *Osservazioni Correlative alla Reale, e Patriarcal Cappella di Lisbona* (1778) in *P-La*, after the earthquake a separation was established between the Royal Chapel, near the Ajuda Palace, and the Patriarcal, which was successively installed in different places in Lisbon. Most of the opera singers belonged to the first institution.
60 AHMF, Livro xx/z/45, f. 33–33v. This letter discusses the eventual contract of the 'amico A ...', the castrato Giuseppe Aprile, who had served under Jommelli in Stuttgart between 1763 and 1769, and was then singing in the S. Carlo Theatre in Naples. In a letter to Martinelli of 30 September 1770 (preserved in *C-Lu* Music GM–AR MZ 288) Aprile says that his greatest desire would be to serve the King of Portugal, and complains of Martinelli's failure to help him in this matter. Replying to Jommelli's offer of an appointment in Lisbon in a letter of 3 February 1771 (*C-Lu* Music GM–AR MZ 287) he says that he is already contracted in Turin for the 1772 Carnival and from then until the 1773 Carnival in Naples, but that after that date he would accept the offer should it still be open. He was never hired for Lisbon.
61 Compare with the Career of Court Singers, 1752–93, pp. 54–5.
62 He was considered too short to serve in the theatre (AHMF, Livro xx/z/46, f. II), but he actually sang in several operas.
63 AHMF, CX. 260, Livro xx/z/46, ff. IV, 5, 19, 25v, 28.
64 AHMF, CX. 260.
65 AHMF, Livro xx/z/45, ff. 2v–3.
66 H. Abert, *Niccolò Jommelli als Opernkomponist*, pp. 76–7.
67 *História da dança em Portugal*, pp. 156–9. He also gives a list of eighteenth-century choreographers and dancers in Portugal in *Apêndice II*, pp. 340–5.

68 'Subsidios para a historia da opera e da choregraphia italianas, em Portugal, no século XVIII'.

69 Cf. ch. 3, note 4, p. 212 below.

70 AHMF, Livro xx/z/46, f. 36v.

71 AHMF, CX. 257.

72 AHMF, Livro xx/z/45, f. 18.

73 H. Abert, *Niccolò Jommelli als Opernkomponist*, p. 70.

74 A. de Gusmão, *Cartas*, p. 139.

75 J. Scherpereel, *L'orchestre et les instrumentistes de la Real Câmara à Lisbonne de 1764 à 1834*, p. 188.

76 *Ibid.*

77 AHTC, Livro 2089, *1778 / Folhas das Rasoes a Dinheiro.*

78 He was later replaced by his son, José Maria de Almeida.

79 AHMF. CX. 260.

80 'Elogio del Jommelli', p. 89.

81 M. P. P. Carvalhais, 'Subsidios para a historia da opera e da choregraphia italianas, em Portugal, no século XVIII'.

82 *Niccolò Jommelli: The Last Years.* Among other sources used, she transcribes the letters from Silva Botelho and Pinto da Silva to Jommelli preserved in the AHMF, and also Jommelli's replies, forty-six letters in all, purchased from Richard MacNutt Ltd, Tunbridge Wells, UK, in 1971 by the Music Library of the University of California at Berkeley. These letters were originally in CX. 260 in the AHMF, where they are mentioned in a list of contents, and it is not known how and when they were removed from there. One chapter in M. McClymonds' study is devoted to 'Italian Opera at the Portuguese Court 1750–1780'. My own research was carried out independently from hers.

83 Livro xx/z/45, f. 10.

84 'Giovanni Cordeiro ... who directs all His Majesty's operas, either serious or *buffe.*'

85 341 soldiers, 86 of whom on horseback, and 96 other extras, according to H. Abert, *Niccolò Jommelli als Opernkomponist*, p. 82. Compare the number of extras used for the same opera in Lisbon, p. 49.

86 Giuseppe Jozzi had been *primo uomo* at Stuttgart between 1750 and 1757. See H. Abert, *ibid.*, p. 73.

87 Livro xx/z/45, f. 16.

88 He must have died sometime between July and December 1802, during which period his salary was paid to his widow and daughter. Besides his salary he received 25$600 rs a year for pens and paper, and 24$000 rs to pay the rent for a stable for his chaise and two mules (Livros xx/z/42, xx/G/19 to 29). A very interesting letter from Jommelli to him, dated 17 October 1769, is preserved in *C-Lu* MUSIC GM–AR MZ 294. It includes comments on *Il Vologeso* and *Fetonte* as well as on the operas of the following Lisbon season. Jommelli expresses fears concerning the performance in Lisbon of so many of his operas in succession, and confesses that he is finding it hard to produce new ideas, especially since he does not know the King's tastes.

89 Letters of Silva Botelho to David Perez of 14 March 1768 in Livro xx/z/45, f. 7, which have been crossed out, probably because they had been wrongly copied into that book.

90 Livro xx/G/19, f. 8.
91 Livro xx/z/45, f. 31.
92 This would amount to 704$000 rs and not to 1:000$000 rs, as E. Vieira states (*Diccionario biographico*, I, p. 550).
93 *Niccolò Jommelli: The Last Years*, p. 121.
94 A new version of *Demofoonte* (1770), *Armida abbandonata* (1770), *Ifigenia in Tauride* (1771) and the serenata *Cerere placata* (1772), for Naples; *Achille in Sciro* and *L'amante cacciatore* of 1771, both for Rome.
95 Livro xx/z/45, ff. 31v–32v. The original text is reproduced on p. 178.
96 Complete transcription in M. McClymonds, *Niccolò Jommelli: The Last Years*, p. 646.
97 *Ibid.*
98 *Ibid.*, p. 702. One of these was the Spaniard Antonio Rodil, who visited London in 1774 (AHMF, Livro xx/z/46, f. 9).
99 Livro xx/z/45, f. 28v.
100 Letters of 16 and 30 October 1770, *ibid.*, ff. 27 and 29.
101 *Niccolò Jommelli: The Last Years*, p. 26.
102 AHMF, Livro xx/z/45. ff. 21v–22. The original text is reproduced on pp. 178–9. This letter shows that the kind of innovations introduced by Jommelli in the *opera seria* and mentioned above by M. McClymonds were by then becoming fashionable even in such remote places as Lisbon.
103 Here probably in the sense of not stressing too much the upper register.
104 J. Scherpereel (*L'orchestre et les instrumentistes de la Real Câmara à Lisbonne de 1764 à 1834*, p. 242) remarks that between 1769 and 1770 ten new orchestral players were hired, including horns, trumpets and bassoons. These, particularly the brass, would have made the orchestra better prepared to play Jommelli's richly orchestrated scores.
105 *Niccolò Jommelli: The Last Years*, pp. 233, 250.
106 See note 44, p. 208 above.
107 AHMF, Livro xx/z/45, ff. 13–13v.
108 Letter of 'Frate Agostiniano' Ignazio Jommelli of 10 November 1774 in *P-Lt*. Pinto da Silva's reply in AHMF, Livro xx/z/46, ff. 18–18v.
109 AHMF, Livro xx/z/46, f. 37v.
110 Livro xx/z/45, f. 27.
111 II, p. 174.
112 *Ibid.*, note on p. 426.
113 'Carlo Goldoni e a opera na côrte de D. José'. Cf. also G. C. Rossi, 'Il Goldoni nel Portogallo del Settecento (Documenti inediti)'.
114 'O teatro de Goldoni em Portugal'.
115 AHMF, CXS. 257 and 5.
116 These and further details on Queluz are extracted from A. C. Pires, *História do Palácio Nacional de Queluz*.
117 *P-Ln* D. 108v, published in *Instrumentos Musicais 1747–1807*, p. 42.
118 *História do Palácio Nacional de Queluz*, II, pp. 170–2. The theatre was also assembled in other places in the gardens.
119 AHMF, CX. 5.
120 In the Ludwigsburg production of 1766 there had been 24 *Ratsherrn*, or ministers, 8 pages, 200 soldiers, 60 spectators on stage, and 250 spectators for

the Amphitheatre scene in Act II (see H. Abert, *Niccolò Jommelli als Opernkomponist*, p. 81).

121 AHMF, CX. 5.
122 AHMF, Livro xx/z/46, f. 37.
123 AHMF, Livro xx/z/45, f. 8.
124 Livro xx/z/46, ff. 38–9; Livro xx/z/47, f. 24v.
125 Livro xx/z/39.
126 *Historical Memoirs*, pp. 11–15.
127 *Travels through Portugal and Spain*, pp. 10–12. Twiss says this performance was
    on 17 November, but if the above calendar (p. 47) is complete it must have been
    either on 4 November or 17 December.
128 Twiss probably means that their faces were not properly shaven.
129 See p. 28.
130 Translated in J. R. Guimarães, *Biografia de Luísa de Aguiar Todi*, pp. 59–65.
131 *A General History*, IV, p. 572.
132 A. S. Bastos, *Diccionário do teatro portuguez*, pp. 300–1, says that in 1768 some
    sheds were built near the Ajuda Theatre which cost 3:550$856 rs, and a house for
    the extras which cost 485$220 rs.
133 C. Beirão, D. *Maria I*, I, p. 174, note 14.

### 3 COURT OPERA AND MUSIC IN THE REIGN OF MARIA I (1777–92)

1 Quoted in C. Beirão, *D. Maria I*, p. 127.
2 I was not able to find some of these books, such as those for the Salvaterra operas
  and for *Nettuno ed Egle* of 1785, which are mentioned in AHMF, CXS. 25 and
  27.
3 AHMF, Livros xx/G/19, f. 75, xx/G/20, ff. 54 and 62.
4 Cf. the list of dancers published in J. Sasportes, *História da dança em Portugal*,
  pp. 340–5.
5 AHMF, Livros xx/G/24, f. 127, and xx/G/20, f. 64.
6 Livro xx/G/22, f. 46.
7 Orti, Reina, Ripa, Torriani and Totti, according to the libretto.
8 Bombelles, *Journal d'un ambassadeur de France*, pp. 153, 167, 225 and 227.
9 For instance on 5 July and 22 August 1782, and 23 August 1785, according to the
  *Gazeta de Lisboa*.
10 Bombelles, *Journal d'un ambassadeur de France*, p. 164.
11 A letter to the Papal nuncio of 3 July 1778 says that, while it was not the custom of
   their Majesties to receive the compliments of the foreign ambassadors while
   staying at their summer residences, and no invitations had been issued for the
   serenata of 5 July at Queluz, he was welcome to attend (A. C. Pires, *História do
   Palácio Nacional de Queluz*, I, p. 183.)
12 At a total cost of 7:189$981 rs (AHMF, Livro xx/G/24, f. 24). M. A. M. Santos,
   *Biblioteca da Ajuda. Catálogo de Música Manuscrita*, IX, p. XVI, says that the
   expenses described there agree with the present aspect of the Sala da Serenata,
   near the Pátio da Física, which would thus be the only room which has
   survived from the old palace (the present palace, whose construction began in
   1802, replaced the Real Barraca which was built in wood to lodge the royal

family after the 1755 earthquake). However, the surviving Sala da Serenata is an oval room which seems too small to have contained a dais and two boxes.

13 Bombelles, *Journal d'un ambassadeur de France*, p. 225.

14 According to the *Gazeta de Lisboa* of 20 and 21 May, there were several serenatas on the days preceding the departure of the Princess Mariana Vitória to Spain, to marry the Spanish Prince Gabriel, both at the Ajuda and the Vila Viçosa palaces. In some of these the Princess herself sang.

15 Pierre Anselme Maréchal established himself in Lisbon around this time, giving his first public concert with his wife at the Assembleia das Nações Estrangeiras on 12 December 1789 (*Gazeta de Lisboa*, 8 December). In 1791 he opened a publishing house with the French printer François Milcent (cf. E. Vieira, *Diccionario biographico*, II, p. 61).

16 AHMF, CX. 29.

17 Eight symphonies or overtures by J. Cordeiro da Silva are preserved in *P-Em*. Four of them belong to his serenatas and it is likely that the remaining four are also copies of overtures to his serenatas and operas preserved in *P-La*.

18 AHMF, CXS. 10, 14 and 22. Attributions based on the scores preserved in the Ajuda library are not possible, owing to the great number of extant operas of the same title.

19 AHMF, Livro xx/G/23, ff. 15–16.

20 CX. 13; Livro xx/G/20, f. 87.

21 W. Beckford, *Journal*, p. 273. This feast, which fell on 22 November, was organised every year by the Irmandade de Santa Cecília, to which all the musicians in Lisbon belonged.

22 *Ibid.*, pp. 274 and 279.

23 W. Beckford, *The History of the Caliph Vathek; and European Travels*, p. 353.

24 *Ibid.*, p. 397. This was the language used by Prince José in a private interview he had with Beckford.

25 AHMF, Livros xx/G/20 to 27, CXS. 13, 14, 16 and 39. More detailed references are not given as these data are marginal to our subject.

26 He was hired at 40$000 a month starting from December 1791 (Livro xx/G/27, f. 115).

27 Livro xx/G/19, ff. 43, 73.

28 Livro xx/G/20, ff. 123, 125.

29 Livros xx/G/24, ff. 10, 133, xx/G/27, ff. 98, 121, 122.

30 A list of contracts for these singers, drawn by Piaggio in Genoa, is preserved in CX. 260. Capranica and Angelelli were both hired at 50$000 a month (Livro xx/G/27, f. 107).

31 The letters of Pinto da Silva are in Livro xx/z/47 and those from Piaggio and the others in CX. 26.

32 Livro xx/z/47, ff. 94v, 117.

33 Marchetti received 240$000 from Piaggio for his expenses and efforts in hiring singers.

34 Cf. M. C. de Brito, 'Conciertos en Lisboa a fines del siglo XVIII'.

35 Correspondence on this subject is also preserved in Livro xx/z/47 and CX. 261.

36 Livros xx/G/20, f. 135, xx/G/22, f. 51, xx/G/24, f. 38.

37 Transcribed in C. Beirão, *D. Maria I*, p. 439.

38 Livro XX/G/24, ff. 43, 85.
39 A. C. Pires, *História do Palácio Nacional de Queluz*, I, p. 314, II, pp. 170–2.
40 Livro XX/G/21, ff. 87–8.
41 Livro XX/G/22, f. 93; CXS. 14, 257.
42 In CX. 257.
43 Salvaterra de Magos lies near the Tagus River, and travel between there and Lisbon was in part by boat.
44 The Palácio dos Estaus, approximately where the Teatro Nacional D. Maria II now stands.
45 Livro XX/G/25, f. 59.
46 All documents relating to the 1786 Salvaterra season are preserved in CX. 258.
47 He was working at the Rua dos Condes Theatre (see p. 108).
48 M. P. P. Carvalhais, 'Subsidios'.
49 This was on 27 January, according to C. Beirão, *D.Maria I*, p. 410. The court returned from Salvaterra on 4 February.
50 M. Moreau, *Cantores de ópera portugueses*, p. 184.
51 A. S. Bastos, *Diccionario do teatro português*, p. 315.
52 During the reign of José I the following operas by Portuguese composers were performed: *L'Arcadia in Brenta* by João Cordeiro da Silva in 1764, *Il mondo della luna* by Pedro António Avondano in 1765, *L'amore industrioso* by João de Sousa Carvalho in 1769 and the same author's *Eumene* in 1773, *Lo spirito di contradizione* by Jerónimo Francisco de Lima in 1772.
53 Cf. J. Scherpereel, *L'orchestre et les instrumentistes de la Real Câmara à Lisbonne de 1764 à 1834.*
54 *Eighteen entire new Lisbon Minuets for Two Violins and a Bass . . .* and *A Second Sett of Twenty-two Lisbon Minuets . . .* , both in *GB-Lbm.*
55 Cf. J. Mazza, *Dicionário biográfico de musicos portugueses*, note 164, pp. 97–8, and 'Avondano' in *MGG*. Two other oratorios by him, *Gioas, Re di Giudà* and *La morte d'Abel*, are preserved in *D-B*, and another with German text, *Die Aufopferung Isaacs*, is preserved in *D-SWl*. The amount of solo instrumental and orchestral music by him, some of it printed, which is also preserved in *B-Bc, D-B* and *F-Pn*, makes him the most important instrumental composer in Portugal in the second half of the eighteenth century.
56 In the palace of the Bemposta, originally built for the widow of Charles II of England, Catherine of Braganza, and which today houses the Military Academy.
57 Cf. J. A. Alegria, *História da Capela e Colégio dos Santos Reis de Vila Viçosa*, pp. 253–4.
58 The libretto is in *I-Bc* and the score in *P-La* 48–III–37/9.
59 *Journal*, p. 271.
60 Private communication of Mr David Cranmer.
61 Further on these composers see E. Vieira and J. Mazza, *Diccionario*(s).

#### 4 COMMERCIAL OPERA 1760–93

1 No. 654/31 in the TNM collection.
2 No. 656/24 in the TNM collection.
3 *Contas do Principio do Theatro da Caza da Opera do Bairro Alto . . .* in *P-Ln.*

4  Translated in J. R. Guimarães, *Biografia de Luísa de Aguiar Todi*, pp. 59–65.
5  *Tartuffe* was translated and performed in 1768 at the instigation of the Prime Minister, the Marquis of Pombal, who wanted to use it as a weapon in his fight against the Jesuits.
6  *Etat présent du Royaume de Portugal*, pp. 171–2.
7  One of the main characteristics of Portuguese adaptations of Metastasian dramas was the addition of a comical subplot, usually performed by three characters: an old man and a couple of young lovers. (Cf. G. C. Rossi, *La letteratura italiana e le letterature di lingua portoghesa*, pp. 70–1).
8  pp. 107–8.
9  From 1776 at least, the music both for the *entremezes* and for other plays includes *modinhas*, popular drawing-room songs of Brazilian origin (cf. F. de Freitas, 'A modinha – portuguesa e brasileira', p. 434). Concerning the above criticisms it must be noted that the French in this period had a generally negative attitude regarding any dramatic works that did not conform to the classical rules.
10  A. J. Saraiva and O. Lopes, *História da literatura portuguesa*, p. 565.
11  *Obras completas*, II, pp. LV, 7–39.
12  M. de Figueiredo, *Teatro de...*, VIII, p. 219.
13  Quoted in T. Braga, *Historia do theatro portuguez*, p. 219.
14  By then the Bairro Alto Theatre had been reserved for Portuguese drama (see p. 96).
15  The original text is transcribed on p. 179.
16  M. de Figueiredo, *Teatro de...*, XIV, note, p. 555.
17  *P-Ln* L 16844P.
18  The vast and little-studied subject of opera in colonial Brazil is too complex to be even broached here.
19  Libretto in *P-Cug* MDLXXVIII (9615).
20  Cf. ch. 3, p. 64.
21  'Carta familiar, e noticiosa; e principalmente critica, sobre a má digestão da armonia da Opera dos Bonecos que por esse tempo se reprezentava na Casa do Devertimento do Bairro Alto' (*P-La* 50–1–13, ff. 171–94).
22  Lisboa, Off. Patriarchal de Francisco Luís Ameno, Anno 1755.
23  *Carteira do artista*, pp. 720–3.
24  On Frei Manuel de Santo Elias see E. Vieira, *Diccionario biographico*, II, pp. 272–3. A sonata by him is published in Autores vários, *Sonatas para tecla do século XVIII*.
25  *P-La* 48–11–33 and 34.
26  *Lisboa antiga*, vol. IV, pp. 136–72.
27  'O Theatro do Bairro Alto'.
28  *Teatro de outros tempos*, pp. 257–61.
29  G. M. Sequeira and M. Moreau (*Cantores de ópera portugueses*) prefer to call the new theatre Teatro do Conde do Soure, to distinguish it from the earlier one. Here the name of Bairro Alto Theatre, or Teatro do Bairro Alto, which is the one used in the librettos, will be retained.
30  Title page reproduced in C. H. Frèches (ed.), Introduction to António José da Silva, *El prodígio de Amarante*, facing p. 40.
31  *Cantores de ópera portugueses*, pp. 186–96.

32 *Contas do Principio do Theatro da Caza da Opera do Bairro Alto* ... in *P-Ln*.
33 This could be the same Pedro António who was hired with his wife by Varela in 1767, with the obligation of acting and dancing (see note 37, below).
34 A copy exists in *P-Cug*.
35 'Subsidios'.
36 M. P. P. Carvalhais, in *ibid.* is of the opinion that this opera was performed at the Bairro Alto in 1770, based on the dubious reason that Nicola and Rosa Ambrosini sang in that year at the Oporto Theatre. A company which included Giuseppe, Nicola, and Rosa Ambrosini appeared in Seville in 1764 (cf. E. Cotarelo y Mori, *Orígenes y establecimiento de la ópera en España*, p. 286).
37 If the above identification (note 33) between him and Mr Antonio remains problematic, it is quite probable that he is the same Pedro António who performed the *Achiles em Sciro* of 1755 (see p. 83 above) and also the Pedro António Pereira who performed *Tartufo* in 1768, and translated several plays (cf. I. F. da Silva, *Diccionario biographico portuguez*, vol. VI, 1862, p. 385).
38 Luísa Rosa de Aguiar had married the first violinist of the theatre, Francesco Saverio Todi, in 1769. On the international career of this great singer cf. the biography by M. Moreau in *Cantores de ópera portugueses*, pp. 50–239.
39 *P-Ln* Cód. 619, ff. 335–6. The originals of this and the following letter are reproduced on pp. 179–81.
40 *Ibid.*, ff. 342v–343v; also transcribed in M. Moreau, *Cantores de ópera portugueses*, pp. 66–8.
41 The Marchioness of Pombal, wife of the Prime Minister.
42 In Portuguese in the original.
43 *Idem.*
44 Gaubier de Barrault also mentions a visit to the Teatro de Graça, where he saw *Guerras do alecrim e manjerona* and an *entremez* entitled *O velho peralta*. According to F. Santana, 'Teatros da Graça', this theatre existed between 1767 and 1780 at least.
45 pp. 94, 96.
46 Again it is not clear whether this new theatre was on exactly the same location as the old one. C. V. Machado, *Colecção de Memorias*, p. 150, says that it was (re)built by Petronio Mazzoni.
47 See Fig. 5. This drawing was originally published in *O Occidente*, vol. V, of 21 June 1882, the year the theatre was demolished.
48 'Subsidios'.
49 Cf. E. Cotarelo y Mori, *Orígenes y establecimiento de la ópera en España*, pp. 197–8. Cotarelo's work amply demonstrates that individual singers and dancers, or often families, rather than whole companies, travelled from place to place. Here only the more significant examples of singers active in Portugal and Spain around the same period will be mentioned (cf. also M. C. de Brito, 'La penisola iberica').
50 Nothing is known of the theatre where this private performance took place. It may have been simply a stage set in the house of the Marquis. Other private theatres may have existed in Lisbon in the eighteenth century. W. Beckford for instance (*The History of the Caliph Vathek; and European Travels*, p. 344), says that he saw a small theatre for operas on the farm at Marvila that

belonged to the Marquis of Marialva. C. Beirão (*D. Maria I*, p. 272) mentions those of the Counts of Sampaio and Almada, the Countess of Anadia, and the Morgado of Assentis.

51  pp. 129–34. The original text is transcribed on pp. 181–3.

52  A French architect who was born in Lisbon in 1754, and was expelled from Portugal in 1808, following the French invasions. He died in 1813.

53  This list, or rather the bound collection of the actual shares, dated 1 July 1771, is preserved in *P-Cul* J.F. 1–9–4. It does not seem to contain any names of members of the nobility. On the other hand it includes some thirty-five foreign names, among them those of Tomás Gildemeester, one of the richest men in Lisbon, Burney's informant Gerard de Visme, (cf. ch. 2, note 25, p. 207), Miguel Verdier, probably the father of Timothée Lecusson Verdier, and Giuseppe Galli, the notary of the Nunciature. It is in fact a sort of contemporary commercial *Who's Who* of Lisbon.

54  The Italian Church in Lisbon.

55  Padre Manuel de Macedo Pereira de Vasconcelos (1762–after 1788), according to A. Pimentel, *Zamperineida*, p. 30.

56  He appears in the cast of *Il tutore ingannato* (Salvaterra, 1766).

57  *Escripturas do Theatro da Rua dos Condes 1772 a 1776* [–1775] in *P-Lt*.

58  *Instituição da Sociedade estabelecida para a subsistencia dos Theatros Publicos da Corte*, ff. 231–47.

59  This is a slightly different name from that used in the collection of shares in *P-Cul*. *Corte* in the eighteenth century could mean either the court or the capital city in the kingdom.

60  On 30 May 1772 a new board of directors was elected, whose members were Inácio Pedro Quintela, Francisco Peres de Sousa, António Soares de Mendonça and Padre Giuseppe Galli.

61  F. F. Benevides, *O Real Teatro de S. Carlos de Lisboa*, I, p. 16.

62  E. F. de Oliveira, *Elementos para a História do Município de Lisboa*, vol. XVII, pp. 401–2. G. M. Sequeira, *Teatro de outros tempos*, says, without quoting his source, that the Society also received 18,000 *cruzados* (7:200$000) from the court.

63  'Subsidios'.

64  *A General History*, IV, pp. 492, 494.

65  'Subsidios'. For the repertoire of this Rua dos Condes company see Chronology.

66  *Zamperineida metrica-laudativa-satyrica* ... in *P-Ln* Cód 8360 and *Zamperineida Macedica, metrica, critica, satirica* in *P-Lan*, Ms. n°. 71.

67  A. Pimentel, *Zamperineida*.

68  He sang in Madrid between 1769 and 1771 (cf. E. Cotarelo y Mori, *Orígenes y establecimiento de la ópera en España*, pp. 200–3).

69  C. Burney, *A General History*, IV, pp. 492, 494.

70  Sister of Francesco and Tommaso Zucchelli, who danced in the court theatres between 1764 and 1774 (see ch. 2, p. 37 above).

71  See pp. 34–5, 50, 67 above. They did not however benefit from any generous pension schemes, as did the court singers.

72  *Historical Memoirs*, pp. 46–8.

73  *P-Lan, Intendência Geral da Polícia / Secretarias*, Book 1, pp. 82–6.

74 He had been appointed to that post on 18 January 1780. His puritanism, allied to the Queen's bigotry, was certainly responsible for the difficulties which affected public spectacles and entertainment during the period (see also M. C. de Brito, 'Conciertos en Lisboa a fines del siglo XVIII').

75 This tribunal, created in 1768, had taken over from the Inquisition the censorship of all publications. Its archive, which has only survived in part, is preserved in *P-Lan*. It includes several manuscripts of plays and opera librettos presented for approval by the censors. Those relevant to our period are mentioned in the Chronology.

76 The view of this theatre reproduced in Fig. 6 is very similar to a drawing published in *O Occidente*, vol. II, no. 42, of 15 October 1879, the year it was demolished. It suggests that it may have been larger, and slightly better, than the Rua dos Condes. Adjoining it there was an arena for bullfights, trained horses, etc.

77 *P-Lan, Intendência Geral da Polícia / Secretarias*, Book III, ff. 264v–7.

78 Cf. M. C. de Brito, 'Conciertos en Lisboa a fines del siglo XVIII', p. 196.

79 *The History of the Caliph Vathek; and European Travels*, p. 404.

80 *Ibid.*, p. 333.

81 *Travels in Portugal*, p. 158.

82 The Bairro Alto Theatre may have been closed by then.

83 pp. 214–17 and 6–16 respectively.

84 At least during those years for which any records survive.

85 AHMF, Livros XX/G/20, f. 120, XX/G/24, ff. 117, 119, 122, 124.

86 Livro XX/G/24, ff. 126, 139. A small poster in the Manuel Ivo Cruz collection announces two performances by the Portuguese company of the Salitre Theatre of (Piccinni's) *La buona figliola* on Monday 8 and Tuesday 9 December. Although the year is not indicated, this may have been the opera which the royal family attended in 1787.

87 *Journal*, p. 178. It is not clear from the text whether the Rua dos Condes or the Salitre is meant.

88 The already named *Licença pastoril* and *Pequeno drama*. Other scores may have survived in Brazil, where Marcos Portugal spent the last twenty years of his life.

89 See E. Vieira, *Diccionario biographico*, II, p. 215.

90 Transcribed in T. Braga, *Historia do theatro portuguez*, pp. 380–2.

91 Milan, 1785–1800. Here quoted from M. P. P. Carvalhais, 'Subsidios'.

92 The way this dancer wore his hair, falling over his forehead, originated the expression *marrafas* in Portuguese.

93 For a list of the dancers who appeared in the public theatres in this period see J. Sasportes, *História da dança em Portugal*, pp. 340–5.

94 Wettin and Wattmann, alias Weltin and Waltmann, were both members of the Royal Orchestra. On the second see E. Vieira, *Diccionario biographico*, II, pp. 409–10.

95 Out of tune, which probably means the same as *scordata*.

96 See note 13, p. 206 above.

97 Lenzi was a horn player in the court orchestra (cf. J. Scherpereel, *L'orchestre et les instrumentistes de la Real Câmara à Lisbonne de 1764 à 1834*, p. 184).

98 For the history of the S. Carlos see F. F. Benevides, *O Real Teatro de S. Carlos de Lisboa*.

99  The form Oporto, adopted in English and some other foreign languages, originated with British residents, who misinterpreted the way the city is referred to in Portuguese with the definite article: *o Porto*, meaning *the* Porto.
100  Namely those in *P-Lan* RMC no. 2292.
101  'Falam velhos manuscritos'.
102  On Setaro see X. M. Carreira, 'Apuntes para la historia de la Opera en Galicia', 'Nicolàs Setaro (Nápoles, 17–/ Bilbao?, 1774)'.
103  'Subsidios'.
104  See p. 18 above. In the Rua dos Condes librettos she appears as Petronilla Trabò Brasili.
105  The original text appears in full on pp. 183–91.
106  This has been interpreted, e.g. by T. Braga, *Historia do theatro portuguez*, as an allusion to the Motim da Alçada, a mutiny in Oporto in January 1757 against the wine monopoly of the Companhia Geral de Agricultura dos Vinhos do Alto Douro, which was severely punished by the authorities.
107  p. 97.
108  pp. 99–103.
109  See p. 86. Two years earlier, on 20 January 1765, an academic Oration which was recited at the Real Academia de Cirurgia Portuense had been followed by a serenata composed by Giacomo Sartori, 'Mestre da Opera do Porto' (libretto in *P-Ln* Res. 1559P (7)).
110  AHMF, CX. 260.
111  'Subsidios'.
112  See titles in the Chronology, p. 144.
113  *Travels through Portugal and Spain*, p. 48.
114  RMC *Proc. Liv. Imp. e outros* in *P-Lan*.
115  José Freire de Andrade and Agostinho Pio da Silva, violinists, Carlo Cosmi, a Neapolitan cello or double-bass player ('rabecão'), José Moreira, horn player.
116  RMC no. 2292$^{9/10}$ in *P-Lan*.
117  R. R. Nogueira, *Reflexoens sobre O restabelecimento do Theatro Do Porto. Em tres Cartas*, in *P-Cul*. The manuscript is a copy and the recipient of the letters is not indicated. The second and third letters are transcribed in full on pp. 191–7.
118  Marina Giordani in *Didone abbandonata* of 1770?
119  Luísa Todi was certainly one of them.
120  The City Governor, Lieutenant-General João de Almada e Melo.
121  'Teatros líricos do Porto', p. 138. He does not indicate his source.
122  RMC no. 2292 $^{6/7}$ in *P-Lan*..
123  Chapter III, p. 54.
124  'O teatro no Porto no século XVIII', p. 107.
125  'Teatros líricos do Porto'. Again he does not indicate his source. The same opera was performed at the S. Carlos in Lisbon in 1794.
126  On this theatre cf. among others J. P. Martins, 'O teatro no Porto no século XVIII'. The present theatre of the same name is a different building, the original one having been destroyed by a fire in 1908.

# BIBLIOGRAPHY

I GENERAL

(Includes only main reference works and a small selection of the works which were useful in the preparation of this study.)

Abert, Herman. *W. A. Mozart*, 8th edn, 2 vols., Leipzig, VEB Breitkopf & Härtel, 1973

'Piccinni als Buffokomponist' in *Gesammelte Schriften und Vorträge*, Halle an der Saale, Max Niemeyer Verlag, 1929, pp. 346–64

Carse, Adam. *The Orchestra in the XVIIIth Century*, Cambridge, W. Heffer & Sons Ltd., 1940

Corte, Andrea della. *L'opera comica italiana nell' 1700*, 2 vols., Bari, Gius. Laterza e Figli, 1923

*Enciclopedia dello Spettacolo*, 11 vols., Rome, Casa Editrice Le Maschere, 1954–68

Fétis, François Joseph. *Biographie universelle des musiciens et bibliographie générale de la musique*, 2nd edn, 8 vols., Paris, Firmin Didot Frères, 1866–70

Gregor, J. *Kulturgeschichte der Oper: Ihre Verbindung mit Leben, den Werken des Geistes und der Politik*, 2nd edn, Vienna, 1950

Grout, Donald Jay. *A Short History of Opera*, 2nd edn, 2 vols., New York and London, Columbia University Press, 1965

*Harvard Dictionary of Music*, 2nd edn, Cambridge, Mass., The Belknap Press of Harvard University Press, 1973

Hell, Helmut. *Die Neapolitanische Opernsinfonie in der ersten Hälfte des 18. Jahrhunderts*, Tutzing, Schneider, 1971

Heriot, Angus. *The Castrati in Opera*, London, Secker & Warburg, 1956

Kretzschmar, Hermann. *Geschichte der Oper*, Leipzig, Breitkopf & Härtel, 1919

Loewenberg, Alfred. *Annals of Opera 1597–1940. Compiled from the Original Sources*, 2 vols., Geneva, Societas Bibliographica, 1955

*Die Musik in Geschichte und Gegenwart. Allgemeine Enzyklopädie der Musik*, 16 vols. to date, Kassel and Basle, Bärenreiter Verlag, 1949–

# Bibliography

*The New Grove Dictionary of Music and Musicians*, 20 vols., London, Macmillan Publishers Ltd., 1981

Robinson, Michael F. *Naples and Neapolitan Opera*, London, Oxford University Press, 1972

Smith, Patrick J. *The Tenth Muse. A Historical Study of the Opera Libretto*, London, Victor Gollancz Ltd., 1971

Stieger, Franz. *Opernlexikon*, 7 vols., Tutzing, Schneider, 1979

Strohm, Reinhard. *Die italienische Oper im 18. Jahrhundert*, Willhelmshaven, Heinrichshofen's Verlag, 1979

Wolff, Helmuth Christian. *Oper – Szene und Darstellung von 1600 bis 1900*, Leipzig, VEB Deutscher Verlag für Musik (Musikgeschichte in Bildern, vol. IV), 1968

York-Longe, Alan. *Music at Court. Four Eighteenth Century Studies*, London, Weidenfeld and Nicolson, 1954

## 2 CONTEMPORARY SOURCES

### 2.1 Manuscript

#### I–Bc

1–4, ff. 20, 21, 23–37; L.117, 165–6. Letters of Gaetano Maria Schiassi to Padre Martini (1735–1753)

1.18.41. Letter of Antonio Maria Mazzoni to Padre Martini (1755)

#### Paris, Archive of the Ministère des Affaires Etrangères

*Correspondence politique Portugal*, vol. 87, ff. 2–6. *Dépêche du comte de Baschi du 1er Avril 1755*

#### P-Cug

J.F. 4–9–5. Ricardo Raimundo Nogueira. *Reflexoens sobre O restabelecimento do Theatro Do Porto. em tres cartas. De . . . 1778*

#### P–La

50–1–13, ff. 171–94. Alexandre António de Lima. 'Carta familiar, e noticiosa; e principalmente critica, sobre a má digestão da armonia da Opera dos Bonecos que por esse tempo se reprezentava na Casa do Devertimento do Bairro Alto'

51–XIII–24, nos. 65–79. Letters of the Secretary of State Sebastião José de Caravalho e Melo to the ambassador in Rome António Freire de Andrade Encerrabodes (1751–2)

52–XIV–35, nos. 79–86. Accounts and other documents concerning the expenses with *Enea nel Lazio* (1767) and *La Pace frà la Virtù e la Belleza* (1777)

54–XI–37, no. 192, *Osservazioni Correlative alla Reale, e Patriarcal Cappella di Lisbona fatte da D. Gasparo Mariani Bolognese per unico suo profitto, e commodo. Quest'ultima mala cópia fu fatta di proprio pugno. In Lisbona. L'anno di Nostra Salute 1788*

*P–Lan*

*Intêndencia Geral da Polícia/Secretarias*, Books I, II and III (1780–93)
R[eal] M[esa] C[ensória] *Proc. Liv. Imp. e outros*
R[eal] M[esa] C[ensória] no. 2292. Advertisements concerning performances in the Teatro do Corpo da Guarda (Teatro Público) in Oporto

*P–Ln*

Cód. 651, f. 78. *Lista de pessoas que podem entrar na platéa segundo as ordens de S. M. Distribuição dos bilhetes nos camarotes nos. 11, 12, 22* [1755]
Caixa 248, no. 36. *Certidão de Medição da obra do Officio de Pedreiro pertencente à Caza da Opera Real que Sua Majestade q̄ D. g. e mandou fazer no Sitio da Tanoaria junto aos Paços da Ribeira desta Cidade pelos Mestres Manoel Antunes Feyo e Manoel Francisco de Souza e mais Socios. Passada em 28 do mez de Abril de 1759* [copy made on 22 May 1778]
Cód. 7178. *Contas do Principio do Theatro da Caza da Opera do Bairro Alto dos annos de 1761 e 1762 e 1763 e 1764 e 1765 athe Julho de 1766* [. . . 1771]
Cód. 619, ff. 331–56. Letters of Gaubier de Barrault to the Count of Oeiras (1771)

*P–Lt*

*Escripturas do Theatro da Rua dos Condes 1772 a 1776* [–1775]
*Seis cartas do Compositor italiano Niccolò Jommelli e do seu irmão Fr. Ignazio, oferecidas ao Teatro Nacional de S. Carlos, em Maio de 1957, pelo Dr. Henrique Viana* (1774–5)

AHMF: Livros

XX/Z/38 List of contracts with dancers and other theatrical personnel (1764–75)
XX/Z/39 *Receita e Despeza Geral das Operas, e mais particulares, de que he encarregado João Antonio Pinto da Silva, Guarda-ropa de S. Magestade e Director dos seos Reaes Theatros etc. etc. Em Julho de 1773* [. . . 1777]
XX/Z/40 Journal of opera expenses (July–December 1773)
XX/Z/41 List of ornaments belonging to the Salvaterra Theatre (?)
XX/Z/42 *1802/Primeiro Quartel/Folha dos Ordenados das Pessoas empregadas em Muzica e Theatro, e tenças às Viúvas e filhos dos q̄ nelles servirão/N17*
XX/Z/43 *1802/Inventario de toda a Fazenda e Moveis que existem no Real Theatro de Nossa Senhora d'Ajuda*
XX/Z/44 List of scores of church music, operas and serenatas kept in the archive of the Ajuda Theatre, with the date 1833 on the spine
XX/Z/45 *Registo de Cartas de fora do Reyno* (1767–72)
XX/Z/46 *Livro de Registo pertencente à Inspecção da Opera, q' principia com o Snr. João Antonio Pinto da Silva Junqueira 22 de Julho 1773*
XX/Z/47 *Livro 1º do Registo do Expediente do Particular Desde 27 de Outubro de 1776 athe 9 de Agosto de 1784*
XX/G/19 *Nº 1/Diario de Receita e Despeza do Particular – De 26 de Settembro de 1776, athe fim de Dezembro de 1778*

xx/G/20 *Livro Primeiro, em Rezumo, de Receita e Despeza do Particular de que he encarregado João Antonio Pinto da Silva, que teve principio em 28 de Setembro de 1776 e findou em 31 de Dezembro de 1782: na forma das Contas que em cada hum dos Mezes deu a S. Magestade; e que no total delles vem a conferir com as do Diario em que vão as ditas despezas por miudo*

xx/G/21 *Nº 2º/Diario de Receita, e Despeza do Particular* ... *Do 1º de Janeiro de 1779, the fim de Dezembro de 1780*

xx/G/22 *Nº 3º/Diario de Receita, e Despeza do Particular* ... *Do 1º de Janeiro de 1781, the fim de Dezembro de 1782*

xx/G/23 *Nº 4º/Diario de Receita, e Despeza do Particular Do 1º de Janeiro de 1783, the fim de Dezembro de 1784*

xx/G/24 *Livro Segundo em Rezumo de Receita e Despeza do Particular* ... *Do Primeiro de Janeiro de 1783 the fim de Junho de 1788*

xx/G/25 *Nº 5/Diario de Receita, e Despeza do Particular Do 1º de Janeiro de 1785, the fim de Dezembro de 1786*

xx/G/26 *Nº 6/Diario de Receita, e Despeza do Particular Do 1º de Janeiro de 1787 the 31 de Março de 1789*

xx/G/27 *Livro Terceiro em Rezumo de Receita e Despeza do Particular* ... *Do Primeiro de Julho de 1788, athe fim de Novembro de 1792*

xx/G/28 *Nº 7/Diario de Receita, e Despeza do Particular Do Primeiro de Abril de 1789, athe 31 de Março de 1791*

xx/G/29 *Nº 8/Diario de Receita, e Despeza do Particular Do Primeiro de Abril de 1791, athe 31 de Julho de 1793*

xx/G/61 *Ordenados e outros pagamentos anuais por ordens particulares de Sua Magestade* (1764–3)

Pasta xx/z/77 –

(11) Letters of Giovanni Piaggio to João António Pinto da Silva (1774)

(14) Accounts of the costumes for *Alessandro nell'Indie, Demofoonte* and Olimpiade

AHMF: Caixas

Containing bills and receipts of the *Particular* (Privy Purse):

| | | |
|---|---|---|
| 1–3 (1755–6) | 20 (1783) | 34 (1787) |
| 5 (1770–6) | 21 (1783) | 35 (1787) |
| 9 (1778) | 22 (1784) | 36 (1788) |
| 10 (1778–9) | 23 (1784) | 39 (1789) |
| 12 (1779–80) | 24 (1784) | 40 (1789) |
| 13 (1780) | 25 (1784) | 41 (1789) |
| 14 (1781) | 26 (1785) | 42 (1790) |
| 15 (1781) | 27 (1785) | 45 (1790) |
| 16 (1782) | 28 (1785) | 46 (1791) |
| 17 (1782) | 29 (1785) | 48 (1792) |
| 18 (1783) | 30 (1786) | 49 (1792) |
| 19 (1783) | 31 (1786) | 50 (1792) |
| | | 314 (1756–61) |

Containing accounts and other documents related to operatic productions:

257 (1768–84)
258 (1786)
259 (1790)

Containing accounts and other correspondence:

260 (1764–91)
261 (1785–92)

## AHTC

Érario Régio, 2089, *1778/Folhas das Rasões a Dinheiro*

Oporto, Gabinete de História da Cidade, *Libro para servir de Receita e despeza que se faz na festividade dos despozorios da Snra Princeza com o Sor Infante D. Pedro por ordem do Senado, 1760*
Lisbon, Arquivo da Irmandade de Santa Cecília, *Livros de Entradas*
Scores and ms. librettos in *P-Em, EVp, La, Ln, VV* and TNM
Drawings of sets by Giovanni Carlo Sicini Bibiena, Giacomo Azzolini and Inácio de Oliveira Bernardes in *P-Ln* and the Museu Nacional de Arte Antiga

## 2.2 Printed

(Includes works published in the first quarter of the nineteenth century and modern editions of contemporary documents.)
Almeida, Francisco António de. *La Spinalba ovvero il vecchio matto*, Opera in three acts, revised and edited by Pierre Salzmann, Lisbon, Fundação Calouste Gulbenkian, 1969 (Portugaliae Musica XII) [score, parts, piano score]
Autores vários. *Sonatas para tecla do século XVIII*, transcriptions by J. Moura, M. S. Kastner and R. V. Nery, study by M. S. Kastner, Lisbon, Fundação Calouste Gulbenkian, 1982 (Portugaliae Musica XXXVIII)
Balbi, Adrien. *Essai statistique sur le royaume de Portugal et d'Algarve*, 2 vols., Paris, Chez Rey et Gravier, 1822
Baretti, Joseph. *A Journey from London to Genoa, through England, Portugal, Spain and France*, 3rd edn, 4 vols., London, printed for T. Davis in Russell Street, Covent Garden; and L. Davis, in Holborn, 1770
Beckford, William. *The History of the Caliph Vathek; and European Travels*, edited by G. T. Bettany, London, New York and Melbourne, Ward, Lock and Co., (The Minerva Library of Famous Books) 1891
  *The Journal of William Beckford in Portugal and Spain 1787–1788*, edited with an Introduction and Notes by Boyd Alexander, London, Rupert Hart-Davis, 1954
Beirão, Caetano (ed.), *Cartas da Rainha D. Mariana Vitória para a sua família de Espanha, I (1721–1748)*, Lisbon, Empresa Nacional de Publicidade, 1936
*Berliner musikalische Zeitung* I (1805)
Bluteau, P.ᵉ Rafael. *Vocabulário português e latino*, 8 vols., Lisbon, Officina de Pascoal da Sylva, 1712–21; 2 vol. supplement, 1727–8

Bombelles, Marquis de. *Journal d'un ambassadeur de France au Portugal 1786–1788*, edited with notes and introduction by Roger Kann, Paris, Presses Universitaires de France (Fondation Calouste Gulbenkian, Publications du Centre Culturel Portugais) 1979

Bourdon, Albert-Alain (ed.), 'Description de Lisbonne extraite de la Campagne des Vaisseaux du Roy en 1755, par le Chevalier des Courtils', *Bulletin des Etudes Portugaises*, Nouvelle Série, vol. XXVI (1965), 145–60

Brasão, Eduardo (ed.), *Diário de D. Francisco Xavier de Meneses, 4° Conde de Ericeira (1731–1733)*, Coimbra, Imprensa da Universidade, 1943

Burney, Charles. *A General History of Music from the Earliest Ages to the Present Period*, 4 vols., London, Printed for the Author: and sold by J. Robson, New Bond Street; and G. Robinson, Paternoster Row, 1776–89

*Music, Men and Manners in France and Italy 1770, Being the Journal written by Charles Burney, Mus. D. during a Tour through those Countries undertaken to collect material for A General History of Music*, Transcribed from the Original Manuscript in the British Museum, Additional Manuscript 35122, and edited with an Introduction by H. Edmund Poole, London, Ernst Eulenburg Ltd., 1974

Cacciò, Giovanni Battista. *Indice de' spettacoli teatrali di tutto l'anno*, Milan, 1760–85 [as quoted in M. P. P. Carvalhais, 'Subsidios para a historia da opera e da choregraphia italianas, em Portugal, no século XVIII']

Carvalho, João de Sousa. *Abertura da ópera «L'amore industriosso» (1769)*, revised edition and study by Filipe de Sousa, Lisbon, Fundação Calouste Gulbenkian, 1960, 2nd edn, 1964 (Portugaliae Musica II)

*Abertura da ópera «Penélope» (1782)*, revised edition and study by Filipe de Sousa, Lisbon, Fundação Calouste Gulbenkian, 1968 (Portugaliae Musica XIV) [score & parts]

Castro, João Baptista de. *Mappa de Portugal antigo, e moderno*, 2nd edn, 3 vols., Lisbon, Officina Patriarcal de Francisco Luís Ameno, 1762–3

Chatelet, Duke de. *Travels of the ... in Portugal ...*, revised and corrected by J. Fr. Bourgoing, translated from the French, London, printed for John Stockdale, Piccadilly, and J. J. Stockdale, no. 41, Pall Mall, 1809

Cordeiro, P.ᵉ Valério Aleixo (ed.), *Memorias da última Condessa de Atouguia*, 2nd edn, Braga, 1917

Corrette, Michel. *Méthode théorique et pratique pour apprendre en peu de temps le violoncelle dans sa perfection*, Paris, 1741, facsimile edn, Geneva, Minkoff Reprint, 1980

Costa, P.ᵉ Agostinho Rebelo da. *Descripção Topographica e Historica da cidade do Porto*, Oporto 1789

Costigan, Arthur William. *Cartas de Portugal 1778–1779*, 2 vols., translation, preface and notes by Augusto Reis Machado, Lisbon, Ática, 1946

Dalrymple, Major William. *Voyage en Espagne et en Portugal dans l'année 1774 avec une relation de l'expédition des Espagnols contre les algériens, en 1775*, Paris, 1783 [translation of *Travels through Spain and Portugal in 1774, with a short account of the Spanish Expedition against Algiers in 1775*, Dublin, 1777]

'De l'état actuel du théâtre au Portugal', *Journal de Littérature, des Sciences et des Arts*, vol. III (Paris, 1781), 387–93 [translated in J. R. Guimarães, *Biografia de Luísa de Aguiar Todi*, pp. 59–62]

# Bibliography

*Description de la ville de Lisbonne où l'on traite de la Cour de Portugal, de la langue Portugaise, & des Moeurs des Habitans; du Gouvernement, des Revenus du Roi & de ses Forces, par Mer & par Terre; des Colonies Portugaises, et du Commerce de cette Capitale*, Paris, Chez Pierre Prault, 1730 [translated in *O Portugal de D. João V visto por três forasteiros*]

[Dumouriez, Charles François.] *Etat présent du Royaume de Portugal, en l'année MDCCLXVI*, Lausanne, Chez François Grasset & Comp., 1775

Ferreira, J. A. Pinto (ed.), *Correspondência de D. João V e D. Bárbara de Bragança (1746–1747)*, Coimbra, Livraria Gonçalves, 1945

Figueiredo, Manuel de. *Teatro de* ..., 14 vols., Lisbon, na Impressão Régia, 1805–15

Formenti, Lorenzo. *Indice de' teatrali spettacoli di tutto l'anno*, Milan, 1785–1800 [as quoted in M. P. P. Carvalhais, 'Subsidios para a historia da opera e da choregraphia italianas, em Portugal, no século XVIII']

Frédéric II. *Histoire de mon temps*, in *Oeuvres Posthumes de* ..., vol. 1, Berlin, Chez Voss e Fils et Decker, 1788

Garção, [Pedro António] Correia. *Obras completas*, 2 vols., text established, preface and notes by António José Saraiva, Lisbon, Livraria Sá da Costa, 1957–8

*Gazeta de Lisboa*, 1715–62, 1778–93

Goldoni, Carlo. *Memorie* [*Mémoires de M. Goldoni, pour servir à l'histoire de sa vie, et à celle de son théâtre. Dediés au Roi*], 2 vols., Florence, G. Barberà, 1907

Gusmão, Alexandre de. *Cartas*, introduction and new edition of text by Andrée Rocha, Lisbon, Imprensa Nacional – Casa da Moeda, 1981

*Hebdomadario Lisbonense*, 1763–7

*Indice de' Spettacoli teatrali per il Carnevale dell'anno 1773*, Milan, Pietro Agnelli, 1773 [as quoted in M. P. P. Carvalhais, 'Subsidios para a historia da opera e da choregraphia italianas, em Portugal, no século XVIII']

*Instituição da Sociedade estabelecida para a subsistencia dos Theatros Publicos da Corte*, Lisbon, na Regia Officina Typographica, 1771 [in *P-La* 97–V–3]

*Jornal Encyclopedico*, Lisbon, 1788–93

Libretto collections in *P-Cug, EVp, La, Lac, Lan, Lcg, Ln, Lt, Mp, Pm, VV*, and TNM

Lima, Francisco Bernardo de. *Gazeta Litteraria ou Noticia Exacta dos Principaes Escriptos, Que modernamente Se Vão Publicando na Europa, conforme a Analise Que Deles Fazem os Melhores Criticos, e Diaristas das Nações mais Civilizadas*, 2 vols., Oporto, Officina de Francisco Mendes Lima, 1761–2

Lima, Jerónimo Francisco de. *Le nozze d'Ercole ed Ebe*, abertura (1785), revised edition by Luís Pereira Leal, Lisbon, Fundação Calouste Gulbenkian, 1973 (Portugaliae Musica XXIII) [score & parts]

Machado, Cirilo Volkmar. *Colecção de Memorias relatives às vidas dos pintores, e escultores, architectos, e gravadores Portuguezes, E dos Estrangeiros que estiverão em Portugal*, Lisbon, 1823, 2nd edn, Coimbra, Imprensa da Universidade, 1922

Machado, Diogo Barbosa. *Bibliotheca lusitana*, 4 vols., Lisbon, 1741–59, modern edn: Coimbra, Atlântida Editora, 1965–7

Mattei, Saviero. 'Elogio del Jommelli' in *Memorie*, Colle, Nella Stamperia di Angiolo M. Martini, 1785

Mattoso, Luís Montez. *Ano noticioso e historico*, 2 vols., Lisbon, Biblioteca Nacional, 1934–8

Mazza, José. *Dicionário biográfico de músicos portugueses*, with preface and notes by P.ᵉ José Augusto Alegria, Lisbon, Revista Ocidente, 1944–5

[Merveilleux.] *Mémoires instructifs pour un voyageur dans les divers Etats de l'Europe*, Amsterdam, Chez H. du Sauzet, 1738 [translated in *O Portugal de D. João V visto por três forasteiros*]

Monfort, Jacqueline. 'Quelques notes sur l'histoire du théâtre portugais (1729–1750)' *Arquivos do Centro Cultural Português em Paris*, vol. 4 (1972), 566–600

Mozart, Wolfgang Amadeus. *Mitridate, Re di Ponto*, Kassel, Bärenreiter (Neue Mozart Ausgabe Serie II), 1966

Murphy, James, *Travels in Portugal; through the provinces of Entre Douro e Minho, Beira, Estremadura, and Alem-Tejo, in the Years 1789 and 1790, Consisting of Observations on the Manners, Customs, Trade, Public Buildings, Arts, Antiquities, & c. of that Kingdom*, London, Printed for A. Strahen and T. Cadell Jnr and W. Davies (Successors to Mr. Cadell in the Strand), 1795

Natividade, Frei José da. *Fasto de Hymeneo, ou Historia Panegyrica dos Desposorios dos Fidelissimos Reys de Portugal, nossos Senhores D. Joseph I e D. Maria Anna Vitoria de Borbon*, Lisbon, Of. de Manoel Soares, 1752

Nery, Rui Vieira. *Para a história do barroco musical português*, Lisbon, Fundação Calouste Gulbenkian, 1980

*Óperas Portuguezas que se representaram nos Theatros públicos desta Corte, Bairro Alto e Mouraria*, 2 vols., Lisbon, Officina de Inácio Rodrigues, 1746

Padilha, Pedro Norberto d'Aucourt e. *Memorias da Serenissima Senhora D. Isabel Luisa Josefa, que foi jurada Princeza destes Reinos de Portugal*, Lisbon, Francisco da Sylva, 1748

Pimentel, Alberto. *Zamperineida. Segundo um manuscripto da Bibliotheca Nacional de Lisboa publicado e annotado por ...*, Lisbon, Livraria Central de Gomes de Carvalho, 1907

*O Portugal de D. João V visto por três forasteiros*, translation, preface and notes by Castelo Branco Chaves, Lisbon, Biblioteca Nacional, 1983

Queiroz, Frei João de S. José, bispo do Grão-Pará. *Memórias de ...*, Oporto, Typographia da Livraria Nacional, 1868

Ruders, Carl Israel. *Viagem em Portugal (1798–1802)*, translation by António Feijó, preface and notes by Castelo Branco Chaves, Lisbon, Biblioteca Nacional, 1981

Saussure, César de, *Voyage de Mons.ʳ ... en Portugal, Lettres de Lisbonne*, edited by the Viscount de Faria, Milan, 1809 [translated in *O Portugal de D. João V visto por três forasteiros*]

Silva, António Diniz da Cruz e. *O Hyssope, Poéma Heroi-Comico*, Paris, Of. A. Bobée, 1817

Silva, António José da (O Judeu). *Obras completas*, 4 vols., preface and notes by Professor José Pereira Tavares, Lisbon, Livraria Sá da Costa, 1957–8

Silva, José Soares. *Gazeta em forma de carta/anos de 1701–1716*, vol. 1, Lisbon, Biblioteca Nacional, 1933

*Sociedade para a Subsistencia dos Theatros Publicos de Lisboa, Apolices dos accionistas*, Lisbon, 1771 [in *P-Cul* J.F. 1–9–4]

Bibliography

*Theatro Comico Portuguez ou Colecção das Operas Portuguezas que se representaram na casa do Theatro Público do Bairro Alto de Lisboa, Oferecidas à muito nobre Senhora Pecunia Argentina por \* \* \**, 2 vols., Lisbon, Officina de Francisco Luís Ameno, 1744

Twiss, Richard. *Travels through Portugal and Spain in 1772 and 1773*, London, printed for the author and sold by G. Robinson, T. Becker and Robson, 1775

Walther, Johan Gottfried. *Musikalisches Lexicon, oder musikalische Bibliothek* (1732), facsimile edn, Kassel and Basle, Bärenreiter Verlag (Documenta Musicologica, First series, III), 1953

Wraxall, Sir N[athaniel] William. *Historical Memoirs of my own Time. Part the first, from 1772 to 1780*, London, T. Cadell & W. Davies, 1815

### 3 MODERN SOURCES

Abert, Hermann. *Niccolò Jommelli als Opernkomponist*, Halle an der Saale, Verlag von Max Niemeyer, 1908

Alegria, José Augusto (ed.), *Bibliotheca Pública de Évora. Catálogo dos fundos musicais*, Lisbon, Fundação Calouste Gulbenkian, 1977
    *História da Capela e Colégio dos Santos Reis de Vila Viçosa*, Lisbon, Fundação Calouste Gulbenkian, 1983

Basto, A. de Magalhães. 'Falam velhos manuscritos' in *O Primeiro de Janeiro* of 28.7, 11.8, 25.8 and 1.9.1950, and 22.1.1954

Bastos, António Sousa. *Carteira do artista. Apontamentos para a historia do theatro portuguez e brasileiro*, Lisbon, Antiga Casa Bertrand – José Bastos, 1898
    *Diccionário do theatro portuguez*, Lisbon, Imprensa Libanio da Silva, 1908

Beaumont, Maria Alice. 'Stage sets by the Bibiena in the Museu Nacional de Arte Antiga, Lisbon' *Apollo*, 134 (1973), 408–15

Beirão, Caetano. *D. Maria I, 1777–1792. Subsídios para a revisão da história do seu reinado*, Lisbon, Empresa Nacional de Publicidade, 1934

Benevides, Francisco da Fonseca. *O Real Teatro de S. Carlos de Lisboa*, 2 vols., Lisbon, Tipographia Castro e Irmão, 1883/Lisbon, Typographia e Litographia de Ricardo de Souza e Salles, 1902

*Bibliotheca Nacional de Lisboa. Inventário Secção XIII – Manuscriptos*, Lisbon, 1896

Bonito, Porfírio Augusto Rebelo. *Os Almadas e o teatro lírico*, Oporto, Empresa de Publicidade do Norte, 1960 [id. in *Boletim dos Amigos do Porto* vol. III]
    'Teatros líricos do Porto, *O Tripeiro*, 6ª série, Year 3, n° 5 (1963), 138–40

Borba, Tomás and Graça, Fernando Lopes. *Dicionário de Música (Illustrado)*, 2 vols., Lisbon, Edições Cosmos, 1956

Boyd, Malcolm. *Domenico Scarlatti – Master of Music*, London, Weidenfeld and Nicolson, 1986

Braga, Teófilo. *Historia do theatro portuguez* – [vol. 3] *A baixa comedia e a opera no seculo XVIII*, Oporto, Imprensa Portugueza – Editora, 1871

Branco, João de Freitas. *História da música portuguesa*, Lisbon, Publicações Europa-América, 1959

Branco, Manuel Bernardes. *Portugal na epocha de D. João V*, 2nd edn, Lisbon, Livraria de António Maria Pereira, 1886

Brito, Manuel Carlos de. 'Alguns dados inéditos sobre instrumentos musicais em

228

# Bibliography

Portugal no século XVIII', *Boletim da Associação Portuguesa de Educação Musical*, 41 (1984), 8–11

Articles on 'B(u)ononcini', 'Lima, Jerónimo Francisco de', 'Moreira, António Leal' and 'Silva, João Cordeiro da' in *Enciclopédia Luso-Brasileira de Cultura Verbo*, vol. 21, Lisbon, Editorial Verbo, 1986

'Conciertos en Lisboa a fines del siglo XVIII', *Revista de Musicología* VII, 1 (1984), 191–203

'A contratação do castrato Gizziello para a Real Câmara em 1751', *Estudos Italianos em Portugal* 45–46–47 (1982–83–84), 281–96

'Domenico Scarlatti e a música em Portugal no tempo de D. João V' in *Domenico Scarlatti ...*, Lisbon, Secretaria de Estado da Cultura (forthcoming)

'Domenico Scarlatti e la música alla corte di Giovanni V di Portogallo', *Atti del Convegno «Domenico Scarlatti e il suo tempo»* (Siena, 1985, forthcoming)

'Fontes para a história da ópera em Portugal no século XVIII (1708–1793)', *II Encontro Nacional de Musicologia – Actas* in *Boletim da Associação Portuguesa de Educação Musical* 42/43 (July/October 1984), 17–23

'Jommelli e a corte portuguesa no reinado de D. José', *V Jornadas de Música Antiga*, Lisbon, Fundação Calouste Gulbenkian, 1984, 34–5

'Musical interrelationships between Portugal and Italy during the Eighteenth Century/As relações musicais entre Portugal e a Itália no século XVIII', *Actas do Colóquio Internacional «Portugal e o Mundo – Processos interculturais na música (O papel de Portugal na música do Mundo desde o século XV)»* (forthcoming)

'Music in Portugal in the Time of Beckford/A música em Portugal no tempo de Beckford', *William Beckford e Portugal, 1787–1794–1797. A viagem de uma paixão*, Palácio de Queluz, 1987, 51–61

'A ópera de corte no reinado de D. José', *Desenhos dos Galli Bibiena. Arquitectura e Cenografia. Exposição temporária*, Lisbon, Instituto Português do Património Cultural – Museu Nacional de Arte Antiga, 1987, pp. 30–6

'A ópera em Portugal antes da fundação do S. Carlos', *S. Carlos Revista*, no 1, n.d. [1986], 26–30

'La penisola iberica' in *Storia dell'opera italiana* a cura di Lorenzo Bianconi e Giorgio Pestelli, vol. 2, Turin, E.D.T. Edizioni di Torino and Società Italiana di Musicologia (forthcoming)

'Portuguese–Spanish musical relations during the 18th Century', *Actas del Congreso Internacional «España en la Música de Occidente»*, Madrid, Ministerio de Cultura, Instituto Nacional de Artes Escénicas y de la Música, 1987, vol. II, pp. 133–8

'Prefácio' to *Biblioteca da Ajuda. Catálogo de libretos*, Lisbon, Biblioteca da Ajuda (forthcoming).

'Presenza di operisti pugliesi in Portogallo', *Atti del Convegno Internazionale di Studi Musicologici «Musicisti nati in Puglia ed emigrazione musicale tra '600 e '700»*, Torre d'Orfeo (forthcoming)

'Relações musicais luso-austríacas' in Ludwig Scheidl and José A. Palma Caetano (eds.), *Relações entre a Áustria e Portugal. Testemunhos históricos e culturais*, Coimbra, Livraria Almedina, 1985, pp. 211–21

Bibliography

'Um retrato inédito do compositor Francisco António de Almeida', *Jornal de letras, artes e ideias*, Year 1, 24 (1982), 20

'Le rôle de l'opéra dans la lutte entre l'obscurantisme et les Lumières au Portugal (1731–1742)/O papel da ópera na luta entre o Iluminismo e o obscurantismo em Portugal (1731–1742)', *Informação Musical*, n.p., n.d. [Lisbon, 1983], 32–43; *idem* in Marc Honegger, Christian Meyer and Paul Prévost (eds.), *La musique et le rite, sacré et profane/Music and ceremony, sacred and secular/Musik und Zeremonie, geistlich und weltlich – Actes du 13ᵉ Congrès de la SIM/Report of the 13th Congress of the IMS (Strasbourg, 29 août – 3 septembre 1982)*, vol. II: *Communications libres – Free Papers*, Strasbourg, Association des Publications près les Universités de Strasbourg/Société Internationale de Musicologie, 1986, pp. 543–4

*Lo spirito di contradizione, Ópera em três actos, música de Jerónimo Francisco de Lima* ..., Lisbon, Teatro Nacional de S. Carlos E.P., 1984

'Symphonic music in Portugal' in *The Symphony in Portugal – Two Symphonies/The Symphony in Spain – Three Symphonies*, New York and London, Garland Publishing Inc., 1983 (Barry S. Brook and Barbara B. Heyman (eds.), *The Symphony 1720–1840, Series F. vol. V*), pp. xiii–xvi

'Vestígios del teatro musical español en Portugal a lo largo de los siglos XVII y XVIII', *Revista de Musicologia*, V, 2 (1982), 325–35

Brito, Manuel Carlos de and Cranmer, David. *Crónicas da vida musical portuguesa na primeira metade do século XIX*, Lisbon, Imprensa Nacional – Casa da Moeda, 1988

Carreira, Xoan M. 'Apuntes para la historia de la Opera en Galicia', *La Opera en España – X Festival de Música y Danza de Asturias*, Oviedo, University of Oviedo, Department of Musicology, 1984, pp. 99–114

'Nicolàs Setaro (Nápoles, 17–/Bilbao? 1774)', *A Nosa Terra*, 289 (27.3.1986, *Músicos de Galiza* nº 29)

'Los orígenes de la opera en Santiago (1768–1773)' (typescript)

Carvalhais, Manuel Pereira Peixoto d'Almeida. *Inês de Castro na ópera e na coregraphia italianas. Separata da obra em manuscripto intitulada: Subsídios à historia da ópera e da coregraphia italianas no século XVIII, em Portugal*, 2 vols., Lisbon, Typographia Castro Irmão, 1908–15

*Marcos Portugal na sua musica dramatica. Historicas investigações*, 2 vols., Lisbon, Typographia Castro Irmão, 1910–16

'Subsidios para a historia da opera e da coregraphia italianas em Portugal, no século XVIII', ms. in the possession of the author's descendants

Carvalho, A. Aires de. *Catálogo da colecção de desenhos da Biblioteca Nacional de Lisboa*, Lisbon, Biblioteca Nacional, 1977

Carvalho, Mário Vieira de. '*Denken ist Sterben* oder Das Opernhaus von Lissabon (São-Carlos-Theater) im Wandel sozial-kommunikativer Systeme vom ausgehenden 18. Jahrhundert bis zur unserer Zeit', unpublished PhD dissertation, Humboldt Universität, Berlin, 1984

Castilho, Júlio de. *Lisboa antiga*, 2nd edn, 5 vols., Lisbon, Antiga Casa Bertrand – José Bastos, 1902–4

*A Ribeira de Lisboa. Descripção historica da margem do Tejo desde a Madre-de-Deus até Santos-o-Velho*, Lisbon, Imprensa Nacional, 1893

*Catálogo de Manuscritos*, 22 vols., Coimbra, Biblioteca Geral da Universidade, 1940–71

# Bibliography

*Catálogo da Colecção de Miscelâneas. Teatro*, preface by Aníbal Pinto de Castro, Coimbra, Biblioteca Geral da Universidade, 1974

*Cathalogo Methodico dos Livros da Livraria do Convento de N. Senhora de Jesus de Lisboa Pertencente Aos Religiosos da 3ª Ordem da Penitencia do N.S. Francisco. MDCXXX, vol. 5. Humanidades*, ms. in P-Lac

Chaves, Castelo Branco. *Os livros de viagens em Portugal no século XVIII e a sua projecção europeia*, Lisbon, Instituto de Cultura Portuguesa, 1977

Cidrais, Maria Fernanda. 'Algumas considerações a propósito de uma colecção de libretos do século XVIII' *A Arte em Portugal no Século XVIII. Actas do Congresso*, III, in *Bracara Augusta*, XXVIII (1974), 65–6, (77–8), 513–20

Correia, Joaquim Manuel da Silva. 'Teatros régios do século XVIII (Algumas considerações acerca dos desenhos da colecção do Museu Nacional de Arte Antiga)', *Boletim do Museu Nacional de Arte Antiga* V, 3/4 (1969), 24–38

*Salvaterra de Magos. O Paço Real, a Ópera e a Falcoaria* (forthcoming)

Costa, Augusto Sá da. *Catálogo da importante biblioteca que pertenceu ao falecido escritor e musicógrafo Manuel de Carvalhaes*. Lisbon, Livaria Sá da Costa, 1928

Cotarelo y Mori, Emilio. *Orígenes y establecimiento de la ópera en España hasta 1800*, Madrid, Tip. de la «Revista de Arch., Bibl. y Museos», 1917

Cruz, Manuel Ivo. 'Ópera portuguesa no Brasil do século XVIII' *IV Encontro Nacional de Musicologia – Actas* in *Boletim da Associação Portuguesa de Educação Musical* 52 (January/March 1987), 39–41

*David Perez e a sua época. Exposição comemorativa do duplo centenário da morte do compositor, por ocasião do Dia Mundial da Música. Na Biblioteca Nacional de Lisboa, 1 a 21 de Outubro*, Lisbon, Direcção Geral do Património Cultural, Serviços de Musicologia, 1979

*Desenhos dos Galli Bibiena. Arquitectura e Cenografia. Exposição temporária*, Lisbon, Instituto Português do Património Cultural – Museu Nacional de Arte Antiga, 1987

Dias, João Pereira. *Cenários do Teatro Nacional de S. Carlos*, Lisbon, Ministério da Educação Nacional, 1940

'Cenógrafos italianos em Portugal', *Estudos Italianos em Portugal*, 4 (1941), 1–12

*A evolução e o espírito do teatro em Portugal. Conferências*, 2 vols., Lisbon, Ed. O Século, 1947

Figueiredo, José de. 'O Teatro Real da Ópera', *Boletim da Academia Nacional de Belas Artes* III (1938), 33–5

França, José Augusto. *A reconstrução de Lisboa e a arquitectura pombalina*, Lisbon, Instituto de Cultura Portuguesa, 1978

Frèches, Claude-Henri. Introduction to António José da Silva, *El prodígio de Amarante. Comédia famosa*, Lisbon, Livraria Bertrand/Paris, Les Belles Lettres, 1967, pp. 23–43

'António José da Silva (O Judeu) et les Marionettes', *Bulletin d'Histoire du Théâtre Portugais*, vol. V, no. 2 (1954), 325–44

'Le théâtre aristocratique et l'évolution du goût au Portugal d'après la «Gazeta de Lisboa», de 1715 à 1739', *Bulletin des Etudes Portugaises*, XXVI (1965), 95–110

Freitas, Frederico de. 'A modinha – portuguesa e brasileira (Alguns aspectos do seu particular interesse musical', *A Arte em Portugal no Século XVIII. Actas do Congresso*, III in *Bracara Augusta*, XXVIII (1974), 65–6 (77–8), 433–8

Giacomo, S. di. *I quattro antichi conservatorii di Napoli. vol. I, I R. Conservatorii di*

*S. Onofrio a Capuana e di S. Maria della Pietà dei Turchini*, Naples, Remo Sandron, 1924

Godinho, Vitorino Magalhães. 'Portugal and her empire, 1680–1720', ch. 16 of *The New Cambridge Modern History*, vol. IV (*The Rise of Great Britain and Russia 1688–1715/25*), Cambridge University Press, 1970, pp. 509–39

*Prix et monnaies au Portugal 1750–1850*, Paris, Librairie Armand Collin, 1955

Guerra, Luís de Bivar and Ferreira, Manuel Maria. *Catálogo do Arquivo do Tribunal de Contas, Casa dos Contos e Junta de Inconfidência*, Lisbon, 1950.

Guimarães, José Ribeiro. *Biografia de Luísa de Aguiar Todi*, Lisbon, Imprensa de J. G. de Sousa Neves, 1872

'O Theatro do Bairro Alto', *Boletim da Real Associação de Architectos Civis e Archeologos Portuguezes*, 4th series, vol. XI, no. 8 (1908), 744–54 (originally published in *Jornal do Commercio* no. 5572ff. of 1873)

*Instrumentos Musicais 1747–1807. Uma colecção à procura de um Museu*, Lisbon, Instituto Português do Património Cultural – Palácio Nacional de Queluz, 1984

*Inventário dos manuscritos (secção XIII) colecção pombalina*, Lisbon, Biblioteca Nacional, 1891

Jackson, Paul Joseph. 'The operas of David Perez: traditional and progressive features of the opera seria in the middle of the eighteenth century', unpublished PhD dissertation, Stanford University, 1967

Kirkpatrick, Ralph. *Domenico Scarlatti*, Princeton, NJ, 1953

Lambertini, Michel'angelo. 'Portugal' in *Encyclopédie de la Musique et Dictionnaire du Conservatoire*, vol. IV, Paris, Librairie Delagrave, 1920, pp. 2401–469

Lemos, Maria Luísa. *Impressos musicais da Biblioteca Geral da Universidade de Coimbra*, Separata from *Boletim da Biblioteca da Universidade de Coimbra*, vol. XXXIV, part 3, 1980

Lindgren, Lowell Edwin. 'A Bibliographical Scrutiny of Dramatic Works by Giovanni and his Brother Antonio Maria Bononcini', unpublished PhD dissertation, Harvard University, 1972

López-Calo, José. 'Portogallo' in *Storia dell'opera*, vol. II, tomo secondo, Turin, UTET Unione Tipografico-Editrice Torinese, 1977, pp. 65–77

McClymonds, Marita. *Niccolò Jommelli: The Last Years, 1769–1774*, Studies in Musicology, UMI Research Press, 1981 (PhD dissertation, University of California, Berkeley, 1978, here quoted in its original typewritten version)

Marques, A. H. de Oliveira. *História de Portugal desde os tempos mais antigos até ao governo do Sr. Marcelo Caetano*, 2 vols., Lisbon, Edições Ágora, 1972/Palas Editores, 1973

Marques, Joaquim José. *Cronologia da ópera em Portugal*, Lisbon. A Artística, 1947 (originally published as a series of articles in the *Arte Musical* of 1874)

Martín Moreno, Antonio. *Historia de la música española. 4. Siglo XVIII*, Madrid, Alianza Editorial, 1985

Martins, António Coimbra. 'Molière no Teatro Real de Salvaterra', *Les rapports culturels et littéraires entre le Portugal et la France. Actes du Colloque*, Paris, Fondation Calouste Gulbenkian, Centre Culturel Portugais, 1983, 201–6

Martins, José Pedro Ribeiro. 'O teatro no Porto no século XVIII', *Actas do Colóquio «O Porto na época moderna»* II in *Revista de História*, vol. III (1980), 99–113

# Bibliography

Miranda, José da Costa. 'Achegas para um estudo sobre o teatro de Apostolo Zeno em Portugal (século XVIII)', *Revista de História Literária de Portugal*, 4 (1974), 5–38; Italian version: 'Notte sulla fortuna di Apostolo Zeno in Portogallo (secolo XVIII)', *Rivista italiana di drammaturgia* 9/10 (n.d.), 135–61

'Ainda alguns apontamentos sobre Goldoni em Portugal', *Estudos Italianos em Portugal*, 43/44 (1980–1), 73–92

'Apontamentos para um futuro estudo sobre o teatro de Metastasio em Portugal, no século XVIII', *Estudos Italianos em Portugal*, 36 (1973), 129–62; Italian version: 'Fortuna e vicende del Metastasio nel Settecento portoghese', *Rivista italiana di drammaturgia*, 1 (1976), 83–105

'Benedetto Marcello, *Il Teatro alla Moda*, apontamentos sobre uma versão portuguesa manuscrita (século XVIII)', *Estudos Italianos em Portugal*, 37 (1974), 25–39

'De uns supérfluos apontamentos sobre teatro de cordel a uma pergunta (inocente) sobre Goldoni', *Revista Lusitana*, new series, 1 (1981), 71–7

'Edições portuguesas do teatro de Pietro Metastasio (século XVIII): distribuição cronológica e significado', *Boletim Internacional de Bibliografia Luso-Brasileira*, XIV (1973), 5–15

'Libretos, libretistas e compositores italianos no Portugal do século XVIII: alguns apontamentos dispersos', *Annali dell'Istituto Universitario Orientale Sezione Romanza*, XXIV, 1 (1982), 127–34

'Novos apontamentos para um futuro estudo sobre o teatro de Metastasio em Portugal, no século XVIII', *Estudos Italianos em Portugal*, 38/39 (1975–6), 125–44

'O teatro de Goldoni em Portugal (século XVIII). Libretos de dramas para música e partituras manuscritas', *Estudos Italianos em Portugal* 37 (1974), 41–77

'O teatro de Goldoni em Portugal (século XVIII). Subsídios para o seu estudo', *Revista de História Literária de Portugal*, IV (1974), 36–85

'Teatro italiano manuscrito (século XVIII): sobre alguns textos existentes em bibliotecas e arquivos portugueses', *Boletim da Biblioteca da Universidade de Coimbra*, XXXIII (1976), 5–27

Mitjana, Rafael. 'Espagne' in *Encyclopédie de la Musique et Dictionnaire du Conservatoire*, vol. IV, Paris, Librairie Delagrave, 1920, pp. 1913–2400

Monteiro, José Gomes. 'O theatro italiano no Porto em 1762', *O Novo Nacional. Jornal Litterario Commercial e D'Annuncios*, no. 84 (11.4.1851)

Moreau, Mário. *Cantores de ópera portugueses*, vol. 1, Lisbon, Livraria Bertrand, 1981

Nogueira, José Maria António. 'Memórias do teatro português (1588–1762)' in *Esparsos*, Coimbra, Imprensa da Universidade, 1934, pp. 37–55; id. as 'Archeologia do theatro portuguez (1598–1762)', *Boletim da Real Associação de Architectos Civis e Archeologos Portuguezes*, 4th series, vol. X (1904), no. 8, 381–91, no. 10, 536–41 (originally published in *Jornal do Commercio*, nos. 5, 6 and 12, April 1866)

Oliveira, Eduardo Freire de. *Elementos para a história do município de Lisboa*, 17 vols., Lisbon, 1885–1911; *Índice dos Elementos para a história do município de Lisboa*, 2 vols., Lisbon, 1942–3

# Bibliography

Pagano, Roberto. *Scarlatti, Alessandro e Domenico: due vite in una*, Milan, Arnoldo Mondadori Editore, 1985

'Le origine ed il primo statuto dell' Unione dei Musici intitolata a Santa Cecilia in Palermo', *Rivista italiana di musicologia* X (1975), 545–63

Petrobelli, Pierluigi. 'The Italian years of Anton Raaff' *Mozart-Jahrbuch* 1973/1974, 233–73

Pires, António Caldeira. *História do Palácio Nacional de Queluz*, 2 vols., Coimbra, Imprensa da Universidade, 1924–6

Prota-Giurleo, Ulisse. *Musicisti napoletani alla corte di Portogallo nel 1700*, Naples, 1924

Resende, Marquês de. 'Descripções e recordações históricas do Paço e Quinta de Queluz', *Panorama*, vol. XII (1855), 210–15

*Pintura de um outeiro nocturno e um saráo musical às portas de Lisboa no fim do século passado*, Lisbon, Typographia da Academia Real das Sciencias, 1868

Ribeiro, Mário de Sampaio. 'El-Rei D. João, o Quinto, e a música no seu tempo', *D. João V – Conferências e estudos comemorativos do segundo centenário da sua morte (1750–1950)*, Lisbon, Publicações Culturais da Câmara Municipal de Lisboa, 1952, pp. 65–89

'À margem da Exposição de Desenhos da Escola dos Bibiena', *Boletim do Museu Nacional de Arte Antiga*, v, no. 2 (1966), 26–31

*A música em Portugal nos séculos XVIII e XIX (Bosquejo de história crítica)*, Lisbon, Separata from Revista História, series A, 1936 (Achegas para a História da Música em Portugal III)

Ribeiro, Vítor. 'O Pateo das Comedias e as representações teatrais (1729)', *Arquivo Literário*, vol. 2°, tomo 7° (1924), 225–30

Rivara, Joaquim Heliodoro da Cunha and Matos, Joaquim António de Sousa Teles de. *Catalogo dos Manuscriptos da Biblioteca Pública Eborense*, 2 vols., Lisbon, 1869.

Rossi, G. C. 'Il Goldoni nel Portogallo del Settecento (Documenti inediti)' *Annali dell'Istituto Universitario Orientale Sezione Romanza*, IX, 2 (1967), 243–73

*La letteratura italiana e le letterature di lingua portoghesa*, Turin, Società Editrice Internazionale, 1967

'Per una storia del teatro italiano del Settecento (Goldoni) in Portogallo', *Studi Goldoniani*, Quaderno no. 2 (1970), 49–89

'Per una storia del teatro italiano del Settecento (Metastasio) in Portogallo', *Annali dell'Istituto Universitario Orientale Sezione Romanza*, X, 1 (1968), 96–147

Salgado, João. *História do teatro em Portugal*, Lisbon, David Corezzi Editor, 1885

Sampaio, Albino Forjaz de. *Teatro de Cordel (Catalogo da colecção do autor)*, Lisbon, Imprensa Nacional, 1922

Santana, Francisco. 'Teatros da Graça', *Olisipo*, 144–5 (1981–2), 1–16

Santos, Mariana Amélia Machado (ed.). *Biblioteca da Ajuda. Catálogo de música manuscrita*, 9 vols., Lisbon, 1958–68

Santos, Vitor Pavão dos. 'A Ópera do Tejo', *História*, no. 8 (1979), 18–27

Saraiva, António José and Lopes, Óscar. *História da literatura portuguesa*, 3rd edn, Oporto, Porto Editora Lda., n.d. [1962]

Saraiva, José Hermano. *História concisa de Portugal*, Lisbon, Publicações Europa–América, 1978

Sartori, Claudio. 'Primo tentativo di un catalogo unico dei libretti italiani a stampa fino all'anno 1800', typescript, Milan, Biblioteca Nazionale Braidense – Ufficio Ricerca Fondi Musicali, 1973–

Sasportes, José. *História da dança em Portugal*, Lisbon, Fundação Calouste Gulbenkian, 1970

Scherpereel, J. *A orquestra e os instrumentistas da Real Câmara de Lisboa de 1764 a 1834/ L'orchestre et les instrumentistes de la Real Câmara à Lisbonne de 1764 à 1834*, Lisbon, Fundação Calouste Gulbenkian, 1985 (originally a PhD dissertation, University of Southern California, 1974, with the title 'Documents inédits sur l'orchestre et les instruments de la Real Câmara à Lisbonne de 1764 à 1834')

Schnoebelen, Mary Nicole. *Padre Martini's Collection of Letters in the Civico Museo Bibliografico Musicale in Bologna: An Annotated Index*, New York, Pendragon Press, 1979

Sequeira, Gustavo de Matos. *O Carmo e a Trindade*, 3 vols., Lisbon, Publicações Culturais da Câmara Municipal de Lisboa, 1939

*Depois do terremoto (Subsídios para a história dos bairros ocidentais de Lisboa)*, 4 vols., Lisbon, Academia das Sciências de Lisboa, 1916–33

*Teatro de outros tempos. Elementos para a história do teatro português*, Lisbon, Livraria Coelho, 1933

Silva, Augusto Vieira da. *As muralhas da Ribeira de Lisboa*, Lisbon, Typographia do Commercio, 1900

Silva, Inocêncio Francisco da. *Diccionário bibliographico portuguez*, 22 vols., Lisbon, Imprensa Nacional, 1858–1923; *Aditamentos* por Martinho da Fonseca, 1927; *Guia bibliográfico* por Ernesto Soares, 1958

Soares, Ernesto. *David Perez, subsidios para a biografia do celebre mestre de musica de câmara de D. José I*, Lisbon, Feira da Ladra, 1935

Sonneck, O. G. T. *Catalogue of Opera Librettos printed before 1800*, 2 vols., Washington, DC, Govt. Printing Office (US Library of Congress, Music Division), 1914

Sousa, Filipe de. 'O compositor António Teixeira e a sua obra', *A arte em Portugal no século XVIII. Actas do Congresso*, vol. III in *Bracara Augusta*, vol. XXVIII (1974), 65–6 (77–8), 413–20

'A música orquestral portuguesa', *ibid.*, 405–12

Stevenson, Robert (ed.) (Autores vários). *Vilancicos portugueses*, Lisbon, Fundação Calouste Gulbenkian, 1976 (Portugaliae Musica XXIX)

Subirá, José. *Historia de la música teatral en España*, Barcelona, Editorial Labor SA, 1945

*Subsidios para a história da Irmandade de Santa Cecília e do Montepio Philarmonico*, Lisbon, n.d. [1916?]

Tengarrinha, José. *História da imprensa periódica portuguesa*, Lisbon, Portugália Editora, 1965

Vasconcelos, Joaquim de. *Os musicos portuguezes – Biographia – Bibliographia*, 2 vols., Oporto, Imprensa Portugueza, 1870

Vieira, Ernesto. *Diccionario biographico de musicos portuguezes: historia e bibliographia da musica em Portugal*, 2 vols., Lisbon, Typographia Mattos Moreira & Pinheiro, 1900

Viterbo, Francisco Marques de Sousa. 'Carlo Goldoni e a opera na côrte de D. José' in *Artes e Artistas em Portugal*, Lisbon, 1892, 214–19

*Subsídios para a história da música em Portugal*, Coimbra, Imprensa da Universidade, 1932

Waxel, Platon von. 'Portugiesische Musik' in Hermann Mendel and August Reissmann (eds.), *Musikalisches Conversations-Lexikon, Ergänzungsband*, Berlin, Robert Oppenheim, 1883, pp. 492–550

# INDEX

# Index

# Index

# Index

Puzzi, Antonio (bass singer), 55, 71
Puzzi, Taddeo (bass singer), 36, 49, 55

Queluz palace, 48, 59, 60–1, 64, 137, 138, 140, 142, 145, 152, 153, 154, 155, 156, 157, 159, 164, 166, 174, 208n42
Queluz Theatre, 48, 51, 57, 64, 69, 70, 77, 137, 141, 143, 147, 149, 153, 174, 208n43
Quilici, Gaetano (singer), 85, 91
Quintanilha, Henrique Silva (owner of the Rua dos Candes Theatre), 104
Quintela, Inácio Pedro (impresario), 92, 93, 110, 182–3, 217n60
Quintela, Joaquim Pedro Quintela, Baron of, 92, 110, 182
*Quinto Fabio*, 62

Raaff, Anton (tenor), 25, 26, 28, 30, 31, 55, 205n6, 207n31
Radicchi, Giuseppe (composer), 62
Raimondi (librettist), 170
Rainoldi, Francesco (designer of combats), 85
Ramos, António de Figueiredo do Espírito Santo (composer), 169
Rastrelli, Andrea (singer), 108
*Il ratto della sposa*, by P. A. Guglielmi, 141
*Il ratto di Proserpina*, by J. C. Silva, 157, 161
Razel, Augusto João (composer?), 111
*Il Re pastore*, by Jommelli, 41, 45, 49, 143
*Il Re pastore*, by L. X. des Santos, 175
Real Academia de Cirurgia Portuense, 139, 219n109
Real Casa Pia do Castelo de S. Jorge, 160, 163, 169
Real Mesa Censória, Tribunal da, 105, 114–16
*Reflexoens sobre O restabelecimento do Theatro Do Porto*, by R. R. Nogueira, x, 116–19, 191–97, 219n117
Reginelle (singer), 12, 176
Reina, Antonio, 34
Reina, Carlo (soprana), 28, 30, 34, 35, 40, 43, 44, 55, 67, 70, 71, 74–5, 178, 179
Reis, Francisco dos (singer), 49
Reispacher, Franz Gottlieb (player), 61
Ribaltone, Antonio (choreographer), 86
Ribeira, Paço de, *see* Paço da Ribeira
Ribeira das Naus, group of the, 97
Ricardino, José Joaquim (= Giuseppe Gioacchino?, dancer), 85
*Riccardo Cor di Leone*, by Grétry, 77, 168
Ricci, Pietro (tenor), 120
Ricciolini, Michele (dancer), 26
*Ricimero*, 62
Rinaldo di Capua (composer), 19, 133, 134, 158
Ripa, Giovanni, (soprano), 55, 65, 71, 72, 74–5

*La risa di Democrito*, 9, 10, 130, 201n51
Rispoli, Salvatore (composer), 62
Ristorini (singer), 35
*Il ritorno di Astrea in Terra*, by J. Palomino, 72, 159
*Il ritorno di Tobia*, by Haydn, 157
*Il ritorno di Ulisse in Itaca*, by Perez, 40, 57, 69, 149, 153
Robinelli, Giuseppe (singer), 38
Robuschi, Ferdinando (composer), 166
Rocchi, Agostino (bass singer), 55
Rocha, Joaquim Manual da (set designer), 84
Rodil, António (flute player), 39, 64, 211n98
Rodriguez, Rosa, *La Gallega* (actress and singer), 3, 13
Romanini, Giuseppe (soprano), 38, 55, 65, 70, 71, 74–5
Romero, Gonçalo Auzier, *see* Auzier Romero, Gonçalo
Ronzi, Antonio (violinist), 61
Rosetelli, Domenico (dancer), 103
Rosignoli, Teresa (dancer), 101
Rossi, Francesco (soprano), 108, 109, 110
Rossi, Giovanni Gerardo de' (librettist), 169
Rossi, Giuseppa (singer), 114
Rossi, Teresa Tizzoni (dancer), 101
Rossi, Venceslao de (dancer and choreographer), 97, 101
*Roubo do Velocino de Ouro*, 134
Royal Academy of History, 5
Royal Chapel, 2, 4, 5–6, 7, 11, 15, 18, 35, 40, 41, 63, 65, 78–9, 93, 208n43, 209n59
Rua dos Condes Theatre, 17, 18, 20, 21, 48, 52, 73, 76, 79, 80, 83, 84, 85, 86, 90–104, 106, 107, 108–10, 110, 111, 132–4, 139, 140, 142, 146, 147, 148, 149, 150, 151, 162, 164, 166, 168, 170, 174, 181, 203n104
Rubbini (dancer), 91
Rubinelli (soprano), 67
Rumi, Pietro (violinist), 75
*O Rustico desprezado*, 115
Rutini, Giovanni Maria (composer), 140

Sá, José Anastásio da Costa e (librettist), 174
Sabbatini, Anna (dancer), 87, 102
Sabbatini, Carlo (dancer), 87, 102
Sabbatini, Vincenzo (dancer and choreographer), 87
*O sábio*, 80
Sacchini, Antonio (composer), 45, 63, 148, 150, 171
*Sacrificio puro*, by Frei M. de Santo António, 164
*Il sacrifizio di Diana*, by Astorga, 125
Sagau, Jayme de la Te y, *see* Te y Sagau, Jayme de la
Sala da Serenata, 59–60, 72, 212n12

# Index

*Il voto di Jefte*, by P. A. Avondano, 78, 171

Wagenseil, Georg Christoph (composer), 32
Wales, Prince of, 126
Waltmann, Jean Baptiste (horn player), 109, 218n94
Weltin, Jean Baptiste (bassoon player), 109, 218n94
Wraxall, Sir Nathaniel William, 50–1, 104
Württemberg, Duke of, 38, 39, 41

Xavier, Francisco (dancer), 120

Zamperini, Anna (soprano), 92–4, 96, 97, 99, 104, 181–3
Zamperini, Antonia (singer), 96, 97, 99
Zamperini, Cecilia (dancer), 103

Zanardi, Teresa (singer), 19
Zanetti, Francesco (composer), 147
Zappa, Domenico (tenor), 114
*Zarzuela*, 2, 3, 4, 9, 120
Zeno, Apostolo (librettist), 42, 147, 150, 183, 188
*Zenobia*, by Perez, 139
*I zingari in fiera*, by Paisiello, 167
Zini, Saverio (librettist), 157
Zoccoli, Anna (dancer), 102
Zoccoli, Pietro (dancer), 103
Zucchelli, Alessandro (choreographer), 108
Zucchelli, Angiola (dancer), 91, 102
Zucchelli, Francesco (dancer), 37, 70, 217n70
Zucchelli, Tommaso (dancer), 37, 217n70
Zucchi, Antonio, 33, 34

254

# Index